PRAISE FOR *THREE CROO[KINGS]*

'*A powerful treatment of an inelegant past that still smoulders.*'
WEEKEND AUSTRALIAN

'Three Crooked Kings *delivers its promised "explosive true story" . . . a fabulous tale of graft, extortion, sex, drugs and mayhem. Condon's deft touch makes [this book] immediate, engaging and riveting.*' THE NEWTOWN REVIEW OF BOOKS

'Three Crooked Kings *paints a compellingly dark picture.*' SYDNEY MORNING HERALD

'*Hailed as the most explosive book of 2013 – a riveting epic and unrelenting tour-de-force which will shock a nation. And it's all true. Compelling stuff.*' THE CHRONICLE

PRAISE FOR *JACKS AND JOKERS*

'*. . . highly readable, well-researched and multi-layered expose of police and political malfeasance in the Sunshine State.*' SATURDAY AGE

Jacks and Jokers '*sprawls and appals in equal measure. Condon's true crime series is not just a compelling read: it is compulsory.*' AUSTRALIAN BOOK REVIEW

'*Praise is being lauded on Brisbane journalist and author Matthew Condon who is backing up his bestselling chronicle of Queensland's underbelly.*' COURIER-MAIL

'*Meticulously researched.*' WALKLEY MAGAZINE

'*An important work of history.*' OVERLAND

'*A fantastic fusion of Frank Moorhouse and Peter Corris,* Jacks and Jokers *is crime writing at its best.*' NEWTOWN REVIEW OF BOOKS

Matthew Condon is a prize-winning Australian novelist and journalist. He is currently on staff with the *Courier-Mail's Qweekend* magazine. He began his journalism career with the *Gold Coast Bulletin* in 1984 and subsequently worked for leading newspapers and journals including the *Sydney Morning Herald,* the *Sun-Herald* and Melbourne's *Sunday Age.* He is also the author of ten books of fiction, most recently *The Trout Opera* (Random House, 2007) and the non-fiction books *Brisbane* (New South Books, 2010), as well as *Three Crooked Kings* (UQP, 2013) and *Jacks and Jokers* (UQP, 2014) — the first two books in his best-selling trilogy about Queensland crime and corruption.

ALL FALL DOWN

MATTHEW CONDON

UQP

First published 2015 by University of Queensland Press
PO Box 6042, St Lucia, Queensland 4067 Australia

www.uqp.com.au
uqp@uqp.uq.edu.au

Cover design by Design by Committee
Cover photo illustration by Josh Durham
Author photo © Russell Shakespeare
Typeset in 11.5/16 pt Bembo by Post Pre-press Group, Brisbane
Printed in Australia by McPherson's Printing Group

Quotes from interviews with Mike Willesee of *A Current Affair* (1984) and Jana Wendt
of *60 Minutes* (1984) reprinted with permission of Nine Network Australia Pty Ltd.

National Library of Australia cataloguing-in-publication
data is available at http://catalogue.nla.gov.au/

ISBN
978 0 7022 5353 9 (pbk)
978 0 7022 5494 9 (pdf)
978 0 7022 5495 6 (epub)
978 0 7022 5496 3 (Kindle)

For my wife, Katie Kate,
and our children —
Finnigan, Bridie Rose and Oliver George

AS HE SAT ALONE *in a parked car, surrounded by splendid Queensland rainforest, a hose running from the vehicle exhaust pipe and into the cabin, did Sydney James Brifman think back to the day, as a young boy, when he found his mother's dead body?*

Just nine-years-old on that Saturday morning – 4 March 1972 – young Syd had gone into the small room off the foyer of the flat in Bonney Avenue, Clayfield, in Brisbane's inner north-east, looking for his mother, prostitute and brothel madam Shirley Margaret Brifman. Sydney and his older sister, Mary Anne, 15, knew their mother liked to sleep in. As a lady of the night she kept odd hours. And if the Brifman kids – there was also sisters Sonia and Helen – made a racket, or had the morning television cartoons on too loud, she often called out from bed asking them to keep the noise down.

On this morning there was nothing but silence. So Syd, and then Mary Anne, went into the room. Upon entering, Syd witnessed his mother's corpse, swathed in a summer nightie and propped up in bed, a hand extended and held in a claw. 'He ran out of there like the roadrunner – with that speed,' recalls his sister Mary Anne.

Less than a year earlier, Shirley, 35, had gone on national television and blown the whistle on corrupt police in Queensland and New South Wales whom she had been paying off for over a decade. A few short weeks before her death she was to testify in a perjury trial against legendary Queensland detective and hard man Tony Murphy. The evening before her body was discovered, she'd received a visitor who had passed her a small vial of drugs. Brifman was warned – commit suicide or say goodbye to your children. The visitor left after midnight.

1

Sydney, the youngest of the Brifman kids, had been born at six months and one week in 1963, courtesy of a botched abortion attempt. Shirley had travelled to the New South Wales capital especially to secure the termination, but it all went horribly wrong. Miraculously, after several blood transfusions, the boy survived. He was named after the city of his birth.

As Sydney was recuperating in hospital, Brisbane's own detective Murphy was gathering evidence to destroy the credibility of witnesses due to appear before the National Hotel royal commission into police misconduct. On this occasion, Murphy took the time to write a letter to Brifman, his long-standing informant, who was due to appear before the commission as its star witness. Over the years the two had become close. Shirley, the former country girl from Atherton in Far North Queensland, would send the detective's children Christmas cards with money inside.

As baby Syd fought through his first few weeks of life, Murphy typed a letter on plain paper at his office in the Woolloongabba CIB. 'Dear Marg,' he wrote, using one of Shirley's many prostitute aliases, 'Your welcome letter to hand the other day. As always I had no hesitation in accepting the information in it as being "good mail".'

Before signing off he added: 'As I want to get this letter in the first mail, I'll close now hoping the young "Briffman (sic) boy" is picking up fast and will soon be out of hospital. Det. Tony Murphy.'

Sydney Brifman was the quiet boy. The good and sweet child who nobody had a bad word to say about. But nine years later, as quick as the roadrunner, Sydney's mother was dead. He wasn't to know that in just a few short years the Brifman curse would strike again.

Within a couple of years of Shirley's sudden death, Sonia Brifman met a young man, got married and fell pregnant. About a month after the birth of her son, Sonia was visiting her big sister Mary Anne, who also had a young son and daughter. It was a special time for the Brifman sisters, sharing early motherhood.

'It was early morning and we were sitting in the kitchen,' recalls Mary Anne. 'Sonia went to reach out to grab the Kellogg's Corn Flakes box and she dropped it. She doubled over in pain.

'I asked her if she was okay. She was in agony for two or three minutes, then it stopped. It was the same scenario the next morning. She couldn't stop crying. She was in agony.'

Thinking her sister may be suffering from complications following her recent birth, Mary Anne rushed her to hospital. 'They said she was suffering from a gut obstruction. That a bit of scar tissue had lodged in the bowel and become infected. I went and saw her in hospital a few days later. I caught a glimpse of her and I had to step out of the ward to get my equilibrium. She was dying.'

Sonia Margaret Brifman developed peritonitis and died in extreme agony ten days later. It was just four years after her mother's death. She was 18 years old.

Syd, not yet a teenager, had already lost two of the women in his family. After finishing school he was taken into the care of relatives in the city and started work at a fruit shop. He lifted crates night and day and seriously damaged his back. The injury would plague him for the rest of his life, although he later went on to marry and have two children. Despite his notorious family history, he lived his life on the straight and narrow and taught his son and daughter the difference between right and wrong. He gave them values. He worked when he could between bouts of recuperation for his bad back, but money was always tight.

When he split from his wife in his late thirties, Syd suffered depression. The torment of his injuries continued unabated. He struggled on, but life had less meaning. In 2002, he drove his car into rainforest near Noosa, a fabled holiday spot for the rich and famous on Queensland's Sunshine Coast, and gassed himself. He was wearing a gold signet ring given to him by his father. It was his treasure. He never took it off.

In death, Syd joined the long list of deceased Brifmans, this Queensland family haunted by crime and crooked cops for almost half a century.

1980s

Squalls

It was a miserable night for New Year's Eve revellers in Brisbane, thanks to a low-pressure system that had developed off the south-east Queensland coast. On the last evening of 1982, a Friday, heavy rain fell across the capital, and trade was down in the city's discotheques and bars. King George Square, at the foot of the City Hall tower, was deserted, its brass lions drenched.

Up in his old Queenslander at 12 Garfield Drive, in the shadow of the Paddington water tower, Police Commissioner Terence (Terry) Murray Lewis was taking in the first of 28 days official leave, sitting quietly at home as the rain drummed on the tin roof, reading editions of the Queensland Police journal, *Vedette*. (Determined to keep up with current affairs within and beyond the force, he may have taken special interest in reports on the development, since 1980, of the state-wide police computer system, modelled on the state government's network.)

Lewis would soon start packing for his annual pilgrimage to the Gold Coast. But the forecast — and some testy natural occurrences — heralded a gloomy opening to 1983. The *Courier-Mail* reported that a vast plague of bluebottles, aided by a strong northerly, had swept onshore at the Gold Coast, stinging swimmers. Beaches at Burleigh Heads, Nobby's Beach, Miami and Greenmount were temporarily closed after sharks were sighted offshore.

It would not deter Lewis. Despite the poor weather, the Lewises had a booking made for their annual break at Broadbeach South Pacific Plaza – room 1504 was waiting for them. A man ruled by routine, the clock and the calendar, Lewis had friends to catch up with. Belfast Hotel proprietor Barry Maxwell and his wife Sheelagh, Deputy Commissioner Syd 'Sippy' Atkinson and wife Norma, Gold Coast City Council alderman Sir Jack Edgerton and former TAB chairman Sir Albert Sakzewski were all pencilled in on his social calendar.

There would also be dinner with developer Eddie Kornhauser, close friend to National Party heavyweight Russell Hinze and the man who claimed, as his monstrous Paradise Centre evolved – a potpourri of hotels, waterslides, shops and restaurants – to have 'virtually made' Surfers Paradise single-handedly. Kornhauser, rumoured to be an associate of notorious Sydney businessman Abe Saffron, may have missed out on winning the Gold Coast bid for a casino the previous year, but he had made a firm friend in Commissioner Lewis. ('Hinze introduced me to Kornhauser,' Lewis says.)

A few squalls couldn't put a dampener on Lewis, who had just celebrated his sixth year as Commissioner, having seen off his nemesis Ray Whitrod and taken the top job at only 48. He had purged the force of pro-Whitrod officers (or Whitrod's 'curly-headed boys', as Lewis calls them) including Alec Jeppesen and Basil Hicks, and put in their place his own acolytes. He had survived police ministers that didn't suit him – most recently the garrulous Hinze, replaced by the affable Bill Glasson. And he had firmly cemented his friendship with Premier Joh Bjelke-Petersen. Lewis had powerful allies.

The Commissioner was in regular contact with his old mate Jack Reginald Herbert, master organiser of the corrupt system known for decades within the force as The Joke – an elaborate, multi-million dollar scheme of kickbacks from illegal gambling, SP bookmakers, brothels and escort services. Likewise, Anthony (Tony) Murphy, so-called member of the legendary Rat Pack along with Lewis and

Glendon (Glen) Patrick Hallahan, who had retired just the previous week at only 55 years of age. Lewis himself was about to turn the same age at the end of February, but retirement couldn't have been further from his mind. He had another decade in him at the very least. He coveted a knighthood, and the Premier had intimated a plush posting in Los Angeles or London after his retirement from the force. Terry Lewis wasn't going anywhere.

Despite his salary – he often bemoaned he was the most poorly remunerated Police Commissioner in Australia – Lewis had, all of a sudden, been making some canny property investments. While he had once toyed with the idea of leaving the force under Whitrod and trying his hand as a real estate agent, and acknowledging his wife Hazel's excellent eye for a property bargain, Lewis had been dabbling in the market. On the advice of his chartered accountant, James Baker, who had an office at 164 Melbourne Street, South Brisbane, the T.M. & H.C. Lewis Family Trust was established in October 1980.

As of 30 June that year, Lewis's asset position consisted of the family home at 12 Garfield Drive, personal effects, furniture and savings to the value of $53,916. In the financial year to June 1981, Lewis had begun his property splurge, purchasing another house in Garfield Drive – number 29, a stucco and orange roof–tiled bungalow. A hundred metres from the Lewis family home, on the other side of the street, its supreme views took in the CBD and the hills of Paddington sweeping over to Toowong and the University of Queensland campus in St Lucia. 'You thought you were setting up things for the future,' says Lewis. '[It] was on the right hand side [of Garfield Drive] … a pigsty. Hazel and the kids … we used to borrow a utility and get rid of the rubbish, cleaned it all up, painted it inside [and] rented it.'

In addition, the Lewises had become aware of two towers of luxury units planned for 24 Dunmore Terrace, Auchenflower, with views of the city and the Brisbane River. It would be known, on construction, as Coronation Towers, replete with tennis courts and a swimming pool. The developers had an 'off the plan' purchase offer in place and Lewis put down deposits on two units in the complex – $8700 on unit 22B, and $9900 on unit 37B. The money for the deposits had come from Lewis's substantial savings. Come December 1981, Coronation Towers was open for business.

Lewis then put a $20,000 deposit on a block of land in Bardon through lawyers Gilshenan and Luton. (And, according to his diaries, he and Hazel would, in just a few weeks' time, be inspecting a 'mansion in Hamilton'.) The property transactions had left the Lewises' savings reduced to $12,349, but in mid-1982 he quickly sold unit 22B for a small loss, keeping the more prestigious unit 37B, and ended the year with a growth in savings to $31,592.

His finances were supplemented, as they had been for some years according to Lewis, with winnings from the racetrack (the bets always supposedly placed by his punting-mad mother, Mona), which accountant Baker later said in a statement 'averaged somewhere in the order of $3000 to $5000 per year'. Not bad, considering the average wage in 1983 for a police officer was $300 a week.

Curiously, Commissioner Lewis gave an interview to a local newspaper in August 1982 telling the reporter he left nothing to chance when it came to his job, and he applied that attitude to his personal and home life. He had the working conditions and welfare of thousands of police officers in his hands, he claimed. Decisions affecting his staff were only made after the consideration of all available facts and information. 'I haven't much interest in punting or lotteries and only rarely can be persuaded to have a fling,' he said. 'Luck hasn't had a part in developing our police force as the most effective and efficient in Australia.' He didn't even have a lucky number, he told the reporter.

Nevertheless, Lewis was more than financially secure come the dawn of 1983. And there were other things in the pipeline for the year. Both Lewis and Murphy were suing the Australian Broadcasting Corporation over its controversial *Nationwide* program of March 1982.

From Lewis's point of view, a legal victory over the ABC just might provide a financial windfall.

In the show, reported by journalist Alan Hall, two former police officers – Kingsley Fancourt and Bob Campbell – had gone on the record denouncing Lewis's police administration and alleging corruption. Following the national broadcast, Campbell had fled Queensland in fear for his life and that of his wife and children, while Fancourt had remained outside Anakie, in Queensland's western gemfields, and ridden out the criticism. He, too, had every reason to be worried. He'd had a couple of close calls since outing the Rat Pack – wheel nuts on his vehicle had been loosened on a number of occasions, resulting in accidents, and the brake line on one of his trucks had been severed.

As the rain shook the leaves of the palm trees that grew along the spine of Garfield Drive, Lewis may also have picked up the New Year's Day edition of the *Courier-Mail*. The front page of the Saturday weekend section carried a huge feature on the Queensland Premier. Headlined: LIFE ACCORDING TO JOH, the preface to the question-and-answer style article, written by journalist John Hamilton, stated that Bjelke-Petersen would turn 72 on 16 January, and that the long-term leader of the National Party had been accused of being too old for the job. His enemies believed he was growing senile.

'I found absolutely no evidence to support this in a long interview with the Premier,' wrote Hamilton. 'The man glows with good health, looks about 50, and his mind is so active it continually races ahead of his mouth, leaving sentences half-completed, thoughts half-expressed. He is, simply, a phenomenon.'

In the interview, the Premier bashed trade unions, suggested the Foreign Investment Review Board be abolished, called for all Indigenous land rights decisions to be immediately halted, criticised foreign aid, made some noise about communists and denied he was an autocratic leader. 'I'm one of those people who believe that one is in God's hands … I don't believe that life is just a game of chance,' Joh said. 'As a believer, I believe that there is a purpose in life and that things are ordained.'

Lewis had a week in Brisbane before he and Hazel headed down to Broadbeach on the Gold Coast. He attended to some correspondence, no doubt typed on his old manual typewriter in his office nook at home; having used the manual since his first days as a constable in 1949.

As the rain continued to sheet down in Brisbane, Lewis took in a movie – *Who Dares Wins*, a British terrorism thriller starring Lewis Collins, Richard Widmark, Edward Woodward and Australia's own Judy Davis. During the closing credits, the socialist anthem 'The Red Flag' was played. 'So raise the scarlet standard high,' the song went. 'Beneath its shade we'll live and die/Though cowards flinch and traitors sneer/We'll keep the red flag flying here.'

As Lewis walked out of the Hoyts entertainment complex at 167 Queen Street, with that song in his head, he must have believed he was precisely the right man in the right job at the right time for Queensland. Since the demise of Whitrod he had proved a good friend to government. His men had dutifully policed Bjelke-Petersen's arcane street march prohibition laws in the late 1970s, for instance, ignoring calls that Queensland had become a police state. If the boss wanted something, then he got it. Dissent from the government line was quashed.

Joh and Terry were on the same page. The red flag would not be flying any time soon in Queensland, Australia, if Commissioner Lewis could help it.

A Late Call

The night after Lewis saw *Who Dares Wins* in the city, an anonymous male caller phoned the Police Operations Centre at North Quay, Brisbane, at precisely 11.12 p.m. Inspector B.A. Pitman was on duty.

The caller asked Pitman if he knew Constable Dave Moore. 'I think you should know, he is a poofter,' the man said. 'I've got evidence to prove it.'

Just as other Australian states were debating the decriminalisation of homosexuality, Premier Joh Bjelke-Petersen and his conservative regime maintained a strong stance against gays and lesbians. The Premier himself described gays as 'perverts', and the criminal law that prohibited sexual acts between males – in place since the beginning of the twentieth century – remained an offence that attracted jail time.

Just a fortnight earlier, on 23 December 1982, the charismatic Moore – a member of the police force's public relations unit who had become an almost accidental children's television star after he was asked to make sporadic appearances on Channel Seven as the face of 'stranger danger' and other campaigns – had once again come to the attention of his colleagues.

Police had raided unit 97 of the Gardens Apartments in Alice Street, the city. The unit was owned by an executive with the Ford Motor Company – Paul John Breslin, then in his early thirties – an associate of Moore's and the popular local ABC radio personality Bill Hurrey. During the raid, police seized a photograph album that contained obscene pictures and photographs of Senior Constable Moore cavorting with some young South East Queensland Electricity Board workers.

At the direction of Deputy Commissioner Syd Atkinson, Moore was questioned by Detective Senior Sergeant Col Thompson and Inspector Jim Sommer in relation to the photographs. According to a police report, Moore 'denied any knowledge that BRESLIN was homosexual – denied any impropriety'.

Moore was warned against associating with Breslin.

But this was not the first time that reports of Moore's questionable behaviour had surfaced. As early as April 1982, an undercover drug squad officer, Constable G.M. Jones, happened to be in the Hacienda Hotel in Fortitude Valley – one of several gay clubs in the precinct, including The Beat and the Silver Dollar – when Moore came onto his radar.

Jones would witness Moore associating with homosexuals in the bar. His report on the incident went up the chain to then Assistant Commissioner Tony Murphy. Jones recorded: 'On Wednesday, the 14th of April 1982, I was performing duty as an undercover agent for the Drug Squad and I was engaged in an operation which centres around the homosexual element of the inner city areas, mainly in the Fortitude Valley area. At about 9.45 p.m., three male persons entered through the front door and I recognised one of them as Constable David MOORE. He and his companions were dressed in casual clothing and one of the male companions was carrying what seemed to be a ladies vanity bag.'

Jones noted in his report: 'It appears obvious that Constable MOORE has homosexual tendencies and I respectfully request that his activities be brought to the notice of his Superiors.'

The report was not acted upon.

Come September 1982, Constable Mike Garrahy of the Juvenile Aid Bureau had interviewed a man concerning allegations that his son Paul – then 17 – was approached by radio celebrity Bill Hurrey and Constable Moore in relation to making 'blue movies'. The boy had become associated with Hurrey through a work offer known as 'Jobs for House Boys'. Paul turned up for duties at a flat at 7/713 Brunswick Street, Fortitude Valley. It was Hurrey's unit.

A confidential police report on the incident stated: '[Paul] … explained he had gone to a unit, performed household duties and was then given liquor to drink and shown hardcore porn magazines. In payment for the work performed it was proposed to take him to dinner at Lennons in the city. He requested that he be paid in cash and subsequently the offers to take part in the movies were made.'

Garrahy submitted the report. Again nothing happened. He would later say he believed the report went to Assistant Commissioner Murphy and that Commissioner Lewis 'would have had to have known' of its existence. He remained bemused that no further action was taken.

Deputy Commissioner Syd 'Sippy' Atkinson later claimed he had heard allegations made against Moore through 1982 and 1983, and that the affable constable had given him 'satisfactory' answers to the allegations. 'I later informed the Commissioner of the allegations I received against Moore,' Atkinson said. 'I believe Moore was allowed to continue his television and public relations work.'

Atkinson conceded that Moore had a good 'working relationship' with the Commissioner. 'In fact, I can recall a couple of occasions when the Commissioner appeared on television with Moore,' Atkinson added. 'Because of this, Moore had easy access to the Commissioner's office and on occasions would appear with the Commissioner at various public relations functions. I am not aware if Moore was on a first-name basis with the Commissioner.'

A former close associate of Moore says: 'Moore had a friend who was in the radio industry and because he was associated with [radio station] 4BC, Moore was introduced to Breslin. He [Breslin] pretended to Moore that he was the government medical officer – a guy called Dr Forde. That was apparently Breslin's modus operandi, his pattern. That was his thing – impersonating police officers. Saying he was the general manager of Ford [Motor Company], saying he was a police officer, high up in government and all this stuff.'

A fortnight after receiving the late call, Inspector Pitman produced a report on the incident and forwarded it to Internal Investigations 'for information and favour of consideration'. The next day, Tuesday 25 January, a copy of the report was sent to the Commissioner's office.

Although Lewis was still officially on annual leave, he was back in Brisbane and coming in and out of the office. On that day he arrived at headquarters around 1.50 p.m., having been out to Marist College, Ashgrove, to enrol his youngest child, John Paul, and have an interview with the headmaster.

He saw Acting Commissioner Atkinson and later had drinks with senior officers, their staff and Police Minister Bill Glasson at headquarters. As for the Pitman report, it made its way to Atkinson's desk by early February and was marked '(1) Seen, (2) File Away'.

Hunting Hapeta

The diligent Licensing Branch undercover officer Nigel Powell, formerly of West Midlands police in the United Kingdom, took to his second tour of duty in the Licensing Branch with gusto. He had arrived out of nowhere in 1979 and, to his surprise, was almost immediately transferred to the Licensing Branch. The rangy, bespectacled Powell made every effort to fit in, but found it difficult to understand how the branch actually worked. The place was steeped in secrets, with hidden connections and loyalties, and Powell wasn't privy to the branch's complex infrastructure. Everyone was suspicious of each other.

Despite this, Powell ploughed forward. A tall man, he became a part of the police basketball team. He was also an accomplished long-distance runner, and joined the police athletics squad, winning a national title.

After briefly returning to the UK in the early 1980s, he was back in Brisbane and Licensing by 1981, and slipped straight into his undercover role. Powell observed that in just a few short years the local massage parlour and escort scene had boomed in his absence. Parlours rashed the city, and escort services were doing a roaring trade. One name kept coming up repeatedly during his police work – Hector Hapeta.

The physically huge Hapeta, convicted criminal and one-time pet food proprietor, had come north from Sydney in 1978 with his de facto wife Anne Marie Tilley in search of a better life in the sun. (Rumour had it that Hapeta had in fact fallen foul of Sydney crime identity Abe Saffron, and had gone to Queensland to wait for the dust to settle.) Within weeks of hitting the ground in Brisbane – and in particular the shady lanes of Fortitude Valley – the pair had established the beginnings of what would become a monstrous vice empire.

The couple lived in a small, decrepit Queenslander at 27 Hill Street, Spring Hill, on the doorstep of the Valley and perched on one of the steep streets that arch east off Gregory Terrace. It was hardly the domicile of the city's leading dealers in prostitution. Then again, Hapeta and Tilley were constantly on the move, he mixing with business partners such as Geoff Crocker, drinking and eating late into the night, catching up with the town's gambling kings – the Bellinos – and trying to broker new business with men like the criminal Roland Short who, since his heyday with swingers clubs like the Matador, was trying to make a fist of it on the Gold Coast. Anne Marie kept busy running their burgeoning number of parlours, drinking in night clubs into the early hours, keeping up to date with the books and in particular the systemic protection payments going back to the Licensing Branch.

Powell informed his superiors in the Licensing Branch of his suspicions about Hapeta but was repeatedly told to direct his attentions elsewhere. It made no sense to Powell: 'It became increasingly apparent to me that the perception in the office that Hapeta had nothing to do with the running of prostitution did not match with the information that I was receiving from people on the street. I observed that Hector Hapeta was never prosecuted for keeping premises ... although he controlled most of the prostitution establishments then in operation throughout Brisbane. Even after I commenced passing on information about Hapeta, I did not see any attempt to obtain evidence against Hapeta in order to have him prosecuted for keeping.'

Powell continued, undeterred. On 26 April 1983 he gathered an information sheet on Hapeta based on intelligence from his informants. It said Hapeta had financed a massage parlour at 608 Wickham Street, Fortitude Valley, and that he was also in receipt of protection payments from a number of escort agencies. Powell handed the sheet directly to Inspector Graeme Parker, in charge of the Licensing Branch.

A week later Powell had more information that he gave to his superior. It provided further details of protection payments and a warning that Hapeta was looking at setting up an illegal liquor outlet 'similar to World By Night' – an unlicensed Bellino/Conte pub and strip club in the city that did a roaring late-night trade.

'During this period I discussed Hapeta with Inspector Parker,' Powell said. 'I told him that I would like to spend some time undercover to find out to what extent Hapeta was involved in various enterprises. Parker told me that his information was that Hapeta was not involved.

'I made a second attempt during this period to be allowed to investigate Hapeta and Tilley. Parker repeated to me that his information was that Hapeta was not involved and that I was not to worry about him.'

Powell told Parker of a distressing development. His informant was able to recite, word for word, phrase for phrase, conversations he'd had with other Licensing Branch officers, including Parker himself. Someone was leaking information.

As Powell's informant was leaving Brisbane, the dutiful officer wanted to get on record as much as she knew, and arranged for her to speak with Detective Senior Sergeant Allen Bulger of the Licensing Branch. In due course, Bulger took a statement from her at the Woolloongabba police station. During the interview the informant repeated what Powell had outlined in his reports – that Hapeta was dispatching protection payments, and owned at least three parlours: Top of the Valley, Fantasia and Touch of Class – and had interests in sex shops.

Powell's diligence in the field was bringing him dangerously close to uncovering the web of corruption that filtered up through the Licensing Branch to the very top of the police force and the desk of Commissioner Lewis himself. He didn't know it yet, but Powell's days in Licensing were numbered.

Laundry

In the early 1980s, Commissioner Lewis wasn't the only one playing the property market. Jack Herbert – the English-born former Licensing Branch policeman, in-line machine salesman and now chief bagman for corrupt police – was buying and selling with aplomb, everything from inner-city apartments to industrial warehouses. The cunning Herbert, maestro of The Joke and recipient of hundreds of thousands of dollars of protection money from growing sources, used real estate transactions to wash his illegal monies.

By 1983, according to Herbert, bribes received from prostitution and illegal gambling totalled around $45,250 per month. He alleged Lewis was taking in $6500 a month, while Herbert himself was pocketing $9679. Something had to be done about the accumulation of black cash. 'Most of the deals involved some sort of scam,' Herbert said in his memoir, *The Bagman*.

Herbert had been dabbling in property since 1970 when he bought his first house at 105 Kirkland Avenue, Coorparoo. This was followed in 1974 by unit 27 at The Dunes, on the Esplanade at Surfers Paradise. In 1976 the Herberts picked up another house and an adjoining block of land at 69 Atlantic Drive, Loganholme, before purchasing the unit he and his family would move into at 49 Laidlaw Parade, East Brisbane.

In the early 1980s they bought houses in Dutton Park and Daisy Hill and in February 1982 purchased two blocks in an industrial estate at 22 Devlan Street, Mansfield, south of the CBD, off a friend who was managing the properties. A 'bodgy' contract was drawn up and Herbert signed. The friend referred to the land as the 'Black and White Estate' because 'so many people were using it to launder illegal money'.

Herbert also bought unit 2 of the Southbank Apartments at 10 Lower River Terrace, South Brisbane, which had splendid views of the Captain Cook Bridge and the Brisbane CBD. Herbert told the estate agent he was in the pinball machine business and had a lot of money he didn't want to be taxed on. He asked if he could use some black money for the purchase. He wasn't knocked back.

In the end, Herbert said he washed about $270,000 through the property market. He claimed he never discussed money with Commissioner Terry Lewis. 'He wasn't a gambling man,' said Herbert. 'He didn't bet on the horses or the trots or the greyhounds. Strange as it sounds, we split more than a million dollars between us and never discussed what we were doing with it. That's how it was with Terry. We had been doing business since the 1960s but I never asked how he disposed of his share.'

Herbert was accumulating so much cash he quite literally didn't know what to do with it. He stashed it around his home. He created secret cavities in walls. He had cemented bundles of it inside besser bricks. Jack Herbert couldn't spend his money fast enough.

And it was exactly how he liked it.

Framed

By early 1983, Queensland's first female detective, Lorelle Saunders, had been languishing in prison for more than eight months on a range of serious offences, including attempted murder. Saunders had come to prominence under the commissionership of Ray Whitrod, and had been a powerful voice for the rights of female police officers. It was this kind of behaviour that had got under the skin of Commissioner Lewis, and even more so the former assistant commissioner, Tony Murphy. But perhaps her biggest transgression had been her involvement, in the late 1970s, in what became known as the Katherine James affair, when photographs allegedly surfaced of the prostitute James in a physical relationship with the high-ranking police officer and Whitrod acolyte Basil Hicks. The pictures claiming to depict Hicks, a dedicated family man, having sex with a prostitute didn't even need to exist. Just the word they did was enough to tarnish Hicks's reputation.

A staunch Catholic, Hicks wanted to get to the bottom of the damning allegations against him. He believed that behind the scenes police were using false photographs as some sort of bargaining chip with the prostitute James. In an attempt to expose the set-up, he headed out to Boggo Road Gaol with Lorelle Saunders, who interviewed James.

When Murphy discovered Saunders had accompanied Hicks, he was apoplectic. Saunders believes that she became the target of a vicious campaign by corrupt police to destroy her career. As an alleged member of the so-called Committee of Eight who had supported Whitrod, Saunders had made several attempts to expose corruption in the force. She had raised the ire of the Rat Pack and had come to understand that revenge was likely, though she could not in her wildest dreams have imagined the form it would take.

On 29 April 1982, Saunders was arrested. An article had appeared in the newspaper, penned by Murphy's old mate crime reporter Brian Bolton, claiming that a senior policewoman had plotted to murder a fellow police officer. The article revealed that detectives had uncovered a plan by a criminal and the policewoman to ambush the officer, murder him and dump his body in bushland outside Brisbane.

'There were headlines in the [*Sunday*] *Sun* alleging very serious matters were being investigated against a female officer,' Saunders recalled. 'This was the first knowledge I had of any such investigation. I subsequently contacted my solicitor.'

Commissioner Lewis made no mention of this extraordinarily grave story in his diaries, but he did note on 28 April that he phoned 'Sir Robert Sparkes re P/W L. Saunders'.

In prison, Saunders was assaulted by both fellow prisoners and warders, and was put in solitary confinement. The charges against her were that she had attempted to procure criminal Douglas Mervyn Dodd to steal money; that on unknown dates she attempted to procure Dodd to conspire with another to kill Saunders' former lover, Superintendent Allan Lobegeiger; and that on 7 March she stole a .357 Magnum Smith and Wesson revolver, a .22 Smith and Wesson revolver, a .44 Magnum Smith and Wesson revolver, an Armalite semi-automatic rifle and a quantity of ammunition, the property of Roy Alfred Coomer. Saunders was additionally charged with attempting to pervert the course of justice, stemming from a tape recording, allegedly found at her home.

Dodd (who had once been Saunders' informant) told police that Saunders had asked him to steal the weapons owned by Roy Coomer, with whom she was in a relationship. Dodd also said Saunders had asked him to procure somebody to kill Lobegeiger. Dodd said he had an incriminating recording of a conversation with Saunders, which he had recorded over the top of music he already had on the tape. When the alleged conversation with Saunders ended, the previously taped music resumed.

It was damming evidence, and Saunders was facing a large portion of her future behind bars.

The Escort and the Casanova

It would have been entirely reasonable if Mary Anne Brifman, eldest daughter of the former prostitute and brothel madam Shirley Brifman, had decided to leave Brisbane and start a new life following her mother's shocking death in the early 1970s. Mary Anne was smart, but hers was no ordinary suburban upbringing. She had been raised in Sydney and witnessed first hand the detritus that comes with being the offspring of a successful big-city brothel madam. Mary Anne had seen things no child should witness. She was at the epicentre of prostitution, drugs, bank heists, bashings, shootings and death. Mary Anne had witnessed her own mother tortured by corrupt police and criminals, and she had been put on the game by her own parents, aged 13.

In 1971, when her mother Shirley Brifman decided to squeal and bring down the corrupt police who had suffocated her life, the entire family fled back to the supposed safe haven of Brisbane. Ironically, it was where Shirley Brifman would meet her death.

As an adult, Mary Anne had a lot of time to reflect on the circumstances surrounding her mother's supposed suicide. Mary Anne knew her mother had not simply taken her own life. She had seen the visitor at the Clayfield flat the night before Shirley's body was found. She'd seen a vial of drugs handed over. She'd heard the warnings.

By the early 1980s, Mary Anne was divorced and struggling to raise two small children. Unable to make ends meet, she did what her mother had taught her so well. By her own account, she was excellent at what she did. 'On the job I was outstanding,' she says. 'I had outstanding skills. My mother taught me. She took me into the bedroom [in Sydney] when I was young and taught me.'

While she disliked the escort life, it was all she knew and she only worked just enough shifts to make enough to cover the costs of food and rent for her and the kids. Unfortunately, like her mother, she couldn't escape getting tangled up with police.

'I went out on a job – it was usually to private homes or hotels – and this job was at Clayfield,' says Mary Anne. 'I did the job. It was good. We had a lot of chemistry. He was nice and polite, but he was a bikie. I was gullible and naive. He saw my green Valiant Charger. He gave me lessons on how to spin around and all those sorts of turns. He was very warm.'

One of the client's friends, however, had recently been arrested and his bail was posted. 'They asked me if I could go over and bail their friend out. I asked them, "What do I do?" I went to the Brisbane watch-house. I was innocent, fresh-looking. You could never tell I was an escort; I was glamorous, clean-cut.

'I went in there and I said to the officer on the desk that I'd like to bail this person out. He was a red-head. He got a shock. He said, "Why would an innocent girl like you be bailing this guy?"'

'He started to flirt with me. He was very charming. This guy liked me a lot. He was so nice to me. He got really friendly with me. He told me he'd left his wife.'

The smitten police constable began phoning Mary Anne incessantly. 'He pursued me, this constable,' she says. 'A romance started happening.'

Something didn't feel right to Mary Anne and she soon discovered that the policeman was living with a woman. He had left his wife for her. The constable told Mary Anne he was not interested in this new woman and was going to leave her, too. 'I asked him to leave me alone. I didn't want to see him again. I asked him very seriously to never call me again. He couldn't help himself. He kept trying to contact me … it was out of hand.'

Mary Anne warned him that if he continued she would take some action, but still he kept ignoring her pleas. In the end, the wife, the mistress and Mary Anne got together and decided to wait for the constable one evening when he came home from work. 'I think it just added to the over-inflated ego he had about himself,' Mary Anne reflects. 'After that he still pursued me and I told him I was going to report him to the police, even though he was a police officer. In the end I did. He ended up being transferred out west.'

Considering her mother's experience, Mary Anne should have known what to expect when she crossed a serving Queensland police officer. She was soon getting visits from members of the Licensing Branch. 'Two detectives came along one Saturday morning and they started insulting me. They called me a whore,' she says. 'They didn't try to arrest me but there was a lot of name-calling and harassment. It was because I put that report in on the constable. It was payback.

'One of them asked me to pay them money. They didn't know who I was. They didn't know I was a Brifman, and I didn't want them to know. I was going under my married name.'

She refused to pay them graft for a very good reason. 'A few days before my mother died she called me into the middle room of the flat [in Bonney Avenue, Clayfield] and made me feel a lump in her groin,' Mary Anne says. 'She said it was cancer and that she was going to die. It was a lump in her groin – it could have been anything – it could have been a cyst, an infection.

'She tried to use it, I believe now, to dramatically grab my attention. She was preparing for her death. She knew she had to die in a few days and she wanted to tell me something. She begged me; she pleaded with me to pledge to her that I would never pay graft to police. I promised her I wouldn't. This was very serious. She had never spoken to me like this before.'

When Mary Anne was asked to pay graft by the two detectives she was in a real quandary. 'No matter what, I could never, ever pay graft, as it was my mother's true dying warning … it was so inculcated and entrenched in me, that by saying yes would have led to eventually being murdered. That day I politely, respectfully, meekly and humbly responded that I could not. Over time they wore me down and I moved house.'

It didn't stop police pursuing the escort who had jeopardised the love life of a local constable. They soon tracked her down. 'I moved into this other place, a small house, and the police found out where I was,' she recalls. 'When I was young I had accrued a lot of driving tickets for speeding and things like that, and I hadn't paid the fines.' The fines had turned into warrants.

'I was in the house and I saw at least six police cars arrive. I thought they were going to arrest me and put me in gaol. I went into the bathroom and hopped into the bathtub. I was shivering and quietly crying. I was very innocent. I couldn't imagine going to gaol. I was laying in the bath and the police were everywhere around the house. They came up to the frosted glass window of the bathroom but they couldn't see me. I could hear them all around the whole house. I didn't know what to do.'

There, alone in the bath, weeping, Mary Anne Brifman resolved that she had to get out of Brisbane. She knew only too well what could happen if you were pursued by the Queensland police. Mary Anne was the same age as her mother had been when she died. It was time to move on.

A Greenhorn in Surfers Paradise

All young Eric Gregory (Greg) Deveney ever wanted to do was become a policeman. He probably had his father to thank for that. Eric Deveney Senior was a respected detective in the drug squad in Brisbane and had worked with the likes of Frank Bischof and Don 'Buck' Buchanan from the 1950s. So when Deveney joined the force in June 1970 – he was the first batch of new recruits under the stewardship of former Commissioner Ray Whitrod – he had high hopes for a long and successful career. In those early years he had heard the rumours about Whitrod – that the boss was incompetent, a pen-pusher, a lofty intellectual who didn't understand the wants and needs of his men at the ground level – but it didn't dampen his spirits. He couldn't wait to serve. Deveney hoped to be as good and honest a policeman as his father.

'I didn't even know bloody corruption existed in the police force,' Deveney recalls. 'You know, I thought it was all honest and fair dinkum and everything else – shining white knights helping people.'

Deveney was posted briefly to Far North Queensland before being consigned to the Gold Coast Criminal Investigation Branch in the early 1980s. He could not have migrated to a more contrasting environment – this jungle was urban.

The Gold Coast had been Brisbane's pleasure pot certainly since the 1940s and 50s – its famous Pyjama Parties a case in point – but by the early 1980s its allure had been discovered by the nation. The Australian film *Goodbye Paradise*, released in 1983 and starring Ray Barrett, may have given Deveney a preview of what he was in for. Set in Surfers Paradise and in and about the coast, the reviewer Dougal Macdonald described the landscape thus: 'The Gold Coast, that place where old Australians go to experience the afterlife before they die, is despite its crassness, commercialism, phoniness and kitsch, a marvellous film location.'

Cheap flights were bringing in the hordes. East-West Airlines ran a successful campaign for a $199 seven-day Gold Coast holiday, including first-class accommodation and free in-flight champagne. The coast already had its 'worlds'. Sea World, the brainchild of entrepreneur Keith Williams, was just about to go up for sale, and Dreamworld opened for Christmas 1981 on the Brisbane to Gold Coast Highway on 80 hectares of bushland at Coomera. Other worlds were on the horizon.

With high-rise apartment buildings rising up across the strip, the high-fliers dined on seafood at Oskars restaurant in Surfers Paradise. Those entrepreneurs like Williams and Mike Gore, men close to Premier Joh Bjelke-Petersen, were dubbed the White Shoe Brigade. As it became increasingly more popular, the Gold Coast simultaneously attracted vice, and the brothel and gambling kings following the money.

Deveney must have been bug-eyed at the Birdwatchers' Bar, the leggy meter maids, the tired but legendary Pink Poodle motel and the strip's not-so-discreet string of massage parlours. When he turned up for work at the CIB offices in downtown Surfers Paradise, home to racy nightclubs, such as The Penthouse and German beer and schnitzel barns, the scales were removed from his eyes. 'I fell out with everybody on the very first day,' he recalls. 'They used to all drink at the Surfers Paradise Hotel [on Cavill Avenue] and they said, "Oh, come on down for drinks after work" … this was about three o'clock and everybody went down. You know we went in the bloody bar and I pulled out my bloody money and put it on the counter. And they said, "Oh, you don't pay in this place mate, it's all free."

'I said, "If they aren't prepared to take my money, I'm not prepared to drink their grog."

'They said, "Don't be stupid, it's all free here, the lot."

'I said, "Nothing is free", and I walked out. That was my first shift. You know, I didn't need that sort of rubbish. Some of them approached me [afterwards] and said, "What was that all about?" I said, "I don't drink free piss … as far as I'm concerned there's no such thing. Anyway, I don't drink when I'm on duty and I don't drink drive."'

His fellow officers didn't quite know what to make of Deveney. They were no doubt aware of his father by reputation, and would have appreciated that he too was a straight-shooter. The greenhorn was given another chance. He was asked to work in the Gold Coast Consorting Squad, and he was partnered with Detective Patrick (Pat) Glancy.

Glancy had spent the formative years of his career in Brisbane, and had worked closely with his mentor, Tony Murphy. He worked on some of the biggest crimes of the 1970s, including the fatal torching of the Whiskey Au Go Go nightclub in Fortitude Valley; it was Glancy who arrested suspect John Andrew Stuart. Glancy had also been a top amateur boxer and had a reputation among fellow police as being not just feared, but ruthless.

Just prior to Terry Lewis being anointed Police Commissioner in November 1976, someone, possibly Murphy, had drawn up a crib sheet of fellow officers under the headings 'Friends', 'Capable' and 'Others'. Along with Ron Redmond, Noel Dwyer, Ross Beer and Graham Leadbetter in the 'Friends' category, was Pat Glancy.

Detective Glancy's arrival on the burgeoning Gold Coast – bristling in the early 1980s with massage parlours and brothels, illegal gambling and SP bookmaking, under the control of Syd Atkinson – was quickly noticed by his superiors. He soon took charge of the Consorting Squad. One local businessman, who often drank with police at the Queen's Hotel in Nerang Street, Southport, said Glancy's reputation preceded him. 'I never took to him, [but] certainly of those fellows, regular police and the other fellows, the local boys, when this Glancy came on the scene … they said, "He's a gun" … He was held in a bit of awe by the local coppers.'

It didn't take long for Deveney to note that only a fraction of prostitutes working on the Gold Coast were being breached by police. He set about changing that and was soon issuing 60 to 70 breaches a month. Again he earned the ire of his colleagues.

'The girls came in and I would give them a warning, a caution, telling them what the go was, and if they wanted to stay in that sort of business they could expect to be summonsed for [assisting to keep] premises,' remembers Deveney. 'And yeah, we just kept trying to keep it as clean as we possibly could.'

One of the more difficult tasks, too, was keeping police out of the brothels. 'We chased uniform and branch fellows and visiting police who were taking advantage of the situation,' he says. 'We stopped all of that, which didn't make us very popular … sergeants didn't like it, especially having a senior constable getting up them in a back alley somewhere.'

Deveney couldn't have known it then, but he would soon have more things to worry about than his popularity in the office.

Salad Days at Shalimar

For Jack and Peggy Herbert, life was great in the new year. The corruption network known as The Joke, and commandeered by

Herbert with the meticulousness of a forensic accountant, was in full gear. The in-line machines were a cash cow – more lucrative than poker machines – and Herbert, with his brilliant organisational skills, was making the most of it.

In addition, he and Peggy had moved into the splendid pale brick riverfront unit block – Shalimar – at 49 Laidlaw Parade, East Brisbane. Their unit sported excellent views up the reach of the river to the skyline of the CBD, and across the river to Merthyr Park. In their unit, Herbert had a bar – he made sure there was a bar in every property he ever lived in – and he utilised it to the full. Guests were forever in and out of the Herbert pad, including Police Commissioner Terry Lewis and his wife Hazel, and former assistant commissioner Tony Murphy. Friends would join Herbert at his bar around 5 p.m., then head out to a restaurant for dinner around 8 p.m.

As for money coming in – it was everywhere. 'He often had envelopes full of cash dropped into his locked letterbox at the unit,' a source says. 'There was so much he didn't know what to do with it. He had bundles of it taped in certain places throughout the unit, even underneath the cutlery drawer in the kitchen. He would count the cash and separate it into the bundles that were going to police and others he had to pay off as part of The Joke.

'But I believe he probably gave away half of what came in for him. He was always giving away money. If he heard that the little old lady across the road was doing it tough, he'd go over and give her $500.

'He was happy, gregarious, and one of the funniest men you'd ever meet. He was always playing on words … he was very funny.'

And the cash continued to pour in from the Hapeta/Tilley and Bellino/Conte consortiums.

'You wouldn't believe the meticulous files he kept on everything,' the source says. 'Everything was filed and cross-referenced. Everything went in there. How much came in. Who the money was going to. When and where money was paid, and by whom to whom. It was just incredible. He used to drive his family crazy. He had to have all his shirts facing one way on hangers in the closet. All his shoes lined up. He was absolutely meticulous.'

Herbert was buying and selling properties with abandon, and on significant purchases like, for example, a boat, he would remark: 'Let The Joke pay for it.'

Herbert regularly made the delivery of illegal monies to corrupt police and politicians like Don 'Shady' Lane, the Member for Merthyr. And sometimes Peggy Herbert made the drops. When the social couple weren't available for the monthly disbursement, a trusted friend would do the job.

'I made the drop at Lewis's house at 12 Garfield Drive on a few occasions,' another source says. 'I would go to the door and Hazel Lewis would invite me in and I handed her the envelopes.'

According to witnesses, Commissioner Lewis visited Shalimar on several occasions – always in plain clothes – where he allegedly discussed the transfer of police officers to various branches and units within the police department. Lewis was also there when Jack and Peggy Herbert celebrated their thirtieth wedding anniversary.

'Jack was a party animal – he loved to be around people,' the source says. 'He was witty and entertaining. To Jack, everything was a joke.'

Fabrication

The trial against the embattled former detective Lorelle Saunders went ahead in May 1983. The crux of the case was criminal Douglas Mervyn Dodd's alleged tape recording of Saunders asking him to procure a hitman to kill police officer Allan Lobegeiger. Dodd claimed he made the secret recording in a park on 19 March 1982.

On the fourth day of the trial, however, Crown solicitor Tony Glynn had some extraordinary news to impart to the court. It appeared that the Dodd tape was a fabrication. A Public Defender's Office solicitor had made an amazing discovery. He studied the background music on Dodd's tape and found a radio station jingle. Further investigation proved that the jingle had first gone to air on 27 March 1982 – eight days after Dodd said he made the tape. 'It thus appears that the only explanation is that the tape was certainly not made at the time and in the fashion deposed by Dodd and appears to be quite clearly a fabrication,' said Glynn.

Justice Shepherdson asked: 'Well, now, Mr Glynn, where does that leave you?'

'That leaves the Crown with no case,' he answered.

Shepherdson directed that Saunders be acquitted. He also directed the Solicitor-General's office to investigate the fabricated tape and find out who was responsible for it. 'Putting it bluntly, really, this man Dodd has plainly committed perjury in respect of this tape,' Justice Shepherdson concluded. 'I don't think it is too strong for me to say that … someone, somewhere, has apparently arranged for this man to fabricate a tape recording.

'I direct that this file, the exhibits and all evidence be referred to the Crown Law authorities for a full and detailed investigation to try to get to the bottom of this whole rather unsatisfactory, sordid affair …'

Ultimately, Dodd was charged with perjury, found guilty and sentenced to six years in prison.

Saunders continued to lobby government and the police department for suitable compensation and was rebuffed, despite then Attorney-General Neville Harper declaring her 'completely innocent of all charges'.

So, who was behind the Saunders scandal? Had such a grotesque and complicated plot really been developed against her because she had supported Basil Hicks in his quest to get to the truth behind the Katherine James photographs? Could her life and career have been threatened because she had transgressed senior police officers close to Commissioner Lewis?

After Saunders was acquitted, Commissioner Lewis consulted two fellow officers. Quite specifically he wanted to know: Could she be charged departmentally?

Member for Archerfield, Kev 'Buckets' Hooper had shouted Saunders' innocence at every opportunity and condemned corrupt police both to the media and on the floor of parliament – he deemed her acquittal one of the highlights of his career. After the trial he called for an investigation. He wanted to know if Saunders had been framed by police and, if so, why. Was it because she fought against corruption?

Saunders was told she could take any complaints she had to either Lewis or the Police Complaints Tribunal. She would spend much of the next decade fighting subsequent suspensions and threats that she'd be sacked from the force. The saga would spill into the 1990s, as Queensland's first female detective continued her fight for justice.

The Aphrodisiac of Power

In the lead-up to the 1983 state election, Terrence Anthony 'Terry' White, the Liberal cabinet minister, was growing concerned by the stench of political and police corruption. White, a working-class boy from Sandgate who, through sheer tenacity, became a successful pharmacist and businessman, had shown an early interest in politics, working briefly on John F. Kennedy's 1960 Presidential campaign in the United States. White was a long-term member of the Queensland branch of the Liberal Party before winning the seat of Redcliffe in a by-election in 1979. He was swiftly promoted to the ministry by Liberal leader Dr Llew Edwards in 1980.

'So, all of a sudden I'm in the Cabinet with these guys,' White remembers. 'And prior to that, within the Liberal Party itself was all these allegations flowing, from the Gold Coast in particular, that were raised by [local MPs] Bruce Bishop and Peter White [no relation] who were outstanding state members. They were raising the whole issue of approvals for suspect developers and there were all these allegations about money being siphoned off to Russ Hinze and the National Party and all that sort of stuff.'

White struggled with what he was hearing. How could he prove it?

Malcolm McMillan, who worked as ALP press secretary for Tom Burns, faced a similar dilemma. Because of the power of Bjelke-Petersen and the Nationals, and because of the Opposition's extended time in the political wilderness, the ALP had to be judge, jury and executioner when it came to matters of corruption. It not only had to present the allegations, but had to have them chiselled in stone to make any sort of headway in parliament and with the electorate. Anything short of that didn't wash.

White was at a loss as the rumours mounted. 'There was the story that some Asian bagman arrived at the National Party headquarters with literally $50,000 in a brown paper bag, and thought the Liberal Party Headquarters was the National Party Headquarters. It was really bad, but you couldn't put your finger on things. It became common knowledge with some developers down [on] the Gold Coast that if you wanted something [a development application to go] through ... you obviously saw the government minister at the end of the day.'

In desperation, White and his colleagues reached out to the young National Party member for Landsborough, Mike Ahern. They trusted Ahern and knew he was straight as an arrow. 'We're talking to Ahern quietly saying, look, we've got to clean this place up or the whole thing is going to go up in smoke,' recalls White. 'And, because Ahern was of a similar age to the rest of us, you know, with Angus Innes and Terry Geiger and Ian Prentice – all those sorts of people – they sort of started to work as a team to use the parliamentary process.

'We needed greater scrutiny and got the estimate committees going ... and of course that's when the divisions occurred in the government because the Liberal Party backbench was doing the job of the Opposition. The Labor Party then was bloody useless, or lazy, or whatever.'

White, too, had been troubled by the fracas the year before, in 1982, over the appointment of the Chief Justice. Indeed, the tension between the government executive and the judiciary had been simmering for over a year. Bjelke-Petersen believed some of the judiciary were not toeing the Party line, and threatened to 'put the skids under them'.

By the time the new Chief Justice was to be appointed, Bjelke-Petersen was determined to get his man home. That happened to be Justice Dormer (Bob) Andrews. Justice James Douglas was first in the line of seniority to take the position. Justice Andrews was seventh.

Bjelke-Petersen got wind that Douglas voted Labor and that was enough for the Premier's trusted confidant, Sir Edward Lyons, to swing into action. He began agitating in earnest for Andrews' appointment to the top job.

White was incredulous. 'It got to the stage where you had "Top Level" Ted Lyons [a trustee of the National Party who was also a member of the Bjelke-Petersen Foundation, which raised funds for the Party] and [Commissioner] Terry Lewis, they used to have lunch every Friday,' says White. 'Anyway, they decided Andrews … was going to get the job whereas Douglas was the recommendation of the Attorney-General [Sam Doumany] and the profession.'

White couldn't make sense of powerbrokers outside Cabinet making decisions on senior government appointments. It defied all he knew of the democratic process. 'I was at a TAB function and Ted Lyons was chairman of the TAB and Lewis was there,' remembers White. 'And he [Lyons] came up and said, "You fucking Libs are not going to have any say, Andrews is going to be the Chief Justice".

'Lewis was in the conversation standing around having drinks. I was a bit of a novice having been in the Ministry only a couple of years. I said: "What do you mean? This is irregular." And I'm carrying on saying, "Look, you know, it's got nothing to do with you blokes. It will ultimately be a decision of Cabinet and it will be based on the recommendation of the Attorney-General".'

In the end the Liberal Ministers made a decision that they would not go along with Joh's recommendation. 'With the exception of Lane. It was Don Lane who blabbed out in Cabinet that Douglas was a "Labor stooge", they were the words that he used, I remember it quite vividly. And we said, "How the hell would you know how Douglas voted?" He said Douglas was overseas and he had a postal vote and somehow or other he [Lane] got hold of it. So Lane was, you know, right in there and none of us ever trusted Lane.'

In the end, the job of Chief Justice went to Wally Campbell. Following that, the appointment of Senior Puisne Judge had to be decided. Again, the Attorney-General recommended Douglas, but Bjelke-Petersen demanded it be Andrews. 'You got your way with the Chief Justice,' Bjelke-Petersen reportedly told his Liberal colleagues. 'Why don't you give me my way with the second position?'

Seven Liberal ministers declined to support the recommendation. Nevertheless, Andrews was selected. The 'flying minute' approving the appointment was taken to Government House and ratified.

The Bar Association did not send a congratulatory telegram, but later made it clear that Andrews had the confidence of the Bar. The Liberal Party State Executive called an emergency meeting over the Chief Justice affair, and narrowly voted to stay in partnership with the National Party. Meanwhile, Bjelke-Petersen and his government were criticised for politicising the judiciary.

The whole affair, however, didn't sit well with White. He couldn't believe the Police Commissioner might have a hand in the internal machinations of Cabinet. 'I've got no doubt that Lewis stymied the careers of a lot of people because of his relationship with the Premier,' reflects White. 'Not long after I was sworn in my secretary said, "Oh, the Police Commissioner wants to see you."

'I thought, what have I done wrong? So, he lobs in the office and it was all about having a cup of tea and just saying, you know, we, the police force, were delighted when the Premier appointed you to Cabinet.

'And I said, "Hang on, the Premier didn't appoint me, I believe that Llew Edwards appointed me."

'"Oh," he said.'

The Flower Farmer of Amity Point

For years, former assistant commissioner of police, Tony Murphy, had been dropping over to the fishing village of Amity Point on North Stradbroke Island, and piecing together a house. He had gone to the island in the mid-1960s with his and Terry Lewis's good mate, Barry Maxwell, proprietor of the Belfast Hotel in Queen Street, and bought at auction two adjacent blocks of land right down the eastern end of Gonzales Street, on the corner of Tosh Street. Maxwell bought a parcel at the corner of Tosh Street and Sovereign Road.

According to Murphy's family, he built a besser brick garage on one of the blocks, complete with a small kitchen and bathroom. The family spent holidays there, enjoying the island life. The three blocks of land overlooked four hectares of Crown Land that, upon his retirement just before Christmas 1982, Murphy leased. He planned to grow a small farm of Geraldton Wax – *Chamelaucium uncinatum* – the hardy, flowering shrub common in Western Australia. The plant, with white, pink and mauve flowers, lasted generously after cutting and was popular with florists.

Murphy first built a besser brick home on one of his blocks and, after a long and colourful career as one of Queensland's most astute and tough detectives, knuckled down to work as a flower farmer. Replacing his suit, he was often seen on his 'farm' at the end of Gonzales Street dressed in khaki dungarees. He cleared much of the acreage and built a small generator, housed in a pale brick shed, to pump water to his bushes. The land was sandy, ideal for growing Geraldton Wax, and he soon had a tractor to help cultivate the block.

Murphy's activities caught the attention of the tight Amity community. Here was a place sparsely populated with holidaymakers, generational fishermen and misfits. People kept to their own business. In a travel story on Amity Point, published in *The Queenslander* in 1899, the author wrote: 'The pure air of Amity was breathed by many a man whose life, so to put it, was his own – many a man who, perhaps embittered and cast aside, lived with no care for the future, with no pleasant thought of the past.'

Murphy may or may not have had pleasant thoughts of the past, but his transition from big city detective to island hamlet flower farmer, was a substantial one. 'We'd made a different life for ourselves down there, growing flowers,' says Murphy's wife, Maureen. 'He was always in the yard to take his mind off things. [It was] hard, hard work.

'He loved it there. Lying in bed and hearing the sound of the birds, the koalas. He wanted to get away from everything. We never made anything off the farm either. Everything was run at a loss.'

Another Murphy family member said: 'He never had any enemies at Stradbroke.'

Still, growing flowers in the village and eventually carting them back to the mainland to sell to florists and at markets was not something that happened every day at Amity. 'We didn't know what that bloke was doing there,' says one long-time resident. 'It was something strange. The island is a long way removed from Brisbane. It's out of the limelight. It may as well be on the other side of the world.'

Murphy's near neighbours in Tosh Street say he was an excellent neighbour and always willing to lend a helping hand. 'He was the best neighbour you could ever wish to have,' they said. 'Maureen and all the kids were lovely. The house was nothing ostentatious. Tony was a good family man. They drove a Black Chrysler; they did not have flash cars.'

Murphy soon joined the newly established Amity Point Community Club, a place for locals to meet and have a social drink. The club convened in an old wooden hall at the end of Gonzales Street, on Ballow Street. Maureen attended a 'cocktail night' with some of the local women once a month. Another local remembers Murphy from the club bar and also the Point Lookout Hotel. 'He stood and drank on his own,' he says. 'He'd look at you, he'd look at everyone that walked in the door and he'd check out who you were. You could tell he was a policeman.'

Author Peter James, who in 1974 published his explosive book, *In Place of Justice: An Analysis of a Royal Commission 1963–1964* – a damning indictment on a young Murphy and Glen Patrick Hallahan at the time of the National Hotel inquiry – remembers coming across Murphy in the hotel at Point Lookout.

James' book had caused controversy on publication, and at one point James was in fear for his life. He received an anonymous threat, and the company that printed the book was mysteriously burned down not long after it was released. In addition, word got back to James that copies of the book suddenly disappeared from Brisbane libraries, even the State Parliamentary Library.

At the hotel, James says he was drinking with friends when Murphy walked in. 'I thought, Oh God, it's Tony Murphy,' says James. 'He looked at everyone in the bar, scanned their faces, but he passed over mine and didn't recognise me.'

By all accounts, a once frenetically busy Murphy settled into quiet village life. He rarely fished, and neighbours reported few visitors. One, however, stood out. 'Terry Lewis did come over once,' a neighbour says. 'I remember Maureen saying, "Mr Lewis is coming".'

The Breslin Cup

One of the most conspicuous and impressive characters who began appearing regularly at the Police Club in the city was a man called Paul John Breslin. He was born and raised in Gladstone where his father, John Edward Breslin, ran a local funeral parlour and was involved in other businesses.

Paul Breslin was a promising student. 'I was very, very good at English ... social studies, ancient and modern history and English, and I was particularly good at logic – top five in Australia for Year 12,' Breslin says. 'It was my own fault because I was lazy. I was pretty good at the more florid subjects, as they say.'

He was also something of a budding entrepreneur. 'I used to run cabarets at the Queens Hotel, which was, believe it or not, above my father's office, simply because the block of land was owned by Castlemaine Perkins,' Breslin recalls. 'On weekends, on a Friday night, I'd run a disco for underage people ... no grog ... and we always had one or two uniformed police officers on the door to ensure there was no alcohol and that undesirables didn't go in.'

Then life changed for the Breslin family – on Sunday 21 April 1974, Breslin Senior committed suicide with a Sterling .22 rifle at the family's home at 11 Bayne Street, Gladstone. He left behind his wife Margaret (known as Peg) and seven children. Paul was the oldest.

'He was an alcoholic,' Breslin says. 'A severely depressed alcoholic. His father killed himself as did his father ... about five fathers in a row. The whole family left after that incident. It was very depressing to go to the graveyard and see all the Breslins.'

(According to the Rockhampton *Morning Bulletin*, John Breslin's father – Edward Matthew Breslin, a respected local businessman and former mayor of Gladstone – died in hospital in 1944 after a short illness. John's great uncle, C.C. Breslin, a merchant, was charged in the Gladstone Police Court in November 1886 with attempting to commit suicide with a razor. The prisoner said he had been unconscious from alcohol on the night in question and 'had not the slightest idea what he was doing'.)

After the tragedy, Paul moved south to the big smoke, Brisbane, and initially settled in the inner-city suburb of New Farm, then a predominantly working-class suburb crammed with wooden cottages bordering Fortitude Valley. He worked as a sales executive for the Ford Motor Company, where he excelled. Breslin displayed an almost obsessive fascination with police – its hierarchy, its work, its uniforms and badges, cars and weapons. If he could have had an alternative career, he would have been a policeman.

Instead, he spent many nights surrounded by them at the Police Club – on the fourth floor of the old Egg Board building in Makerston Street – an initiative that had been shut down during former Commissioner Frank Bischof's era (in the days of the wet bar at the old Roma Street police station near Turbot Street), but revived by Ray Whitrod. The troops, Whitrod believed, needed a place to talk and relax, and Commissioner Lewis had kept the doors open. The club itself was immensely popular for its conviviality and its food. Indeed, a contingency of police used to fly up from Sydney specifically for the crab pot lunches.

The Police Club president at the time, John Cummins, vividly recalls Paul Breslin. 'Breslin was brought to the Police Club, I don't know by whom,' he says. 'Police had to bring guests. We had plenty of journalists. He [Breslin] represented himself as the used car manager for the Ford Motor Company. He was a likeable sort of fellow.'

Cummins remembers discussing potential business with Breslin. 'He said Ford would like to do something with the police – put up a mirror wall in the club at his expense,' says Cummins. 'He did that. And he donated a cup – The Breslin Cup – to the footballers. They used to play the fire brigade and the ambulance [for the cup honours]. He sort of came out of the forest into the place. He wanted to impress everybody all of the time. He was a bit of a mystery man. It was as though Breslin had been sent from outer space to help [the club].'

A Ford colleague remembers a bright young man with a stellar future. 'He would come to a dealership and he would report to Ford the appearance of the dealership and in turn the whole layout, how the business was operating, and he would take orders on behalf of Ford Motor Company from you, for supply,' he remembers. 'As a rep he went as far as Coffs Harbour, he did Lismore, Grafton and all those and back to the Gold Coast, and he in turn would inspect police cars for Ford somewhere along the line, and so he was always fraternising with the police …

'[Breslin was] a big fella. Could have passed for a copper. Six foot and probably 16 or 17 stone. He was well educated and well spoken.'

It was at the Police Club, at least on one occasion, that Breslin met Police Commissioner Terry Lewis. 'I think I met the man once at the Police Club at a Ford do,' Breslin recalls. 'Ford was introducing a new model, I think it was at the Royal Show, because I'm a life member of the RNA, and I think we put on free drinks at the Police Club which used to be on top of the CIB at North Quay, and I met him there once. Ron Redmond introduced him.'

It was where Breslin claims he also met, for the first time, the popular local television personality and police public relations maestro, Constable Dave Moore. 'Strangely enough, Terry Lewis introduced me to David Moore at the Queensland Police Club,' says Breslin. 'If the Commissioner introduces you to someone socially, you obviously think they must be important. Lewis called Moore over and said, "David, there's someone I want you to meet."

'He [Lewis] promulgated me far above my level. At that stage I didn't know of his [Moore's] TV show. It wouldn't be something I'd have been at home to watch.'

(Breslin would later claim a strong acquaintance with senior police officer and future acting commissioner Ron Redmond. In a statement made to lawyer Chris Nyst years later, Breslin said he had met Redmond and other detectives at the Police Club for drinks and the case of the infamous Whiskey Au Go Go case came up in conversation. Breslin said in his statement: 'He [Redmond] said a number of things about the case and suggested that [John Andrew] Stuart was right for the Whiskey Au Go Go fire. He said words to the effect that [James] Finch was a mate of Stuart's and that he was such an animal that they had to get him off the streets, so they "bricked" him. Redmond repeated a couple of times his assertion that he had "bricked" Finch. None of the other officers there seemed particularly surprised.')

By early 1983, however, Breslin himself had already been the object of an undercover police operation, resulting in a raid on his Alice Street apartment, overlooking the old Botanic Gardens in Brisbane city. There, police found photographs of Constable Dave Moore cavorting with young men and dressed in a South East Queensland Electricity Board workers uniform.

Moore, the public face of the Queensland police, was subsequently questioned by his superiors and the incident was deemed 'nothing offensive'. He was warned off associating with Breslin.

Breslin claims he was at the end of a police conspiracy. 'My barrister … Pat Nolan … there was some ridiculous charge that I was remonstrating with people at a swimming pool wearing a Queensland Police uniform …' says Breslin. 'One day when I was at Metro Ford, I clearly remember this, I put my Fairlane in for service. I walked back to my unit. By the time I got there it was about an hour, [I] talked to a couple of people on the way, there were about five detectives in there planting stuff. I burst the door open and said, "What the fuck's going on?" They had all these search warrants.'

Breslin says he was told that Ron Redmond had organised the raid. 'I'm saying that I certainly didn't do any of the things that I'm alleged to have done,' he says. 'I'm not coming out and telling you that I haven't walked on both sides of the fence, I certainly don't get involved in that sort of rubbish.'

Police Club president John Cummins was alerted to the mounting Breslin situation. 'The next thing I know about him I get a telephone call from a very senior policeman,' he says. 'I was told that Breslin was under investigation. I got him out of the club as quickly as I could . . . I told him I didn't want him there anymore. He got barred.'

A Rendezvous in Montague Road

In early 1983 Geoff Crocker and his wife Julie were running a number of successful escort agencies across the city when the pattern of business suddenly changed – someone was telephoning him and warning him of police raids on his girls. Crocker suspected the calls were coming from Licensing Branch officer 'Dirty Harry' Burgess. He also got a feeling he was about to be hit up for protection payments.

He was right.

Burgess phoned once more and asked Crocker and his wife to meet him at the south-western end of Montague Road in West End, where the Brisbane River takes a dramatic sweep around Toowong towards St Lucia. Burgess said he'd rendezvous with them 'under a big fig tree with a table and chair sitting under it'.

'Julie and I went down there and Harry Burgess was already sitting at that table, so we got out of the car,' Crocker would later tell investigators. 'He had another officer with him … I didn't know him.'

Burgess came to the point. 'Things are going to change,' he supposedly told Crocker. 'You've been getting phone calls telling you about busts and that.'

'That's right. I thought that might have been you.'

'It was,' Burgess said.

'Why? What's going on?'

'From now on you've got to pay somebody,' said Burgess.

'What, you?'

'No,' he clarified. 'You won't be paying any police.'

'I won't pay police, I never have and I never will.'

'Well, I'm telling you now what's got to be done,' Burgess went on. 'After this discussion today, you'll get a phone call and you'll be told how much money to leave at a certain spot, each time of the month, and if it's not there I'll bust you and put you in gaol. If you don't cooperate, Julie, your wife …'

Crocker arced up. 'Don't you frighten Julie because there's no need to …'

Crocker saw that his wife was shaking.

'No need to be, if you just do what you're told, it'll be alright. It'll be a lot better. I guarantee you, you won't go to gaol … but if you don't cooperate and you do anything silly, you could easily be found face down.'

Crocker asked if this was 'heavy, big-time stuff'.

'Yes, it is,' Burgess warned him.

'Julie and I can't end up dead out of this,' he said.

'Well, if you don't do as you're told, you can, by all means.'

Crocker and his wife took a moment to digest the threat. He told his wife in front of the two officers that she wasn't to go back to the escort agency. 'Bullshit,' she said. 'I'm there … what's the difference, if you're dead, I might as well be dead anyhow. We're together. That's it.'

For the next two weeks after the meeting with Burgess under the ancient Moreton Bay fig, Crocker's business ran smoothly – it attracted no attention from police. None of the Crocker girls were busted. Then he got another phone call. He was told he owed $7560 in kickbacks for the month.

'That's a lot of money,' Crocker exclaimed.

The voice at the other end of the line said: 'That covers as many escort agencies as you wish to have.'

Crocker asked if the fee covered him starting up some OP or 'on premises' agencies.

'So long as the boys don't find out that you're doing jobs on the premises, you don't advertise as a massage, it will be classed as escort and comes under the $7560,' the anonymous caller said.

'Who am I talking to?'

'It doesn't matter. You need never know.'

'Are you a police officer?'

'No, I'm not.'

Crocker was given instructions about where to drop off the money. 'He told me there was a toilet block at Davies Park South(s) Football Club, just inside the fence,' recalled Crocker. 'I was to take it into there, put it in the actual pedestal cubicle behind the pedestal, wrapped up in a brown paper pack. There was just a urine trough and a cubicle. Six o'clock in the evening on the dot … don't be late, don't be early …'

Crocker was short of cash come the day the money was due. The following day his places were raided by Harry Burgess.

Ante Up

In February and March of 1983 the Bjelke-Petersen Cabinet gave approval to build the Gold Coast's Jupiters Casino and parliament discussed the Jupiters Agreement Bill. The casino tender had been awarded to Jennings Industries Ltd on behalf of Jupiters Hotel Ltd. The huge Jennings construction company had been founded by Sir Albert Jennings, father to Doug Jennings, the National Party member for Southport. One of Jennings' brothers also worked for the company. The family connection had forced Jennings to make a personal explanation to parliament the year before.

'When I left school I joined AVJennings construction company,' he told the House. 'My father founded the company 50 years ago in 1932. I worked for the company for 13 years before deciding to go out on my own … My brother is a director of Jennings Industries, but I make it clear once again that I have no physical or financial involvement with that Australian-owned public company, although I am certainly proud of its achievements.'

During the debates over the Bill, Jennings would clash with the Treasurer and minister responsible for the casino, Dr Llew Edwards. Edwards accused Jennings of attacking the Casino Control Bill.

In turn, Jennings did not agree with aspects of the Bill, nor with Edwards' 'dictatorial powers' in relation to safeguarding the casino against corruption, something Jennings felt would 'create the reverse situation and provide a perfect recipe for graft and corruption and frighten off investors'. The argument underlined the now open warfare between the coalition partners.

As for Edwards, his zealotry in ensuring the new casino remain corruption-free may have been linked to what he was observing behind closed doors. He noticed that the issue of 'political donations' to the National Party was getting out of hand. Word was rife, too, that ministers were being asked favours in exchange for money.

Other members, such as Nev Hewitt (NP, Mackenzie), Ron Camm (NP, Whitsunday) and Fred Campbell (Lib, Aspley) were also concerned. The National Party system, Edwards believed, was severely flawed. 'I think they were very loose in the way they ran that side,' says Edwards. 'In the Liberal Party, we have a … and it wasn't me who did this, it was Tom [Hiley, former Queensland Treasurer] did this years before – that if a minister received … an offer of funds … they expected their resignation, and we all adhered to that view.

'The moment we were offered some money for something, you would have to report it to your leader, and I had a couple of very nasty, or very attractive offers, which I declared very, very quickly and we excluded them on the casino decision.

'There were, you know, a large number of people who had applied for the casino licence in Queensland, and that was one of my worst periods ever.'

Edwards also recalls being approached by police who were concerned about corruption in the force, but none would commit anything to paper. Edwards says that time and again he went to successive police ministers with concerns he'd picked up in the course of his work, and consistently hit dead ends.

'In the police force it seemed as if … something went in, [and] it never sort of came out, and so our job, I guess, was to, you know if we did hear a bad story, to please let our colleagues know and they'd say, "They tell me it's fixed up anyway. It was a bit of a misunderstanding." I probably feel that perhaps a lot of us had too much confidence in the integrity of the police.

'People feared that if they did go public they'd be victimised. I am certain in retrospect that quite a bit of that did go on, and so a knowledge of some query, call it corruption, just didn't go very far.'

All That Glitters

Nigel Powell had been hitting a brick wall with much of his investigative work for the Licensing Branch. Many of the reports he was submitting to his boss, Graeme Parker, had been ignored. In late May 1983 he was telephoned at home before his shift. It was work. They needed him to 'dress up' appropriately for a job on the Gold Coast. It was a strange request, but Powell did as he was told and put on a three-piece suit. Powell was wary of the Gold Coast. He had working girls as informants down there, and they would tell him of police getting 'freebies' and on occasion giving the prostitutes 'back-handers'.

The job on this occasion, along with the Gold Coast CIB, was to take a look around a penthouse suite that had been turned into a bar and strip club.

Powell and three other Brisbane Licensing Branch men drove down to Surfers Paradise. 'With another officer, I go in there, it's

9.30 p.m.,' says Powell. 'We're standing out like dogs' balls. We've had a few drinks. We get up to this place, knock on the door, [but] it's still way too early. A woman comes to the door. They're still setting up behind her.'

Powell told the woman he would come back later, but she asked him to wait. 'Then the guy who's running it [the club] comes to the door. He says, come in. He looks at the three-piece suit. I haven't got a story worked out or anything.'

A topless waitress approached Powell's group and asked them if they'd like a drink. They observed a 'bit of gaming, bit of porn, a sex show, but no evidence of prostitution'.

Nevertheless, Powell believed he had enough to lay some charges and made his excuses so he could go directly to the nearby Gold Coast CIB offices to obtain the necessary warrants. Before he left, he asked: 'That blonde in the show, does she do anything else?'

'She'll be waiting for you when you get back,' he was told.

'How much?' he asked.

'I'll find out.'

Powell returned with the warrants and men from both the local CIB and the Brisbane Licensing Branch. There was a ruckus at the door as they entered the club. Everyone was asked to keep calm.

Powell later said in evidence to the Fitzgerald Inquiry: 'While the investigation was proceeding and the penthouse was still full of customers and potential defendants, Detective Pat Glancy of the Gold Coast CIB stood in the middle of the penthouse and abused me savagely, calling me a fucking cunt and accusing me of "giving up my mates".

'I was allowed ... to go downstairs and look after the liquor exhibits. As I was checking the truck with the liquor exhibits in it, I saw members of the Gold Coast CIB exit through another door towards their vehicles, which were on the other side of the building.' Powell says, 'the scales are falling from my eyes at this point'.

He later learned that a cash box from the club containing up to $2000 had vanished. 'It was apparent to me that [Glancy] was extremely agitated at the thought that Licensing Branch detectives were on the Gold Coast,' Powell said in the statement.

Powell returned to Brisbane and mentally filed away the penthouse experience. Not long after, he received a phone call at home from his boss, Graeme Parker. 'He told me I was transferred to Woolloongabba,' Powell said. 'I asked him if there was any particular reason for the transfer and he said that there was not.'

Parker explained to Powell later that one of the Lucas Royal Commission recommendations from the 1970s was that Licensing Branch officers should stay only two years in the branch to avoid any possibility of institutionalised corruption. Powell knew that Parker himself and colleagues Bulger and 'Dirty Harry' Burgess had all been in the branch longer than two years.

Despite this, before his transfer took effect, Powell continued his investigations into Hector Hapeta's growing empire. He typed up yet another report on Hapeta's plans to set up a club without a liquor licence called Pharaoh's.

'In that information sheet I identified a person whom I believed worked in the Hapeta/Tilley organisation who may be a "weak link" who could eventually provide evidence sufficient to prosecute Hapeta for his illegal activities,' said Powell. 'I put the information sheet in an envelope and put it under Inspector Parker's door.

'The next day I was working day shift and I went to see him. Inspector Parker threw the information sheet back at me. Parker's attitude to my report was dismissive.'

Just days after this incident, Powell went on sick leave. When he returned to work the next month, he was ordered to report for duty at Woolloongabba. He'd been sent back to uniform.

Flying Lessons

By 1983, Joh Bjelke-Petersen had been Premier for close to 15 years, and while he was still immensely popular with the public, and seen on a national level as something of a country bumpkin, an eccentric who could be counted on for a laugh, there were those closer to home who felt the job of running Queensland did not always attract the former peanut farmer's full attention.

Dr Llew Edwards remembers the Premier being missing in action from annual budget preparation meetings. 'Joh wouldn't even turn up, you know, and if he did turn up he'd be there for five minutes and get bored and leave,' Edwards says. 'He'd never read any of the pre-preparation papers and there was a senior group of Ron Camm, me and Joh, and I don't ever remember Joh attending those budget preparation meetings, or budget profiling meetings.'

In essence, Edwards was left to run Queensland as Bjelke-Petersen went off on his flights of fancy. 'He trusted me and I had a good relationship with him, and we had some very nasty differences, but we never let it go beyond that difference,' Edwards recalls.

Edwards says it took some tactical, behind-the-scenes manoeuvring to manage the Premier and some of his more quixotic decisions. 'We would try to jump in ahead of him and raise issues in the pre-Cabinet decision discussions ... it might be about building a new airport or something,' Edwards recalls. 'If there was something we knew was going to go off the track ... Ron Camm and I were extremely close and he'd back me up before Joh would get ... he wouldn't even know what we were talking about at this stage still, and we would then get the Cabinet sort of all expressing views.

'If it was something we were worried about that would bring disgrace to the government, you know, that was how we had to handle it. Looking back, it wasn't the best way to run a government. But it was fairly successful.'

At one point, Premier Bjelke-Petersen literally went missing without explanation. He didn't show up to Cabinet meetings for six weeks in succession.

Edwards asked: 'Where's the Premier?'

Nobody had an answer.

Troubled by this, Edwards vowed to meet Bjelke-Petersen face to face in his office and get an explanation for his absence. He rang the Premier's office and asked for a meeting. He was pencilled in for 3 p.m. one day.

A convivial Premier was there to greet Edwards. 'Look Joh, we're all getting very anxious,' Edwards informed him. 'You haven't been to Cabinet for six weeks, we don't get an apology, and your office won't tell us where you are.'

Bjelke-Petersen interrupted him and said: 'Llew, I'm learning to fly a helicopter, and the only time they can fit me in for lessons is on a Monday morning.'

Edwards was incredulous. 'I thought, you know, it showed two things at the time,' remembers Edwards. 'The trust that he had in us, we could say that, and I think he did, and secondly, he put these individual priorities above anything else. I think that summates the kind of man he was. That he would suddenly desire to do something, and would break every rule in the world, every regulation and not necessarily law ... to achieve that, and that's why I think he was, you know, with a background of leaving school at nine ...

'He had a very introverted approach to most things and couldn't cope with the modern world and the demands of that world in many areas.'

The Sheriff of Mareeba

In the tiny town of Mareeba, 417 metres above sea level on the Atherton Tablelands in Far North Queensland, its place name Aboriginal for 'meeting of the waters', Lindsey 'Ross' Dickson was a no-nonsense policeman who was liked and respected. Here, where the Granite and Emerald creeks met with the Barron River, was a place of abundant sunshine, a place that winter didn't visit, and the perfect location to grow everything from pineapples, coffee and bananas to lychees, cashews and mangoes. It was also the ideal landscape to grow marihuana.

Dickson, known as the Sheriff of Mareeba, had racked up some remarkable statistics in his two-and-a-half years as head of the local four-man CIB. His crime clean-up rate hovered around 84 per cent. By comparison, the Queensland average was a dismal 49 per cent.

Dickson had been sworn into the Queensland Police Force on 26 April 1966, and initially trained in the Legal Section before being seconded to Mobile Patrols and the CIB as an Education Department Liaison Officer. He was appointed a Detective Constable in April 1974, before being transferred to the Gladstone CIB. He then went to Yeppoon before being promoted to Detective Sergeant 2/c and placed as head of the Mareeba CIB on 19 October 1981.

Dickson would soon uncover evidence of organised crime and its involvement in the drug trade in the vast district under his command. He was shocked at what he found. 'We didn't look past the day-to-day thing sometimes,' Dickson says. 'I said to a few of the blokes, we're all running around locking up bad guys, and we're looking at bad guys only, but there's this group of people who are supposed to be good guys who are running around watching us, in case we get in their way, and we're not even seeing that.

'It's like people are so busy with the day-to-day operations and they get tied up with [trying to solve] petty things or smaller crimes and organised crime just goes along. Nobody can have a look at it because everyone's got so much [other] crap to do.'

The Italian involvement in the drug trade was obvious. They'd been engaged in vice in the region since the 1930s. 'I remember a fellow saying to me once – everyone will tell you the Mafia doesn't exist … he was a policeman … but every now and again something happens and you start wondering again if it really does exist. We all knew it did. [But] it was a deniable thing in the 1970s and 80s. The Mafia? Don't be stupid.'

Dickson took to naming his North Queensland beat The Badlands. By 1983, he was impelled to inform his superiors about what was happening in his district. He began writing long and detailed 'Confidential' reports to his superiors. 'The drug problem in this area is enormous as is the area covered by Detectives in this District,' Dickson reported. 'Drugs such as cannabis, heroin, LSD and cocaine are readily available in this area in any quantity desired and no doubt the Police Department is well aware of the drug industry operating in this area and the fact that it is much larger than probably any other area in Queensland.'

The Mareeba CIB alone, he claimed in his report, had information involving 41 separate people or groups actively involved in drug dealing. During a single quarter in 1982, drugs arrests increased by 500 per cent. Dickson pleaded for some undercover operatives to support his team. 'It is absolutely essential that undercover drug officers work in this area if there is to be any headway made against large-scale drug operators,' Dickson wrote. 'If Detectives from this office are able to make numerous drug arrests and gather information easily on the activities of drug offenders … the results following undercover drug investigations should be very productive.'

Dickson's report wasn't only not acted on, he received no acknowledgement that it had even been read by the police hierarchy. Undaunted, he tried again, citing a similar report he had submitted in late 1982 – a year after he had started work in Mareeba – seeking more staff. He had pointed out that criminals were escaping prosecution because there was not enough manpower to properly process numerous drug cases.

Dickson was getting angry. 'No additional staff were supplied,' he noted of his earlier plea. 'No one gave any decision on the request.

No reply was even forthcoming from the department and the report was apparently ignored in the hope that police would continue to work on and the period of increased workload would pass in the following months.'

The Sheriff of Mareeba was exasperated. In a single week the Mareeba CIB had proffered 220 charges against offenders. The situation was out of control.

Dickson couldn't comprehend the blatant indifference to the drug trade coming out of police headquarters in Brisbane. 'There was no money and no support for investigating drugs,' he says. 'We woke up that it was to limit us in what we were doing. We were having some absolutely major successes, massive plantations, you know? It was like we didn't exist. If it happened in Brisbane, there'd be a week of news.

'We'd ring up and say to the boss in Brisbane, we've got $8 million worth of plants, we need a botanist here, what are we going to do with them? They said, "Fucking burn them".'

Dickson's superiors, also, were tiring of his repeated requests and complaints. The detective faced endless paperwork. It was one way they could keep him in line. He started receiving orders to get his clerical house in order. A memo from District Officer P.L. O'Shea to Dickson was marked 'For urgent attention'. 'You are instructed to attend to the within matters without any further delay,' it said, referring to cases set to go before the local magistrates court. 'You are required to furnish a report to this office when the within matters have been attended to. Your attention is drawn to the requirements of G.I.4.237 in the Queensland Police Manual in relation to the compilation of Court Briefs.'

Dickson responded: 'This section is severely hampered especially in the past two months by investigations in outlying areas and the staff are finding themselves increasingly bogged down with the additional serious investigations that do require immediate attention.'

Dickson was fed up. His protesting reports became longer and more detailed. In one, he saw fit to criticise a superior District Officer.

Dickson was treading on some very dangerous ground. His most agitated memo to date, initially about the necessity for overtime for his men, was addressed to Superintendent Alan Walker.

During the 1982-83 period the workload of this office increased by 44.28 per cent with no increase in staff and without any outside assistance despite numerous verbal requests to the Police Department and directly to the Drug Squad as well as several written requests which in my opinion were ignored.

At the present time we have 182 separate drug investigations being conducted in relation to different persons or groups of persons and quite frankly at the present time and for the past months nothing has been done in relation to drug matters and will not be done in the coming months because of the extremely heavy workload, subsequently hundreds of drug offenders come and go as they please and even serious drug investigations are not being investigated and large scale criminal organisations growing cannabis flourish in this area because there is no time to combat the problem, no equipment to organise ourselves with and no manpower or outside assistance to work with.

Dickson wasn't sure the Police Department hierarchy fully understood the adversity he and his men faced on a day-to-day basis. He said he and his men worked in 'hostile conditions'.

We have an enormous area consisting of mostly gravel roads and very dirty and uncomfortable conditions in the Gulf of Carpentaria due to dense jungle in coastal areas ... we have in the past found sharpened bamboo stakes and trip wires near drug areas we are investigating which could cause serious injury however no equipment is supplied.

Dickson asked for an investigation into the working conditions of the Mareeba CIB. He argued his men were frequently put in danger 'because of the attitude of the Police Department'. He said he often clashed with his district officer over these issues. 'The Police Department is to blame for this situation arising by placing a man in charge of such a volatile district who was incompetent and well known to be incompetent,' said Dickson. 'I take full responsibility for this report if it upsets anyone but quite frankly I have had enough of Police Politics ...'

Dickson was subsequently instructed that he and his staff could only work business hours Monday to Friday. In response, he posted a sign on the door of the Mareeba CIB: 'If you're going to get raped, mugged or murdered, please do it between 9 a.m. and 5 p.m., Monday to Friday.'

Dickson couldn't work out the puzzle before him – why did he and his men feel like they didn't exist? Why was their work ignored? Why were they ordered repeatedly to pull their heads in?

'I talked to police I trusted,' Dickson remembers. 'I said, they think we know something, and we don't know what it is. But they think we know. One day one of us is going to have to put his hand up for all this and there'll be a fucking big stink.

'I talked to my wife about it, you know, [I told her] I know it's going to be me. It's going to happen to me. I was the most vocal.'

Dickson could have been guaranteed his antics would upset people. Indeed, his apparent recalcitrance would make it all the way to the desk of Commissioner Lewis, 1746 kilometres south, in Brisbane.

An Audience with Miss Bell

One night on the Gold Coast, officers Pat Glancy and Greg Deveney were on patrol when they pulled up outside a unit at Palm Beach. Once inside, Glancy introduced his partner to a prostitute called Miss Fox. There was another woman there – a Miss Bell.

According to Deveney, Glancy went into a room with Miss Fox. Miss Bell then grabbed Deveney's hand and led him into another room. 'At that stage that girl, as far as I was aware, wasn't a working girl. She was a bloody housekeeper and that's all,' says Deveney.

'Greg,' she told him inside the room, 'are you aware of the fact that I'm now working?'

'What?' he replied.

'I'm now working [as a prostitute].'

'How long have you been working?' he asked.

Miss Bell said it had only been a matter of weeks. 'I'm sorry, Greg,' she said. 'I've been made . . . forced . . . to do this to you.'

When Deveney walked out of the room he encountered Glancy and Miss Fox. He claims both were laughing at him. 'Don't worry about it, Greg,' Miss Fox supposedly said. 'It only hurts the first time. It gets better the more you do it.'

Glancy suggested they get going. Deveney was devastated. While he described his actions of going with Miss Bell as 'stupid', he believed he was set up by Glancy. 'When we were driving back to Surfers Paradise, he [Glancy] said, "At least now I've got something on you." And I said, "What do you mean?"

'He said, "You've had sex with a prostitute tonight." I said, "Listen, you've got nothing on me, Pat." I said if anybody asked me about it I'd admit it.'

They drove the rest of the way to Surfers Paradise in silence. As they got closer to the station, Glancy supposedly said: 'I think I've made a big mistake in having you with me today.'

The next morning Deveney headed to the office early and requested to see his superior. He didn't want to work with Glancy anymore. In fact, Glancy had beaten his young partner to the punch. He'd come into the office even earlier and asked to be taken out of the Consorting Squad altogether.

Incredibly, Deveney was then put in charge of the squad on the recommendation of Glancy. Deveney asked if there was anyone he could trust to partner him in Consorting. He requested Detective Constable Murray Verrell.

Glancy, meanwhile, continued working on the Gold Coast. 'Glancy just did his normal pub scenes and everything else that they all did down there,' he says. 'We were having a rash of armed hold-ups at that time, too, and set up all these special patrols. The only two people doing special patrols were Murray and myself. The others were all in the pub.'

The Mater Miracle

He was known, for reasons he never initially understood, as the Mater Miracle.

John Stopford, born in Brisbane's Mater Hospital in the city's inner-south in 1956, arrived with club feet and also suffered spina bifida. He had died and been brought back to life. But he was a fighter. His parents couldn't care for him. They were fighting, too, but in the way of domestic disharmony; his father was a heavy drinker. So, Stopford was sent to the Xavier Home for Crippled Children in Cavendish Road, Coorparoo. It was here, in the converted 1890 mansion 'Erica', designed by architect John Jacob Cohen, where Stopford spent the first eight years of life. He slept in a steel cot and came under the watchful and caring eye of a particular Catholic nun at the home. The order of nuns became known as 'The White Sisters'.

The nun that took a shine to Stopford had a brother who ran a Marist Brothers home for boys in Sydney. Stopford was sent there when he was almost nine – his parents' marriage having disintegrated – and returned to Brisbane a few years later to live with relatives at Sunnybank. By his mid-teens, however, he was suffering with chronic pain from years of operations for his condition, and ended up in the Lowson

House psychiatric clinic at the Royal Brisbane and Women's Hospital. He had repeatedly tried to self-harm by slashing his arms and legs, and was depressed.

At Lowson House, he met a young girl, Joanne, and when both were released they married. A short time later, in the mid-1970s, Joanne got a job as a receptionist at the Polynesian Playground massage parlour on Logan Road in Woolloongabba. The place was run by the legendary brothel madam Kerry Kent. Stopford was asked if he'd like to do some maintenance work around the place, and he agreed. He would fix windows, paint and patch leaks in the roof of the old Queenslander. The job became virtually full-time, and Stopford was working happily until one day the Licensing Branch paid a visit.

The naive Stopford had broken an unwritten code – the only males to be found on the grounds of a massage parlour were to be customers. A senior Licensing officer approached the maintenance man and put his service revolver to his head. 'This is the kind of thing that happens to people who want to muscle in on things that are bigger than they can handle,' the cop said. He added that if he found him there again, the gun would be loaded.

When Stopford's own marriage broke down, and with his back pain relentless, he was put in touch with criminal Roland Short on the Gold Coast. By the late 1970s, Short was steadily building a vice empire that involved swingers clubs in Brisbane, such as the Matador. He also dabbled in various business ventures on the side. One of those was a small, illegal card game he set up in a house in Leonard Avenue, Surfers Paradise. Another was Gold's Gym in the heart of Surfers, not far from the famous Pink Elephant Bar. Stopford was asked to manage the gym. In addition, he became the card dealer at the exclusive games in Leonard Avenue on a Friday and Saturday night. He had no idea this was the beginning of him being drawn into Queensland's underworld.

One day Short said he had a meeting not far from the gym. He asked Stopford to come look for him if he hadn't phoned in an hour and a half. The meeting was between escort agent king Geoff Crocker and leading massage parlour heavy Hector Hapeta. 'They were trying to sort out advertising jurisdictions,' says Stopford. 'Who could advertise in what booklet and publication. And of course some of the other minor trouble happening at the time, but Roland was never forthcoming on that. Hapeta at that stage had the Gold Coast sewn up.'

For a variety of reasons Stopford left the Gold Coast and was offered a job as a driver in Geoff Crocker's organisation in Brisbane. He shifted into a sprawling old Queenslander at 27 Sankey Street, Highgate Hill, out of which Crocker ran his girls. 'I found him alright, man on man,' says Stopford. 'As a person generally he'd just bully females, including his own wife Julie.

'He [Crocker] looked like a two-bob gangster. The gold chain. A pair of shorts that I'd wear to the beach. And he loved the Italian mesh shirts, the ones where you can see skin through the holes, he thought the white and gold looked good together.'

Stopford drove the girls to their jobs in the company car. The business catered for every walk of life, from legal silks to labourers. The women were delivered right across Brisbane. 'Geoff wasn't happy unless it was 30 jobs a day,' recalls Stopford. 'Probably eight girls for those jobs. Girls in town, if they were lucky, were only getting 40 per cent of the money. I think an hour was $100, and I think a half-hour was $60 or $70. An all-nighter was $150. At least $3000 a day. His best girls were earning $1500 a week. They'd be getting one day off.

'I was enjoying life. My wage was $5 a drive. I was earning say, $350 to $500 per week – cash. I was on call 24 hours a day. You could only relax if you were lucky enough to have to drive Geoff somewhere.'

In time, through the early 1980s, Stopford would end up with his own escort agency, working with his new partner Wendy. 'Geoff didn't like the idea that Wendy and I had got together and by this time he had pretty big faith in me,' says Stopford. 'He wasn't coming in to the parlours as regularly. So I think he could see the writing on the wall and he offered to Wendy and I that we open a new escort service over at Crosby Road, Albion. It was on top of a TV repair shop [Robin White's Rentals].'

Despite all of their hard work, Stopford alleges Crocker took the bulk of the profits. He pulled out of the deal. 'I do remember when I pulled the plug,' Stopford says. 'Crocker rang my Mum and made threats to her. "He won't get away with this, and if he tries to start up by himself ..."'

'We were killing it, me and Wendy. We were pulling, on Thursdays, Fridays and Saturdays, we were pulling in 35 jobs a day. [But] we were working outside the arranged payment plan; outside Hapeta, Bellino, Crocker, the police. It made me very vulnerable. That's when the retribution began.'

Stopford would find all of his telephone lines into the brothels ripped out. 'And they were sending [the] Licensing [Branch] my way. I learnt from Geoff that we could go past the Licensing building in those days and find out who the hell was on that night. So we knew if we were in for a rough one or the usual courtesy call.

'I tried to pay them graft. I had to. They didn't accept, openly. But cash found its way into certain hands. We were raided. Sometimes I was tipped off, sometimes not.'

Stopford was not only being harassed by the Licensing Branch, and in particular Sergeant Harry Burgess, but he was copping 'heat' from Hector Hapeta. 'Burgess said to me that his boss could tell them – if they didn't stop the rubbish they should drop off or they would get the heat,' Stopford later recalled. 'He explained that Hapeta and Crocker are the big men in Brisbane but they still take orders from the Licensing Branch.'

When Burgess was moved out of escort agencies and onto massage parlours, Stopford was told to deal with Sergeant Neville Ross. One evening, Ross, accompanied by two detectives, visited Stopford at his home in Laurier Street, Annerley. Ross asked him how he was going to 'survive'. Stopford thought Ross meant survive the onslaught from Hapeta. Ross corrected him. How was he going to survive with the Licensing Branch?

'You may as well give us money,' Ross supposedly said.

'What sort of money?'

'It is normally $400 to $500 per month per house … it has to be ready at the end of every month and picked up then or at the start of the new month. Police hierarchy are not impressed with you starting a new agency without permission.'

Stopford later remarked: 'If you're getting $500 off every house you must be making a lot of money.'

'Of course,' Ross replied, 'it's about $100,000 a month.'

By now, Stopford and Wendy had had a child – Jay. But Stopford, in part due to his chronic pain, was addicted to heroin. So was Wendy. They moved to 35 Green Terrace, Windsor. By 1983, with Jay less than a year old, they were forced to start up an escort agency out of their home to finance the heroin. It didn't work. The cost of the addiction was outstripping the business income.

On 7 June Stopford was sent to prison for bankcard fraud. His life, thanks to drugs, had reached a dead end. He had tried to play with the big boys and lost.

In gaol he thought a lot about his infant son, and his own difficult early years of life, a reject in the crippled home for children. He made a vow to make a better life for his son once he got out.

Fate would also make this pimp and junkie a vital figure in the collapse of the corrupt regime known as The Joke.

Whitrod Reflects

Former assistant commissioner, ace detective, union agitator and now flower farmer, Tony Murphy, was enjoying his retirement in the fishing village of Amity Point on North Stradbroke Island, spending hours on the back of his tractor and clearing native forest on his leased land, when a ghost from the past triggered his temper.

It was former Queensland police commissioner Raymond Wells Whitrod who shattered Murphy's idyll. In early July 1983, newspapers published an interview with Whitrod, who had returned home to Adelaide after working as an academic in Canberra. The picture accompanying the story showed an obviously older, but svelte, Whitrod. He had taken up marathon running.

Meanwhile, the report said, Whitrod had taken to reflecting on his 'Queensland Years'. He said bluntly his career ambitions had ended on his resignation from the Queensland force in November 1976. He also said he had been 'forced to resign'.

Whitrod did not spare the rod. 'It was a strain in Queensland,' Whitrod said. 'It's a turbulent state. That's the nature of the society. It's still very much a developing, pioneering state. The other states, with the exception of Western Australia, are more mature. [Queensland is] not an intellectual state. People are engaged busily in making a very good income in farming, cane, cattle, mining etc. There isn't much time left for reflection.'

As for his opinion of the state's police department, his estimate went to rock bottom. He advised young men and women not to join the Queensland police force. 'I would advocate they join another Australian force,' he said bluntly. 'From the three state forces I know well – South Australian, Victorian and Queensland – I think Queensland must rate the lowest.'

Integrity was essential in the force, he added. 'Police corruption is not a matter of a few rotten apples,' said Whitrod. 'What you really have in any police force is a case full of susceptible apples. For many years now, there has been an east coast network of corrupt police officers in key positions who have run operations worth a lot of money to them and their associates.'

It was a clear swipe at the Rat Pack. Murphy, the flower farmer of Amity Point, was outraged. The *Sunday Mail* of 3 July 1983, re-ran the Whitrod article, and in its front news pages offered a strident rebuttal by former assistant police commissioner Murphy. The article, by journalist Peter Hansen, quoted Murphy as saying that Whitrod was talking 'hogwash', and that his old boss was guilty of 'geriatric griping' and 'never-ending sniping'.

'Mr Whitrod's seven years in the Queensland Police is insignificant compared with my own 38 years' service,' Murphy trumpeted.

Incredibly, after so many years, Murphy continued to spruik the line that Whitrod himself had been 'used' by a very small group of ambitious and 'devious police' within the force. Murphy was referring to Whitrod's trusted team, all of whom had either been forced to resign, had their characters assassinated or were exiled across the state during the early years of the Lewis regime. Murphy believed Whitrod had resigned because he was 'embarrassed' over incidents such as the Southport Betting Case, in distant 1974, and the student demonstrations in the winter of 1976, when a female undergraduate was clubbed over the head by a police officer.

The article then offered a dot point list of great achievements by the Queensland Police Force since the demise of Whitrod, it being the only force to 'physically arrest' Mr Asia, Terrance (Terry) John Clark. Here, more than two decades after they started the practice, a member of the so-called Rat Pack was using the local press to distort history and disparage their enemies. Murphy's rant was ludicrous. It failed to mention Premier Bjelke-Petersen's involvement in the resignation of Whitrod and elevation of Lewis. Nor did it take into account the true story of the Clark arrest and its outfall, courtesy of another poorly judged release of bogus information to a local newspaper reporter by Murphy himself. It had been Murphy's leaking of confidential information about police interviews with Douglas and Isabel Wilson that directly led to their murders by Clark in the late 1970s.

Commissioner Lewis failed to mention the little press spat in his official diaries, but equally incredibly, Ray Whitrod was never far from his mind. In the week leading up to Murphy's brain snap, Lewis received information from a police officer that Bjelke-Petersen had ordered that the leader of the opposition, Keith Wright, was 'not to view [his] file in Special Branch'. That same day: 'To Belfast Hotel, luncheon with B. Maxwell, R[eg]. Tegg, A[nthony] Murphy and H[orrie] Robertson.'

Just days before the article in the *Sunday Mail*, the commissioner 'saw Det. B[rian] Marlin re: appln for CIB, Mackay'. The next day, Lewis toddled over to the Executive Building and saw an official 're detail needed in submissions for Imperial and Aust[ralia]n Awards'. And two days after the newspaper story, Lewis was in discussion with Liberal parliamentarian Terry White regarding a particular police officer being 'very outspoken in favour of ALP and Mr Whitrod, against Govt'.

Lewis had been Commissioner for more than six-and-a-half years, and still Whitrod rankled him. Either that, or the former honest commissioner had become simply a byword for everything that stood against the Bjelke-Petersen regime.

Whatever the source of the rancour, it soon dissipated. On the Wednesday after the Murphy tirade was published, Lewis was off with his wife Hazel to inspect a property owned by a Mr Zendler for sale on Waterworks Road, and a few weeks later, after an afternoon at Doomben races with Judge Eric Pratt, the couple went to see another house for sale in Aspley.

Despite the Lewises' interest in property hunting, other news kept the city in thrall. Agro, the 'hairy little police helper' and star of Channel Seven's *Super Saturday Show*, co-starring police officer Dave Moore, was formally being promoted ahead of many other more qualified members of the Queensland Police Force. The picture story featured prominently, also in the *Sunday Mail*.

'After only three years' service, Agro is being promoted to sergeant, and the Police Commissioner, Mr Lewis, gave Agro a couple of hints by showing him the examination papers!' the newspaper said. 'Mr Lewis met Agro ... at police headquarters in Brisbane to celebrate Agro's third birthday.'

In the cute and cuddly photograph accompanying the story were Agro in his police hat, flanked by Commissioner Lewis in suit and striped tie, and Constable Moore, his left hand clutching Agro's elbow. Both men are grinning broadly.

Night of Knives

In the winter of 1983, popular St Joseph's College Nudgee student Peter James Walsh went out on the town with friends to celebrate. His and other Nudgee Rugby teams had had some recent victories, and it was time to fly the college flag in the bars and clubs of the city. Walsh, 17, was in his senior year at school, and was one of a long line of Walsh boys who had gone to Nudgee. One of eight children, Walsh's father, the well-known solicitor Peter 'Pappy' Walsh, was also an Old Boy of the college.

The Walsh's was a strict Catholic household. Pappy went to Mass every day, and he parented with a firm hand. Young Peter had been named after his father because Walsh Senior had been gravely ill at the time he was born. To everyone's relief, Pappy pulled through.

Peter Walsh Junior also had a nickname. He was called 'Father', or Father Walsh. His mates reckoned that any Irish Catholic family with eight children should have at least one priest among its siblings.

It was Saturday 30 July, and dozens of the revellers drifted from bar to bar. At around 10 p.m. the group of 60 or more drank at the St Paul's Town Inn in Leichhardt Street, Spring Hill, before heading down into St Paul's Terrace to Bonaparte's Hotel, towards Fortitude Valley. By the early hours of the morning Walsh and a mate, Chris

Herbert, had run out of money, and were wandering around the pub finishing off other people's drinks.

Walsh then left Bonaparte's around 2.30 a.m. with a mate, caught a taxi and was dropped off at Gympie Road, about 150 metres from the family home in Fifth Avenue, Kedron. Stupefied by this stage, he ran across Gympie Road and plunged headfirst through the plate-glass window of a nearby motor mower shop. He cut his hands on the glass. He then staggered home, retrieved knives from the kitchen, and went to the house of close neighbour Stephanie Ryan.

Ryan, 32, was a quiet, book-loving teacher. She was the daughter of the former Queensland Solicitor-General, Bill Ryan. Stephanie had known Peter Walsh since he was a baby. There was a gate between their back fences. She had helped the boy with his homework, on occasion, and now and then Peter would mow Stephanie's lawn.

It was one of Peter Walsh's daily chores to buy a fresh loaf of bread every morning on waking. He would often cut through the Ryans' backyard to Sixth Avenue then across to the corner store on Eighth Avenue and Leckie Road.

In the early hours of 31 July however, the usually well-mannered, polite and moral Peter Walsh, taking the knives from his mother's kitchen, knocked on Stephanie Ryan's door. He asked his kindly neighbour if he could stay the night at her house as he'd lost his house keys and didn't want to wake up his parents.

Stephanie agreed and let him in. She was standing at the linen closet, getting clean sheets to make up a bed for the teenager, when he viciously stabbed her in the back.

Walsh, crazed, repeatedly stabbed her in a struggle that ranged throughout the house. She would go on to lose over a litre of blood. She later reported that Walsh had ground her face into the carpet, leaving a shoe print on her skin.

'I was shocked,' she later said. 'I was disbelieving. There was no reason for it. I knew the boy. He kept saying he would kill me. He spoke in a firm voice. I think he had control of the situation. That was what frightened me.' She said Walsh had 'a watery haze over his eyes'.

Walsh's actions were inexplicable. He had absolutely no history of violence or substance abuse. And he had a long-held affection for Stephanie Ryan.

She pleaded with him, telling him she wouldn't tell his parents what had happened. She feared she might bleed to death.

Meanwhile, dog squad officer Sergeant John Casey was on patrol around 2.30 a.m. when he received a call to attend Sixth Avenue as a woman was reportedly screaming. When he arrived at the house he heard loud, frantic screams. He called for the door to be opened and heard a woman's voice: 'Help, I am bleeding to death.'

The officer kicked down the door to be faced with Ryan, covered in blood, and a man running from him. Casey then heard the sound of glass breaking. Again, Walsh had crashed through a window, this time upstairs in Ryan's home, and made his way back to his house.

Casey's dog tracked Walsh to the family home in Fifth Avenue. The police officer spoke to Pappy Walsh. Peter had made it to his bedroom and was in his bed when the police arrived. Soon after, at the kitchen table, he was observed sitting in a daze, reading a newspaper held upside down. He had a towel wrapped around one of his injured hands.

Pappy Walsh called on an old friend – senior barrister Des Sturgess – for legal help. Over decades, Sturgess had risen to the top of the Queensland legal fraternity, and had earned a reputation as a fine criminal barrister. During a colourful career in Brisbane, he was the first defence pick for many police and for major criminal trials, and had represented police such as Glen Patrick Hallahan – member of the so-called Rat Pack – charged with corruption in the 1970s. He at various times gave legal counsel to the likes of former Licensing Branch officer Jack Herbert, along with Commissioner Lewis and retired assistant commissioner Tony Murphy.

After taking a call from Pappy Walsh, Sturgess, with solicitor Pat Nolan, arrived after dawn at Fifth Avenue. Walsh was reportedly instructed not to answer any questions.

Peter James Walsh, Nudgee schoolboy, was charged with attempted murder and burglary. The local scandal would take a year to get to court. When it did, it would feature a surprise witness for the defence who was extremely familiar with the world of drugs and underage drinking, and was enmeshed in the Queensland police culture with friends in high places.

Transfer

Greg Deveney continued to do his best cleaning up Gold Coast vice, but the odds, and his honesty, were against him. His partner, Murray Verrell, had been sent a message to see a Surfers Paradise madam by the name of Gay Buckingham. He and Deveney paid her a visit.

Buckingham asked Deveney what he was doing there. 'I wanted to talk to Murray alone,' she said.

'Why?' Deveney asked.

'I don't believe I can trust you anymore.'

'Why is that, Gay?'

'You're on the take,' she said. 'You're copping money.'

'Gay, you know me,' he said in his own defence. 'I don't – I'm not involved in that sort of activity.'

Buckingham told him another detective had informed her that Deveney was not only taking kickbacks but he was indulging in free sex with prostitutes in her brothels.

Deveney asked who her informant was. She said it was Detective Senior Constable Pat Shine of the Gold Coast CIB. He later said: 'Well, it took us a while to settle Gay down and for her to build her confidence to talk to me, but she explained that she had been paying this particular detective money over a period of time and that it had reached the stage where she had not any funds available to pay for her electricity.' Deveney learned that Buckingham had been forced to use candles for lighting. She also hooked up an extension cord from her mother's house next door to keep the refrigerator going.

Deveney reported Shine, who was sent back down to uniform.

By mid-1983 Deveney was promoted and assigned to the Juvenile Aid Bureau (JAB) in Brisbane – the brainchild of corrupt former commissioner Frank Bischof, and run by Terry Lewis from its inception in 1963 to the mid-1970s when Ray Whitrod transferred Lewis out to Charleville in western Queensland. Before his new position took effect, however, Deveney worked with his replacement on the Gold Coast – Detective Senior Constable Tegwyn Roberts.

A week before moving to the JAB, Deveney, Verrell and another officer dropped in on a new brothel on the coast. It was a wet, windy day, and the three plain-clothes officers were welcomed inside. 'The girl thought that we were three clients,' Deveney later recalled. 'We got into the room, the lounge room, and I introduced myself to her and the other two police officers and informed her that we were from the Consorters [Squad] and we wanted to interview all the girls who were on those premises.'

She replied: 'The boss is upstairs waiting for you.'

Deveney proceeded up the stairs and into a room. A man was waiting there. The man shook Deveney's hand then gave him a roll of bank notes. It was hundreds of dollars. 'What's this for?' Deveney asked.

'That's from our conversation on the telephone this morning,' the man replied.

Deveney was nonplussed. 'Do you know who I am?' he asked.

'Teg Roberts,' the man said.

'Hang on,' said Deveney, 'I'll get my mate to come up so he knows what this money is for.'

Deveney shouted out for Verrell to join him. 'Look at this,' Deveney said, showing Verrell the notes. 'This bloke thinks I'm Teg. Come on.' The two detectives went back into the room. 'This is Detective Verrell,' Deveney said. 'Would you mind just repeating to Murray why you have given me this money?'

The man repeated the story about the phone call earlier in the day.

'Do you know who I am?' Deveney repeated.

'Teg Roberts.'

'No,' said Deveney. 'My name is Detective Deveney. I am the officer in charge of the Consorting Squad on the Gold Coast.'

'Teg Roberts told me he was in charge,' the man retorted.

'No, Detective Roberts is on the squad, and from next Monday he will be in charge of the Consorters but up until then, I am.' He further informed the man that the Consorters were honest, did not take kickbacks, and didn't accept free sex with prostitutes when he was in charge. Deveney returned the money, but he left the Gold Coast a nervous wreck.

While his integrity might have raised an eyebrow with Pat Glancy, Deveney's reporting of fellow officer Pat Shine was a step too far for his Gold Coast colleagues. He was deemed 'a dog' – someone who dobbed on his mates. Other officers barked at him when he was in the office. The word 'dog' was crudely written across one of his folders. Dog shit was left on his desk. At home after a shift he would arm himself, fearing retribution. He stalked the shadows around his house when his own dog barked at night.

Deveney's shift to Brisbane and the JAB didn't end the matter. The same harassment, and his personal fears, continued. He was terrified he would be planted with drugs. He checked under his car whenever he went for a drive. He worried that his house would be torched. Eric Gregory Deveney had joined a long line of police men and women who paid for their honesty.

Although he couldn't have foreseen it, he was facing another decade of torment before he opted out of the only career he had ever wanted.

Bikie Bandits Case

In the spring of 1981 police had arrested two heroin addicts who had launched a series of terrifying bank robberies across Brisbane. They became known as the Bikie Bandits, given they used a motorcycle as a getaway vehicle. Detectives made a number of coordinated raids throughout the city, with one suspect fleeing and leading police on a high-speed chase before being apprehended at gunpoint. The Bikie Bandits were Alfred Thompson, 21, unemployed, of Spring Hill, and Steve Kossaris, also 21 and unemployed, of Ashgrove. Following their arrest, they were taken to the watch-house and put in separate cells. That night, they made statements to police, but later told their legal representatives from the public defender's office that detectives had given both of them heroin to inject before they made their admissions. 'You both look pretty sick,' a detective allegedly told the two heroin addicts. 'I can give you something to fix you up.'

Thompson would go on to allege that one of the officers '... then held my arm while I injected. The heroin was a very good quality. Kossaris then injected himself.'

At their trial a year later, a clinical pharmacologist from the Princess Alexandra Hospital, Dr P.J. Ravenscroft, was called to give evidence and concluded that blood sample analysis confirmed that the defendants had heroin in their systems during the time they were incarcerated in the Brisbane watch-house following their arrests. Thompson and Kossaris were found guilty and sentenced to lengthy prison terms. Justice Connolly made no finding adverse to police.

Straight after the trial two senior public servants had lodged a complaint with the relatively new Police Complaints Tribunal, headed up by Justice Bill Carter. This scandal became known as the Brisbane Watch-house Heroin Affair. Carter, with the approval of then Police Minister Russ Hinze, used both internal resources and outside investigators to probe the case.

The police officers investigated by the Tribunal were: Detective Sergeant 2/c Ronald Douglas 'Ug' Pickering; Detective Senior Constable Robert Matthew Pease; Detective Senior Constable Cameron Bruce Gray and Plain-Clothes Constable 1/c Ian Roland Claridge. All were members of the Special Crimes Squad attached to the metropolitan CIB.

The report alleged that while Thompson and Kossaris were in the watch-house they began suffering heroin withdrawal symptoms and were offered it by police. A needle, one of a type usually reserved for taking police blood samples, was retrieved and given to the two men to inject themselves. The Tribunal report said: 'The heroin was mixed with water in an ashtray on a table in the room, and Thompson and Kossaris, with the assistance of the police officers, then received three injections of heroin each. Having received heroin and having been relieved of the symptoms associated with withdrawal, each of the prisoners then wrote statements admitting their involvement in all of the alleged bank robberies. They were later taken to their cells.'

Tribunal chairman Carter was unequivocal in his recommendations and concluded that there was 'a body of cogent evidence available' to establish that both Thompson and Kossaris were indeed supplied heroin by police, and furthermore that all four officers along with Detectives Raymond Frederick Platz and Vicki-Leigh Teresa Greenhill, had allegedly committed perjury at the trial of the two bank robbers.

The six officers were subsequently committed for trial on a variety of charges, including supplying a dangerous drug and perjury. In late 1982 Lewis organised for the union to pay for their legal funding.

In mid-June 1983 Senior Crown Prosecutor Frank Clair wrote to the Solicitor-General, Denis Galligan. 'The solicitors acting for all the accused except Pickering have written to the Attorney-General [Sam Doumany] asking him to investigate the evidence with a view to exercising his discretion to discontinue the proceedings against all of the accused,' Clair stated.

On Friday 5 August, Solicitor-General Galligan, QC, sought for himself and Attorney-General Doumany the opinion of Chief Crown Prosecutor Angelo Vasta, QC, on the matter. Vasta, in turn, phoned his old mate Police Commissioner Terry Lewis that weekend, but later said they had had no significant discussion about the case.

It was Vasta's ultimate view that, despite the possibility there was a prima facie case available, the evidence was unsatisfactory and that it would be dangerous to proceed to trial.

Another opinion was sought from Cedric Hampson, QC. After securing further scientific information on heroin residue in the human body, Hampson agreed that the charges should be dropped. In the end, a nolle prosequi was entered.

For the police concerned, it was time to celebrate, and a party was arranged at Ron Pickering's place at Mansfield, near Carindale. Present were all six officers who had been charged with various offences. Also in attendance were Police Commissioner Terry Lewis, his deputy commissioner Syd Atkinson, and Chief Crown Prosecutor Vasta. Another special guest was Sir 'Top Level' Ted Lyons.

Lewis and Lyons arrived at the party together at about 5.30 p.m. and left at 9 p.m. Lewis would later say that the police involved thanked him for not suspending them during their ordeal prior to, and subsequent of, them being charged. Vasta said it wasn't put to him that the drinks at Pickering's house would be a 'celebration'. Ted Lyons would later not be able to offer any explanation as to why he was even there at the party.

Agent Wanted

In the early weeks of spring, just a fortnight before the state election, the *Courier-Mail* newspaper carried a curious flurry of advertisements that on the surface showed a rigorous democracy at work. On Saturday

8 October 1983, for example, the National Party wanted to make sure everybody was ready to get behind the Premier. An ad – with a mug shot of Joh Bjelke-Petersen – shouted HOW TO VOTE, and offered multiple telephone helpline numbers in Brisbane and up and down the Queensland coast. It also casually suggested, if you didn't want to use the telephone, to call in person at the National Party Office, Brisbane City Mall, 209 Queen Street, Brisbane. 'Now, more than ever,' it concluded, 'Queensland needs Joh and the Nationals.'

In the same issue, in the book review pages, was a large advertisement for the recently released authorised biography of Bjelke-Petersen – *Jigsaw*, by Derek Townsend. It claimed to be the most explosive book ever written about an Australian statesman and spruiked over 12,000 copies already sold. It retailed for $19.95.

Townsend was a curious choice as biographer. His previous publications were primarily travel guides and books on how to make home movies or master underwater photography. One of his radio programs for the British Broadcasting Corporation was titled *8mm Film Versus 16mm Film*.

In the same edition of the newspaper was a review of *Jigsaw* by writer Peter Trundle. It was remarkably uncritical of Townsend's hagiography. 'Because it gives a one-sided viewpoint of Joh by someone who admires him to the point of adulation, it cannot be regarded as a definitive work,' writes Trundle. 'But having recognised that, it is a useful source of information about [how] Mr. Bjelke-Petersen came to be the way he is.'

Further back in the newspaper's classifieds, there was an advertisement for the World By Night strip club and restaurant – run by Gerry Bellino – at 548 Queen Street, boasting not just a full a la carte menu, but 'Our Bathing Beauty MIRANDA', and a topless waitress service.

Then even further back was a notification from the Totalisator Administration Board (TAB) seeking an agent for its outlet at Dunwich on North Stradbroke Island. 'The successful applicant will be in the 25 to 40 years age group, of smart appearance and pleasant manner, capable of promoting the Board's business and image, and who is pared (sic) to make service to the public the first priority,' the ad read. 'The person to be appointed must be able to provide a working capital of at least $1500 and a Security Deposit of $500.' It explained the agency's weekly remuneration: an hourly rate for hours worked; commission based on weekly turnover; a fee for each [betting] ticket handled. The deadline for applications was just a week hence – Friday 14 October 1983.

On the Saturday the position was advertised, Commissioner Lewis was in Townsville on official business, along with his wife Hazel. He inspected police stations in the region as well as the local water police and dog squads before attending a function with general staff at the Townsville Police Social Club.

He was back in Brisbane on Monday 10 October, and went to the fabled Milano's Restaurant, eatery to politicians, the judiciary and the rest of the city's wannabe A-list, under the watchful and attentive eye of wine master Gino Merlo. That day, Lewis dined with his old friend from the Belfast, Barry Maxwell, Reg Tegg, also a publican who was currently before the courts on various charges, former police officer Jack Herbert, the Commissioner's personal assistant Gregory Early, and the flower farmer from North Stradbroke, Tony Murphy.

At the time of the TAB notification, former president of the Police Union and knockabout detective Ron Edington was working part-time for the board in its headquarters in Albion, just north of the Brisbane CBD. (In fact, Lewis had secured Edington the position through his good mate Sir Edward Lyons, chairman of the TAB. Lewis says: 'When I was the boss he used to ring me from time to time … he took optional retirement at 55. He used to ring me to try and get a job. I got him a job at the TAB out at Albion. Probably got old Ted Lyons to get it for him.')

Edington remembers the Dunwich vacancy coming up, and he in turn thought of his old mate Tony Murphy, living over at Amity Point on North Stradbroke.

'When I left the police I got a job at the TAB as a security officer, at Albion, at the headquarters ... they had a newsletter and this newsletter used to come out every week and I saw ... the two girls that had the agency at Dunwich had a split and they were calling for applicants. So, I rang Tony Murphy and I said to him, "They're advertising for Dunwich." [Murphy's wife] Maureen used to work for the TAB. Maureen's a lovely person ... I said [to Murphy], "Why don't you apply for it? You live at Amity Point."'

Murphy took Edington's advice. His application was dated Tuesday 11 October, and was received at Head Office on the Thursday. There were 27 applications for the agency, which were whittled down to four interviews. 'I said to him [Murphy], "Just get onto Terry, Terry will get onto Sir Edward Lyons," I said. You couldn't fucking miss,' recalls Edington.

Lewis confirms that he helped out Murphy with the position. '... when Murphy got in touch with me when he left the job and wanted to get a TAB at ... whatever island he was on,' he says. 'And I didn't mind ringing old Ted Lyons and saying, look, he is a worker.'

Lyons didn't just pull strings for Murphy, he ordered that Lewis's mate get the agency. Former TAB general manager Charles Harriott had sighted the application and believed that Murphy was too old to run the Dunwich outlet; the job was six days a week. 'It's very, very rare to put someone his [Murphy's] age into the job,' Harriott later said. 'He's the only former police officer we've ever appointed to that position.'

Harriott did not agree with the appointment, but changed his recommendation to the board on the instruction of Lyons. As a 'servant of the board and the chairman', he felt he had no choice.

Murphy got the job.

The TAB office itself was in a small, rectangular brick building on the corner of Shepherd Lane and Rous Street, opposite the Dunwich state school. The dreary besser brick building housed three shop spaces with identical sliding doors at the front, a stainless steel sink, and a small window at the rear near the back door.

'But it wasn't worth nothing,' remembers Edington 'They only used to open three days a week and ... $300, nearly $400 a week, it was worth ... and then he employed one of the girls that had the split with the other girl because he didn't know much about the TAB himself.'

Maureen Murphy says the family made no money from the agency. 'It was ... we didn't make anything out of it ... it was pitiful,' she says. 'We applied for it and we got it. I don't know whether anybody else applied for it. It was more of a hobby sort of thing, and so was the farm.'

A Letter from the Frontline

Meanwhile, Queensland's political landscape had seen some pyrotechnics leading up to and after the 1983 state election, held on 22 October. The Liberal–National Party Coalition had dissolved, an ambition of Premier Joh Bjelke-Petersen since the late 1970s, and new leaders stepped up – Keith Wright for the ALP and Terry White for the Liberals.

Labor had hoped to capitalise on the Coalition split, but Bjelke-Petersen won a sixth consecutive term. The Liberals lost 14 seats in an electoral wipe-out. Joh fell one seat short of a majority. The result had no impact on the ebb and flow of Brisbane's underworld.

A month after the state election, the irascible and newly returned Labor member for Archerfield, Kev Hooper, again rose in Parliament House and did what he had been doing, relentlessly, for a decade – he tried to prompt government action on matters of vice. Hooper being

Hooper, he sprayed the parliamentary chamber with a volley of random barbs before he knuckled down to the point. He took aim at the Police Minister, but his real target was crime and corruption, inside and outside the Queensland Police Force. 'It is common knowledge that where there is organised prostitution there is organised crime …' Hooper continued, with what must have seemed like endless déjà vu, '… I have pointed out on many occasions that the prostitution industry in this State is the soft underbelly of the Queensland Police Force.'

Hooper highlighted the Gold Coast and its booming trade. 'I have received many calls from elderly residents on the Gold Coast who have purchased units on the coast for retirement only to find several prostitutes operating from the building in which their units are situated,' he said. 'These elderly folk are very upset about harlots using their premises as a house of assignation.'

As ever, Hooper left the best till last. He alerted the chamber that he would read a letter 'from a police officer I have no reason to doubt', regarding the 'non-existent' brothels and casinos in Fortitude Valley, Brisbane. The letter was dated 12 October 1983. In addressing Hooper, the officer asked: 'Why is no Police action taken against illegal businesses conducted by the Jeri [sic] Bellino family? This family is the state's biggest operator of illegal casinos, massage parlours, escort agencies and unlicensed bars.'

The officer nominated three casinos in Fortitude Valley 'within walking distance of the Valley Area Office Police Headquarters', another in South Brisbane and one each in Cairns and Townsville that operated 'unhindered'. Hooper read the letter aloud:

Despite the [Brisbane] *Sunday Mail* having published the actual addresses of these casinos why is the only Police presence at some a red Falcon sedan (attached to the CIB Consorting Squad), driven by the same notorious, grossly overweight Detective Sergeant?

Why is it that this officer … and his sidekick a Detective Senior Constable, also of ample proportions, drink, gamble and disappear into back rooms of these premises with management but not take any action to close same?

Why do the same Consorting Squad duo plus many other detectives and indeed members of the Queensland National Party drink and socialize at the following Bellino controlled premises – premises which sell alcohol well after 3 am despite having no liquor licence to trade to 3 am?

Hooper, courtesy of the anonymous author, named the World By Night strip club at Petrie Bight, Pharoah's nightclub in Adelaide Street, the Hollywood Disco in Elizabeth Street and the Cockatoo Bar in Ann Street, Fortitude Valley.

There were a few final questions from the whistleblower: 'Why is it when Jeri [sic] Bellino was recently confined to bed for a series of examinations at Auchenflower's Wesley Hospital that two National Party ministers as well as the ever vigilant Consorting Squad duo call on him to cheer him up?'

The officer wasn't done with the Bellino family and the inference that some members of the National Party were on friendly terms with an alleged vice king. 'A final parting question,' he wrote, 'that only a body outside of Queensland, such as a Federal Senate Select Committee of Inquiry can answer truthfully, is: Did the National Party Queensland State Director receive a $50,000 cash donation at his Spring Hill office on the morning of Thursday Sept. 8th, and was this donation from the Bellino family?'

The officer concluded his letter: 'I regret that I cannot authorize the publication of my name and address; I have a family to support and we would all like to live a little longer.'

Hooper deemed that if such an inquiry was held, it would open a Pandora's box that would 'bring the government down'.

The impact of Hooper's damning allegations was close to nil. After his speech, parliamentarians greeted distinguished chamber visitor Dr S. Langi Kavaliku, Minister for Education, Works and Civil Aviation, Disaster Relief and Rehabilitation in the Government of Tonga.

That day, Commissioner Lewis recorded in his diary that he had a meeting with Premier Joh Bjelke-Petersen and Police Minister Bill Glasson where they discussed a range of topics, including 'loyalty of most Police'.

The following week, Lewis's usual peripatetic schedule saw him fly to Canberra for the day on a conference, take in an early round of Yuletide parties, dine with his assistant Greg Early and Michael Gambaro at the famous restaurateur's seafood eatery in Caxton Street, and visit as usual his old friend and advisor 'Top Level' Ted Lyons in his offices in Queen Street, the city.

Life didn't just get back to normal; it had never been interrupted in the first place.

Interlopers

As Royal Commissioner Frank Costigan, QC, began delivering his interim reports following years of investigating the Painters and Dockers Union, tax evasion schemes and other related criminal activities, debate arose over the establishment of a crime-fighting body on a national scale. Former prime minister Malcolm Fraser was behind the idea, as was his successor Bob Hawke. The idea was to have the National Crime Authority (NCA) up and running by late 1984, when Costigan would have handed down his final reports. Costigan's findings, along with those of Justice Stewart and his own commission of inquiry into Terrance Clark and the Mr Asia drug syndicate, highlighted the need for a more sophisticated approach to tackling organised crime.

In September 1983 Federal Cabinet agreed to convene a joint Attorneys-General and Police Ministers' Conference to discuss the establishment of the NCA and how it would work. From the outset, the Queensland government resisted the idea and foreshadowed not cooperating with any Federal crime body.

Bob Gibbs, the Labor member for Wolston, couldn't understand the National Party's reluctance to joining the fight against organised crime. He took Queensland Minister for Justice and Attorney-General Neville Harper to task over the issue. 'A number of weeks ago without any consultation with the Federal Government and very little consultation with his departmental officers … he [Harper] made one of the most ridiculous attacks that I have ever heard on the proposed establishment by the Federal Government of a national crimes authority in Australia,' Gibbs told the House.

'The authority is an absolute must if there is to be a combined effort by the State and the Commonwealth to combat organised crime, particularly the activities of organised drug rings in this nation. The Minister [Harper] said that he would not support it and that the Queensland Government would not support it.'

Gibbs informed the House that any investigation carried out in Queensland by the NCA could only be executed with the consent of, and in consultation with, the State Attorney-General. Gibbs added that he was 'amazed' at the government's lack of support for the initiative, given that prior to the recent state election it spruiked how it would take a hard line against drug peddlers. 'Yet, when the government has the opportunity to join with the other state governments and with the other Attorneys-General to discuss the guidelines for the National Crime Authority, it rejects the proposal out of hand,' Gibbs went on.

'I wonder why? Is it, as some of my colleagues have implied in this Assembly previously, that there is some sort of link between the National Party and organised crime in this state?'

Falls the Shadow

Lewis was always a busy Commissioner, rarely pinned behind his desk and constantly on the move, visiting remote police stations throughout Queensland, briefing his minister, taking on board operational matters, and fitting in a dizzying calendar of social events that ranged across charities, businesses, government and community events.

In November 1983, he continued to work at full throttle. According to his diaries, on Monday 14 November, for example, he got a phone call from the head of Queensland Rugby League, Ron McAuliffe, 're: money to keep M[al] Meninga in Qld as Souths Club has gone broke'. Later that evening he telephoned the Premier in relation to '3 queries by him'. They included: '… Painters and Dockers involvement in Drugs; Comalco or Capalaba branches of Westpac loaning money for drugs, & Drug Squad cooperating with Costigan Royal Commissioner'. The following day he squeezed in a lunch with local kung-fu school director and businessman, Malcolm Sue.

On Wednesday 16 November, Lewis had lunch with 'Hon. [Don] Lane' and discussed 'Police Union, Police Minister, Summ. Offences Act'. The following morning the Commissioner 'phoned Wayne Goss re meeting snr. officers', then he headed down to the headquarters of the *Sunday Sun* newspaper in Brunswick Street, Fortitude Valley, for a 'luncheon with Ron Richards, 6 staff and 4 other guests including Premier'. On Monday 21 November, he had lunch with his former assistant commissioner Tony Murphy.

A week later, Lewis recorded: 'With Snr. Officers saw W.K. Goss, D.J. Hamill and P. Comben, ALP members for Salisbury, Ipswich and Windsor re liaison generally.' The following day in State Parliament, the young Goss, opposition police spokesman, acknowledged the meeting with the Commissioner of Police – on the eve of Lewis's seventh year anniversary in the top job – and used the moment to fire a shot across the bow of the government.

I am pleased to have had an opportunity to meet with the Police Commissioner [Mr Lewis] and his senior officers and also separately with the Police Union Executive. I am confident that contact with such men will ensure that I am better equipped to carry out my role as Opposition spokesman.

However, I sound a note of warning and warn the police force to guard against further attempts by the Premier to manoeuvre the police into a partisan political position for his own dubious political motives. For it is both the community and the image of the police force which suffer when the Premier gives illegal and improper directions to the police force, whether they be to prevent citizens from exercising basic rights of free speech and assembly, or whether they involve vexatious and spiteful investigations against his political opponents.

Goss also saw fit to quote T.S. Eliot's famous poem, 'The Hollow Men'. 'There is a yawning gap between what this Government says and what it does, between the flowing promises and the actuality, between the expensive public relations brochures and the truth,' said Goss.

Goss then castigated the government for ignoring the 1977 Lucas Report, describing it as a 'discarded rag doll that is occasionally thrown around when some new outrage surfaces'. Lucas had recommended that police records of interview be tape recorded to avoid the possibility of police verballing.

Furthermore, Goss declared that there was a 'shadow' between 'the laws that this government is prepared to pass to regulate the freedoms of its citizens and the absence of regulation when it comes to powerful interests'.

In a colourful but stinging address, he quoted the words of American actor James Cagney as befitting the Bjelke-Petersen regime's mentality: 'Steal a buck and they put you in gaol, steal a million and they call you sir!'

Goss was just 32. He was the new member for Salisbury. A lawyer and civil libertarian, he had an intellectual brio that seemed a natural progression from the larrikinism of Kev Hooper. And he lost no opportunity to remind Bjelke-Petersen that the Premier's regime belonged to a lost era. It did not sit comfortably in modern Queensland.

'I am of a generation of Queenslanders whose adult life has never known any system of government other than the present unresponsive and shambling machine,' Goss said. 'Too long a period of arrogant and unresponsive rule can numb the mind and deaden the heart. We must work hard to overcome this.'

I'll Tell You What to Say

Commissioner Terry Lewis was criss-crossing town in late 1983 during the usual hectic Christmas Party season. His appointments diary was a blizzard of lunches, dinners and cocktail parties. On Monday 12 December he had a lunch aboard the MV *Mantaray* as a guest of solicitors Power and Power, then it was over to Parliament House for one of the big ones of the year – the Police Minister's Christmas function. There, Lewis met Minister Bill Glasson's new press secretary Robert Stewart.

Stewart would later recall the moment. 'Being new to the position, I made a point of introducing myself to the various people present at this function and at some point found myself in the company of the Police Commissioner, his assistant Greg Early and as I recall, the Commissioner's driver,' Stewart said.

'During my discussions with the Commissioner, I recall him saying words to the effect "that insofar as statements by the Minister regarding police matters are concerned, I'll tell you what to say".'

Stewart was taken aback.

'While I was aware that some matters had to be checked with the Commissioner's office, I gained what I viewed as a clear impression to have everything checked with the Commissioner's office before the Minister issued a statement,' he said.

'In my mind the comments made by the Commissioner were presumptuous and I indicated to him in quite clear terms that I would only be guided by the Minister. My recollection is that I told him words to the effect that I would check facts and figures with him, but what the Minister said was strictly a matter for the Minister.'

Stewart was naturally suspicious of Lewis, and the two would cross paths in the future. As for the Commissioner, Glasson's Christmas drinks only held him until 6 p.m.

As his diary recorded: '… with D/C Atkinson to TAB Bldg, Albion re The Totalisator Administration Board of Queensland Cocktail Party …'

Bubbles

The prostitute Katherine James had learned a hard and expensive lesson when she tried to set up her own massage parlour outside the strict jurisdictions of the Brisbane vice scene in late 1982. By that stage, brothels, escorts and illegal gambling were in the control of two groups – the Hector Hapeta and Anne Marie Tilley consortium, and 'the Syndicate' run by the Bellinos and Vic Conte.

James thought that her independent enterprise, Xanadu, in Stanley Street, Woolloongabba, had been given the nod by corrupt Queensland police, so she went ahead with costly renovations. The brothel happened to be a short distance from a rival Hapeta/Tilley establishment.

Within weeks Xanadu was receiving so much police attention that it was impossible to conduct any sort of business. It was dead in the water before it had even started. James had messed with The Joke and its tangled relationship with the city's vice figures. She never went out on her own again.

After the Xanadu experiment failed, she briefly went overseas before returning to Brisbane. She knew if you couldn't beat them, you joined them, so she started work with the syndicate. 'I approached Geoff Crocker [who ran the escort agencies and brothels for the group] ... and asked for a job,' she recalled years later. 'He employed me ... for the next 18 months . . . I did work for all of the houses which were in the syndicate.'

Other brothels in the empire to that point included the big house on the steep slope at Sankey Street, Highgate Hill, a house in Duke Street, Kangaroo Point, Club 29 on Sandgate Road at Albion, Caesar's Bathhouse in Wellington Road in East Brisbane, another old Queenslander at 81 Sylvan Road, Toowong, and Bubbles Bath House beneath the illegal casino at 142 Wickham Street.

'The reason that I say I was working for a syndicate was that all of the houses that I worked for ... were linked by two-way radio and every house had a list of other houses which the manageress could ring to get assistance with staff,' said James.

Eventually, James became a trusted member of the group. Every Wednesday at 10 a.m. she attended a meeting in an office under Bubbles Bath House in the Valley. At that meeting the money from the brothel network was counted and the books balanced. She said Geoff and Julie Crocker did the books for the massage parlours. Others covered the escort agencies, strip clubs and gambling houses. She claimed that every fortnight, on average, Gerry and Tony Bellino would drop by during the meeting.

'You had to gain entrance to the office from the side street,' James remembered. 'There is no internal access from Bubbles Bath House on the floor above. There is one fairly large room which had lounge suites in it. This big room would also contain bits and pieces such as filing cabinets up one end and some gym equipment. The office where the meeting took place also had in it a large board with keys on it. These were the spare keys to all the parlours and other businesses which were run by the syndicate.'

James estimated that the syndicate was taking in – across its various interests – about $100,000 per week. She said about 20 per cent of that went to corrupt police. 'I knew this from conversations that I had with Geoff and Julie Crocker and Gerry Bellino ... nobody told me, however, to whom the monies were paid or when,' James said. 'I saw evidence of payments myself in that it was obvious to me that the owners were never prosecuted for prostitution offences. In fact, the receptionists [who] were booked for keeping offences had been paid $500 for taking the booking and also had their fines paid for them.'

She said police were constant visitors to the syndicate's brothels. 'During routine visits by police, it was commonplace to give them food and drink,' she remembered. 'We had fridges upstairs and downstairs and there was always food available for the clients. I don't recall that the girls got booked there very often at all . . . I was never booked while I was with the syndicate.

'I do not recall any searches by the police for drugs. I recall occasions when the police would come in and see a girl was stoned on drugs. In those cases, they would simply order the person in charge of the house to send her home.'

Meanwhile, across the river in the Police Club, Commissioner Terry Lewis was telling leading businessmen, senior police, hoteliers and journalists that Queensland had one of the 'highest crime clean-up rates in the world'. Lewis put the state figure at 51 per cent. 'We are fortunate in this state in having the support of a very large proportion of the public,' Lewis crowed. 'This has certainly made our job easier – and assisted the clear-up rate.'

A proud Commissioner Lewis said the local academy was turning out 'some of the finest police officers in Australia'. He added: 'While

I am on record as saying that we are understaffed and could well use an additional 450 officers immediately, our relatively small handful of 4600 police officers – spread throughout this vast state – is doing a magnificent job.

'I have read most of the annual reports of police forces around the world, and the only ones I could find with a slightly better clear-up rate [than that of Queensland] were a couple of small ones in England.'

A Curious Case in Dunmore Terrace

Peter Gallagher was a no-nonsense style of copper. He joined the Queensland force in 1964, starting out in radio communications, then worked out of Roma Street headquarters. After a couple of stints in Ipswich and then Charters Towers in the far north, Gallagher was brought back to Brisbane. He worked on the drunks wagon for a while before joining Commissioner Frank Bischof's notorious Bodgie Squad, tasked with keeping the city's recalcitrant youth on the straight and narrow. 'We used to ride the last buses at night, the last trains, looking for trouble,' remembers Gallagher.

He was soon working for the Burglary Squad which, in turn, evolved into the Consorting Squad. He would later do a stint on the Gold Coast before being promoted to sergeant 2/c at the CIB in Brisbane. 'I used to get a lot of shoplifters because I knew the security officers at David Jones, Myer, McDonnell & East,' he remembers. 'So they used to ring [me] because they knew that I would bloody-well go prosecute the bastards.'

Gallagher's reputation for hard work was so fierce that younger officers would call in sick if they were rostered on with him. 'They knew that we'd bloody work eight hours,' he says.

On Thursday 19 January 1984, Gallagher arrived at work just prior to 6 a.m. to find a distressed young Indigenous man sitting in the foyer of police headquarters. The boy had a complaint he wanted to make. 'Ricky Garrison was his name,' recalls Gallagher. 'I said, "What's your go?" And he said, "Oh, I was picked up by a bastard named Breslin [in the early hours of 19 January] … and they took me to this place in Auchenflower …"'

'My ears pricked up because I knew [Paul John] Breslin was an impersonator of police and also a … harbourer of police. A lot of the deadbeats used to go down there and get grog at his place when he lived down near the Botanic Gardens [in Alice Street, the CBD].

'I said to this kid, "How did you get down here?" He said they let him go and he got a taxi … and I said, "Can you take me out to this place?" and he said, "Yeah, yeah … I'll take you out."'

In his statement Garrison alleged that he had been picked up the night before near the Victoria Bridge and taken to the salubrious Coronation Towers at 24 Dunmore Terrace, Auchenflower. Paul Breslin, the Ford Motor Company executive and friend to several Queensland police, courtesy of his Police Club membership, had purchased unit 24 off the plan, although he still had the unit in Alice Street. The Coronation Towers unit, in the early 1980s, was occupied by his mother, Margaret Rose Breslin, known to everyone as Peg.

Gallagher and a team of police headed for unit 24 along with Ricky Garrison. By this time it was mid-morning. 'I went to the body corporate, the manager, to get a plan of the unit so I knew when the fellows that I took with me went in, I could say you go there, you go there, you go there and do this,' says Gallagher. 'And you wouldn't believe it, [according to the manager] the bloody unit was owned by [Commissioner] Terry Lewis.' (The manager was mistaken. Lewis had once owned unit 22B, an investment property in the other tower from Breslin's unit, and had sold it years before the Garrison incident.)

The police proceeded to unit 24. 'We knocked on the door and there was no answer and there were three deadlocks and an ordinary lock on it,' says Gallagher. 'I walked over to this manager and I said, "Who's the bloke in there?"

'"Oh," he said, "that's Breslin", and his car was … Garrison pointed his car out … in the garage underneath. As I was coming back I happened to look up at the unit and I saw some bloke looking out through the curtains. So this is nice, three deadlocks and a bloody ordinary lock … Christ, what do I do now?'

Former Special Branch operative Barry Krosch was also on the raid. 'This Aboriginal boy walked in and said he had been kidnapped while he was walking across one of the [cross river] bridges,' he says. 'I think he said he was drugged and then sexually molested in a unit. This boy actually showed us the unit … I think he left a mark of some sort on it when he left or escaped.

'About six detectives attended. We knocked on the door and there was no response. The senior officer [I think] was an old-school detective, Senior Sergeant Gordon Duncan, also known as 'Burri' Duncan. Burri telephoned a locksmith mate of his. The fellow arrived and opened the door. The allegation was so serious you could do that … in law, it's called "fresh pursuit".'

The police stormed the unit and eventually discovered Breslin in the bedroom. 'Anyway, we raced in and Breslin is in bed, he's pretending he's in bed, and he's got … these airline masks, that they give overseas people, on and he's [saying] … "Oh, what's wrong? What's wrong?"' says Gallagher.

'I went into his room and he had some Vaseline type of stuff there. I said, "You got the market cornered for this stuff? Who else was in here?"

'He said nobody, so I had a look … I took possession of this lounge where the kid was and [the] scientific fellows found sperm on it and the kid's shirt, they found sperm on it. And they'd masturbated on his face and all this type of shit.'

Krosch recalls: 'We searched the unit. I found a photo album containing pics of [Constable] Dave Moore in various states of undress. In one, he wore his police cap. In another, he had his police baton stuck between his legs a la penis. I also clearly remember picking that photo album off a book case. I clearly remember two pics ... especially one of Moore on his back ... in the nude ... with the baton stuck between his legs.'

Gallagher says there appeared to be immediate heat on him over the Garrison investigation. 'The harassment started,' he says. 'They kept saying to me – I think there were five inspectors – called me over for an interview because of taking this lounge suite. And I said well, you know, it was lawful, the thing was found on it. I said I didn't act unlawfully at all ... anyway, we got the lounge suite back to him and ... I took out a summons for him, for Breslin.'

Krosch adds: 'I know that photo album was shown to the Commissioner of Police the next day.' (Lewis's Commissioner's diaries, however, place him on the Gold Coast on annual leave. He would not return to the office until Thursday 26 January.)

It wasn't until Friday 9 March that Lewis recorded in his diary he'd been telephoned by Welfare Services Minister Geoff Muntz 're raid on Paul Breslin on 19.1.84 re Drugs'. Breslin had in fact been charged with administering Garrison with stupefying drugs on or around 19 January.

It wouldn't be until the end of the year that the public had any inkling about the Breslin and Moore scandal.

Breslin says the allegations against him were a fabrication. 'I was collateral damage,' he claims.

In Strictest Confidence

In early February 1984, Kevin 'Buckets' Hooper, the member for Archerfield, was hitting his straps during the first sittings for the year in state parliament, railing at police corruption and the vice dens in Fortitude Valley.

He was also taking his characteristic pot shots at the National Party. Nobody was safe from a Hooper arrow. While discussing the Police Act Amendment Bill, Hooper told parliament that the Police Ministry was too important to be merely tacked onto a long list of other ministerial responsibilities. He said it should be dealt with singularly, and by a senior minister who was 'underworked'. 'The Deputy Premier and Minister Assisting the Treasurer [Bill Gunn] comes to mind,' Hooper quipped.

Hooper again blasted Police Minister Glasson and Commissioner Lewis's department by stating that 'some of the dens in Fortitude Valley' – the illegal games and massage parlours that 'didn't exist' – were not raided frequently enough.

'I will stick my neck out by telling the Minister about one high-ranking police officer who visits some of these places regularly,' Hooper went on. 'He drinks beer there and even plays some of the gambling games. I refer to Detective Sergeant Ross Beer of the Consorting Squad ... If he frequents a place and drinks with the proprietor, he must know what is going on. The Minister should immediately get Commissioner Lewis to ask Detective Sergeant Beer what he is doing on licensed premises without making an arrest.'

Two days later, Police Minister Glasson chastised Hooper in parliament, calling his attack on Beer and other police 'cowardly'. 'Does Mr Hooper expect detectives to find criminals attending church on Sunday?' asked Glasson. 'Obviously, in this line of work, Consorting detectives must visit places where criminals congregate. To imply that they are abusing their role as police officers by doing so is again a malicious slander. Detective Sergeant Beer is a fine and efficient officer.'

Beer told the *Telegraph* newspaper that Hooper's informants had 'given him a bum steer'. 'I deny all of these allegations, and can only assume Mr Hooper and his informant have me mixed up with some other person. I am not a punter except for one or two bets a year on the Melbourne Cup or a big race. As for gambling, I can't even play 500 or euchre, so I would have no hope of mastering complex gambling games.'

Commissioner Lewis recorded in his diary that he got a call from Judge Eric Pratt about Hooper's comment 're D/S Beer'.

Was there anything that could stop the irascible Kevin Hooper?

His electorate office in Inala, south-west of the Brisbane CBD, had become over the years a virtual confessional for disaffected police, prostitutes, street spivs and people on the fringe of the underworld. They all beat a path to his door, the working man's friend, who regularly offered his ear.

His desk was invariably covered in an assortment of paperwork, Spirax notebooks and ruled Queensland Legislative Assembly stationery, all covered in his large, unwieldy handwriting, the tableaux flecked with question marks. Who ran prostitution and gambling in Brisbane? Was this apparently wealthy suburban businessman the city's leading drug dealer? How did drugs get into Queensland? And how could certain people escape prosecution in the full glare of police attention?

As Opposition Police Spokesman, Hooper received wave after wave of tip-offs. Often, the data was as imprecise as his handwriting. As early as 1978, for example, he was being told seemingly tall tales of the 'Mr Bigs' in the state's drug scene and the going rates for various services in Brisbane brothels ('Topless hand relief = $15; Full oral = $50'). At one point he was also the recipient of anonymous notes, pointing to the suspect real estate portfolio of a senior National Party minister. It was all grist to Hooper's mill.

In early 1984, around the same time he was going into battle on the floor of parliament with Police Minister Glasson, Hooper received a 15-page, single-spaced typed document that was so rich in detail, so frighteningly wide-ranging, that even he must have been astonished. The document, complete with an annexure, was compiled by a group of serving Queensland police officers, concerned about rampant corruption within the force, and its impact on the future of the police department. Indeed, the Police Commissioner would often make mention of Hooper's 'police' informants in his diaries – disaffected officers who ran to Hooper to air their grievances, just as they had once consulted the former Labor MP and attack dog, barrister Col Bennett.

But this was different. The manifesto that landed on Hooper's desk in 1984 appeared to be a 'coda' to the corrupt system known as The Joke, outlining its history, its internal workings, its primary players and specific details of who did what within the system. At the top of the document it read: 'In Strictest Confidence'.

'It is our belief whether rightly or wrongly, that you were the man behind the resignation of [former assistant commissioner Tony] MURPHY and it was your influence that prevented his obtaining further promotion in the Queensland Police,' the document stated. 'If this be true we can only thank you. His name is synonymous with organised crime, fear, set up's [sic] and murder.'

The document claimed that Murphy, then retired and living at Amity Point on North Stradbroke Island, was making a bid to replace Merv Callaghan as secretary of the powerful Queensland Police Union. 'We're sure, Sir, that we don't have to tell you how disastrous that would be for the Queensland Police and in fact the citizens of this State,' the document stated. 'In that position, MURPHY would in fact control the Queensland Police Department. His control would be more absolute than if he were Deputy Commissioner. The man is so sick with a "power" complex that [it] is frightening.'

The authors then went on to explain that organised corruption in Queensland was so 'intricate and controlled that it would do justice to any security agency'. It made explicit reference to the system of graft payments rife in the force, outlining the operation of The Joke. 'The overall commander is called "The Godfather" and is, of course, ex–Assistant Commissioner Tony Murphy. Under Murphy's able leadership this group controls most of the organised crime in this State. They are also affiliated with a similar group in the New South Wales Police Department … in Police circles the Queensland Police has the reputation of being one of the most corrupt Police Departments in the Western world, second only to the New York Police Department.'

The document pointed out that the corruption within the force could be traced all the way back to faction fighting within the force in the 1950s – the Irish Mafia versus the Masons. It said Commissioner Lewis had kept 'a foot in both camps' and had the 'great backing' of former commissioner Frank Bischof.

Hooper would have been stunned by the history lesson. The document claimed that high-level corruption only existed and thrived because of high-level political influence.

The men of the Rat Pack have been able to 'corrupt' politicians, men of other government departments and leaders of industry by using the resources of the Police Department for non-police purposes.

Illegal tapping of phones and use of sophisticated electronic surveillance gear, control of illegal gambling, prostitution at all levels and the keeping of comprehensive files on citizens of prominence are all ways in which this group of men are able to get appointed to high rank in the Department.

These men are able to exert influence over not only politicians but members of the Judiciary, Magistrates, Trade Union leaders, Businessmen and Jurors. There is not a level of society that these men do not have contacts and informants who work for them either through fear of exposure or for monetary gain.

The document also gave an unprecedented insight into how The Joke was structured. Beneath the top level were a series of structured cells. One person, known as the 'control', was in charge of each cell.

> For example, at level 3 a 'control' may have six persons who answer to him. These six persons know only their 'control'. Their 'control' would answer to a 'control' on level 2 ... and not deal with any other person.
>
> The groups are known as 'cells'. The same principle is operated by organisations such as the KGB and CIA ... in the case of the Queensland Police if there is a Royal Commission this type of system makes it virtually impossible for any evidence to be obtained against the 'top echelon' of the Rat Pack ... there may be many rumours as to who the men in overall control are ... but no concrete evidence.

The document's 'annexure' offered a potted history of The Joke and its primary figures.

> The Rat Pack ... [are] predominately Irish Catholic, also known as The Irish Mafia. Controller ... ex–Asst Commissioner Anthony MURPHY, known as the 'Godfather'. Commissioner Terry LEWIS ... subordinate to MURPHY but on 'the board' that makes major policy decisions re group activities.
>
> Inspector Kevin DORRIES ... did control the Sunshine Coast area, primarily in the supply and distribution of drugs. Controls Gold Coast and Brisbane.

The document stated that Dorries was a part-owner with other police of the Zodiac Massage Parlour at West End. It named several other police officers before presenting a list of major crimes that had been mounted by corrupt officers on the orders of the 'Godfather'. The allegations included: the death of the principal witness [Shirley Brifman] against the 'Godfather' on conspiracy charges over the National Hotel inquiry; the death of the police officer [John Connors] in the grounds of the All Nations club at Mareeba; the Whiskey Au Go Go fire, 'for the sole purpose of destroying the credibility of COP [Commissioner of Police] WHITROD with the government of this State'.

Other cases cited were the murder of National Hotel manager Jack Cooper, armed hold-ups, drug and fauna smuggling, major robberies in south-east Queensland and the disappearance of brothel madam Simone Vogel ('... the Godfather is believed to have ordered her silence at any cost including her death if necessary').

The document also firmly recommended that 'the honourable Don Lane not be trusted with any information involving entrapment of corrupt police'. It concluded:

> Legally we realise that a Royal Commission is the only answer. We do hope you or the Police Minister may be able to initiate some sort of action that will enable the Queensland Police to begin to become a non-corrupt force and one in which honest officers won't be afraid to stand and be counted.

The letter sent to Hooper was a bombshell document, giving the greatest insight to date into The Joke, its structure, operation, breadth and membership.

Hooper, however, would never get the chance to raise the allegations in parliament. Just over a week before he was due to enter hospital for a basic medical procedure, he stood in parliament and discussed the case of Senior Constable Lorelle Anne Saunders – whom he had championed – and the appalling conspiracy to pervert the course of justice in relation to her being charged with attempting to procure to unlawfully kill a fellow officer. Hooper wanted to expose the Queensland police behind the conspiracy, and see them charged and gaoled.

The confidential document in his possession went into detail about the policemen behind the Saunders scandal, including former assistant commissioner Tony Murphy, and the anonymous allegations would have almost certainly bolstered his stance. He may have taken some comfort in the 'coda', given he had been tracking the same protagonists for years, and been howled down by police and the National Party for his troubles.

But as for the rest of the extraordinary material about The Joke and its players, it did not see the light of day on the floor of parliament via Hooper, who went into hospital for a routine biopsy and never went home.

Frozen into Shivering Immobility

Early in 1984, in what was to be a major cultural event in Brisbane, the University of Queensland Press were set to publish the second volume of historian Ross Fitzgerald's *A History of Queensland*. The first volume – *From the Dreaming to 1915* – had been released to critical acclaim two years earlier. Now, the bulky *From 1915 to the Early 1980s* was ready to be launched.

It was a big deal for the small but prestigious press, under the leadership of the estimable Laurie Muller. It had published some of Australia's greatest writers – David Malouf, Peter Carey, Frank Moorhouse, Roger McDonald and Barbara Hanrahan. It was also reprinting the novels of the brilliant and irascible Thea Astley, who had never shied away from portraying the political and social realities of her home state of Queensland.

Astley had written of the bordellos of Brisbane, for example, from her teenage memories as a citizen of the city, and when she settled in Far North Queensland, she relished in the frontier nature of life, sparing the sensibilities of no one. She was once asked what she thought of the city of Cairns, and she replied it was 'full of real estate agents and hookers'. The quip unleashed a storm.

As for Ross Fitzgerald's book, a launch was organised, and the book was to be sent into the world by then state secretary of the ALP Peter Beattie.

Ross Fitzgerald, about to turn 40, was born in Melbourne and completed his PhD in political theory at the University of New South Wales in the late 1970s. He was erudite, thought well on his feet and had the skill to reduce complex political argument and analysis into something digestible to the public. In early 1977 he had been offered a position as lecturer in political philosophy at Griffith University in Brisbane. Come the state election in November, he was immediately picked up by Channel Seven as a political commentator for the election coverage.

As he settled into his new life with wife Lyndal Moor, herself a former top fashion model and ceramicist, at their home in Kenmore, it dawned on Fitzgerald that a comprehensive history of Queensland had never been written. He became acquainted with the last published effort – *Triumph in the Tropics* by Sir Raphael Cilento and Clem Lack Snr, released in 1959. Cilento was a noted public health administrator and barrister. Lack was the Nicklin government's State Public Relations Officer who had also written a book of verse.

Triumph in the Tropics was a peculiar volume that even appeared outdated for its time. In its introduction, the authors wrote: 'The story of the self-governing State of Queensland is essentially the record of the white man's triumph over climate and his taming of the tropics.'

In a section on 'The Bush Blacks', they concluded: 'Like his own half-wild dogs, he could be frozen into shivering immobility or put to frenzied flight by people or things that provoked impressions of terror; or moved to yelps of delight or to racing around, or striking grotesque poses, or to expressing frantic excitement by any sort of clowning ... in his bushland home he lived in such insecurity that his immediate response to any situation of surprise was almost a conditioned reflex – instantaneous: to strike, to leap aside, to fall and roll.'

Fitzgerald was incredulous that this was the last official history of his newly adopted state, so he set to work on his two-volume history. When UQP sent out review copies to the press, they were anticipating another success following the triumph of the first volume. Instead, Fitzgerald and the publishers received almost instant fury from the then Chief Justice, Wally Campbell, and the then Attorney-General, Neville Harper.

On page 354, Fitzgerald had written about the controversial appointment of Campbell as Chief Justice over Justice James Douglas in 1982. In concert with Campbell, Harper threatened Fitzgerald and the University of Queensland with criminal libel. (A case on such a charge had not been seen in Australia since the scrap over Frank Hardy's political novel *Power Without Glory* in Melbourne in 1951.)

The threat from Campbell was delivered to Muller in the publishers' offices on campus at St Lucia. The irony was that Campbell, in threatening the university with libel and potential prison, was in fact indirectly suing himself – at the time he was the Chancellor of the University of Queensland.

UQP had printed about 3000 copies of the book. Around 1000 were in public circulation when the legal threat arrived. The publishers immediately attempted to recall the media review copies (surprisingly they got back the vast bulk of them from journalists) and pulped the edition.

Ross Fitzgerald had no idea what he'd stumbled into in Queensland. A history book had almost financially ruined him and threatened to send him to gaol. He had heard stories of fellow academics in the Sunshine State who had been set up on false drink driving charges because of their adverse views on the Bjelke-Petersen regime. And Fitzgerald himself was warned that a public exposure frame-up would not be beyond the realms of possibility, given that he had been for years a sober alcoholic.

The amended volume was finally published in late 1984. The Campbell passages were deleted.

While there were two Campbells cited in the newly revised index, Walter Campbell was not one of them.

Laurie Muller says the publicity probably did them and the book a favour. The second print run of the book was bigger than the first. 'I'd taken on the job of publisher at UQP as apolitical as you can get,' he says. 'After the monstering of Ross Fitzgerald's book, I decided to get proactive. Let's get stuck into them. I'm just about sure my phone was tapped then for close to a year.'

Queensland had become a state where, if historical fact between the covers of a book was unpalatable to the regime, it was summarily removed.

The Little Man's Friend

On Sunday 4 March 1984 it was business as usual in the Inala household of colourful MP, Kev Hooper. Hooper's wife, Terri (he gave her the unusual nickname of 'Knackers'), had prepared a Sunday roast, and Hooper's brother John (he called him 'Jackie') and his wife Helen had popped over for dinner.

During the meal, Hooper complained of feeling unwell. His face was ruddier than usual, and his neck was swollen. 'What do you think it is, Knackers?' he asked his wife.

'You look like you have the mumps. You should see your doctor.'

Hooper said he'd already done that, and was booked in to hospital later in the week for a biopsy. Brother John promised to pick him up and take him. The brothers spoke by telephone during the week before the appointment. Kev asked his brother if he had a suitable 'port' or carry bag he could take to the hospital. John borrowed one off their sister Marie.

Early in the week Hooper stopped to have a chat with a journalist in the corridor outside the Press Room in Parliament House. 'You know, I'm not well, but I've just got to go in for this simple operation,' Hooper supposedly said. 'All it is, is a blockage in a vein and they just have to bypass that. Anyway, it will all be over in a few days.'

On Wednesday 7 March, Hooper met *Sunday Mail* journalist Ric Allen at the Breakfast Creek Hotel. Allen had beer. Hooper drank soda water. The two men discussed the stories they'd done together over the years, from the Lorelle Saunders saga to 'Teddy Lyons and his problem with drink-driving'.

The next day, John Hooper picked up his brother and they headed into the city. 'You know, Jackie,' Kev said thoughtfully. 'Apart from the gash on my bum and the odd hangover, I have never really been sick in my life. I have never had a headache.'

The brothers arrived at the entrance to the Prince Charles Hospital in Chermside, just north of the city. 'I opened the boot to get his port and he said he wanted to carry it himself,' says John. 'When he bent over to pick up the port he was purple. As we walked through the front door I realised why he wanted to carry the port. All the wardsmen were saying, "Good day, Kev". They would have been members of the Miscellaneous Workers' Union.'

At the hospital reception, Hooper was asked to fill out the usual admission forms. One asked him to nominate his 'religion'. 'I'll put none,' Kev said.

'Hedge your bet,' John said. 'Just to be on the safe side, put Roman Catholic.'

Hooper went to his room and John returned to see him later that evening. 'He was sitting up in bed in his new pyjamas and dressing gown,' John remembers. 'He told me he was thirsty and asked me to get him a soft drink. I got him two cans of lemonade. We had a natter and he said he was having his biopsy early the following morning.'

They discussed what the doctors might find. 'If there is anything sinister there I wouldn't want to linger,' Big Kev, as he was known, confided in his brother.

'At this stage it's only a biopsy,' John said. 'We can cross that bridge when we come to it.' The two men shook hands. 'Mate, you'll be okay,' John assured him. 'I'll see you after the biopsy tomorrow.'

The next morning, John and his wife were urgently summonsed to the Prince Charles. There they met Terri.

'Kev's gone,' she said.

John could not comprehend that his beloved brother had died as the result of such a simple procedure as a biopsy. 'I was taken down to the operating theatre on my own where I was met by a very young doctor who took me to Kevin,' John recalls. 'He was lying on a bed. He had been cleaned up and looked like he was sleeping. I was very upset and kissed his forehead.'

John asked the doctor what had happened, and was told the tumour on Hooper's right carotid artery was bigger than expected. The bleeding couldn't be stopped.

'Are you telling me he bled to death?' John asked, incredulous.

The doctor further advised that Hooper had been suffering Hodgkin's Lymphoma.

News had already started to get out. John says Peter Beattie telephoned to offer his condolences to the family. Naturally it made page one of the *Daily Telegraph*: HOOPER DEAD.

'Grand old rascal, fighter for the underdog, master of parliamentary wit, and working class family man whose castle was a Housing Commission house at Inala – Queensland, and State Parliament in particular, will never be the same without Kev Hooper,' the *Courier-Mail* reported. 'Those he tirelessly attacked and exposed will breathe a sigh of relief at his sudden death – he would have been extremely disappointed if they did not.'

Hooper was described across the board as a 'scallywag'. His funeral was held at St Mark's Catholic Church in Inala. Father Frank O'Dea, of the parish, said of Big Kev: 'He will be remembered as the cricketer who played on the footpath with the kids of Inala. He was a tough politician and a gentle family man. He was intoxicated with people.'

Insubordination

Tension had been building for months between Detective Sergeant Ross Dickson, the Sheriff of Mareeba, in Far North Queensland, and his superiors over numerous work-related issues. Dickson was overworked and his CIB was understaffed. Having written numerous memos to his superiors in an effort to resolve matters, Dickson hit a wall. All his pleas had been ignored.

The situation finally boiled over in mid-March 1984. Dickson's boss, District Officer W.J. [Bill] Bergin, had two run-ins with Dickson that necessitated him lodging a confidential report to his Regional Superintendent. Dickson was cited for insubordination on both counts. Bergin did not plan to take the matter further, he simply wanted it on record.

The first run-in involved Bergin attempting to arrange assistance for an officer from the Atherton CIB in apprehending a possible drug dealer. A forestry worker had been threatened by the dealer, accusing him of harvesting his cannabis plantation. The dealer ordered the crop be delivered back to him at a specific time and place. Detective Sergeant R.J. Wall, according to Bergin, sought help in apprehending the dealer.

Bergin wrote: 'At about 6.30 p.m. ... I attended my office at Mareeba for the purpose of supplying arms and ammunition to the C.I. Branch personnel from Mareeba to take with them to Atherton ... Detective Sergeant Dickson arrived at my office and told me that he was also going to Atherton. This would have been on overtime.'

Bergin said: 'Ross, there is no need for you to go as there are already enough police going along.'

Dickson allegedly replied: 'Look, boss, I'm a detective and have been for 14 years. You don't know anything about detective work, it's out of your field, you don't know what you are talking about.'

Dickson said he had spoken to 'Wallie' who wanted him present on the scene.

'You're not going,' Bergin repeated.

'I'm in charge of the C.I. Branch and I will do as I please,' Dickson supposedly said. 'You don't know how to run anything. If I want to go there I will.'

'Get out of my office,' Bergin told him.

In the end, Bergin allowed Dickson to head off to Atherton. 'I'm sorry about before, boss,' Dickson allegedly remarked, 'I just get het-up at times.'

The other matter involved Dickson wanting to go out on the scene of an incident involving a women threatening to kill her husband. Bergin ordered him to stay in Mareeba.

'You're fucking wrong and it will be on your shoulders,' Dickson supposedly told him.

Dickson was ordered to Brisbane to undertake a mental health examination with the chief medical officer. 'They were trying to get me for being mentally ill,' he recalls.

Solicitor Pat Nolan organised for him to see a specific doctor. alleging that the chief medical officer at the time was 'Lewis's man'.

After he was examined, Dickson was asked if he wanted the results. 'This bloke [the doctor], he was paranoid, he wouldn't tell me in his office, we went out onto the street. He said, "You're the sanest man

I've ever met, and I'll be putting that in my report." But he was very concerned that his office was bugged, you know?'

Then, on 5 April, Dickson alleged he had been given an extraordinary verbal direction by Bergin. Dickson and the CIB were told to lay off investigating drugs and serious sex offences. Dickson was gobsmacked. So much so that he wrote one of his lengthy missives to Commissioner Terry Lewis himself.

Dated 9 April, Dickson's letter informed the Commissioner that he had been instructed that his office 'was not to pursue the investigation of serious sex offences in relation to numerous children by four men, only one of whom has to date been interviewed'.

He had been further instructed that other children and suspects involved in the case were not to be interviewed and he would have to proceed to court with information already obtained. Dickson described Inspector Bergin as 'unreasonable and inexperienced'.

'Inspector Bergin has also told me that he is keeping a special file on me and when he has enough evidence I will be charged with insubordination towards him,' wrote Dickson. 'Inspector Bergin also told me that I was the subject of a special file being held by the Police Department and that all my overtime was being investigated.'

He informed the Commissioner that he had been told he was being investigated even further by two Queensland parliamentarians over his excessive overtime – a claim Dickson didn't believe.

Mr Lewis, you as head of the Police Department I feel have no idea what is happening here and some other police districts because you are not being told.

I have tried my best to do my job and the results speak for themselves but if you want this situation to continue and it is done with your approval then I tell you now that whoever is responsible for wrecking the working performance of good Police Officers has won, as I just cannot cope with the constant threats and pressure the Police Department is placing on us NOT to do our job and because we are doing it to be constantly suspected and accused whilst those men who choose to be lazy and never do any work are never subjected to anything to make them work and live the life of Reilly at our expense.

Dickson complained that Bergin was harassing him.

I feel that a deliberate attempt is being made to curb the activities of this section because we are too active and someone wants us to be slowed down for some unknown reason that we can only guess at. If no decision is made to change anything from this section then I would respectfully request written directions that I am not to persue [sic] investigations along the lines that I have already been directed …

Again I personally request you [sic] assistance in this matter as I am at a loss to know what to do from here on.

A week later, Dickson wrote a sharp rebuke to Bergin, saying that if he hadn't instructed the office not to investigate drug matters, then two local drug dealers – the subject of constant complaints from the public – would have been already charged with serious drug offences.

Bergin wrote back: 'I do not want any further comment verbally or otherwise about my direction in this connection.'

Dickson now says he believes Bergin was acting on instruction from Brisbane to try and cut down on expenses.

'Was there police involvement in the drug trade? I didn't see it that way, no, not then,' he says. 'They were trying to knock us back for overtime. Bill was a decent bloke. Bill just did whatever they told him to do. I really think he was trying to limit expenses.'

But the saga was about to turn nasty.

The Italian

Down in Canberra, on the fourth floor of the unremarkable National Mutual Building on London Circuit that surrounds City Hill in Civic, an officious, bespectacled sergeant was sifting through reams of statistics on his desk at the Australian Bureau of Criminal Intelligence (ABCI).

Peter Vassallo, a trained engineer before he joined the New South Wales Police and was then seconded to the ABCI, had come to crime fighting relatively late. He had been living in Sydney's eastern suburbs and working successfully as an engineer when he learned of a drug problem at his daughter's high school. Incensed, Vassallo approached local police and asked them what they planned to do about it. They were indifferent. So, he warned them – if you do nothing, then I'll join the force myself and exact justice.

And that's precisely what he did.

Vassallo was in his early thirties when he went through the academy and qualified as a police officer. At the ABCI, however, he was tasked with collecting data on illegal marihuana production and sale in Australia in the wake of the Stewart Royal Commission into the Mr Asia syndicate, headed by heroin dealer Terrance Clark.

Because of the prolific number of Italian families believed to have been involved in growing the marihuana, and profiting considerably from the enterprise – to the point where their grand houses were colloquially dubbed grass castles – Vassallo's one-man operation became known as 'the Italian desk'.

Fortunately, Vassallo had a brilliant mind for statistics and data. Already in his research he had delineated that particularly gruesome murders were occurring, year after year, at roughly the same times of year in places associated with the large-scale cultivation of marihuana, specifically Griffith in New South Wales and Far North Queensland. Why?

Vassallo worked out that the violence erupted around the time that crops of dope were being harvested and packaged for sale. There would be disputes over money. Fights over quantity. Vassallo would study these patterns, as a meteorologist might pore over weather data and make a forecast. What will happen tomorrow? What does all this mean? Vassallo's investigation became known as Project Alpha.

Given his expertise, Vassallo was chosen to undertake an elite intelligence analyst's course at the National Intelligence College in Manly, Sydney, in late 1984. His roommate for the duration of the course was Queensland Undercover Detective Jim Slade. Slade was probably Queensland's finest intelligence officer, trained by and large by retired assistant commissioner and legendary detective Tony Murphy. 'We were doing the intelligence analyst course that was run there,' says Vassallo. 'We were learning the actual processes involved in any form of discipline, in that there was conventions. We all had to learn the conventions of intelligence analysis, be it strategic intelligence or tactical intelligence.

'[It] basically deals with … the Venn flow charts, link charts, entities, how you describe an entity. A confirmed link and an unconfirmed link – and we all take it for granted these days a confirmed link from one entity to another entity diagrammatically is described or depicted as a straight line. An unconfirmed link is a broken line.'

He liked Slade. And their work shared some common ground. 'We got on there and we had a few beers and the bottom line was that Jim was really concerned about … a trip up north,' recalls Vassallo. 'Things had happened to him and he realised that he was being pressured by the administration. He told me certain things and I said, well, I'm your counterpart … he didn't quite understand that I was a New South Wales copper. First of all, he thought I was a Federal copper and he realised he could not get help from within, right? He needed an outside ally and he was looking at … me, because I worked at the bureau.

'We got on well, we understood each other … everything he was telling me was gold in that I'd read a lot about where the data was coming from, and there was nothing coming from Queensland.

'So, I now had a fountain of information, and he'd just come back from a major exercise up there and he's telling me all this shit. So I'm just sucking it in and I'm having my Southern Comforts and he's having his beers and, you know, over the course of two weeks, apart from doing our courses and doing exams and ... finally getting our qualifications, we partnered up often.

'I was very interested in what he had to say but what I couldn't tell is, you know, is this all bullshit? Was it fantasy?'

Vassallo quickly concluded that Slade was on the level. 'In that first sense I believed everything he was saying because of the colour and detail of what he was saying,' Vassallo adds. 'The places that he had been, the fact that I was aware of certain things in certain places. And notwithstanding illegal things, I knew for example that in the southern states the growing of marihuana was seasonal; in the northern states you could grow it during the winter.

'Well, the growing of tomatoes and the growing of marihuana have lots of parallels and our Italian mates started off in soldiers' plots in Griffith growing tomatoes. And later on oranges, and putting marihuana plants between wine-grape vines or tomatoes was beautiful camouflage, and that's what they used to do in the old days.

'From Jim's perspective, he had this skill with people ... you know, he was a chameleon. I could see in his mannerisms, I could see the passion ...'

Courtesy of the recommendations of the Williams and Stewart Royal Commissions, Slade had been tasked to investigate drug plantations and drug importation in Far North Queensland. His work was dubbed Operation Trek. Trek involved numerous bureaus and bodies, both state and Federal, including the ABCI, National Parks and Wildlife and the armed forces. It also utilised elements of the Queensland Bureau of Criminal Intelligence (BCI) under the control of Alan Barnes.

In early 1984 Slade and his partner Ian Jamieson went on patrol in the far north for more than three months, setting up a network of information sources. They included fishermen, boat skippers, property owners, pilots, teachers and local police. Both men gathered an enormous amount of intelligence. Much of it even stunned these two seasoned investigators. How had this corrupt industry been allowed to flourish for so long without coming across the radar of police?

When Slade and Vassallo came together, so too did some of the pieces of this monstrous puzzle.

Transfer

Mareeba Detective Sergeant Ross Dickson's specialty was the drug trade, and he'd built up a vast network of contacts throughout the region. He knew who was doing what, and was making headway in the fight against drugs and organised crime.

It was incomprehensible to him to be directed to not investigate the drug trade, as he alleged he had been instructed by Inspector Bergin. Dickson was having some success in what was probably the capital of marihuana production in Australia outside of Griffith in rural New South Wales, and he and his men were told in unequivocal terms to back off. Why?

Dickson had known he'd wanted to be a policeman since he was a child. He was proud of his work. So, after typing up his concerns in a letter to the Commissioner of Police, Terry Lewis, asking why he had been given an instruction that he considered unlawful, he waited anxiously for an answer in writing.

He got one. Just weeks later he was notified that he was to be transferred to Townsville. The transfer officially came through on 30 April, the notification was signed off by then Acting Commissioner Syd 'Sippy' Atkinson.

Dickson immediately penned an 'Application to have Unapplied for Transfer Cancelled'. He said such a move to Townsville would cause him and his family financial hardship, his daughter was receiving specialist treatment for an ailment and needed a further 18 months treatment, that he was accepted by the local community and that he still had some major court cases and investigations on the go. He also had another reason he should stay put: 'Knowledge of the criminal element as a whole in particular, and organised crime in this area particularly relating to the Griffiths [sic] Drug Organisation plus the value of informants cultivated will be lost.'

The application was rejected.

Dickson stood his ground, and by doing so set himself on the same perilous path as many before him, those who had dared to upset the status quo in the Queensland Police Force, including Kingsley Fancourt, Bob Campbell, Bob Walker, Lorelle Saunders and others. His fate was sealed when he gave a series of media interviews.

One of the first was to the veteran reporter Mike Willesee who hosted the popular Channel Nine program, *A Current Affair*. Introducing his report, Willesee referred to a Queensland policeman 'who appears to be paying a penalty for being too good at his job'.

Willesee posed the question – how did Dickson get a reputation for being a 'crime buster' in a town as small as Mareeba, population 5000? In answer, he went on to inform viewers that Mareeba was the police base for an area approximately the same size as Victoria. 'It's close to South-East Asia, it has disused World War II airstrips, it has properties so large that the owners often haven't seen all of what they own,' Willesee informed his audience. 'Accordingly, it's an area which has attracted drug growers, drug smugglers, drug dealers and smugglers of illegal immigrants.'

Willesee explained to viewers that Dickson was now being transferred from Mareeba against his will. When Willesee asked Dickson why this was so, Dickson responded, 'I don't know, nobody will tell me.'

Willesee: So you have a high rate of crime, a high rate of clean-up, but you're being transferred. It seems to me that something is terribly wrong.

Dickson: I say that myself. I've been trying to find out what's been going on. I've been put under a lot of pressure all of this year. I've put a report in to the Commissioner and I have made sure it was hand-delivered to him, asking him if he knew what was going on.

Willesee: Was there a reply?

Dickson: Yes. I was transferred.

Willesee: How do you read that?

Dickson: Well, I don't read anything sinister [in]to it. I said in the report to the Commissioner about the pressure that was being applied to us not to investigate major offences, but I suspected that we were perhaps too close to the executives of certain organised criminal activities and perhaps they thought we knew more than we did know.

Willesee: Do you mean you were asked not to investigate certain alleged offences?

Dickson: Yes, I was instructed on the fifth of April, under no circumstances were we to investigate any further drug matters at all at Mareeba.

Willesee: How can you possibly explain that?

Dickson: I can't explain it, it's an unlawful instruction and I went straightaway and typed a personal letter to the Commissioner telling him this and telling him that if he wanted me to … obey this instruction, that I required that instruction in writing.

Willesee suggested that the action was almost an open invitation to drug dealers to head to Mareeba and set up shop, so long as they didn't work regular office hours. Dickson added that trying to contain the drug industry was an almost impossible task.

'We're all trying to work in together, we're trying to stretch a thin blue line around an enormous area and, unfortunately, there's a lot of gaps in it and we're just doing the best we can,' said Dickson.

Dickson believed his imminent transfer was a way for the police administration to set an example. It suggested: 'Pull your head in or the same will happen to you as happened to Dickson.'

In Channel Nine's Brisbane studio, Willesee crossed to Queensland Police Union spokesman Detective Sergeant John 'Bluey' O'Gorman. Was the transfer good news for Queensland criminals? Willesee asked.

'I'd say that if I was an executive, if you like, of a large drug-growing, marketing venture,' said O'Gorman, 'I couldn't have achieved a better result ... than if I'd gone out and shot Ross Dickson personally.'

Problematically, Dickson continued talking to the newspapers and television reporters. The night after the Willesee story, he popped up on Channel Seven's current affair program *Today Tonight*, and was interviewed by Mark Suleau.

During the interview Suleau asked Dickson: 'Are there men in the marihuana industry powerful enough to put external pressure on the police force?'

'Yes, well, going from experience where we've seen the rest of Australia we all realise that there are people with a lot of influence connected with the drug industry ...' Dickson replied.

Dickson's name also began to light up in Commissioner Lewis's diary. On 1 May he fielded a call from Police Minister Glasson 're D/S/ Dickson transfer'. Three days later Lewis took a call from *Tablelands Advertiser* journalist Ken Pederson who confirmed there was 'little support for D/S Dickson in Mareeba'. On 6 May he sat down with union representatives and told them Dickson's transfer was 'to stand'.

Old friend Ron Edington also appeased his boss by phoning Lewis and discussed 'general poor image of D/S/Dickson'.

But the media interviews just kept coming.

The young Opposition Police Spokesman Wayne Goss told journalist Chris Allen of Channel Seven's *State Affair* that another police officer – Constable Hurrell – had been transferred after investigating a cattle stealing case that involved a former police officer and two other serving officers. 'The clear message coming from the Commissioner to police is that if you move into, if you investigate sensitive areas, then this government will sack or transfer you,' Goss said.

Goss then appeared on Seven's *Today Tonight* on 6 June. Reporter Chris Adams asked Goss if he thought there was corruption 'at a very high level' in the Queensland Police Force.

'Well, it can only be one of two things,' Goss replied. 'It can only be corruption or it can only be some misguided notion of mateship – a friend of a friend – that is protecting people who have been involved in activities warranting investigation by police.' Goss openly wondered if the whole affair wasn't 'a question of incompetence at the administration level' of the force.

The conflagration grew, and on the day Goss did his interview with Adams, Commissioner Lewis noted in his diary: 'With A/Dep Comm McDonnell saw Messrs Chant, McCaul, O'Gorman and Hannigan [of the Police Union] re D/S R. Dickson – transfer to stand.'

Lewis now appreciated the sort of damage Dickson could wreak on the department. The next day, 7 June, he telephoned '… Judge Pratt re false statements by Mr Goss MLA on 6th inst, on Glen Taylor show'. Lewis then contacted lawyer Pat Nolan regarding Goss's criticism of him and the force. Could Goss's comments provide enough substance for a defamation case?

Lewis decided to speak out on Friday 8 June. 'Mr Dickson is well aware of the reasons for his transfer,' the Commissioner said. 'In fairness to him, I do not propose to discuss them publicly.' Lewis said it involved 'internal departmental discipline'. The Mareeba detective had already had his files confiscated and his colleagues had been interviewed by senior officers.

Over the next week the big guns were drawn into the mounting crisis. Lewis phoned the Premier's Department over the matter, and former detective and friend to Lewis, Tony Murphy, called in with information about the 'Union Executive and D/S Dickson'.

Police Minister Glasson, who had failed to satisfactorily answer the crucial question – Why was Dickson transferred from Mareeba to Townsville? – finally delivered the reason at the heart of the controversy. Dickson, he said, was being transferred for 'disciplinary reasons', including defying an order from a senior officer. 'The transfer of Det. Sgt Dickson – and all police officers – is not solely decided by Police Commissioner Lewis,' the Minister explained. 'But is ... recommended to Commissioner Lewis by other senior commissioned officers. If I intervened, it would indicate that I had no trust in Commissioner Lewis, nor his senior officers – which is patently not correct – and it would be the thin edge of the wedge of breaking down the transfer system.'

Glasson threw down a challenge to Opposition Police Spokesman Wayne Goss and to Dickson to 'put up or shut up' if they had any information on drugs and organised crime in North Queensland. Glasson was talking tough.

Dickson hit back. He dared the Minister to publicly issue any damaging information he had on him, in exchange for a complete waiver from defamation proceedings. 'There is a backstabbing campaign against me, and I have been told that when parliament resumes in August there will be allegations made under parliamentary privilege to discredit me,' said Dickson. 'I am prepared to give the Minister a written guarantee that I will not take any legal action if he will make a full statement so that the public can be told everything right now.'

Goss, backing Dickson, said he had been told by sources within the force that 'the department intended bringing an internal charge against

Dickson in a couple of months and that, after an internal investigation, he would subsequently be sacked. Similarly, the Queensland Police Union came out guns blazing in support of Dickson, placing large notices in the *Courier-Mail* newspaper. IT IS TIME FOR SOME ANSWERS, read the headline on the advertisement. 'Dickson has stood up, this Union supports him. The people of Queensland need to know the truth ...'

Another union advertisement stated: 'We still do not have any tangible reason for the transfer of Detective Sergeant Ross Dickson.'

On Friday 15 June, Commissioner Lewis got a relieving telephone call in his office. 'Premier phoned re Cabinet's support for our stand on D/S Dickson.' Later that day, Lewis and lawyer Pat Nolan sat down together with the department's press officer, Ian Hatcher, and five assistant commissioners, and 'viewed a series of TV programs re: D/S Dickson, Mr W. Goss and others'.

Lewis would also come into the possession of the full transcripts of all of Dickson's television interviews. Lewis remembers Dickson as a 'hot little worker'.

'Bright bloke, he was a cadet, I think three years a cadet ... very bright. Hard worker, but [a] hot worker. He was, I think he was a uniform man at Mitchelton, he was pinching anything that breathed, and then later when ... [Ray] Whitrod came in, and I think briefly, at the Juvenile Aid Bureau we'd caution a lot of youngsters, and I still think rightly, very rightly so, and we'd put a return in at the end of the year – X number cautioned – but that wasn't classed as an arrest. That didn't suit statistically mad Whitrod. So he got the idea of forming this education liaison unit, and that's when he put Dickson on it.'

Lewis believes the group was formed by Whitrod to intentionally undermine his JAB. 'That's the only way of describing it [the liaison unit], and any youngsters they got, they'd be charged, and of course they [the Whitrod administration] relished that,' says Lewis. 'They charged them with stealing a pencil ... and it got the stats up nicely, and that's when sort of ... I ... I don't know what they wanted to do, I think Whitrod wanted to close us down or something.

'But getting back to Dickson ... well it probably would have happened when I came back [from Charleville in 1976 and became Commissioner]. I would have got rid of the bloody education liaison unit and got the JAB going, and Dickson was back in the CIB ... [he was] up there [in Mareeba], and he was an arrogant little possum. He fell out with [an inspector] who was an absolute bloody gentleman – wouldn't say, "shit" – and anyway, to cut a long story short, somehow it came to [my] notice.'

Dickson travelled to Brisbane and asked to see Commissioner Lewis and Police Minister Bill Glasson so that a reason for his transfer could be offered face to face. Both men refused to meet with him.

On 17 June the high-rating current affairs program *60 Minutes*, hosted by Jana Wendt, got in on the story. During the interview Dickson alleged that the police department was keeping a secret file on him, and that two politicians were investigating him. He wanted to know why he was being investigated. He conceded that his stand against the transfer would probably tarnish his career for good.

'And there's nothing in it for me, not a single thing in this for me,' Dickson said. 'I will be ... I will suffer, probably for the rest of my service, for what I'm doing.'

'So what is your future, do you think?' asked Wendt. 'Where will you be in a couple of years' time?'

'Dunno,' Dickson replied.

The First Guest

In the middle of the enthralling attempted murder trial of Brisbane schoolboy Peter James Walsh, another event was titillating the city's social set. The Sheraton was due to open its first international-quality hotel in the Queensland capital.

Despite being a 'soft' opening and not the 'formal' one (that would go ahead in October, attended by the Premier, the Police Commissioner Terry Lewis and his wife Hazel, and a myriad of home-grown celebrities, business identities and socialites), it was still a major event by the city's standards. It gave the local citizenry an excuse to boast over Brisbane's increasing cosmopolitanism and sophistication – a perennial debate – and the government bragging rights in relation to tourism and employment creation. On a practical level, there was a posh new watering hole in town.

Befitting such a spectacle, the immensely popular ABC radio announcer Bill Hurrey was brought in on the morning of Thursday 12 July 1984 to broadcast his morning show from the sparkling Sheraton lobby. Local public relations maestro John Lyneham was responsible for securing good media coverage. 'I did liaise with Billy Hurrey,' Lyneham recalls. 'Hurrey had built up a listenership and I wanted him there. We got him. His technicians set up the night before.'

The $63 million hotel – the State Government Insurance Office held a 90 per cent stake – was the first to be built in the city in more than ten years. It boasted Royal and Presidential Suites in its exclusive 'tower' section. These rooms – at $350 a night – gave guests access to, among other delights, toilet paper holders finished in 24-carat gold.

Reporting on the event was the *Courier-Mail*'s popular 'Day by Day' columnist, Des Partridge. His page-three column the following day was headlined: FIRST GUEST VERY IMPRESSED. The article quoted a Mr Paul Breslin from Sydney, who had booked the room six months in advance, and was the first person to sample the hotel's service. 'It's as good as anywhere I've stayed in the world,' Breslin reportedly said.

Breslin claimed he was a businessman who travelled overseas regularly, and that Brisbane 'now had a hotel it could be proud of … It compares very favourably with the Vista International – recently named the world's number one hotel by the *Business and Travel Magazine*.' The chuffed guest gave a big tick, also, to the friendly room service and soundproofing of the rooms, declaring his stay 'a perfect first night'.

Extraordinarily, while Paul Breslin, well-travelled businessman 'from Sydney' was enjoying the largesse of the Brisbane Sheraton, Paul Breslin of Coronation Towers, Auchenflower, appeared that very week as a star witness in the Peter James Walsh trial.

Indeed, just the day after the *Courier-Mail* reported on Breslin the impressed hotel guest, it carried a report of the trial hearings and the evidence given by 'Paul John Breslin of Auchenflower'. At the time of Walsh's trial, Breslin was still awaiting a hearing date for his own charges relating to the alleged assault of Indigenous minor, Ricky Garrison, in January.

What could explain the fact that Breslin, of Brisbane, was appearing as a witness in a major trial in the city, while at the same time turning up in the newspaper as a well-heeled and well-travelled businessman purportedly from Sydney?

The Assistant

Apart from his wife Hazel, Commissioner Lewis had no more loyal an associate than Gregory Early, his personal assistant.

Early had grown up on a series of dairy farms in the Kilcoy region, about 100 kilometres north-west of Brisbane. He had wanted to become a carpenter but his father directed him towards a career in the police. He joined up in 1956 and showed considerable organisational flair. He also became an accomplished shorthand writer. During the 1970s he was personal assistant to Commissioner Ray Whitrod before Whitrod's resignation, and upon Lewis becoming Commissioner in November 1976, Early slipped into the same role.

Given the animosity that had developed between Whitrod and Lewis, and the latter's pained efforts to ultimately exorcise all Whitrod acolytes from the force, it appeared a minor miracle that Early was kept on by Lewis. One police colleague recalls: 'With Greg it wasn't a case that he made a decision to sit on the fence whoever the boss was. He didn't. He was just one of those people who offered his loyalty.'

Early, too, was a master of discretion. His job was never dull, and the variety of tasks was extraordinary. 'On many occasions I used to field telephone calls from Mona Lewis, the Commissioner's mother,' Early says in his unpublished memoir. 'She was quite aged and had a son named Gary. Gary was on a disability pension and generally was a pain in the arse to Mona and anyone with whom he came in contact. He was a half-brother to the Commissioner. [Assistant Commissioner] Ron Redmond knew Mona well from seeing her at the races and I am sure that after Lewis became Commissioner Redmond and Jim O'Sullivan, both regular race attendees, used to give Mona a lift home to her flat at Hamilton or nearby.

'I recall occasions when I have rung [Ron] Redmond or [Jim] O'Sullivan and asked them to go down and quieten Gary down or lock him up. I also recall Mona telling me that on occasions Redmond and maybe O'Sullivan used to give her a bottle of whiskey, which she claimed to like.'

Early also accompanied his superior on sporadic tours into far-flung regions of Queensland. Lewis was adamant that he visit every single police station in the state during his tenure. It spoke volumes in terms of Lewis's almost fanatical attention to detail.

'It took him four-and-a-half years to visit every police station in the state. That had never been achieved by a Commissioner before and probably will never be done again,' says Early. 'This was when there were about 320 stations with over 200 of them being one and two officer stations.

'Originally we used to do a district at a time and have no social function at the district headquarters. But after a couple we realised the worth of such a function, to which officers and spouses were invited. We used to get information up on each station before we went out and this enabled us to know who was at the station, what they had asked for and what had been denied or was still outstanding.'

It was during one of these trips that Early experienced the rarely expressed wrath of Terry Lewis. On a visit to the Proserpine police station in North Queensland, Commissioner Lewis had somehow arrived at the station before Early. There had been a schedule mix-up. 'For some reason the Commissioner got there before us and was embarrassed because he had not read up on the station and, more particularly, who was in charge,' remembers Early. 'He was not impressed and told me so. However, he was not one to bear grudges or mull over things. He made his point, which was accepted, and we moved on.'

Early says Lewis was grooming him for the position of Commissioner on his retirement, just as Frank Bischof had groomed Lewis. 'One morning during our usual session [the] first thing he said to me [was] words to the effect: "When the time is right I am going to recommend that you replace me as Commissioner. You should start thinking about anything which you would like to implement as Commissioner and make a list of these things so that if I can I will start on them myself to make it easier for you."

'He was quite definite in his advice to me as though it was just a matter of time – not if or maybe. I have thought now that he mentioned a couple of times staying on as Commissioner to beat the record of Frank Bischof and at this time I am pretty sure he had passed Bischof's record.

'Over the years several people have mentioned to me that I was being groomed to become Commissioner but I used to brush off any suggestion to that effect because I had seen officers be built up to anticipating promotion and to not get it.'

Birds and Drugs

Undercover operative Jim Slade was entering the heart of darkness when it came to the criminal underworld. He was discovering rampant drug and wildlife smuggling in his investigations in Far North Queensland, and murders on the fringe of the industry. It was a very similar story to that being revealed on a national scale by his friend and confidant, Peter Vassallo, down in the Australian Bureau of Criminal Intelligence (ABCI) in Canberra.

Slade was also speaking to a colleague he trusted in the Brisbane Bureau of Criminal Intelligence (BCI). At one stage the friend asked if the situation was really as bad as it was beginning to look. 'I predict that it's going to be the frontier, the future frontier,' Slade told him.

'What are you talking about?'

'Well, illegal immigrants, and you know … drugs.'

Slade remembered his time in Far North Queensland when he had reported directly to former assistant commissioner Tony Murphy. His boss had expressed disbelief at the magnitude of the drugs and wildlife smuggling operations. Murphy had told Slade 'the economics are not there'.

'What do you think about that [now]?' the colleague asked Slade.

'Well, I completely disagree.'

'How do you reckon it works?'

Slade had just spent a month on a petrol barge in the Gulf of Carpentaria, and had worked as a prawn spotter on trawlers. 'I'd been through there and bloody talked to people, completely undercover and no one knew, you know, what I was doing,' Slade remembers. 'I was just gathering intelligence, and what I found out – and it made so much bloody sense – is that all the boats would come out of the Gulf of Tonkin [off the coast of North Vietnam and southern China] and down, and what they would do is they would fill up with fuel, they would fill their freezers, or what freezers those shonky boats had.

125

'They'd come down to Australia, and ... clean out all of ... their tanks. What was happening was that prawns, they came in boxes ... probably ten kilogram boxes, you know, maybe a bit less.'

The fishermen worked out that there was more money in heroin than prawns. They could pick up a kilo of heroin in Asia for a couple of hundred dollars, then on-sell it in Australia. The worth of the drugs on Australian streets was many hundreds of thousands of dollars. The fishermen were happy, and so were the dealers.

Slade also discovered that dealers could score a kilogram of heroin in exchange for about 300 native Australian birds. Slade recalled that Murphy had been incredulous upon hearing this news. He didn't believe Slade's intelligence. 'Well hey, excuse me, you know, that's complete bullshit, because those 300 birds, some of them could be worth up to $1000 each,' Slade recalls responding. 'Maybe not to ... the end user, and it's the same with the heroin. You know, by the time it's cut, a kilo of heroin becomes five kilos becomes, you know, half a million bucks.'

Slade's colleague in the BCI headquarters that day was equally as stunned. 'Have you got anything that you can back this up with?' he asked Slade.

'Yes, I have,' Slade replied. 'In a couple of weeks I can give you an analysis report, which you'll be able to use to really get things going.'

In a short period of time Slade's information brought together representatives from the Victorian and New South Wales Police, Customs and Immigration. Alan Barnes was put in charge of Operation Trek. And soon, Graeme Parker would head up the BCI.

Slade recalls: 'I got up and gave this presentation to the group, and the group said, "Let's think about this, this is really worthwhile." So, within a very short period of time, all those organisations had a representative to work under Barnes at the BCI.

'Operation Trek started; at the time I was in charge of the field operations, collecting intelligence. We collected all this information, and brought it back to this group in the BCI. Now, I don't know what happened, but we got a lot of information on Bellino, a lot of information on drugs, how the crops were being grown and harvested, all this interchange of money and people between Griffith and … all this sort of bloody thing.'

Slade was breaking new ground with Operation Trek, but its revelations were not greeted with enthusiasm by some of his superiors.

The Trial of Peter James Walsh

Almost a year to the day after his frenzied attack on his neighbour and teacher in the northside suburb of Kedron, Peter James Walsh, now 18, stood trial for attempted murder.

Since the bizarre stabbing in the winter of 1983 after a night out with school friends in Fortitude Valley, Walsh had been staying with his parents at a friend's house at Burleigh Heads on the Gold Coast. He was kept away from his victim, Stephanie Ryan, a teacher, who had known him since he was a child. The Walshes in Fifth Avenue, and Ryan in Sixth Avenue, shared a back fence.

Walsh's father, Pappy, had employed the services of friend and leading barrister Des Sturgess, assisted by Pat Nolan. 'Pappy was about the same age as me, [and] as young fellas we'd see something of each other,' recalls Sturgess of Brisbane's convivial legal past. 'From time to time he joined me or somebody else who I was having a drink with, things like that. I don't recall ever receiving a brief from him except for the brief from his son.'

Sturgess says Walsh Junior's behaviour leading to the charges was spectacularly out of character. 'He was still a schoolboy,' says Sturgess. 'He wasn't any sort of ruffian; he was well brought up. They were very staunch Catholics, and you know, he was filled with Christianity I suppose, a pupil at Nudgee. He loved his football.

'Pappy gave evidence and said he was one of the lads that gave him the least trouble from any of the others. [But] this night he went absolutely berserk. You've never seen anything like the inside of that house, there was blood smeared everywhere.'

During the trial there was a sudden, and extraordinary, development. A man called Paul John Breslin appeared out of nowhere to assist the defence. Breslin, until only recently, had been an ambitious and respected senior executive for the Ford Motor Company, and had socialised with senior police, including Commissioner Lewis. Then in January 1984 he had been charged with sexually assaulting a minor, and a raid on his Auchenflower apartment had uncovered explicit photographs of police officer David Moore.

While he was awaiting a court appearance on the assault charges, he somehow scored a position with the Family Court and its security division, and was making claims that senior political figures had asked him to take on the job. It all simply added more pieces to the puzzle that was Breslin.

'What happened was, we were right in the middle of the trial and he [Breslin] rang me up,' says Sturgess. 'He was a court orderly then at the Family Court, and he said he had important information to give me. I went post haste ... to see him with Pat Nolan, my instructing solicitor, and Breslin gave us a story.

'There'd been some trouble in the Family Court. I think a Family Court judge had been killed down south, murdered, and Breslin's story was ... he didn't usually do this orderly work, you see, but the Commonwealth Attorney-General [Senator Gareth Evans] had asked him, because of this act of terrorism down south, to act as orderly in the court.'

In early July, Pearl Watson, the wife of Family Court judge, Justice Ray Watson, had been killed when a bomb tore through the family's home in harbourside Greenwich, Sydney. The assassination was one of a long line of threats and murders involving the Family Court dating

128

back to 1980, when Justice David Opas was shot dead at point blank range at his home in Sydney's eastern suburbs.

In March 1984 Justice Richard Gee's home had also been targeted by a bomb. He escaped with injuries. A month later, Parramatta's Family Law Court building had been damaged when sticks of gelignite were hurled at the front entrance. There were no injuries. Police believed at the time the incidents were all linked to a single child custody case.

Breslin's story, therefore, appeared plausible. His unlikely appearance as a credible witness, halfway through the trial, was a boon for Walsh's case. Breslin told Sturgess that he had, by chance, been drinking at Bonaparte's Hotel the year before on the very same night that Peter James Walsh and his friends were out celebrating their football victories and chanting the school song.

Sturgess recalls: 'Breslin said he was down there that night at the hotel and he saw drinks being spiked … so Pat and I went away and sort of … we thought we'd really struck a treasure … Pat went out to see him on the Saturday morning and got some more particulars, and also got particulars from a policeman friend of his … which revealed that he had a very chequered history. I remember I spoke to the policeman involved and he said, "Oh Christ, you're not going to rely on him, are you?"'

Breslin, the man who would be publicised as the new Brisbane Sheraton's first guest, and who was concurrently awaiting his own trial for the alleged sexual assault of a minor in his flat in Coronation Towers, Auchenflower, was suddenly putting up his hand in defence of Peter Walsh.

Sturgess was in a quandary. 'I got a telephone call from Des Breen, he was a barrister, and he'd acted for Breslin in some of his travails, and he gave me information, all of which was to Breslin's detriment,' says Sturgess. 'We thought long and hard about calling him [as a witness]. I myself was against calling him.

'I said, "Listen Pat, I think Pappy better make the decision on this one." So we put it all before Pappy, told him all about Breslin, about what Breslin was saying and sticking to his guns about.'

A source says Peter James Walsh had never heard of Breslin. 'Halfway through the trial, that's when everyone heard of Breslin,' the source says. 'There was a conversation as to whether he should be used, it was sort of like, you know, it was a risk but it had to happen. Someone had to get up and say that [about the drinks being spiked]. This guy came forward.'

A meeting was held between Pappy Walsh and Pat Nolan. It was agreed that Breslin would be called. 'Peter [Junior] had no say in the decision,' the source says. 'Everything was out of [his] hands.'

Paul John Breslin has a different recollection. 'I remember Des Sturgess approaching me with a barrister … he was acting for the Walsh family,' he says. 'I was a security manager for the Commonwealth of Australia at the Federal Family Court. It used to be in Adelaide Street, I think. And he appeared a couple of times and I helped him … I think Pat Nolan … I think he might have seen me working in the court, too … being security I'd be wearing a name badge.

'They knew I ran … that I was President of the Queensland Prisoners Aid Society, I think it was called, [who] had a halfway house at Wooloowin, a property owned by the Main Roads Department, which we leased for $1 a year. We took people, when they were released, and gave them a place to stay so they could find accommodation. They could stay from memory for one or two months. They were pretty closely supervised, as you can imagine.

'I was asked … I didn't know Peter Walsh from a bar of soap.'

While acquaintances of Breslin noted that he was a person who often enjoyed being the centre of attention, and that he had a habit of 'big-noting' himself by alleging he had friends in high places, these characteristics didn't explain why he would engage in a high-profile trial and volunteer crucial evidence about the night of Walsh's attack and the hours leading up to the alleged offence. Given his own legal problems at the time, why would he step up to help a complete stranger, and voluntarily place himself at the epicentre of the trial's landscape?

Angus Dodds, the Crown psychiatrist, was the main witness at the trial. He examined young Peter Walsh shortly after his arrest and he thought there was more to it than just aggression. It was a risky manoeuvre. If Breslin's past was brought into proceedings, it could be fatal to the Walsh case. 'I had my fingers crossed through all this. I thought a lot of it would slip out in cross-examination, but it didn't,' says Sturgess.

Sturgess denies that he contacted Breslin first. 'That's a lie. He contacted us. I remember that distinctly. We couldn't believe our good fortune when we first heard of it,' says Sturgess. 'I wouldn't attempt to give any explanation as to why he did what he did. Personally, I wish he had kept the hell out of it. I can understand Pappy Walsh's view. He was crazed with worry ... All I knew was that he [Breslin] could be dynamite if I called him, he could blow the case out of the water.'

There were further curious anomalies during the trial. On Thursday 12 July, Drug Squad Detective Frederick George Maynard gave evidence that hallucinogenic drugs were not available in Brisbane at the time of the Walsh incident. Maynard said cannabis and heroin were prevalent, but not LSD and similar drugs. He confirmed that they were rarely dissolved in drinks. 'There was no LSD in Brisbane last year,' Maynard told the court. 'I think it became a fact of life that a lot of drug users would not use LSD. They became frightened of it.'

This did not marry with the defence's mounting argument that Walsh consumed spiked drinks in Bonaparte's on the night in question. However, the following day, Maynard was abruptly recalled to the witness box. This time he admitted that the drug squad had purchased large quantities of LSD in Bonaparte's in early July 1983, just weeks before the Walsh incident occurred. It was a complete about-face, and went a long way to corroborating Breslin's allegations.

'The evidence I gave on Thursday was based on my recollection,' Maynard said by way of correction. He had checked the drug squad files before giving his earlier evidence and couldn't find anything relating to hallucinogenic drugs. Now he had information about the dealer in Bonaparte's who had 1000 'tabs' of LSD for sale.

In the end, Walsh was found not guilty on the grounds of 'unsound mind'. Sturgess had successfully argued that at the time Walsh was suffering 'pathological intoxication', brought about by alcohol and triggering a brain disorder. The jury took just minutes to bring down their verdict after the 11-day trial.

Justice Williams ordered that Walsh 'be kept in strict custody until Her Majesty's pleasure be known'.

'Pat Nolan had lined up legal aid [for Walsh],' says Sturgess. 'Pappy Walsh wasn't a wealthy man. He was a solicitor, had a fair sized practice but a whole tribe of kids, educated at Nudgee. There wouldn't have been much left over. Peter Walsh was entitled to legal aid.'

But that was not the end of the controversy. A month after this curious scenario, Deputy Opposition Leader and Member for Lytton, Tom Burns, unloaded a barrage of accusations in parliament.

Burns labelled Breslin a 'publicity seeking ... homosexual crook'. He cited the *Courier-Mail* column on the Sheraton's gala opening. 'To give Breslin some form of credibility in the [Walsh] trial and especially during the period when he was such a vital witness, someone arranged a page-three story in the *Courier-Mail* in which this businessman, who had stayed in hotels around the world and was the Sheraton Hotel's first guest, was given prominent coverage, quite a convenient way of giving Breslin a more respectable image than he deserves,' Burns told parliament.

He added: 'I would like to know whether Breslin, at the time he gave evidence, was on a charge relating to administering a stupefying drug to a minor who was handcuffed and chained to his bed?

'If that is true, was Breslin, whilst on this charge, reported to have been interviewing young boys and demanding government aid to provide a form of shelter for young people? Is Breslin involved in some way as an officer of the Prisoners Aid Society? Is there disquiet over his role in this society?'

Pointedly, Burns asked: 'Was Breslin offered any inducement to give evidence for Walsh? Has a person hearing charges against Breslin made some orders restricting publication of court details?'

As for Walsh, he was transferred to a psychiatric hospital in Chermside in the city's north, where he read a lot of books and played a lot of ping pong. He was granted conditional release early the following year.

In the week Breslin managed to be both a Sydney businessman and a witness in the trial of Peter James Walsh, no mention of any of this was recorded by Commissioner Lewis in his diaries. Lewis, of course, was acquainted with Breslin through the Police Club. In late 1983 he had sent one of his Commissioner's Christmas cards to Breslin, in the latter's capacity as president of the South Queensland Prisoners Aid Society.

'Dear Mr Breslin,' he handwrote in the card, 'and members of the Society.' Then the standard printed greeting – 'Best wishes for a Happy Christmas and peace and prosperity throughout the coming years'. It was signed 'Terry Lewis'.

At the time of this controversial trial, Commissioner Lewis had his usual frantic schedule, including attending a local Australian Crime Prevention Council conference on child abuse and the criminal justice system. In fact, he delivered a paper titled – 'Child abuse – is police involvement necessary?'

Rebel Cop

Detective Ross Dickson continued to make a lot of noise about his transfer. Once he had been labelled the Sheriff of Mareeba. Now they called him the Rebel Cop. He finally moved to Townsville in late July, against his wishes, but still the scandal wouldn't go away.

On 30 August in parliament, ALP member for Windsor, Pat Comben, continued to stoke the fire. Comben wanted to know if senior police officers had been sent to Mareeba to seek out possible complaints against Detective Dickson and to check his old files for the purpose of bringing departmental charges against him.

Police Minister Bill Glasson called the question 'astounding'. Glasson alleged Dickson was being used as a puppet by the union in an attempt to appeal against unapplied for transfers. 'It would be impossible for the Commissioner of Police to control the police force if appeals against unapplied for transfers were allowed,' Glasson argued.

'Are you going to charge him [Dickson]?' Comben pressed.

'Senior Sergeant Ross Dickson arrived in Townsville on 21 July this year,' Glasson answered. 'Therefore, he conformed to the requirements of his transfer, and no charges are pending against him in regard to that transfer.'

Glasson unwittingly misled parliament. There was indeed an investigation underway into Dickson and it involved checking 'old files', as Comben had queried. A subsequent nine-page report was produced, titled 'Complaints Against Sergeant 2/c L.R. Dickson'.

The examples cited went all the way back to 8 April 1968.

1. Complainant: James McKAY, 37 Prospect Road, Gaythorne.

Nature of complaint: Constable DICKSON arrived at the complainant's residence in a two-tone shirt, shorts and bare feet. He spoke to the 13 year old daughter of the complainant and demanded to know where 'Glen' was.

When the daughter said he was not there, DICKSON threatened to use other measures. DICKSON then searched the residence, did not find Glen and went away.

Result: No further action taken.

None of the subsequent dozen or so complaints against Dickson were ever substantiated.

Glasson was also misinformed about charges being laid against Dickson. The *Courier-Mail* reported in an exclusive page-two report on 20 September that Dickson was set to face 83 departmental charges, with others pending. He was to be interviewed by internal investigators.

'The charges stem mostly from his public criticism of the police force, and his refusal to carry out police orders ... he is also in trouble for taking a TV news crew on a drug raid,' the newspaper said. 'Det. Sgt Dickson had claimed he was transferred because he wanted to reopen the investigation into the mysterious death of a Mareeba detective six years earlier.' (This referred to John Connor, a young officer who was found dead of a single gunshot wound to the head in his car near the Mareeba RSL on 15 October 1978. That day, Connor reportedly met up with some colleagues at a hotel and told them excitedly that he was going to make an arrest that would 'shake Australia', presumably a figure related to the drug trade. Late that night his body was found, and the death was deemed a suicide.)

'Det. Sgt Dickson claimed he was being moved because of his activities in trying to break up the drug trade in North Queensland.'

Police Minister Glasson made a ministerial statement that day in parliament. He said he was concerned over the *Courier-Mail* article. 'The truth of the matter is that Inspector Ryan of Cairns has been investigating the alleged furnishing of false crime statistics for the Mareeba district during the period Detective Dickson was stationed at Mareeba CIB,' Glasson said. 'Inspector Ryan's enquiries have nothing to do with Detective Sergeant Dickson's criticism of the police force, nothing to do with any reopening of investigations into the death of Detective Senior Constable John Connor six years ago, and nothing to do with his taking a television crew on a drug raid, as has been claimed.

'It is wrong to say Detective Sergeant Dickson will be departmentally charged, as he has not yet been given the chance to answer the allegations.'

Lewis recalls the Dickson affair: 'He [Dickson] was topping the state [with his crime clean-up rate] ... and then I don't know how we found out, [but] somebody brought to [our] notice what he was doing,' says Lewis. 'So, I sent two blokes up there, two inspectors, and they ... found out ... he was just furnishing false reports, and the worst ... part of it was those people were on police records, they hadn't done anything, but if it came up in the future, how were they going to disprove it?

'And then, you know, he said the only reason they got rid of him [was] because he was trying to expose corruption and ... that was utter, utter bullshit.'

Fun at Pinky's

By 1984, Geoff and Julie Crocker had scaled back their escort operations. The police kickbacks were taking their toll on business operations, and after all expenses and bribes, the pair was, at times, only bringing in an income of $1000 a week.

While they still had their escort operation at 27 Sankey Street in Highgate Hill, and another in 81 Sylvan Road, Toowong, their newest operation was proving to be immediately lucrative. Pinky's was an 'on premises' massage parlour located at 625 Main Street, Kangaroo Point, near the corner of Bell Street and a short walk from the Pineapple Hotel.

Pinky's was a classic Queenslander worker's cottage, though under the house had been built in with brick. A clutch of palm trees stood in the front yard. The project was Julie's baby and she immediately took control, painting the exterior bright pink. It couldn't have failed to attract the attention of commuters on busy Main Street, an East Brisbane artery that fed traffic north across the Story Bridge and straight down into the cesspit of Fortitude Valley.

The owner of another popular Brisbane massage parlour, and friend to Geoff Crocker, was called in to give some advice on fitting out the place. 'I told Geoff that if I was a customer I wouldn't want all those bright lights, and they needed to get some plants in there,' she recalls. 'My place was doing well because we were offering clients some food and drinks. Pinky's hadn't been officially opened but it was open for business, and one of the girls went and got a packet of corn chips and offered the clients a beer. It was very funny. Geoff had a good sense of humour.'

The property was renovated, four spa baths were installed – two small ones upstairs and two large ones down – and it was soon open for official trading. The Crockers threw a party at the brothel to celebrate. 'It wasn't actually a party to celebrate the opening of Pinky's ... to us it was ... but to the customers it was just a party,' Crocker later recalled. 'Julie used to come up with all these weird ideas ... let's have a Whiskers and Warlock night, or let's have a Halloween night, so one of those sort of things fell into what was commonly known later on as the opening party at Pinky's.

'There were quite a few people there ... a lot of our personal friends were invited over cause it was just going to be a sociable group and fun night, and if anyone wanted a lady they could do business.'

The opening night party had a 'gangster' theme. Some of the girls on shift that night wore 1920s-style outfits. Several police from the Licensing Branch and the Drug Squad attended, leaving their unmarked cars parked in Main Street.

According to prostitute Katherine James, who was working that day, (she was one of ten prostitutes hired to service about 30 guests) – the party went for eight hours. 'There were different people going to spas and bedrooms together and drinking and eating together,' she said. 'All the food and alcohol was supplied and the girls were paid [$300 each] to give sexual favours for the whole night. There were three full-sized spas that eight people could fit into. Many people, including police officers, got their clothes off and got in the spa baths.

'Gerry Bellino called in for about five minutes ... I remember that Geoff Crocker began to take a couple of photographs but he stopped because everyone freaked out. There was not only police there but people pretty high up in real estate, medicine and law.'

The party was a huge success, rivalled only by another Pinky's sex fiesta on Melbourne Cup Day in early November. 'Julie arranged for ... girls to start at Pinky's at ten o'clock in the morning on Melbourne Cup Day,' Crocker remembered. 'At probably midday Julie rang up [the brothel] and said – did the girls show up? Are they all dressed up nicely for the ... party? I'd been and got grog the night before ...'

By mid-afternoon the party was raging. According to eyewitnesses, eight Licensing Branch officers were at the party. The prostitutes were wearing lingerie and several had sex with police. There was also a wet T-shirt competition. At one point guests were drinking champagne out of men's top hats.

Crocker arrived late, knowing the party would still be going, 'to make sure that I'm still going to earn some money without the party interfering with business'. He observed that 'the coppers were all pretty pissed, very pissed, some of them'. Crocker was, by nature, cautious of drunken Licensing Branch detectives. 'When these guys got a bit pissed they didn't like people like me very much,' he remembered. 'When they were sober they were better because they knew they were being looked after ...'

The party had been a great success, although several of the officers were too drunk to return their official vehicles back to headquarters. The party would prove a turning point for Katherine James. She said not long after the infamous party, Licensing Branch officer 'Dirty Harry' Burgess came into Pinky's and told Crocker to get rid of her. 'Harry said to me, "I wield a fucking big sword and if you get in my way I'm going to chop your head right off." I don't really know why he took this attitude, except to say that he may have taken exception to me inviting the Woolloongabba CIB [to the party].'

If anyone had been sober enough to notice, the Melbourne Cup that day was won by Black Knight, ridden by Peter Cook, trained by George Hanlon, and owned by millionaire businessman Peter Holmes à Court. On retirement from racing, Black Knight, a dark bay, was employed as a police horse in Victoria.

The Line in the Sand

By 1984, the local petty criminal John Stopford was attempting to get his act together. He had worked for the likes of Roland Short and Geoff Crocker, and operated on the fringes of Brisbane's vast vice scene, and had gotten hooked on heroin. Now he had a son to consider – young Jay.

'I suppose the biggest impact on my whole life came when Jay was 18 months old,' Stopford recalls. 'He contracted meningitis. He was in isolation and we'd gone home to get a bit of rest and got a phone call about 11 p.m. The nurse said, "He's not doing too well, we notice on here you've registered that you're a Catholic … is he baptised?"

'I said, "No".

'"Well," she said, "you might want to arrange it."'

It was a bad sign, and Stopford knew it. He and his wife Wendy, whom he'd met in one of Crocker's escort agencies, raced to the hospital. 'I don't know what time it was, after being there a little while Wendy [said] … I can't wait here any longer, I've got to go and get on,' says Stopford. 'That's when I knew … that's when it dawned on me that this is not going to be a lasting relationship. I got quite upset over that. I told her to go.'

Stopford was in a quandary. He was going to have to do this by himself. He asked the hospital chaplain if he'd baptise Jay. He refused, given Stopford had not annulled his first marriage. Stopford telephoned his loving mentor at the orphanage for crippled children, where he'd grown up, and asked for her help. 'I had a priest there within half an hour,' he says. 'That's when the most famous thing happened, take it whichever way you want.

'I got a photo of Jay being baptised in her [his mentor's] arms ... they brought him [Jay] out of intensive care so he could be baptised. They wanted to take him straight back. Within 40 minutes of Jay being back in isolation, he was on the mend. By the end of the day, he was taken out of isolation.

'So, yeah. That's where I drew the line. I made a promise to Him, if he saved Jay, he could take me whenever he liked, but I would no longer use heroin.'

Making his pledge to God, when his son recovered from his near-fatal illness, was 'easier said than done'.

'The only thing I could do was return to my family doctor, be upfront with him ... I ended up as a registered user and on methadone,' he says. 'The [escort] businesses had started to deteriorate. I'd lost control. I was in and out of hospital a bit. I did 26 weeks in traction.'

Unwittingly, Stopford's health took him out of the parlour and escort scene. Even so, he spent enough time on the inside to be one of a small number of people who knew at least the basic machinery of Brisbane's illegal gambling and sex trade. By proxy, that not only made him dangerous, but could potentially put him in danger as well.

Troublesome Boys

For more than two years rumours had percolated through the Queensland Police Force about the sexuality of Constable Dave Moore, the national television celebrity and public relations officer, who had gifted the department more positive publicity than any orchestrated campaign in its history.

Despite being married with children, gossip continued to grow that Moore was in fact a homosexual, and had been engaging with some unsavoury adult characters in supposedly procuring underage boys for sexual mischief. He had been variously linked with popular ABC radio personality Bill Hurrey, and also with former Ford Motor Company businessman and head of the local Prisoners Aid Society, Paul Breslin.

Indeed, word of Moore's salacious reputation had made it to the offices of then Assistant Commissioner, Tony Murphy, and that of Deputy Commissioner Syd Atkinson. Atkinson had in fact counselled Moore as early as 1982 to keep away from bad influences. Atkinson later swore that after each incident involving Moore, he passed the information on to Police Commissioner Terry Lewis.

In September 1982, Senior Constable Mike Garrahy interviewed a juvenile who told him he had been approached by both Moore and Hurrey to make homosexual pornographic movies. Garrahy filed a confidential report to the then officer in charge of the Juvenile Aid Bureau, Detective Inspector Frank Rynne.

In his report, Garrahy requested permission to view the files on the notorious paedophile from the late 1970s, Clarence Osborne, who gassed himself in his car in late 1979 after he came to the attention of police. Osborne, it transpired, kept meticulous records – including measurements and photographs – of his more than 2000 victims. One was a 14-month-old baby.

The Osborne files had been moved to JAB headquarters in the old Egg Board building on Makerston Street and secured in a strongroom. Garrahy believed the information he was gathering on paedophilia 'may be related to the activities of Osborne's known associates'. The young officer also asked permission 'to carry out the necessary surveillance on Hurrey and Moore and any associates'. Garrahy had stumbled upon a case, by chance featuring a high-profile serving Queensland police officer, that may have had links to one of the most abhorrent and extensive examples of paedophilia in Australian history.

Rynne, on taking up his position at the JAB, perceived a 'growing paedophile problem' in Brisbane and wanted something done about it. When he first stumbled upon the shocking Osborne cold case he was alarmed. 'My eyes were opened to the Osborne team ... the thing that amazed me was that nothing had been done about it,' he says of the earlier investigation. 'I think it was apathy.' Rynne says there was a sense at the time that 'nobody believed it was happening, nobody could believe that's the way people behaved'.

He instructed Detectives Brian Wiggan and Kerry Kelly to reassess the Osborne material. 'While Garrahy had uncovered information concerning the involvement of a police officer, I received his report as being part of the overall context of paedophilia intelligence, which was being collated and investigated,' Rynne later recalled. 'Bearing that in mind, I did not want any impediments to the overall paedophilia investigations. I decided to continue our investigations into paedophilia and also to investigate the extent, if any, of Moore's involvement through surveillance.'

Rynne's officers unearthed a lot of information 'because there were all sorts of idiots around the town at that stage, you know. So it was a fascinating time but unfortunately I got pulled out [of the JAB]. I asked why and I said, well if I'm not doing the job ... [and his superiors said] no, you did an excellent job.'

Commissioner Lewis had, in the late 1970s, been drawn into the Osborne scandal through his friendship with criminologist and academic Dr Paul Wilson, who was writing a book on the controversial government court reporter. Osborne had approached Wilson with some of his writings and photographs, and they intermittently engaged in conversation over several months until Osborne, by chance, came to police attention with regards to his sexual activities in late 1979. After an initial police interview, Osborne had been released and later that night gassed himself in the garage of his Mount Gravatt home.

Wilson sought permission from Commissioner Lewis to peruse

Osborne's seized files for the purposes of researching his book, later published as *The Man They Called a Monster*.

On 5 November 1984, Constable Kerry Kelly took a statement from the youth who had given information to Garrahy in 1982 over the blue movies. Out of this, a Detective Sergeant M.R. McCoy of the JAB compiled yet another confidential report dated 9 November, this time including allegations from several youths about the behaviour of Moore and Hurrey.

McCoy's report was delivered that same day to Commissioner Lewis by the then head of the JAB, Lewis's old mate Detective Inspector Don Braithwaite. The report was subsequently forwarded to the Internal Investigations Section.

After years of procrastination, the matter suddenly caught fire. Hurrey was arrested and charged with ten counts of alleged sexual offences against boys. He was taken off the air from his popular ABC breakfast radio program, but not sacked. He was remanded to appear in the Brisbane Magistrates Court on 6 December.

To date, there had been no link in the public eye between Hurrey's activities and Senior Constable Dave Moore. But Lewis was mistaken if he thought he could keep this matter behind closed doors; he was on the precipice of one of the most turbulent periods in his career. If his diary entries are anything to go by, a slumbering giant was awakening. On Monday 5 November he wrote: '... saw Hon. [Bill] Glasson re ... arrest of Billy Hurrey and mention of S/C D. Moore.' Lewis then went with 'D/C Atkinson ... saw Insp. Munn and S/C D. Moore re association with Bill Hurrell [sic].'

The next day Lewis '... phoned D/I Braithwaite re Hurrey investigation'.

Incredibly, on Thursday 8 November – the day *before* McCoy was to lodge his confidential report on Hurrey and Moore – Lewis pre-recorded a segment for an upcoming *Super Saturday Show*, featuring Dave Moore. 'Taped birthday greeting, 4 years, for Agro.'

The next day, when McCoy's report was allegedly forwarded to the Commissioner of Police, Lewis made no mention of the matter in his diaries. Instead, he recorded on that day that he had farewelled the police force's basketballers who were heading to the national titles in Darwin, had luncheon at the exclusive Brisbane Club, then headed over to the Queensland Cultural Centre 'building handover' in the presence of Premier Joh Bjelke-Petersen. As was Lewis's habit, later that day he popped over to the offices of Sir Edward Lyons in Queen Street for a drink and a chat about Cabinet, and murders on the Gold Coast, among other things.

A rumour of the dimension of the one that circulated around Dave Moore was impossible to contain in a city the size of Brisbane, and on Wednesday 14 November, Ron McLean, the Labor member for Bulimba, directed a sequence of questions to Police Minister Bill Glasson. 'I ask the Minister for Lands, Forestry and Police: Is he aware of widespread reports that a police officer who is responsible for police campaigns among children has been involved with persons charged with offences against boys, and that pornographic photos of that officer swapping uniforms with a male SEQEB employee posing in handcuffs in a compromising position have been circulated?'

McLean claimed that reports of the officer and his activities had been drawn to the attention of his supervisors – he wanted to know what action would be taken to ensure the officer would not pose any threat to young boys.

Glasson, taken by surprise and befuddled, shot back: 'The honourable member referred to a police officer who was charged. With what?'

'He was not charged,' McLean repeated.

'I ask the honourable member to put the question on notice. I will certainly not deal with the future of a police officer until I know the background to the question,' Glasson asserted.

The Opposition smelled blood and the following day the pummelling continued. Leader of the Opposition and keen lawn bowler, Nev

Warburton, wanted some clarification: 'How long have senior police known about the constable's activities? Is it as long as three years? At the earliest, was it brought to the attention of police following a raid in 1982 by the Consorting Squad on a home unit owned by Mr Paul Breslin in Mary [sic] Street, Brisbane?'

Glasson floundered. He had clearly not been briefed to the same depth as the ALP. He conceded that '... it is some considerable time since suspicion arose in relation to the activities of the officer'.

Warburton wasn't done: 'Why was no action taken when this matter was brought to the attention of the Commissioner and other senior police? Why was the officer not transferred from his duties in the public relations section, which necessarily brought him into contact with thousands of Queensland children? I suggest that the Minister ought to be in a position to answer that question today.'

Glasson's response was curious. It revealed both his frustration over being caught out over the sudden scandal, and the imperative that he at least appear to support his Commissioner and the police force in general. Glasson had not just been poorly briefed, but clearly information had been withheld from him.

'This morning I spoke to both the Commissioner and the Deputy Commissioner,' Glasson stumbled on. 'Investigations have been taking place ever since the allegations against and rumours about the police officer first began. If it is necessary, I will make an in-depth report of the actions taken by the Commissioner and his deputy in endeavouring to have someone come forward with evidence.'

Then, on 20 November, Opposition Police Spokesman Wayne Goss went for the jugular, detailing new evidence about the drama. He relayed instances of the unnamed police officer engaging boys in pornographic photo shoots and of schoolboys being picked up from Indooroopilly Shoppingtown in exchange for money.

Goss also went into detail about the case of Paul John Breslin, and the charges against him over the alleged assault of Richard (Ricky) Garrison at a unit in Coronation Towers, Dunmore Terrace, Auchenflower, at the beginning of 1984. 'The Commissioner now complains that this matter should not be the subject of discussion while an investigation is underway,' Goss railed. 'As far as I am concerned, that is humbug. The Commissioner conducted an investigation previously, and it was ineffectual. The matter was buried; no action was taken. The constable was not even removed from the position of trust that he occupied in the Public Relations Branch. It was only – and I repeat "only" – when this matter was revealed to the public last week that the government and the Commissioner of Police moved.

'It has gone on for two years too long. The duty of the Minister and the Commissioner is not to avoid embarrassment for the police department and the government. On the contrary, their duty is to act to enforce the law.'

The witch-hunt began.

After Goss's scathing assessments that day, Lewis, along with his deputy Syd Atkinson, approached Detective Sergeant John O'Gorman, Police Union Spokesman. Lewis wrote in his diary that O'Gorman denied 'contacting Mr Goss, MLA' with information on Moore.

That day, Constable Dave Moore was working on the police department's annual Christmas float for Brisbane's yuletide street festival. He got a phone call from a journalist asking him if he was aware of all the allegations that Goss was putting out in parliament.

Soon after, Lewis saw David Moore 'regarding resignation'.

The Danger of a Job Well Done

It was a difficult time to submit a controversial report. Jim Slade and his partner Ian Jamieson had finally completed their field work for Operation Trek and compiled their findings. The journey had been an epic one. 'We had worked in four-wheel-drives, planes, boats,' remembers Slade. 'We went from Cairns to Karumba, we covered Cape York Peninsula and also the Torres Strait. Our job was to create a network of intelligence gatherers, and we had discussed this with our senior officer, Inspector Col Thompson.

'We received assistance from the North Queensland CIB – Roy Wall in Atherton, Ross Dickson in Mareeba and Paul Priest in Cairns. We formulated a report that was dated 21 November 1984, which was forwarded to the Bureau of Criminal Intelligence. The report was compiled in Brisbane.'

Slade sent a copy of the report and tape-recorded interviews with an informant to Peter Vassallo at the Australian Bureau of Criminal Intelligence (ABCI), 'Italian desk', Canberra. He remembers the period of the mid-1980s where activity in the drug trade became more widespread. 'The Bellinos really started changing their interest from gaming and prostitution to drugs. A lot of the work that I did was to identify competition. Everything was good until the Bellinos came in, and then violence started to really erupt.

'When Vassallo started puddling around in the dirty water … it wasn't until I put the report in relation to the Bellinos that my whole life changed. I just wish something had been done about it. There was enough evidence in the report to spend the money to do a proper investigation. I'm not saying there was enough there to arrest anyone, but there was definitely enough evidence there to support a decent push in regard to what was going on up there.'

Slade's work was already having a curious impact. When he and Jamieson were in Cairns for work they invariably stayed at the Inn the Pink Motel in Sheridan Street, North Cairns. It was known as a hotel for travelling police on business. Incredibly, it was also the lodgings that the Bellino family used to put up visitors and business associates.

They stopped using the motel when Slade submitted his report. 'I had tape recordings, piles and piles of documents, eyewitness accounts. When I put the report in, they commissioned this bloody senior officer, insignificant bastard of a bloke … instead of finding more evidence … they visited everyone and threatened them and bloody squashed it … I can see his face … he was one of these ineffectual officers, drinks all day, arrests someone, produces no evidence and wonders why they're not successful in court.'

Informants were physically threatened. Evidence went missing. Slade's report was privately lampooned and labelled 'embellished' by some senior police. The report was on its way to being buried.

However, law enforcement agencies outside of Queensland were exceedingly interested in the work of Slade and Jamieson, especially the Australian Federal Police and the ABCI. Vassallo remained an important sounding board for Slade – his Queensland mate's report was dovetailing with his own analysis. He had included the name Bellino in his confidential Alpha report. This was a family that had been familiar to corrupt police for many years. They controlled the syndicate in Brisbane – that network of illegal gambling and vice that formed a vital part of The Joke. If the Bellinos were exposed, so too would be an equally intricate network of police corruption. And if that happened, the kickbacks stopped.

Slade had always been regarded highly by the force's senior administration, but that was about to change. Soon, Slade was going to need every friend he could get. '[A draft report of Operation Trek] was given to Alan Barnes,' remembers Slade. 'Within a fortnight, that whole group was sacked, a guy was chosen to write the report, and that report was then done in a week and was submitted and nothing ever happened from Operation Trek,' Slade says.

'And do you know what? I'm sure that there would be inspectors and people retired now in Victoria that would have that report, because they were absolutely pissed off that Operation Trek had so much money spent on it, it was a model of how cooperation should bloody exist, and yet … the report was squashed and re-written. Barnes was the officer in charge of the intelligence analysis.'

But it made absolutely no sense to Vassallo – given what he was learning month after month from Slade – that there was no intelligence coming out of Queensland. 'As soon as I went back to the bureau [after the analyst's course] I did a few checks based on what Jimmy had to say, and of course there was nothing there,' Vassallo recalls. 'Which caused a bit of consternation, how could this be correct? And then it suddenly dawned on me [that] Slade was also talking about corruption and that he was having problems getting documents to us. You know, this is at a time when I'm … solidifying my connections with people interstate I haven't met yet, and our professional connection is over the phone.'

Vassallo was beginning to wonder, too, about the Queensland police representatives who worked for the ABCI. Could there be a spy in the ranks? Or someone deliberately blocking the exchange of data between the Canberra office and the Sunshine State?

Suddenly, nobody knew who they could trust.

Implosion

Back in Brisbane, the Moore saga continued to gather heat. In the midst of the mayhem, Police Minister Bill Glasson received a telephone call from a television station asking for his reaction to the resignation of Moore. Glasson claimed he knew nothing about it. He later said he felt 'such a fool' that Lewis had not kept him informed. Lewis's diary for Friday 23 November, however, includes the notation that he 'phoned Hon. Glasson re acceptance of resignation by S/C D. Moore'.

That night, Moore was served notice that his resignation had been finalised. According to a close friend, Moore felt 'this great burden had lifted' when he resigned. 'He went home and went out for dinner that night … he was emotionally a wreck … he got back home about 11 p.m.,' the friend says. 'About ten minutes later there was a knock on the door and there was an inspector of police and a junior police officer. He had a letter signed by Lewis, and Moore's resignation was effective immediately, and he was there to retrieve Moore's uniform. He felt so betrayed. The knives were out.

'Lewis never said one word to him. He never spoke to him … He [Moore] had devoted his cause to him [Lewis] and what he represented, he was his boss, he showed him loyalty in the sense that he did his job and he did it well.'

Lewis says he was shocked by the Moore saga and denies allegations that he had been 'protecting' Moore during those years.

Despite the incident inflicting enormous damage to the credibility of the government and Lewis's police force, there would be more collateral damage. Glasson was furious that he had been made to look foolish over the Moore resignation. And Lewis wasn't happy with Glasson's support of the force, or more specifically, his perceived lack of support during the scandal.

Former police minister Russ Hinze had earned Commissioner Lewis's ire in the early 1980s and been removed. Now it was Glasson's turn. In Lewis's diary for 23 November, the Commissioner intimated for the first time his displeasure with his Minister. 'Premier phoned re progress on investigation,' Lewis wrote, 'told him I am disappointed over lack of support re S/C Moore matter in House.'

Lewis then got on the telephone to Glasson. '… expressed my displeasure at lack of support in refuting false statements by Mr Goss MLA, re Moore matter'.

As was his custom, Lewis batted off criticism from outside the department over the Moore incident, and began building a narrative that the whole thing just may have been a political conspiracy.

He had another face-to-face meeting with Glasson about various matters, the Moore scandal the top priority, on Monday 26 November. He wrote in his diary that he talked to Glasson about 'D/C [Deputy Commissioner] Atkinson phoning re confidence in Admin by Minister and Government; no known comp[laints] by a parent or child whilst

Moore was in Pub. Rel.; Goss's personal attack to try to influence coming decisions re … Dickson; report of 4 pages re … D. Moore as requested by Doug Stewart on Hon Glasson's behalf on 22.11.84; Breslin's criminal history …'

By the next day, Glasson seemed to have digested the peril of crossing swords with Commissioner Lewis. He rose in the House and offered a spirited defence of the government, the police force, even Dave Moore, and en route tried to blame the whole sordid affair on Wayne Goss and the Opposition. 'Not only has he [Goss] orchestrated this character assassination against this former officer, but also, at the same time, he has smeared the overall good name of our Queensland Police Force.'

Glasson found it regrettable that at the Australia versus West Indies cricket test that had just concluded at the Gabba (the Windies won by a comfortable eight wickets), officers on duty at the ground were jeered and taunted with the crowd chanting Dave Moore's name. He firmly blamed Goss.

'To put it bluntly, not only does Mr Goss now have the general public ridiculing members of the police force going about their everyday duty,' Glasson fulminated, 'but also, he has totally ruined the life of a young man … without presenting one iota of legally acceptable evidence.'

He continued:

He has forced this young man, with a family of three and a wife expecting another child, to resign from the police force – so far, through nothing more than innuendo.

To allow Mr Goss the opportunity to clear himself of these most serious charges that I have laid against him, I request, here and now, that he present his evidence to the appropriate authorities or to this Chamber – which I hope and trust will stand up in a court. If he does not, or cannot, do that, he stands condemned by every member in this House for what he has quite obviously done to this young man.

Personally, I must be guided by reports from the Police

Commissioner [Mr Lewis], who has top Internal Investigations section detectives working on the case. As late as this morning, Mr Lewis advised me that the police had been unable to substantiate even one of Mr Goss's allegations to the point of sustaining a criminal charge against this young man.

Glasson refuted Goss's accusations that Moore had featured in compromising photographs found at Breslin's unit in Alice Street, in the city, and later at his apartment in Dunmore Terrace, Auchenflower. 'Last Wednesday afternoon, I spent a little over half an hour looking through what I could only describe as the disgusting products of very sick minds,' Glasson went on. 'At my request, the Police Department provided all the photographs in its possession seized in raids on two premises ... photographs which Mr Goss and other members of the Opposition ... insinuated involved this former officer in a compromising position. However, I found not one shred of evidence of any involvement by any police officer ...'

According to a source close to Dave Moore, the cache of photographs shown to the Minister had contained pornographic pictures unrelated to Moore, and ones that may have been planted in order to lend more gravitas to the case against Bill Hurrey and Paul Breslin. 'There were never child pornography photographs. There were never photographs of Moore with children. There were never photos of Bill Hurrey with children. There was never anything like that whatsoever. That became the media frenzy,' the source says.

'What they did with Bill Glasson at the time was, they had paraded, mixed the photographs up with other photographs that were not even associated with the Bill Hurrey thing. When they showed them to Glasson ... they put Moore's photograph in there with the SEQEB worker, and there were other photographs of males engaging in sex ... not children engaging in sex ... but overaged people. And Glasson made the statement, I've seen the photographs and they'd make you vomit.'

There was a suspicion, too, that some of the pictures provided to shock Minister Glasson had come from the extensive files of Clarence Osborne, still held in the Juvenile Aid Bureau's strong room.

Despite Lewis's misgivings about how Glasson handled the crisis, Premier Bjelke-Petersen stood by his Police Minister. Sir Joh told the *Courier-Mail* that Lewis had kept Glasson informed of the general issues but there 'could be one or two things' Mr Glasson had not been told.

'It has been disclosed that complaints were first made about the officer two years ago but no action was taken,' the newspaper reported. 'Sir Joh said yesterday he wanted the police to follow their investigation through normal legal processes.' He added, 'I'm very satisfied that Terry Lewis and the police boys are doing all they can.'

The Premier supported Glasson and said it was not unusual for Commissioner Lewis to talk to him directly about police matters. 'I discuss different issues from time to time with Mr Lewis. It's a process that goes on right down the years,' Sir Joh said. 'Different things come up and I've got to know the background. It doesn't always result in anything.

'As Terry Lewis said to me, if the Labor Party thinks we can just grab a bloke and charge him, they don't know the legitimate processes.'

The Christmas Card

With only weeks until Christmas, Commissioner Lewis was caught up in his usual whirl of official functions and corporate cocktail parties. Some were more elaborate than others. On Saturday 8 December, for example, he and wife Hazel hopped aboard an Ansett 767 and flew to Hamilton Island as guests of tycoon Keith Williams. Way back in January 1977, Williams had hosted Lewis and the Bjelke-Petersen family on his yacht moored in the Southport Broadwater, not far from his Sea World resort. Now Lewis was back for the stage one opening of Williams' ambitious resort in the Whitsundays.

'Nice room, 126,' Lewis recorded. 'Then in mini-bus on tour of inspection, to be huge building programme. Seafood buffet dinner. Official opening by Sir Joh Bjelke-Petersen ... Entertainment by Chris Kirby, ventriloquist [whose dummy, it transpired, was also named Terry], Island dancers and Peter Allen until 11.30 p.m.'

The next morning at breakfast in the Dolphin Room, Williams discussed with Lewis the need for police to be based on the island, particularly water police. Lewis then had a confidential meeting with Bill Glasson, who'd also made the trip, and the Premier. This was a matter of the gravest concern.

Since the Moore scandal had erupted, the rumour-mill within the force had gone into overdrive. Indeed, someone in the force had dared to commit to Queensland Police stationery a raft of allegations about Lewis, Moore and others for the benefit of the Labor Party.

Somehow, this damning gossip had made its way into Glasson's office. The allegations were explosive. They involved homosexuality, paedophilia, perverting the course of justice, bribery, cover-ups and tampering with police evidence. The typed accusations were posed as a series of questions.

The document began: 'FURTHER QUESTIONS FOR POLICE MINISTER GLASSON 28/11/84.'

The first query centred on a standard Christmas card sent by Commissioner Lewis to Paul John Breslin in late 1983 when the latter headed up his Prisoners Aid Society shelter for young offenders. 'In view of the enclosed Xmas card,' the document asked, 'what exactly is the relationship between Breslin and Mr Lewis? This card was seized by police on 19/1/1984 in Dunmore Terrace raid.'

And another: 'On Tuesday, April 24 this year, did the Commissioner at the request of [a homosexual police officer] ... attend a function at an inner-city hotel that was a gathering of gays known as The Society of Friends? Did Mr Lewis give Mr Breslin a lift to this gathering in the Commissioner's departmental Statesman Caprice?

'Was a Family Court judge, a Supreme Court judge, two Magistrates and a number of senior and junior police present among the 150 men present? Did the Commissioner not tell them that what they did in their own bedrooms was their own business?'

The document further alleged that Lewis had given Breslin a police headquarters photo identification card, allowing him 24-hour access to the building. It then looked at the investigation by Detective Sergeant Peter Gallagher into Breslin and his alleged assault of a teenager in his Dunmore Terrace unit in January 1984. 'Is it true that in the current investigation of Breslin by … Gallagher … items of evidence have been stolen or are missing? … Are the executive of The Society of Friends so powerful that Det. Sgt. Gallagher actually had to take exhibits home with him each night to prevent their being stolen/tampered with?'

Gallagher confirms that he made sure he kept close the controversial photographs found in Breslin's Dunmore Terrace unit during the police raid in January 1984. 'I used to post the photographs away, send them over to Darwin and return address to me and I'd send them out to Cairns, I'd send them to Sydney, I'd send them to Perth, any bloody where. Just so as I wouldn't have them in my possession,' says Gallagher. 'They tried to order me to give them in and I said no, no, no, I can't, I haven't got them with me, I haven't got them on me.

'So anyway, the next thing I had to go down and see Bill Glasson …'

Lewis strongly denied the gossip. He wrote in his diary: 'On Sat[urday], saw Premier re inform. on Christmas card to Breslin, and other allegations re lift in car, permission to drive Police cars, meeting Breslin etc. all false except Christmas Card. Hon. Glasson present re same matter.'

Breslin denies he had any form of friendship with Commissioner Lewis. 'Never spoken to him by phone,' says Breslin. 'Never faxed him. Never had him call me or leave a message on my answering machine …

'Am I alleged to have been a member of The Society of Friends? Isn't that Quakers? That's the only Society of Friends I know of … I've seen Lewis socially maybe twice. I saw him once at police HQ, a tender briefing for a new model [of Ford motor vehicle] – he was part of a selection panel.'

Girls Working

Geoff Crocker continued to run a tight ship with his brothel Pinky's and numerous escort services, but he had to remain vigilant when it came to working girls and drugs. He had made a promise to his mother years before that he would not tolerate drugs, and in Brisbane the word soon got out that if you were a druggie – even taking prescription drugs – you needn't bother asking Crocker for a job. 'I've had a few work for me over a period of time and when I … realised they were bringing needles to work and everything … sacked on the spot, you know, they were just never reliable,' he said later in an interview.

'If you had ten girls working and two of them were druggies you can bet your life those eight that weren't druggies would be there on time to start work. The druggies would turn up two hours later, you know, and then they'd go to sleep on the lounge … you couldn't send them off on a job because they would be off their face so you just let them sleep it off …

'There were plenty of girls popping Serepax and all that sort of shit … I thought they were worse off on that than bloody heroin. They were hopeless when they were on Serepax … falling down and things … Valium, they were always on that. You'd find most of the girls in parlours are on them.'

156

Crocker revealed a scene that had changed little since the days of Shirley Brifman in the 1960s, when she ruled as one of Sydney's most famous brothel madams, her life a haze of cops, johns and prescription drugs, secured in bulk from friendly pharmacists in Potts Point. By the 1980s in Brisbane, the work – as ever – was relentless.

'If a girl was genuinely tired and done a day shift and a night shift together – what we call a double – if it was quiet she'd go upstairs and pick a room and have a sleep,' remembered Crocker, 'and if it got busy, she'd be woken up and used again.

'If she'd made good money on the previous shift and there was three girls still handling the flow, we wouldn't wake her up, we'd let her sleep all night until it was time to go home, so we tried to be very fair with the girls, but you'd have to have her there in case you got that busy you needed her.'

Crocker was also sensitive to family holidays like Christmas. 'Every year Christmas time comes and the girls have got no family here in Brisbane – they're from down south or up north or wherever,' Crocker said. 'Our house was open to them at Christmas time for the Christmas dinner and all that, and my family would all be there and all the working girls would be there and we'd have a great Christmas party and you get a bit of grog in them and so on and so forth and they'd sit down and start pouring out their ex-life to you ...

'A big percentage of the girls had been tampered with by their step-fathers and real fathers ... and it actually shocked me to know how many of the girls had carnal knowledge and [were] abused by their parents. A big percentage of them ... were interfered with.'

Drugs, though, were his bugbear. He once found one of his staff at Pinky's overdosed in a car parked near the brothel. 'Julie and I walked out to the car and she [the employee] was in the car stretched out across the front seat with a belt around her arm and a needle lying beside it,' Crocker recalled. 'She'd overdosed. God only knows how long she'd been there for.

'... I never touched the car because as soon as I saw the belt and the needle on her ... she could be dead ... I didn't know. Julie said to me, "Oh, you better get her up to the hospital or something." And I said, "I don't want to touch the bitch. I hope she's friggin dead." That's the words I used, and I said, she's never coming back on these premises again.

'Now, Julie would have arranged for one of our drivers or someone ... to take her off to the hospital ... but I didn't touch her or her car or anything. When I saw that, I wanted nothing more to do with her.'

Male to Male

During the height of the scandal over former policeman and TV star David Moore, two journalists over in the red-brick headquarters of the *Courier-Mail* at 41 Campbell Street, Bowen Hills, began a unique investigation. Senior journalist Tony Koch, and a junior, Matthew Fynes-Clinton, started looking into the world of male brothels in Brisbane. They were also interested in child pornography and prostitution.

Weeks earlier, both journalists had met with Opposition Police Spokesman Wayne Goss in the Grosvenor Hotel, on the riverside corner of George and Ann streets. The Grosvenor had long been the watering hole for the legal profession, given its proximity to the law courts. It was also a favourite of the police. Goss had an interesting document to show them. It was the two-page list of damning allegations compiled anonymously that had so interested Police Minister Glasson in relation to his Police Commissioner and Paul John Breslin.

At the bottom of the document a question was posed: 'Is it true that during a recent police undercover operation observing the operation of a male brothel, known as Brett's Boys, of 206 Kelvin Grove Road,

Kelvin Grove, both Messrs (X) and (Y) were observed making late-night visits to the premises?'

The unnamed men were allegedly both members of state parliament. If true, the allegations could floor the government.

Escort agency owner and operator Geoff Crocker would later reveal in an interview that he had once had discussions about the male sex worker industry with Hector Hapeta. 'I was led to believe Hector was involved with Brett's Boys and to this day I reckon he was, because I remember a conversation with him once that there was big money in male massage ... and I said to him: "How would you know, have you got one?"

'[He said,] "Yes, I'm a partner in Brett's Boys".'

Crocker delineated, through his own escort business, that there seemed to be a demand for male prostitution: 'Quite a few guys rang up a lot of my escort agencies wanting a job to do male-to-male stuff and I've always told the receptionist not to entertain the thought of even talking to them on the phone, we don't want to know about it, and some of them got really dirty and said, you know, it was male, what do you call it [discrimination] ...'

On Monday 10 December the *Courier-Mail* ran the first part of its investigation into male brothels and paedophilia under the headline: THE MEN OF EVIL WHO PREY ON CHILDREN.

The article claimed there were at least four male brothels operating and advertising openly in Brisbane and the Gold Coast. The report detailed how 'respectable' men would pick up boys – the bulk of them aged between 14 and 18 – from pinball parlours and the streets. They were then taken to motels and homes for 'pornographic photos and homosexual activity'.

In the case of male brothels, the young prostitutes would often be flown in from other states but locals were also recruited. One of the brothels the report targeted was Brett's Boys. Another was the House of Praetorian at 1/86 Rialto Street, Greenslopes.

The journalists interviewed ten prostitutes and were told that the main drug supplier to street kids and the gay community was 'Mick' of Inala, who they claim was protected by corrupt police.

'Most Brisbane brothels, male and female, are owned and operated by a man known as "Hector",' the report said. 'Hector has operated the brothels in Brisbane since 1974. Most are massage parlours in Fortitude Valley. Prostitutes employed in the Hector chain say he is notorious for reneging on payments to his staff.'

The story went into detail about the high incidence of children selling barbiturates on the street, and how the pornographic photography of boys in homosexual acts was done for profit.

On page three, the investigation continued with another story by Koch on the notorious paedophile Clarence Osborne, 61, who supposedly gassed himself to death in 1979 after he came to the attention of police. Koch, as part of his enquiries, spoke to gay men at the Hacienda Hotel in the Valley, who told him the media had exaggerated the recent paedophile ring allegations. 'The boys are willing, and even though they might be 14 or so in years, in the "street" sense they are older than you or me,' one man said. 'They are never forced, and more often are the aggressors.'

On the day of the shocking newspaper report, Commissioner Lewis went and saw his minister, Bill Glasson, about 'Breslin matters'. Later that evening he would attend Parliament House for Glasson's Christmas party.

The following morning the *Courier-Mail* reported that the Police Complaints Tribunal, by now under the control of Judge Eric Pratt, would investigate whether police were involved in child sex and child pornography. Pratt's inquiry would be held in camera.

Glasson said he had asked Lewis to investigate the newspaper allegations and report back within three days. 'If the allegations are true, it would be of concern to every parent in Queensland,' Glasson stated. 'And as for a male brothel operating opposite a school [Kelvin Grove

Junior], if that is true it is of grave concern … I cannot understand that it has not surfaced before.'

There was significant support in Cabinet for a wider inquiry, but the government was prepared to wait for the Lewis report before deciding further.

The head of the police department's child abuse unit, Detective Sergeant David Jefferies, told the newspaper: 'There is definitely child pornography being made in Queensland. At this stage we don't think it is being made in commercial volume but we have found photographs of local children in overseas pornographic magazines.'

Opposition leader Nev Warburton simply called for an independent judicial inquiry. The *Courier-Mail* editorial applauded the tribunal inquiry but wasn't so complimentary of the government and police. 'While it is difficult to believe that the Queensland Police Force did not know of these operations, it is more difficult to understand why they were not closed down. The apparent lack of activity has been matched by the Queensland Government. Mr Glasson and Mr Lewis have both declined to answer questions …'

On the Wednesday, Koch and Fynes-Clinton reported that the allegations of a child pornography ring had been stirred by police factions wishing to discredit Commissioner Lewis. 'Some information accused Mr Lewis of having supplied a man [Breslin] facing charges with an official pass which allowed him 24-hour access to police headquarters; having allowed him use of police vehicles; having accompanied him as guest speaker to a "clandestine gathering of gays"; and having tried to make something sinister of a handwritten Christmas card, signed by Mr Lewis, which was found in the man's flat in a police raid.'

The *Courier-Mail* straightened the record. The official pass was an Australian Journalists' Association card; Breslin sometimes delivered police cars as a former employee of the Ford Motor Company; as for the gay meeting, the newspaper said it had sighted Breslin's passport and he wasn't in the country at the time the meeting was said to have taken place.

Lewis, with the help of media officer Ian Hatcher, issued a press release: 'This morning, two squads of detectives … raided premises at Greenslopes and Kelvin Grove. While a certain morning newspaper may claim credit for forcing this police action, the raids were in fact the culmination of two months' intensive investigation by the Juvenile Aid Bureau into male escort agencies and possible links with child pornography.'

Bowing to public pressure, the government approved a broader public inquiry into child pornography and child prostitution, although Premier Bjelke-Petersen, in London, was not so sure. He told reporters a full inquiry was 'not a foregone conclusion'.

'I'm not usually in favour of inquiries,' the Premier said. 'What do these inquiries do? Get on with the job and intensify police activity.'

On Saturday 15 December, the *Courier-Mail* reported on a Lewis television appearance the night before. Lewis had denied that police should have acted sooner on the allegations against constable David Moore, who was awaiting charges by summons in relation to two alleged cases of indecently dealing with boys aged 15 and 16.

Defending himself on Channel Seven's *Today Tonight* program, Lewis said, 'You have got to know the full story before you can make a judgement like that. It's not quite as simple to deal with anybody without adequate evidence.' He claimed nobody from the media or police force had ever complained to him about the gentlemen concerned, and what's more, he found it rather surprising that everyone claimed they knew everything, but nobody ever spoke about it before.

Despite the barrage – both internally from his own Minister and Premier, and externally from the media – Lewis continued on, seemingly unruffled. The next day, he was in his office at headquarters by 11 a.m. 'Saw Insp. Early and viewed Channel Nine programme, very fair presentation of interview and comments.'

The following week, Cabinet appointed Brisbane barrister Des Sturgess as the new Director of Prosecutions and approved his appointment as Queen's Counsel. Attorney-General Nev Harper said Sturgess's 'first official duty' would be to inquire into child pornography and prostitution in Queensland.

The Opposition labelled it a 'cynical token of an inquiry'.

Des Sturgess remembers that he was 'unencumbered by procedure' when he began investigating child sex abuse and prostitution for his much-anticipated report. 'The Moore, Hurrey and Breslin thing had gotten the government interested,' he says. 'I received considerable assistance from the Juvenile Aid Bureau. It wasn't a formal inquiry in a sense. People just came to see me. People telephoned and I had letters from prisoners. I went out to the gaols. I went to Sydney to see the gay mardi gras. I went to Long Bay prison and interviewed prisoners.'

He says he received little help from Queensland's Licensing Branch. 'The branch was shot through with corruption at that stage,' Sturgess says. 'I became aware of this and had been aware of it for some time. I didn't get the cooperation I expected from the Licensing Branch. Stuff was held back and not given to me. Information was held back.'

A Secret Meeting with the Minister

Police Minister Bill Glasson had been thumped by the controversy over former police senior constable Dave Moore, and the whole issue had pitted him against Commissioner Terry Lewis.

Lewis had expressed his concerns about Glasson's loyalty to the force and had denied any impropriety in relation to the affair, but Glasson was not convinced of Lewis's claims that he had not heard of allegations against Moore prior to 1984. He convened a top secret meeting with someone who might shed some light on the whole mess – Constable

Mike Garrahy, the young JAB officer who had come across victims of Bill Hurrey and Dave Moore as far back as 1982.

Glasson's press secretary, Robert Stewart, recalled: 'During the latter part of 1984, allegations concerning then police officer Dave Moore started to surface. I recall there being a number of statements made by the Commissioner to the Minister that such allegations were unfounded.' Determined to get to the bottom of the issue, Stewart arranged to interview Garrahy in the presence of his Minister.

The interview was held on Wednesday 19 December in Glasson's ministerial office. Garrahy was nervous. When he was offered a cup of coffee he asked for it white, with two sugars. He requested permission to smoke during the interview, then proceeded to unload the background of the sordid saga. Off the bat, he alleged that a file on the case forwarded to the Crown Law Office was 'incomplete'.

Stewart: If you could just explain to the Minister what you told me over the phone the other day about your meeting with [police officer] Kerry, Kerry Kelly.

Garrahy: Right, I was in contact with Kerry Kelly and Kerry told me that the file that was sent from the Police Department to the Crown Law office was incomplete. It wasn't the full file that had been put in.

Stewart: Now that file went from him [Kelly] to the Commissioner's office ...

Garrahy: To the Commissioner's office to the Crown Law office.

Stewart: So no one else would have access to it.

Garrahy: Not that I know of.

Stewart: [It] went to the Commissioner's office and any interference to the file must have happened in the Commissioner's office?

Garrahy: Well I'd say so. Anyway, what happened was Kerry

told me that he was called down to see the person who was doing the adjudication on the file at the Crown Law office and there were gaps in the file that had been sent down by the Police Department and that he subsequently produced all the missing pieces of the original file that he had and handed them over.

Stewart: In other words, he had a duplicate file with him?

Garrahy: Yeah, yeah, and filled in all the gaps.

Stewart: Do you know, from what he told you, were they sensitive sections that were missing?

Garrahy: Apparently so, yes, he wasn't game to say very much because like a lot of the fellows at the minute, you know, they're all fairly worried and they're playing this very close to their chest 'cause word's out if anyone talks, well, that's going to be the end of us.

Stewart: If we approached or ... ah ... had somebody approach Kerry do you think he'd be prepared to give us the full story?

Garrahy: No, he won't.

Stewart: He won't?

Garrahy: No, I've already tried.

Stewart: So, they're actually scared for their own future and their career?

Garrahy: That's right.

The young constable revealed how his original report on Hurrey and Moore from late 1982 had vanished into the system and had only reappeared since the arrest of Hurrey. He said he had no idea what had happened to the report in the 'missing' years. Garrahy told Stewart that after he had submitted his report to Inspector Frank Rynne the report had been taken to police headquarters by Rynne. When Rynne returned Garrahy was given a verbal instruction to concentrate on Hurrey instead.

Garrahy said he knew little of Moore and had never really mixed with the young constable.

Stewart: You didn't have any association with or working association with Breslin at all?

Garrahy: No. No, the only, my only association with Breslin was when we followed him a couple of times.

Stewart: And you had suspicions then?

Garrahy: Oh yeah. What happened was, um …

Glasson: Was Breslin under direct surveillance by instruction?

Garrahy: No. No, what happened was we received some confidential information that Breslin had allegedly got a police officer full of grog at the Police Club and taken him down to his unit down at the Gardens [in Alice Street] and had sexually assaulted him and this copper was too ashamed to report it and we started, for other reasons, we started to think, well there's got to be some tie up here, and we followed, I think we followed Breslin twice and the third time I got sprung and he turned round and he said to me, ah g'day, how are you? Because I'd seen him in the club a couple of times and said g'day to him. I said, oh not bad, I've had a few I said, I'm going to go down and catch a cab and go home. He said, oh why don't you come down to my place for drinks and I said, no I've had too much and I've got to go to work in the morning. And that's the only conversation I ever had with Breslin.

Glasson: Now why … what astounds me is there seems to be this incumbent fear, what reason is that there? Your jeopardy of your whole future career, is that what you're concerned about?

Garrahy: Not only that … ah … there are stories that we've
             been told about and whether they're true or not
             we'll never know, about things that have happened
             in the department over the last few years and even
             if some of them are true they … the boys all feel
             that they're just too much of a risk.

Stewart: That's a risk to their careers?

Garrahy: And their personal safety.

Focus returned to Garrahy's explosive confidential report on Hurrey
and Moore in 1982. Garrahy revealed that a couple of weeks after
he'd submitted it, he learned that Moore had been tipped off about its
contents. Word had got back to Garrahy that a detective inspector had
filled Moore in on the guts of the report and warned him to lay off and
stay away from Hurrey or else there'd be trouble.

Cheesed off, Kelly and Garrahy put in a request to put surveillance
on Hurrey and Moore. Garrahy claimed he had then received an
instruction to lay off Moore and concentrate on Hurrey.

Stewart: So, someone going along your lines, someone in
             the Commissioner's office, be it [then] assistant
             commissioner [Tony] Murphy, knew of your
             concern at that time?

Garrahy: That's right.

Stewart: And do you think that the Commissioner himself
             would have been made aware of it?

Garrahy: He would have had to have known.

Stewart: Why do you say that?

Garrahy: Because I can remember we all said at the time
             it's going to be a bombshell when it goes off and
             none of us wanted to pinch Moore because he's
             a … well … another constable. That's why we said

that if we got enough evidence to pinch Moore
we'd have to get a couple of inspectors from Internal
Investigations to do it.

The constable said he couldn't comprehend that nothing had been done about the allegations against Moore and Hurrey, and he agreed there was an internal cover-up to protect Moore.

Because of work stress following the Hurrey and Moore investigation, Garrahy said he had a nervous breakdown and requested a transfer to Tara, on the Darling Downs, 300 kilometres west of Brisbane.

That night, Commissioner Lewis and his wife Hazel joined businessman Kevin Driscoll and his wife Thelma for cocktails. According to Lewis's diary, 'he [Driscoll] said one of Hon. Glasson's staff said they were going to "chop my head off".'

Lewis had faced tougher threats than that. He wound down the year in his usual punctilious fashion. He worked right up to Christmas Day. On the day itself he had the Lewis clan over for lunch, but still managed to read the October edition of *Police Chief* magazine. On Boxing Day he received a call from the Premier who told him a man in Zurich was telling him 'he is on East German "hit" list'. Lewis began two weeks of official leave on 31 December and didn't manage to get down to his usual holiday haunt, the Gold Coast, until 7 January 1985. A short time later, Don 'Shady' Lane rang Lewis to let him know that Glasson was 'knocking me behind my back'.

It had been a rough year for Lewis – the Bikie Bandits scandal, the extraordinary trial of Peter James Walsh, and the furore over Senior Constable David Moore. Each of those spot fires involved some suggestion of police cover-ups. Interstate, the Australian Bureau of Criminal Intelligence was starting to have its doubts about the Queensland Police Force and its proactive desire to keep any national investigating bodies outside state borders.

Lewis, in his own inimitable way, had weathered all storms. To his mind it was time to remake his nest at 12 Garfield Drive, Bardon. With his wife Hazel, the couple had a grand plan to remove the old Queenslander that sat on this prime parcel of real estate and build something that would last – a place befitting the status of the Commissioner. There was nothing safer as an investment, too, than good old-fashioned bricks and mortar.

Terry and Hazel would only have the best for the house in which they would grow old together. It would be designed by Queensland's most famous architect, the mastermind behind the Queensland Cultural Centre, the Queensland Art Gallery, the Queensland Performing Arts Centre, stage one of the new Queen Street Mall, the State Library of Queensland and the Queensland Museum.

In his diary for Friday 11 January 1985 Lewis had a single entry: 'Robin Gibson called re plans for new house.'

The Ranks of the Medically Unfit

The troublesome Rebel Cop, Ross Dickson, was on Christmas holidays with his family in the first week of January 1985 when he was served with 14 departmental charges involving 168 instances of 'knowingly furnishing false reports whilst stationed at Mareeba'.

Syd 'Sippy' Atkinson, Acting Commissioner while Commissioner Lewis was on recreational leave, issued a press release stating 'the charges are not trivial and technical such as typing omissions and errors, as some people would have the public believe'.

The force was out to destroy Ross Dickson, despite Atkinson's assurances otherwise: 'Vindictiveness associated with the investigation and charging of Sergeant Dickson is strongly denied by the police administration.

'During the hearing of these charges, it will be alleged that as a result of these false reports by Sergeant Dickson certain juveniles and other persons are recorded in departmental records as having made confessions to certain crimes, whereas in fact not only did those persons not confess to those crimes, but the crimes were never committed.'

The case Atkinson was referring to involved two young women who had recently gone on a break-and-enter spree across Far North Queensland. Dickson arrested them and took them in for questioning. 'Those girls did hundreds and hundreds of burglaries up and down the coast,' Dickson remembers. 'We charged them. One was a criminal and the other one was a rich bitch, only a kid really, [she] came from a really well-to-do family. She denied everything; she was a real smartarse. We had enough on her to put on about ten or 20 break-and-enters, the other one was copping hundreds.'

Dickson used a time-worn strategy. He told the 'rich' girl that her friend was putting it all on her. They wired the friend and sent her into the cell with her partner in crime. 'Over the course of hours and hours, we got her to talk about all the jobs they'd done – the break-and-enters.' Dickson suggested her solicitor drop into the police station before court. 'He heard the tapes. He made her plead guilty. We had so much on her,' Dickson says.

Dickson waited to be interviewed by his superiors over the incident. He was never approached. '[Then] they turned up and laid all these charges on me,' he says. It was a tried and true method, used for decades within the Queensland Police Force against outspoken officers. If you couldn't get an officer to keep quiet, you could bring them down over minor transgressions of police rules, especially when it came to keeping paperwork updated, or an official diary in order. More often than not, busy detectives would get behind on their paperwork.

Atkinson said a 'legally constituted inquiry' would be held as soon as possible in North Queensland. 'If proved, the punishment could be dismissal from the Police Force of Sergeant Dickson,' the release stated. 'He was suspended from duty because of the seriousness of the charges.'

Dickson protested to the press about the 'manipulated and concocted charges' against him. He said the minute he spoke out on the police department's reluctance to tackle organised crime he became a 'marked man'. He also lashed out vociferously at both the police department and the government. Shockingly, he claimed he could name two state politicians who were involved in organised crime.

'I'm not going to say who controls all the girls and gambling in this State,' Dickson told the Rockhampton *Morning Bulletin*. 'Every person who investigates major crimes says that major crime cannot flourish without senior police officers and politicians being involved. These officers tell you quite openly when you are doing jobs with the big-time drug dealers and the smugglers and every other sort of vice: "Pull your head in or you're gone."'

Two days later, on 8 January, Atkinson sent a confidential memo to Police Minister Bill Glasson: 'I recommend that the Judge appointed to make the [Dickson] investigation under the Police Rules be Judge [Eric] Pratt, QC, of the District Court.'

However, just days before Dickson's hearing, the former Sheriff of Mareeba was examined by doctors and deemed medically unfit to continue as a police officer.

'They were doing a real number on my wife,' Dickson remembers. 'I'd go to work in Townsville and they'd ring her up and say: "Tell him to pull his head in", "He's going to die", "He won't come home from the shift", "He's dead, we'll get him tonight."'

'They came out to the house and turned the power off when she was home alone, pregnant with a little baby.

'On New Year's Eve 1984, they made some really determined threats to her. She told me about it and I thought, this is it, we've done enough ... there was no point in getting bloody killed over it.'

One examining doctor concluded that Dickson suffered from stress anxiety and paranoia. Another diagnosed that he suffered from angioedema – the often rapid swelling of the throat and tongue – and severe bouts of itchiness. It necessitated that he carry ampoules of adrenalin for self-injection.

His lawyers at Gilshenan and Luton wrote to Commissioner Lewis saying they'd appreciate it if he could expedite Dickson's application as soon as possible. 'Our further strong advice to our client is that in the future as a police officer or not, it is our opinion that it is in his best interests not to engage in public statements or debate on matters concerning the Queensland Police Force,' the lawyers wrote.

'Pat Nolan, the solicitor, let them know about all my tapes, he hinted to them that I had a lot more tapes than what I did have,' says Dickson. 'Normally it takes six to nine months to go out medically unfit. From the time I put the report in, it took 19 days,' Dickson recalls.

A statement was issued saying that he would not 'hereafter issue any statement to the media or to any politician concerning matters pertaining to the Queensland Police Force or my service therein'.

Dickson's application to the Medical Board featured often in Lewis's police diary, and it wasn't just him and Police Minister Glasson who were interested in the Dickson case. On Thursday 7 February, Lewis recorded: '… Premier phoned re … D/S Dickson appln'.

The problem that had been Ross Dickson quietly retired from the force. He had joined the ranks of the medically unfit, as so many agitators, whistleblowers and truth-tellers had before him. As for the inquiry into his departmental charges, Judge Pratt adjourned it 'indefinitely'.

Lewis remembers: 'I charged him [Dickson] departmentally with 154 charges, and I had to sign the charges for those sort of things – the furnishing of false reports and so on and so forth – and the rotten little bastard got the union onto it … and they got a couple of doctors or something on side … anyhow, he went out medically unfit.

'He got his … payout … and bought a bloody fish shop or something up at Hervey Bay or somewhere.'

Dickson later said: 'I loved my 21 years with the police force … but I don't miss it … I still haven't been told the reasons behind my transfer.'

Gallagher in the Cesspool

Since that early morning in January 1984, when teenager Ricky Garrison had fronted up to police claiming he had been sexually assaulted in a unit in Auchenflower, police officer Peter Gallagher had entered a twilight zone of sexual deviancy in Brisbane. Gallagher, who took the original complaint, and who was on the team that raided the unit, owned by Paul John Breslin, was wading deeper into the cesspool.

Gallagher was uncovering some disturbing stories based on information supplied by an informant in the gay community. The informant had told Gallagher about Senior Constable David Moore, and he knew the ins and outs of paedophilia networks in the city, of child prostitution and the production of child pornography. 'He spilled a lot of beans,' Gallagher remembers. 'This fellow told me that he would organise for me to get a job on. They used to go to Indooroopilly, pick up the kids, take them to this address in Indooroopilly, give them $200 for a session and put them out in the street. So in those days, you know, $200 – Christ, that was a lot of money at the time.'

The informant said children were picked up from around Indooroopilly Shoppingtown or the nearby railway station, taken to the address of a senior airline executive, photographed, and the pictures were flown interstate.

Gallagher executed a warrant on the executive's safe at work but found nothing. 'My informant said there are photos in his safe ... so I took a warrant out and like a fool I told a bloody couple of people down there, and when I got there the safe was ... not a thing,' says Gallagher.

Gallagher was still posting to himself the photographs seized from Breslin's Auchenflower apartment, depicting lewd shots of Constable Moore. There was nobody Gallagher felt he could trust. Alarmingly, too, the whole affair was becoming increasingly political.

After Gallagher was hauled in to speak with Police Minister Bill Glasson, he was then summoned by the Deputy Police Commissioner. 'I went over and saw [Syd] Atkinson,' says Gallagher. 'I'd worked with Syd and … had a lot of respect for Syd because Syd was a good detective in his day. I said, "Syd you know what's happened with bloody Moore? You'd better do something. You'll have to do something about it."

'"Oh, she'll be right Pete, she'll be right", he says [to me].'

One of the primary concerns over the scandal was how confidential facts were being leaked to the Opposition. Gallagher was next asked to be interviewed by Judge Eric Pratt, the chairman of the Police Complaints Tribunal. 'They questioned me for a while and asked me questions and … did you leak?

'"No, no, no," I told them. I said, "If I'd have known that this was going to happen I would have bloody leaked."

'As I was leaving Pratt's office he says, "I'll probably see you again."

'I said, "I'm sure we will."'

In the middle of all this, Gallagher took annual leave. When he reported back for duty at the city CIB, they told him he no longer worked for the branch. He was transferred to uniform duties at Beenleigh, the 'punishment' station for troublesome officers, south of the CBD.

'They weren't sure how much more I knew,' says Gallagher. 'While we were waiting for the [Breslin] trial, I was sent over to Woolloongabba for a while on night wireless. When I got there … there was a phone call for me. They said, "Oh, we've got so and so [my informant] locked up here and he wants to get in touch with you."

'I went over and sure enough it was this bloke. I said, "What are you doing in here, in the watch-house?"

'He said, "Well, I don't know."

'They came knocking at his door, a couple of uniform fellows, and they grabbed him and locked him up.'

Gallagher rushed over to the communications room to check the job card for the arrest. There was none.

He Can Offer No Information

It was the last thing Commissioner Lewis needed during a hectic festive season, but a small debate had bubbled to the surface within the police department regarding the managing of massage parlours and brothels. This had been a point of discussion with police since the first bordellos had emerged in wooden Queenslanders over in South Brisbane, nestled among the fish factories and pubs, in the first quarter of the twentieth century. But in modern Brisbane the scene had exploded, and some officers were getting worried; the recent scandal over male brothels in the city had put the vice industry under the spotlight.

Detective Inspector Col Thompson of the Bureau of Criminal Intelligence (BCI) wrote a memo expressing his concerns. The two-page document was headed: 'Prostitution – associates and criminal activities: A subject for intelligence gathering by the Bureau of Criminal Intelligence.'

In the report, Thompson drew attention to the noticeable lack of intelligence gathering by the BCI in relation to the activities of prostitutes and their associates. He had been under the impression that such matters were to be left entirely to the Licensing Branch but claimed that copies of the daily running sheet, which only listed the names of people who had been spoken to or arrested, was the only information he ever received.

Thompson conceded that occasionally information on drugs and standover methods and assaults on working girls filtered in, and that he had also heard that a 'very well known southern criminal' was attempting to take over the entire massage parlour scene on the Gold Coast prior to the official opening of the new casino at Broadbeach.

'Through lack of contacts in this area, we are unable to confirm or deny these rumours,' he reported. 'I have discussed this with Inspector [Allen] BULGER, relieving in charge of the Licensing Branch, and he can offer no information that would assist. He advised me that the

Licensing Branch do not maintain records of the Gold Coast area and only go there on specific jobs.'

Thompson acknowledged that with the large number of people now involved in massage parlours and other forms of prostitution, 'there must be a wealth of information available' in the drug and other criminal fields. He pointed out that the Victorian BCI had three officers working full-time gathering intelligence from the prostitution industry.

Assistant Commissioner (Crimes and Services) Bill McArthur contributed to the debate with a confidential memo. 'The area of complaint from detectives charged with the fight against general crime is that, more and more, there is indeed a great deal of criminality in and on the periphery of the massage parlour and associated industries. There is no in-depth intelligence gathering of that aspect of criminal activity. My view is that our overall fight against crime is hampered by present policy.'

McArthur recommended that a selected 'cell' of officers (perhaps two) from the BCI be allowed to operate within the massage parlour industry to gather intelligence.

But what some knew, and many didn't, was that an embedded 'cell', as described by McArthur, would very quickly detect the vast corrupt network, known colloquially as The Joke, and the reach of its tentacles.

Detective Inspector Graeme Parker, in charge of the Licensing Branch, also added to the discussion. He said there were only 14 massage parlours in Brisbane, involving an estimated 70 prostitutes. He claimed 'it had been the practice of members of this branch to elicit information from these persons' and pass it on to the BCI.

He also assured Assistant Commissioner McArthur that officers of the BCI, the Drug Squad and the Licensing Branch had 'joined forces' and gathered intelligence on the Gold Coast.

He concluded: 'The suggestion of BCI members visiting areas of the prostitution scene in Brisbane is worthy of consideration, however, the final decision would no doubt be a police matter for the department to consider.'

Assistant Commissioner (Operations) Ron Redmond put in his two cents worth. He believed the policing of the 14 massage parlours in Brisbane should remain the responsibility of the Licensing Branch. 'It is my view that we must retain the present policy of this department in only permitting Licensing Branch personnel to police the parlours,' he declared. 'Should we allow police from other establishments to enter the parlours in a policing role, I am sure that we are only inviting trouble insofar as allegations of graft, standover tactics of the girls operating the parlours and other obvious reasons.

'It is also the government's view that policing of massage parlours must remain the responsibility of the Licensing Branch,' he concluded.

The final word, of course, went to Commissioner Lewis. 'It is considered that the present system is working well,' he declared.

Every Little Bit Helps

It had been three months since Jim Slade had formally submitted his dynamite report on the drug trade in Queensland. The report had gone to Queensland's Bureau of Criminal Intelligence and was then forwarded to Peter Vassallo on the Italian desk of the Australian Bureau of Criminal Intelligence in Canberra. Somehow it had gotten out of the state without being 'choked off'.

Without doubt, Slade's focus on the Bellino family had gotten around the department like a brush fire, yet Slade had received no blow-back through the Christmas and New Year period.

Commissioner Lewis had been preoccupied with the Dave Moore scandal since late 1984, and continued to try and manage the damage into the New Year. On top of that, Queensland was suffering from a major clash between the government and South-East Queensland

Electricity Board (SEQEB) electricians. Bjelke-Petersen had denied them a wage rise and squared up for a brawl with the Electrical Trades Union (ETU). Hundreds of electricians went on strike causing major power blackouts from December.

The strike dragged on. Then, on Thursday 7 February 1985, the Premier – having learned of its political effectiveness during the Springbok Rugby Union protests of 1971 – called a State of Emergency. Once again, Queensland police became the government's muscle in a protracted arm wrestle.

Lewis was called to attend a Cabinet meeting in the Executive Building in George Street, Brisbane, the next day. 'State Emergency proclaimed over Power Strikes', he recorded in his diary. 'Police to ensure safety and peace at 83 SEQEB depots.'

That night, and unbeknown to Commissioner Lewis, Detective Constable Jim Slade was winding down with a few drinks in the Police Club at North Quay. He was joined by one of his superiors, Senior Sergeant Alan Barnes, of the Bureau of Criminal Intelligence.

'It was fairly late at night, around 10 p.m., as far as I can remember,' Slade later recalled. 'At one stage Alan Barnes and myself were left alone and Alan said: "How would you like a bit of extra money?" and I said, "Yes, every little bit helps."

'He said, "As you know I have got my ear to the ground and I can organise most transfers that people want", and I said, "Yes, I'm aware of that".'

Barnes then mentioned a number of officers who 'met at Jack Herbert's place and that is where most of these things are sorted out'.

Slade was stunned by Barnes' revelation. The following day, he discussed the Barnes offer with his colleague Ian Jamieson. He also telephoned his friend Peter Vassallo in Canberra.

The next month, on Saturday 30 March, Slade was again approached by his boss. Slade had just stepped off an Ansett flight from Mount Isa, and Barnes picked him up from the airport in his silver Commodore.

'We had some conversation re[garding] the job in Mount Isa, and before Alan Barnes started the car he put his hand into his pocket and removed a number of $20 notes,' recalled Slade.

The $100 bribe was clearly related to Slade's Operation Trek report and his information on the Bellino family. When Slade got home to Marsden, 27 kilometres south of the Brisbane CBD, he took notes of the conversation and transaction with Barnes.

Back at work on Tuesday, Slade confidentially informed Inspector Col Thompson of what had happened in the car with Barnes. 'I got the impression from Col Thompson that he was going to take it further with his superiors.'

Four weeks later, Barnes approached Slade again. At 2.48 p.m. on Monday 29 April (as recorded precisely by Slade), he was in the BCI Queensland office. 'About halfway up the corridor Alan Barnes stopped and turned and handed me a folded pack of $20 notes.'

'Here you are,' Barnes said.

'Thanks, mate,' Slade replied.

'Everything alright?'

'Yes, no worries,' Slade replied.

'You haven't told anyone about our little thing?'

'Oh no, mate, no way,' said Slade.

'I trust you,' Barnes said. 'You know what would happen?'

'Yes,' Slade replied. 'No worries.'

'Keep it like this, a hundred a month. A hundred a month is not bad for doing nothing.'

'I'll say, mate. I'm happy.'

Slade returned to his desk. That night he and Ian Jamieson went to the Police Club for a drink after work. It was around 6.10 p.m. Barnes was at a table with colleagues just inside the door. Slade had some whiskey and sodas. Barnes later summoned him to the end of the table. 'Listen, I picked the boss [Thompson] up this morning … [he] put it on me that I had told you to lay off Gerry [Bellino],' Barnes said.

'Oh, shit mate,' Slade replied, 'that's not right.'

Barnes explained that when Thompson got in the car and before they headed off to pick up another Assistant Commissioner, he asked Barnes if he'd ever asked Slade to back off Gerry Bellino.

'Shit, that doesn't make sense,' Slade countered. 'We haven't got a job going on Gerry, have we?'

'No,' said Barnes. 'Anyway, he doesn't have to get his money illegally, he is making a fortune out of that marble up north.'

'Yes, that's right,' said Slade. 'Listen, Alan, are you worried about that?'

'No, not at all,' he replied. 'The only thing is not to tell a soul about this.'

Slade and Jamieson made to leave when Barnes called him back. 'Will you swear on the Bible you haven't told anyone about the money I have given you?'

'I haven't told a soul,' Slade said, 'but I am really worried about what the boss said.'

Barnes reassured him that 'no one knows about you'. And added: 'The bloke I get the bread off knows I give $100 of the $300 I get off him to another bloke in the squad but he doesn't know your name. But for Christ's sake, don't say a word.'

Slade had now taken two wads of cash. He packed the notes in exhibit bags and slipped in each bag a note recording the date, time and place the money was received.

Slade discussed the conundrum with his wife Chris. He was in a difficult position. He had liked and respected Barnes, and to rat on a fellow officer was against every professional fibre in his being. But it was impossible to accept the cash.

'Only when Barnes offered that money, that's when it affected me, that's when I had to do something about it,' he says. 'If they hadn't made it so fucking obvious, just after my report [for Operation Trek was submitted] … I used to take it [the cash bribes] home and I'd say to Chris … that mongrel Barnes wants to give me more money. We sat and talked about it and we put the money under our waterbed mattress. We were trying to work out what to do with it.'

Slade grew fearful for his family. He started sleeping with a gun under the bed.

The Shade of Nazis

In the final weeks of February, as Commissioner Lewis's fifty-seventh birthday loomed and Slade was ruminating on the underbelly of corruption that he was unwittingly being dragged into, the ramifications of the government brawl with the Electrical Trades Union workers was being felt. Following the sacking of 1000 workers, the government found it difficult to quickly replace the huge number of retrenched linesmen and power supply from the stations was cut by half. The community tension, by this stage, was palpable.

On Tuesday 19 February Lewis wrote in his diary: 'Premier phoned re security required at suite in parlt. Annex (sic) and at home in Kingaroy.' And later: 'Phoned Premier re addit. security arrangements.'

The next day, Lewis was discussing the possibility that police would be called upon to 'perform functions at power stations', and he talked to his deputy about 'using Police to protect persons serving court orders on power workers'.

In parliament, the debate over the SEQEB crisis hit fever pitch. The brawl was bitter and long. 'Queenslanders are absolutely tired of being held to ransom by dictatorial union leaders, supported by the Labor Party, who are quite content to see people suffer physically, mentally and financially while they practise their own form of industrial blackmail, which they are so expert in doing,' the Premier fired. 'Such action in essential industries will no longer be tolerated in the modern age.'

One of Bjelke-Petersen's great political strengths had been to seize an issue and simplify it into an easily digestible narrative for his conservative followers. He did it well with the Springboks rugby fiasco in 1971. This time the story was not about fair rights for ordinary workers, but a tale of barbarians holding hostage good, hard-working families, over something as essential as electricity. His remedy was to change legislation to ensure the electricity industry was a 'strike-free' zone.

Leader of the Opposition Nev Warburton retaliated. He accused Bjelke-Petersen of deliberately prolonging the dispute in order to use the strike as a mask for the government's hopeless economic mismanagement in general. He countered that 'the Premier and his Cabinet of faceless men have deliberately set a course which has promoted hatred and division in our community'.

ALP member for Ipswich, David Hamill, rose to debate the issue of the State of Emergency, still in place and possibly, as hinted at by Bjelke-Petersen, to remain until May. He also questioned the Premier's use of Police Commissioner Terry Lewis and his men in the dispute.

'I now want to examine the role of the police and the other agencies that the government has employed to be the tools of its political action,' he said to a heated House. 'The action of the government is not industrial conciliation and arbitration. The action of the government is political action and ideologically based action.'

Hamill made references to the campaign of harassment of the families involved in the striking. 'It was interesting,' he noted '… that the Queensland Police Union yesterday acknowledged that the police had been used in a manner that was both scandalous and detrimental to the esteem in which the public would hold the force.

'The Police Union yesterday undertook to make sure that there was a discontinuance of those intimidatory tactics for which the police were used in some areas. The Police Union recognised that the police had been used callously by the government for its own political ends …'

Hamill said he had received intelligence that Special Branch officers were also taking photographs of meetings of the sacked linesmen. 'The government should hang its head in shame,' he concluded.

During proceedings, an Opposition member called out: 'Shades of Nazism.' The Opposition may as well have been shouting into a well. The Bjelke-Petersen government didn't just maintain the status quo in response to those who dared question its authority, if anything, they intensified their approach.

On April Fool's Day, 1985, Lewis and his assistant, Inspector Greg Early, were summoned by the Premier to the Executive Building in George Street. As Lewis's diary notes: '... before 16 Cabinet Ministers advised our Police were not active enough against picketers and persons annoying SEQEB workers'.

Lewis clearly took the advice on board. That month, the Premier had expressed a degree of pressure in the job to Lewis, and also underlined the closeness of their friendship. In an early morning meeting, Lewis wrote in his diary that the pair discussed '... security at Kingaroy home and 2 extra police; Sir Edward Lyons and TAB; disloyal Police; thankless jobs with threats to self and family; press bias; left wing unionists and politicians; average 70 hr week; not staying if you leave ...'.

Not staying if you leave.

Clearly, by the autumn of 1985, the careers of the Premier and the Commissioner of Police were obliquely entwined, for good or ill.

The Perth Briefing

On Sunday 28 April, Commissioner Lewis and Sergeant First Class Clark headed to Brisbane's Eagle Farm airport at about 3.15 p.m., boarded Ansett Flight 1029 to Sydney, before transferring to Flight 220 to Perth, arriving at 9.40 p.m. local time. Lewis checked into the

Parmelia Hilton International Hotel in Mill Street, in the CBD and a short walk to the Swan River. He settled into room 834, which he considered 'very clean and comfortable, but noisy'.

Lewis was in Perth for the annual conference involving the Australian Police College Board of Control, the National Police Research Unit Board of Control, and most importantly, the Australian Bureau of Criminal Intelligence Management Committee.

He spent the next day discussing numerous agendas with the various committees. The unexpected star turn of the short conference, however, was to be an address by Sergeant Peter Vassallo of the ABCI's 'Italian desk'.

For years, Vassallo had been investigating the hugely lucrative cannabis trade in Australia, with the intent of identifying the major players and the volumes of cannabis being grown and sold. The data would ultimately make its way into his top secret report, Project Alpha, which in turn would stun law enforcement authorities with not just evidence of several Italian families behind the drug trade, but the attendant murders and corruption that went along with an illicit industry of this proportion.

In Perth, Vassallo took the opportunity to fly some of his findings across every police commissioner in the country, and Australian Federal Police boss Major-General Ron Grey. He was initially insecure about presenting the material and worried about how it might be received by the state commissioners.

'Trust me when I tell you that when this was happening to me I was shitting my pants, right?' recalls Vassallo of the Perth briefing. 'I had put all this [Alpha material] together in my head. I had bits and pieces of paper. I had no notes because that's how I protected my information. The notes and the information were always there in the systems or in microfiche or whatever, because I always acted on information.

'But there's one thing I did that no one had done before me. Coppers go looking for crime, analysts go looking for information. Analysts work on information from sources that are verifiable or not, the admiralty system right? What do lawyers and judges work on? Evidence. My audience was going to be senior politicians, senior commissioners and the National Crime Authority, full of fucking lawyers, the joint was run by lawyers. Therefore it dawned on me that I'd have to come up with an analysis and a pictorial representation based on fact.'

Vassallo's research revealed that a prominent Italian family had taken control of the cannabis trade in North Queensland and that there were links with them and organised crime figures interstate, particularly in Griffith in western New South Wales.

Commissioner Lewis, sitting at the briefing that day, must have put two and two together – that one of his own officers, Jim Slade, had uncovered similar intelligence through his lengthy Operation Trek, submitted to Queensland's Bureau of Criminal Intelligence just months earlier. What Lewis did not know at that point, was that Vassallo and Slade had been confidentially trading stories, and documents. In addition, Slade had shared with Vassallo how he had been offered a bribe by colleague Alan Barnes in February.

If his diaries are anything to go by, Lewis remained unfazed by the Vassallo presentation. Late on that first night of the conference, he shared a quiet drink with Tasmanian Police Commissioner Max Robinson until midnight. The next day he attended a meeting of senior officers of the Australian Police Ministers' Council, and had late afternoon drinks with Victorian Commissioner Mick Miller and his counterpart in New South Wales, John Avery.

Lewis was back on a plane for Brisbane the following morning, but had to return to Perth a month later, this time with his Police Minister Bill Glasson for a national police ministers meeting.

Vassallo gave the same briefing to the ministers. 'Well, Glasson is at the meeting and the bottom line is it's exactly the same briefing, there's not a word added extra,' says Vassallo. 'He just took it all in very professionally, he thanked me very much; I met them all.'

Glasson got back to Brisbane and was clearly disturbed by Vassallo's revelations, particularly in relation to Queensland. Vassallo received some inside intelligence that Glasson wanted to see some action. How could this, after the Moore fiasco, have happened on his watch without him knowing anything about it?

'And immediately Glasson came back [to Brisbane] he started to agitate, he said this is not right,' recalls Vassallo. 'This is when Jimmy Slade rang me up because Jimmy is still … at this stage he hadn't been attacked. But it was after that they figured out that Jimmy and I went to the course together [in Manly, Sydney]. Jimmy and I … he was passing information to me, we were talking. They probably started surveillance on him. And they would have looked at the [phone] numbers that he was ringing and of course the ABCI number was the one … and then there's my extension.'

Vassallo was right behind Jim Slade but he knew, in the world of corrupt police, how these things could go bad. 'Jim did the right thing, he knew he had to do the right thing and he knew he had a problem since September of 1984 when I met him,' recalls Vassallo. 'And he simply saw me as a lifeline because I was outside of the state.

'He quickly realised that I had the same opinions as he did. You know, the only way organised crime can survive is if good men do nothing, okay? I said to Jimmy my target will not be the Bellinos, my target will be the people protecting the Bellinos. Until we neutralise them we can't attack the Bellinos. So hence why, at all times, I didn't see the government as the enemy, I actually saw the police as the enemy because they were the obvious enemy.'

The way Vassallo viewed it, corrupt police had now approached Slade, and by that action they had become 'overt'. They were aware Slade was leaking intelligence to Vassallo. That put them both in danger. 'Suddenly I was thought to be a threat because Jim was supplying information to me. They could control Jim, but they couldn't control me and I had a fucking audience that was unbelievable, okay?' says

Vassallo. 'And once they became aware of these things, that gave me a certain amount of pull, so I could use it strategically.'

As for Slade, he knew precisely why the National Crime Authority could not get a foothold in Queensland, and why they were always repelled at the border. The Joke was by now so extensive that there was little in government or in the police force that it didn't touch.

'Murphy and Lewis wouldn't allow [the NCA in Queensland],' recalls Slade. 'Queensland was the only state in Australia where nothing was happening in relation to external agencies. Peter Vassallo knew there was something wrong. It was my meeting with Peter, where he took some of my stuff to the commissioner's meeting in Perth, where the shit really hit the fucking fan.

'I was hauled over the coals by [Inspector in charge of the Licensing Branch] Graeme Parker. "What the fuck are you doing giving bloody documents away?"'

Only later would Slade discover that the bulk of his reports and sensitive documents were all bundled together and kept in Parker's safe. 'They weren't going anywhere at all,' reflects Slade.

High Fliers

Despite these dark and potentially deadly machinations operating below the surface, Commissioner Terry Lewis took to his appointment diary with aplomb, his life a dance through the light of celebrity and power, as afforded by his position.

He lunched on the Gold Coast with a number of high fliers, including Minister Russ Hinze, Sir James Ramsay and Sir Edward Williams, where the Commissioner was called upon to offer a toast to the health and future of horse racing. Lewis also continued his convivial Friday afternoon drinks with Sir Edward Lyons in his office in Queen Street. In his ninth year as Commissioner, their tete-a-tetes over a few tumblers of Scotch had become almost solely political. As Lewis records in his diary: 'Saw Sir Edward Lyons and discussed Rothwells; Channel Nine; TAB Chairman; Carbine Club luncheon; apt. of next Governor; no early elections; redistribution; Expo leadership; Justices for Supreme Court and Sol[icitor]-Gen[eral] from outside.'

Lewis was now so much a part of the National Party fabric that it must have appeared natural to him to be in discussion about senior judicial appointments and election strategies. He also displayed his usual punctilious courtesy when it came to getting in touch with people who might be worth cultivating for the future. Following local council elections, Commissioner Lewis went out of his way to personally telephone the newly appointed mayors and deputy mayors of numerous shires.

On a quick trip to the Gold Coast, Lewis contacted Sea World employee Peter Doggett 're pass for John', presumably his son John Paul Lewis. During the same trip, he managed to squeeze in a meeting with high-powered real estate agent Max Christmas 're Japanese investing and visiting Queensland, but fear of crime'. Later, he went to drinks at Sir Edward Lyons' Gold Coast pad and joined guests such as Sir Thomas Covacevich and Justice Dormer (Bob) Andrews.

Back in Brisbane the following week, Lewis was invited to Government House on Fernberg Road to dine with the Duke and Duchess of Kent, Sir James and Lady Ramsay, Sir Richard Buckley and other notaries. As he strutted the stage, concerns were developing within Treasury that the financial management of the Police Department had devolved into a farce. The department was bleeding money through over-spending and a constant demand for staff and resources.

Treasury had had enough. A senior public servant in the Police Department said the spending was profligate and there was very little official accounting performed. 'I remember one day we got an absolute blast from Leo Hielscher [then Deputy Under Treasurer of Queensland] about the spending and lack of accountability,' he said. 'We were up until midnight trying to prepare an explanation in response to that, to get some sort of document together before the Cabinet meeting the following Monday. We put in all sorts of things to explain where the money had gone.'

Under each of his police ministers, Commissioner Lewis had, year after year, petitioned for a greater budget and more officers. It was an annual feature of his tenure. Yet it was clear to Treasury that there had been little fiscal scrutiny of the Police Department, and that the budget was out of control. Lewis had been in the top job for nine years, yet it appeared few in government were looking closely at the department's books.

Slade's Dark Night

At 11 p.m. on Friday 7 June, after both of the revealing conferences in Perth, Senior Sergeant Alan Barnes phoned Jim Slade at home and asked to meet. Slade agreed but his wife Chris wasn't keen.

Slade rang his boss Col Thompson to inform him of the call. The Slades then waited for Barnes to arrive but close to midnight the phone rang again. It was the police operator at the Beenleigh station telling Slade someone called Barnes was on the line for him.

Slade told the operator to tell Barnes he would meet him at the shopping-centre car park on the corner of Browns Plains Road and Chambers Flat Road. He knew there was bushland nearby where he could observe if it really was Barnes who wanted to meet. 'I was concerned for my safety and my family's safety,' Slade said.

Arming himself for the rendezvous, he told his wife: 'Ring Col Thompson and tell him, you know, where I've gone and if I'm not back within half an hour, three-quarters of an hour, ring him again and, you know, do something about where we've gone to.'

Barnes was there on his own. Slade recalls: 'I met with him and saw that he had been drinking very, very heavily and I saw that he was of no threat to me and my family in the state that he was in … Alan and I had a general conversation about the police force … I decided I would ask him to come back home to talk about the matter there; firstly, to alleviate my wife's concern about where I was and, secondly, so Col Thompson would know that he didn't have two dead police officers on his staff.'

At the Slades' home, the pair sat in the lounge room and talked. It was around 12.30 a.m.

Barnes eventually got around to the purpose of the meeting: 'Why did you go … why did you tell Col Thompson about the money I gave you?'

Slade denied he had told Thompson.

The two men talked about loyalty between police officers. Barnes became emotional. 'There was nothing in the money that I gave you,' he told Slade. 'I never asked you to do anything or not to do anything.' Barnes was drinking a combination of coffee and cask wine that he had brought with him; he drank it straight out of the foil bladder. He told Slade that the Bellinos only ran a few games in Brisbane and that there was nothing wrong with them. 'Why did you do it?' demanded Barnes. 'Why did you do it to me?'

At that, Chris Slade interjected and demanded of Barnes: 'Why the hell have you done it? Well, why have you done this to us?'

Slade had already made a decision that he would not record their conversation. He still considered Barnes a mate, and believed that to record him covertly would have been a form of betrayal. The emotional conversation between the two men ended after 3 a.m. and Barnes left.

In the end, the bribe money was returned to Barnes, who claimed he had given the money to Slade as a loan. No internal charges were laid. Barnes was transferred to Longreach. Slade remembers: 'I don't think Barnsey could ever kill anyone. We all had guns. Potentially there was a lot at stake, you just don't know. At that time I was very desperate and saw I had one chance of survival. We talked about what we were going to do. We didn't know who to turn to.'

Slade's problems, however, were only just beginning. He was sent down to the 'punishment' station at Beenleigh. 'The greatest thing was that every shit-stirrer against [Commissioner] Lewis was in Beenleigh,' he recalls. 'In town [the Brisbane CBD] you were treated as a dog. You had to be careful. I was fully armed all the time. They threatened me continually.

'I had to take certain action … if not, I'd be in gaol. It was the only time in my whole life that I have ever been extremely ultra-violent. From that point on nobody ever touched me again. It was probably a good move, unbeknown to me. I was being threatened by everyone.'

Slade still refuses to divulge the violent action he was involved in.

'As soon as I came down to Beenleigh I was told – these are the rules,' he says. 'The inspector said to me, "I don't know what you did down there, but congratulations. I don't want any bullshit. I don't want you to bring any skeletons in here. Work hard. You do not leave Beenleigh unless one of us is with you. You do not go into town by yourself." They really looked after me.'

Slade, one of the state's top investigators, knuckled down and policed his new beat, but it didn't last long. All of a sudden, a new detective was put in charge of Slade's unit and the whole thing changed. 'I was very lucky. I wasn't subject to the terrible things that happened, the first six months after I reported Barnsey. Fucking childish … all to protect this fucking Joke. Can you imagine if the effort that was put in[to] The Joke was put into policing …'

Slade's career was on the rocks, and the threats remained. In desperation, he contacted his old mate, Peter Vassallo, in Canberra.

'You're in deep shit, you've got no one. You know what they're capable of,' Vassallo told him.

'Yes, my arse is grass,' said Slade. 'In no time at all I'll be in court on a major crime, no doubt about it.' Slade feared being framed. 'From this stage on,' he said to Vassallo, 'if there are dead bodies found and I'm one of them, you'll know why there is. There's no way in the world I'm going to be charged on a criminal offence that I've been fitted up with. No way in the world.

'I'm going to be around for as fucking long as they are.'

I Know It Was Murder

Des Sturgess, the respected lawman and Director of Prosecutions, had been working on his inquiry into child sexual abuse, prostitution and pornography for about six months when he sat down with two working Brisbane prostitutes and heard their story. What they told him was so shocking that Sturgess felt impelled to alert the Queensland police to the allegations.

Detective Inspector R. Dargusch and Inspector B. Webb met with Sturgess on 17 June 1985. The legal eagle said he was greatly concerned over the dramatic growth in the number of escort agencies and massage parlours, and expressed the opinion that this was only possible if it had been allowed by the Licensing Branch.

Sturgess, in turn, provided the officers with two unsigned statements from prostitutes, Dawn and Jennifer, and arranged for the two officers to interview the women in his office. The revelations were astonishing – what both women provided, in essence, was a window into The Joke.

Dawn, 24, of North Road, Woodridge, had been a driver for the proprietor of an escort agency since January 1984. She told police his name was Alan Miller and he lived on Scenic Drive at Tweed Heads, just over the Queensland border. Dawn had driven cabs for three years and when she saw the position advertised in the *Daily Sun* newspaper she applied for the job and got it. Her job was to drive prostitutes to their jobs. She was paid on a commission basis – $5 for a half-hour job and $6 for an hour. Miller had three cars for such purposes, she said. She worked from 6 p.m. until the early hours of the following morning.

'Miller owns one agency located at 150 Logan Road, Buranda,' Dawn informed police. 'It was called "Just a Tough" and is now called "Champagne Escorts" … When I started there were 14 girls working there. I was also told that [the] Licensing [Branch] only permits six girls.'

Dawn would arrive for work at 5.30 p.m. and make sure the cars were clean and filled with fuel. She sat and watched television until the jobs came in. The cars had two-way radios. 'The fees charged were $70 [for a] half hour and $110 [for] one hour,' she told police. 'Prices went up and down with what Licensing said. Licensing fixed the prices. Prices never went any higher than $80 [for a] half hour and $120 [for] one hour. Bisexual acts were charged more.'

Dawn worked with Pepper, Alice, Jodi, Tammy, Debbi and others. 'The girls seemed to get younger in the last five or six months,' she said. 'The youngest girl [Jemera] who started work there was very tall and we became friends and shared a flat at Greenslopes. She told us she was 18 but her birthday came around in April and she said she was only 16. I later found out that police caught Jemera in possession of marihuana and took her to the Juvenile Aid Bureau … they found out she was 14 years old. She had worked for Miller for at least six months. I told Miller to get rid of her. He said no.

'There were three girls who we knew were underage. Licensing used to come to see identification of girls. [When] they didn't come as often, it was easier for Miller to turn a blind eye to the age of the girls.'

She said Miller had a high staff turnover rate. Many of the girls were not even paid. Miller got 50 per cent of each job. The working girls got the other half, but had to pay the drivers. Dawn gave a detailed account of the involvement of the police. 'Licensing Branch came around on a Tuesday night before 8 p.m.,' she said. 'They came two to three times a month. A phone call would be taken by the receptionist, sometimes the call came from Miller, warning him they were coming. Licensing [officers] would arrive. They would walk in, have a look around and leave.

'Licensing had an occasional phoney bust. They would ring Miller and tell him to have a girl ready tomorrow night. She would be booked into a room at the Southern Cross [Motel], Kangaroo Point. The girl goes there and is busted and charged with soliciting. Miller would pay the fine and the girl would be given $500 for taking the rap.'

It appeared, too, the Licensing Branch and uniformed officers used massage parlours as personal clubs, day or night. The code for officers from the branch was 'black'. Regular, uniformed officers were 'blue'.

'Licensing would walk in and say hello,' Dawn said. 'They would check that no one was running out. They would take a list of names. They would ask for identification and ask how business was. They would always have a beer, which was kept in the fridge for them, and then leave.

'Over a 14-month period I guess there were 30 to 40 times when uniform police would just arrive, pull up, come in, have a beer and stagger down the front stairs when they were on duty. They used to stay for hours and drink and flirt with the girls.'

Dawn also noticed an increase in drug use among the working girls, including heroin. 'I found a girl dead in a flat at Kangaroo Point,' Dawn recalled. 'Her name was Barbie [working name]. Her real name was Lisa.

'John, the manager, said he had had a phone call from Miller to say there was trouble at Lisa's place. We arrived at her place and the door fell open and she was dead – had been dead for three days. She was black and blue and fully dressed. She was 18 years of age. The cause of death was said to be a heroin overdose. We know that she had not touched heroin for months. She was into pills and marihuana. Lisa was to be a witness in the trial of … an agency owner. She had gone to the police and she told them she would give evidence.

'Police insist it was a heroin overdose. I know it was murder.'

As for Jennifer, she told police she had worked in the escort business for about five years. She reported that Miller's businesses were earning him up to $10,000 a week. 'Most men ring up and ask how old the youngest girl working there is,' Jennifer said. 'I would say 18'. They would ask if there were any girls who looked younger than 18. They would ask if there were any girls aged ten or 11. I would say "no" and they would say that they would ring where they knew they could get somebody that young. I would get five to six calls like this per night.'

She knew of girls as young as 14 working in the industry. She gave a withering description of the police, verifying Dawn's information. 'Licensing is a total joke,' Jennifer said. 'They come in once every four to six weeks for an official visit.

'They would make a false booking for one of the girls to go to a hotel and bring her back in their car. It was arranged for one of the girls to take the rap. There were standard questions asked and standard answers given. They would take a statement from the girl and leave, and business carried on as usual. They would come back the next night with the typed statement and the girl would sign it and after it went to court you would get a fine in the mail.'

Jennifer offered an alarming insight into Brisbane's vice industry. 'Hector [Hapeta] is violent towards girls,' she said. 'He owns parlours and escort agencies, Brett's Boys and Bubbles [Bath House].

'The organisation and Licensing [Branch] control the whole operation – prices, conditions etc. The members of the organisation all sit at the top table at Bubbles. None of them are under 45 and all of them look to be Greek or Italian. The organisation would control all massage parlours in Brisbane one way or another.'

Her statistics were wildly at odds with official police data. She said there were 'hundreds of prostitutes' who worked in Brisbane, with some parlours employing up to 20 girls per shift.

The scenarios as outlined by Dawn and Jennifer were refuted at length by Superintendent Graeme Parker – head of the Licensing [Branch] from April 1981 to August 1985 – in a formal written and signed statement. He said the average citizen could easily be confused by the complicated legislation surrounding charges in relation to escort agencies, parlours and prostitutes.

Parker said the Licensing Branch Escort Staff had to visit escort agencies 'to collate information on girls employed there so their movements from Agency to Agency or Agency to Massage Parlours could be monitored'. To this, he added most emphatically: 'The Licensing Branch has nothing at all to do with how these areas of prostitution operate or the prices or conditions applicable. Licensing Branch personnel have the responsibility of collating all available information and the enforcement of those statutes relating to prostitution.'

In the end, Dargusch and Webb concluded their investigation into the stories of Dawn and Jennifer: 'Our investigation failed to reveal any evidence to substantiate any impropriety on the part of the Licensing Branch.'

Revolting by Community Standards

Paul John Breslin's trial for indecently assaulting Aboriginal teenager Ricky Garrison finally came before the courts in July 1985, after numerous adjournments. He was represented by Shane Herbert, QC, known among his legal colleagues as 'Sid Vicious', after the member of the 1970s punk rock band the Sex Pistols.

Breslin, 36, by now unemployed of 30 Jarrup Street, Jindalee, was charged with intent to facilitate the commission of an indictable offence by administering to Garrison a stupefying drug, namely Quinalbarbitone; that on 19 January 1984, in an apartment in

Coronation Towers in Auchenflower, he indecently dealt with Garrison, a boy under the age of 17 years; and that he unlawfully assaulted Garrison and did him bodily harm.

Breslin pleaded not guilty.

The exhibits tendered included a drawing of the accused's unit, photographs, a brown-painted baton, the complainant's jeans, shirt and shoes, two sets of handcuffs with keys, samples of Garrison's urine and blood, some sofa vacuuming's, the rear seat of Breslin's Ford Fairlane, pubic hair and a photograph of Breslin's press pass. He was found guilty of the second two charges.

During the trial, the arresting officer, Peter Gallagher, having been transferred out of the city to Beenleigh, south of the CBD, was ordered by his superiors to stay away from the trial. After giving his evidence he wanted to return to the trial to see the outcome of the case. He was told to keep out of the court.

Gallagher recalls: 'So I said – you're interfering with the course of justice, aren't you? I'm going on my own day off and I'm going to ask the prosecutor if I can stand up before the judge and relate that you forbid me to go to the court. So they had to back off.'

Justice Paul De Jersey delivered his judgement to Breslin. 'You have been found guilty of serious offences, one of induced dealing with a boy under the age of 17 years and the other of assault occasioning bodily harm,' De Jersey told the court. 'I intend to sentence you on the basis that the act of indecent dealing was not carried out with the consent of the complainant. That is clearly the proper approach because of the allied conviction for assault occasioning bodily harm.

'Further, I consider it proper for me to assume, notwithstanding the not guilty verdict on count one, that the jury accepted the boy's evidence that he was taken to the unit against his will. The acts carried out by you, on the evidence, which led to the conviction are revolting by any ordinary community standard, especially I refer to the placing of the penis in the complainant's mouth and the subsequent masturbation and ejaculation over his body. There was a similarly deplorable allied assault to the inner leg of the complainant with the baton.

'The fact that the complainant had a stained history before the events does not lead me to the view that I should reduce the sentence which I would otherwise impose. The law, providing that such conduct amounts to offences, is for the benefit of all children, sullied or innocent.

'I accept that for the present purposes there is nothing particularly significant in your criminal history. I also accept that you have in the past made a worthwhile contribution to some aspects of community life. On the other hand, the commission of offences of this character has to be deterred. The sentence I impose must reflect the obvious concern of the community that this sort of thing must not occur. I consider that a fine or a community service order would be an inappropriate response by this Court to the sort of conduct of which you have been found guilty.

'In the respect of the count of indecent dealing I imprison you with hard labour for a period of two years. In the respect of the count of assault occasioning bodily harm I imprison you with hard labour for a period of 12 months. The sentence will be served concurrently.'

Breslin still declares his innocence. 'I couldn't believe what had happened to me … that I'd been through all that, that it was still me, like watching someone else. It's very hard to describe,' he says.

'You're a high flier and you're doing all these things and you can pick up a phone and access anyone, and all of a sudden you're dirt and no one wants to talk to you.'

Breslin says he was a naive kid from Gladstone who didn't know how to handle the big city. '[I was the] first-born child with bonny blue eyes and all that stuff … I was the boy from the bush made good, and then had the shit kicked out of me,' he reflects. 'I've had a rich life in some respects, but [made a] poor choice in compadres …'

Alpha

Sergeant Peter Vassallo of the Australian Bureau of Criminal Intelligence (ABCI) in Canberra finally started compiling his Project Alpha report in July 1985. Ultimately, the 56-page report would contain a special section titled 'Queensland Crime Group'.

Vassallo had never heard of the Bellino family of Queensland before he started his investigations. The Sunshine State was not his turf. So he began to test the information he was receiving. 'I used their names with absolutely nothing to go on ... this was when I decided to set up my counter-intelligence operation by myself, and started flagging the name to see what the response would be,' he says. 'Because if they were protected people and special people, as Jimmy [Slade] was saying they were, then if I started mentioning them ... I should get a response.

'If they weren't and I got yawns, well, maybe Jim is not on the line. So that was one way of testing and validating Jim as an informant, if I can use that term. Because I didn't know who the fuck the Bellinos were ... what went on in other states was all news to me.'

Vassallo's report was done by the end of July but the bureau didn't want to release it straightaway. The report nominated 21 individuals or 'targets' involved in the production and sale of Indian hemp in Australia. The ABCI hierarchy, however, questioned the age of the targets – they were too old, they were all pensioners. Could this be true?

'Boss,' Vassallo said to his superior. 'You're an Assistant Commissioner, yeah? You've got a year or two before you go off on a pension. People with power and influence, yeah, they're fucking pensioners, they're not the young Turks on the streets.'

Vassallo was undeterred. 'There was a lawyer who worked for the National Crime Authority [NCA] who lived in Canberra,' says Vassallo. 'Every Monday he'd drive to Sydney and every Friday he'd come back for the weekend. And Justice Stewart was the guy that I dealt with there [at the NCA] and briefed ... and he was the one that wanted it. He was driving the NCA thing.

'This guy living in Canberra, he called into the ABCI and asked if the report had been approved for release, could he pick it up? I said the director hasn't released it yet.'

The lawyer badgered Vassallo for weeks. He asked for an unofficial copy. In the end Vassallo showed him his own personal copy. 'I had my own copy of the bloody thing because I was the author of it,' he remembers. 'I wanted him to know and see it because I knew he'd go and report back [to Justice Stewart] you see.'

About six weeks after Vassallo completed the report, Justice Stewart personally telephoned the Director of the ABCI [Alan Watt]. Robin Chalker, the Deputy Director, called Vassallo and ordered him to the Director's office on the sixth floor. 'Up I go and the Director is almost speechless and Robin is there, his face is flushed,' recalls Vassallo. 'He [Chalker] said, "Mr Watt here has just had a phone call from Justice Stewart from the National Crime Authority, he said he's threatened Watt that if the report isn't on his desk by Wednesday he'd ... have the ABCI shut down."'

'They knew I was stonewalling, that I would not agree to any changes and I was in some heated arguments in various rooms. I was a sergeant of police ... the author of the thing, I was the guy who went around the country; I was the guy that mentioned all the games. And now we've got, you know, people who are administrators ... wanted to drop the thing because of legal fucking reasons, I thought no, I'm not playing this fucking game. Kick me out of the bureau if you must but no, I won't answer it.'

Vassallo asked them: Did they really believe that a sergeant of police could influence a Supreme Court judge to ring the Director of the ABCI and threaten to have him closed down by going to Prime Minister Bob Hawke?

The report was on Stewart's desk the following Wednesday. 'Stewart wanted it because he wanted to go to Brisbane and lobby up there and have it under his wing to get the Attorney-General to sign off the special reference [to give the NCA operational presence in Queensland],' says Vassallo. 'The special reference under the Act allowed the NCA to use coercive powers. And it allowed them to do telephone intercepts; it allowed them to do covert surveillance.

'And of course this is a Commonwealth-funded agency, you know, it's a national body and it's now acting independently of the Queensland or a state police force. It acts independently from the government and it has all its powers coming from the special reference, not from local government. Right?

'So when you're thinking of constitutional law and all the rest of it, who is in fucking charge and who is running the joint right? From Joh's perspective … you're a disciple of the fucking devil, the Labor Party is in charge … so it was purely political. It had nothing to do with the traditional supporting or not supporting organised crime, it was a political statement that Lewis was saying to the Attorney-General – run these bastards out of town. And that's exactly what happened. They were run out of town.'

Once the report arrived in the offices of state police commissioners, it elicited an immediate response from Queensland. 'There were three representatives from Queensland who came down,' says Vassallo. 'And when the list of targets was nominated by the National Crime Authority, they read them out and there was, you know, everyone got a guernsey as they say, except Tasmania.

'The Bellino brothers were the target names in question and suddenly the spokesman for the Queensland representatives challenged it.'

Assistant Commissioner (Crime) Graeme Parker, the Queensland Police Force's liaison officer with the ABCI, attended the bureau's briefings and received information bulletins. In addition, he was liaison officer with the NCA and the Australian Federal Police. 'Parker and Lewis had access to everything that was going on in Australia,' says Vassallo. 'Those guys had access to all the information.'

The Queensland representatives said the Alpha report had relied on Slade's Operation Trek report, which they claimed had since been discredited and was no longer valid. Vassallo told them he hadn't relied just on the Trek report. 'They actually went there and they sought to attack it [the Alpha report] with a view to having those three [Bellino] names removed from the target list,' says Vassallo.

'I told them that Queensland wasn't the source of the information, [that] there were other agencies involved, and they were dumbstruck. And of course there was fucking silence in the room. I told them the names on that report, the names of the Bellinos in that report, were as valid as every other name.'

The impact of the bond between Slade and Vassallo had been underestimated by Slade's superiors. While the Operation Trek report had been re-written and dismissed by senior Queensland police, some of its contents mirrored Vassallo's research. And while Slade was being lured into The Joke by Alan Barnes, possibly because of the enormous knowledge of the drug trade Slade had accrued through the Trek investigation, Vassallo had completed his own sensitive report.

Vassallo was methodical. For years he'd been gathering details on people arrested and charged in relation to Indian hemp plantations dating back to 1974. He discovered at least 250 such cases, and by careful deduction established that 15 Italian family surnames had major connections to the Australian marihuana industry.

Vassallo would eventually conclude: 'Antonio Sergi ... residing in Griffith, New South Wales, is identified as having the most association links to persons arrested on plantations. The second most important person identified using this analytical method ... is Luigi Pochi ... of Melba ACT.'

A further purpose of the analysis, was to establish not only a relationship between families and persons arrested on plantations, but to test the theory that solid family relationships existed within this Italian crime group. 'From an analysis of inter-marriage and blood relationships it can be shown that all of the 15 Italian families except [one] are interrelated.'

Vassallo did something else that was utterly unique. He put an estimate on the number of plantations across the country from year to year, and the estimated street value of the drugs. For 1983, for example, he estimated the number of crops at a staggering 46, with a net worth of $376.3 million, given the average price for a kilogram of Indian hemp was valued at $1000.

He also produced some hair-raising data. Murders with links to the industry and Italian crime families occurred by and large on an annual basis between April and August – the non-growing season. This was leading up to and including harvest time, when the drugs were packaged and transported, and the money started rolling in. Disputes were commonplace. Vassallo also concluded about the murder zone: 'One reason for this could be that the persons responsible do not want police investigations being pursued during the growing season.'

This made complete sense in relation to the slaughter of drug dealer William (Paul) Clarke, 36, and his Latvian wife Grayvyda (Maria) in their house off Pinnacle Road in the tiny hamlet of Julatten, Far North Queensland, on 24 May 1981. Doctors later recovered 132 pellets from the lower right-hand side of William Clarke's chest, and 80 from Grayvyda's body. The killer or killers splashed fuel around the house and torched it, the fire so intense it melted metal and burned off the heads and limbs of the Clarkes.

The murder was investigated by a team from the Mareeba CIB, under the direction of regional superintendent Tony Murphy. The double murder remained dormant until Vassallo started connecting a few dots on behalf of Alpha.

Little attention had been paid to the Queensland cultivation scene but Vassallo was convinced the Clarke killings had Italian underworld connections.

Vassallo would later conclude:

As a result of the CLARKE murder inquiry, documentation was submitted by Queensland Police, which was used by the ABCI to analyse the organised criminal activities of persons in Queensland and their involvement in the commercial cultivation and distribution of Indian hemp in that State.

The main objective of the analysis was to identify the associates of CLARKE and his wife prior to their murder on their property at Pinnacle Road, Julatten, Queensland in 1981 thus exposing the extent of William CLARKE'S drug dealing.

Analysis shows that CLARKE and others had a drug oriented association with the BELLINO group.

Vassallo exposed a number of companies who used to launder the enormous profits of the drug trade. He also identified Clarke's many associates, including drug dealer Terrence Sichter.

He added: 'Antonio SERGI makes business trips to Queensland to visit his brother-in-law Antonio PALUMBO in Mareeba. In May 1981 SERGI was at Mareeba at the time of the CLARKE murders. Unsubstantiated information has, in the past, nominated the visits by SERGI resulting in transportation of Indian hemp to the southern area of Australia.'

Vassallo, working long hours in Canberra, had established a compelling portrait of the marihuana trade across the country, and the Mr Bigs who controlled it. A copy of the top secret report went to every state police commissioner in Australia.

The reaction to Alpha in Queensland was extraordinary. But not in the way anyone expected.

Slings and Arrows

On Monday 29 July, just as the Alpha report was set to be released, Commissioner Terry Lewis travelled down to Canberra for some meetings with staff of the Australian Bureau of Criminal Intelligence (ABCI). He checked into the Capital Motor Inn, and the next morning was in the ABCI offices in London Circuit for another meeting of the management committee to discuss computers and costs.

He then travelled out to the 'AFP College, Weston', for a briefing on outlaw motorcycle gangs and organised crime 'involving La Cosa Nostra'. Later that night, he attended a cocktail function hosted by Jim Sturgis, 'FBI rep in SW Pacific'.

After an early morning flight the next day, he was back at his desk in headquarters by 9 a.m. That morning, Lewis 'advised snr officers re Canberra briefings'.

On Monday 5 August, Lewis telephoned Director of the ABCI Alan Watt 're presentation of "Alpha" project to Cabinet'. In short, Peter Vassallo was being summonsed to Queensland to give Cabinet, including Premier Joh Bjelke-Petersen, a confidential briefing on his cannabis report.

While Glasson had been shocked by the briefing Vassallo gave in Perth earlier in the year, the Police Minister may have impressed on the Premier the importance of the Alpha report and Queensland's role in a national drug industry.

Vassallo says the request to address Cabinet stemmed from Lewis's call on the morning of 5 August. 'Lewis rang up saying that the Premier had directed me to come up after I gave that briefing to the Police Ministers' Council. He wanted to hear it too,' recalls Vassallo. 'Of course, there was no way in the world you would ask any questions. It was simply, "Yes, sir."'

That done, Lewis had other things to focus his attention on for the rest of the month. He saw Sir Sydney Schubert 're Honours and awards'. He farewelled Detective Superintendent T.J. Wightman on retirement, who told him 'I am the best Comm. he has worked under' and 'Force is free of any organised crime'.

He had a small telephone spat with Australian Federal Police head Major-General Ron Grey. 'Phoned Comm. R. Grey re difference of opinion re arrest of J.K. Brook at Ringwood, our Snr Police say AFP not truthful, Mr Grey said his police "pissed off" with some of our Police.'

And of course he had another annual Ekka to attend and perform official duties, including inspecting the mounted police. He was present for the opening of the third session of the 44th state parliament, then stayed for afternoon tea. He recorded in his diary: 'Premier said he would submit my name on Honours recommendation but I must maintain secrecy.' Later, Lewis moved on to Police Minister Glasson's parliamentary suite for drinks.

In five days' time, however, ABCI analyst Sergeant Peter Vassallo was due to tell local politicians that Queensland, despite its claim to a unique separateness from the rest of Australia, was part of a national network of illicit drugs worth hundreds of millions of dollars. After years of repelling outside crime investigation authorities, why had Queensland suddenly rolled out the red carpet for an interloper like Vassallo, and one bearing grim news at that?

The Confidential Cabinet Briefing

On the second last weekend of August, 1985, Commissioner Lewis, accompanied by his wife Hazel, had a whistlestop tour of Townsville, and Quilpie in western Queensland, along with his Minister Bill Glasson. In Quilpie, Glasson opened the annual district show.

On Saturday 24 August, they returned to Brisbane in the government jet. Lewis then spent his day of rest reading '32 Journals, Reviews and Gazettes'. It was a normal end to the weekend.

The next morning, however, Lewis was in his office at 6.40 a.m. That was relatively early by his own exacting standards, and may have been for two reasons. The first, according to his diary, was that his son Tony had been 'arrested U.I.L. [Under Influence Liquor], 4.02 a.m., .17%'.

The other reason was the arrival of Peter Vassallo of the ABCI, in Brisbane to brief Bjelke-Petersen and his Cabinet on the growing menace of drugs, and the implications for Queensland.

Vassallo had arrived in Brisbane on the Sunday afternoon as Lewis was reading his gazettes. He was greeted at the airport by some Queensland police, and on the way to his hotel in Wickham Terrace, Vassallo's hosts treated him to a meal and some beers at the Breakfast Creek Hotel. The cheery party then moved on to Brothers Rugby League Club at The Grange. Vassallo was alert to any dangers, despite the camaraderie.

'Jimmy [Slade] told me to watch myself because the usual modus operandi [MO] was that I could be set up there with someone coming to my [hotel] room. Then that person, who is a druggie, alleges that I've made an offer to them and all that sort of stuff. He warned me about that. It was an MO for Queenslanders.'

Vassallo had with him a single piece of equipment that he used for all of his briefings – a large map. The top secret map had been loaded onto Vassallo's flight from Canberra only after all passengers and luggage were on board. The loading was supervised by Vassallo and an Australian Federal Police officer.

There was a similar procedure on his arrival in Brisbane. 'The plane would land at my destination, the AFP would come up the gangway, the doors would open, everyone would be told to sit in their seats, and my name would be called out,' says Vassallo. 'I would go to the front with the AFP copper and we'd go downstairs, round the side where the hold was, and ... we had to supervise the opening of the hold – they weren't allowed to open it until we were there. And then the first thing that came out would be this tube that would be given to me and I'd be escorted through the bloody bizzo into a car to wherever I had to go.'

The map was a tool vital to Vassallo's presentation. It was also highly dangerous – Vassallo's research was underpinned by a long list of interconnected murders across the country. Here, the dots were beginning to come together.

'What was important for the briefing that I gave was to show the geographic distribution of where the marihuana plantations were,' recalls Vassallo. 'I had four PVC plastic overlays and the old trick of having, you know, you bring down one on top of the map to show something ... then you bring over the next one which adds to the first, gives it more meaning. And finally the last one. The map would have been six foot long and about eight foot wide ... a picture tells a thousand words ...'

On the day of Vassallo's presentation, Lewis recorded in his diary: 'Saw Sgt. Peter Vassello [sic], ABCI re briefing for Cabinet.'

Vassallo was picked up at his hotel that morning and taken the short distance to Commissioner Lewis's office at headquarters. The two men were, of course, familiar with each other, given that Vassallo had conducted the confidential briefing before Lewis a few months earlier in Perth at the ABCI management conference.

'... so here I am thinking I'm going to the fucking lion's den,' Vassallo recalls. 'Because at this stage I'm convinced that he's a crook and there's a whole bunch of crooks and I've got to play this game. And so I've gone up into his office.

'He [Lewis] was very courteous, he was very professional. He said, "Look, have you met Sir Joh?"

'I said I'd seen him many times on television.

'He said, "He's a nice man, don't be overawed by him in any way." He said, "He'll listen, he may ask you some questions ... just answer honestly."

'Lewis was definitely trying to put me at ease.'

Lewis and Vassallo then headed for Parliament House in George Street in Lewis's official Commissioner's vehicle. 'I requested to make sure we go early enough for me to verify everything was set up correctly, which he acceded to,' says Vassallo. 'I went in to set up the room … and when I was satisfied … I waited outside for Joh to turn up.

'Joh was introduced and he walked in and we followed in behind. When we walked in the door – Lewis, [Graeme] Parker, [and] a third, all in white shirts … here was a third senior police officer of a similar rank to Parker.'

Parker, former head of the Licensing Branch since 1982 had, exactly a week earlier, been promoted to Superintendent Third Class. Within five months he would be elevated to Assistant Commissioner.

Incredibly, Lewis and his trusted men were permitted to sit in on the confidential Cabinet meeting. 'They stood on the wall facing the Cabinet table and I was to their right,' recalls Vassallo. 'So when I was giving my briefing, basically I positioned myself with my back to them … and I always focused on Joh Bjelke-Petersen. I never focused on anyone else. I'm briefing to one person, I'm convincing one person, that's it.'

The briefing ended. Vassallo had displayed, on his large map, the names of the Bellinos as being associated with drug production in Queensland. He says there were no questions from Cabinet about the Bellinos. None of the government ministers had any queries, not even Police Minister Bill Glasson. Nor did Premier Joh Bjelke-Petersen.

It was a deliberate strategy on Vassallo's part. 'I left the impression that there was really not much going on in Queensland,' he says. '[It was] very sketchy information because I knew who was listening out on the left, they needed to hear that. They needed to understand that I wasn't a threat. And that's exactly what I was doing consciously. I wanted to fulfil the task that I was given in that a summons had been issued for my appearance. I appeared your worship, right? So I just told them things they needed … they wanted … to hear.'

After the briefing, Vassallo was taken back to headquarters where he was asked to conduct the briefing again, this time to senior police. Vassallo says he was taken to an auditorium where hundreds of officers were waiting. He had not been expecting to brief the top echelon of the Queensland Police Force. 'I do recall seeing Parker and a whole row of white shirts, you know, the trumps at the front,' recalls Vassallo. 'And I remember ... because I'd met Parker – he'd come to the bureau [ABCI] to be briefed – and I knew he, with a couple of others, was trying to change certain information that I'd put on the database [back in Canberra].

'[I went] straight in to the auditorium where everyone has been summonsed and ... I walk on stage, and it was an elevated stage, everyone is there ... it did cause a buzz ... the fact that here was a guy that was from out of town, at an agency that's only been going two years and suddenly here they are talking about the fucking Bellino brothers. You know, these were untouchables. I didn't appreciate that, I just didn't realise and, of course, I didn't give a fuck – that was all part of a test.'

Vassallo and his map were driven back to the airport. The officers escorting him stopped, as was the custom, for a drink on the way. He made an excuse that he had a lot of things to do and wouldn't be imbibing. '[I] got on a plane and went home and I was glad to get home,' he says. 'The thing that worried me the most was now a lot of Queensland police officers, including some of the senior ones other than Lewis, could put a face to [my] name.

'They'd heard the name but now they had a face.'

An Overdue Arrest

While Peter Vassallo was relieved to be back on home turf in Canberra after his Queensland adventure, the impact of his Project

Alpha report and briefings had an immediate impact. In his report, Vassallo had gone into great detail about the shotgun murders of marihuana grower William (Paul) Clarke, 36, and his wife Grayvyda Marie Clarke, 35, in their home at Julatten, near Mareeba, on 24 May 1981. Both were blasted to death in their bed and their house had been torched.

Robert 'Dave' Berrick, a North Queensland hippie with a record of petty drug offences, knew Paul and Grayvyda well. Berrick had grown marihuana plantations with Clarke at Idlewild Station. Some of the crops were worth in excess of $1 million. Indeed, Berrick owned the property at Julatten where the Clarkes were murdered. Berrick says Clarke had a premonition of his own death. 'He told me that he'd seen it, that he wasn't going to live too long,' Berrick remembers. 'He sensed the danger. He knew what was coming. The big one. Paul told me he was dealing with the Mafia. I kept out of it.'

At the time of the murders Berrick had initially been a suspect. Detectives had flown to Sydney where Berrick was renting a small flat in Elizabeth Bay in the city's inner-east. Berrick was taken to a local police station and interviewed. 'They said I did it,' recalls Berrick. 'I told them – "I think you blokes did it". They took me back up to North Queensland for a look around. I told them everything. After all, Paul and his wife had been murdered, there was not much point keeping secrets.'

Alpha painted a dark and dangerous picture of the drug trade in Queensland – something that would have been news to many of Premier Bjelke-Petersen's members of Cabinet. How could this have been allowed to develop in God-fearing Queensland?

Vassallo wrote:

Invariably, violence is associated with any major organised crime group and the police investigation into the murder [of the Clarkes] has exposed a major organised crime network which has flourished in that area for over a decade. Companies have been incorporated to hide the movement and acquisition of the vast profits generated.

From the police inquiries conducted during the CLARKE investigation it became quite apparent that many people in the northern Queensland area were aware of the activities of CLARKE and his associates.

Vassallo's conclusions certainly pointed towards the need for a more thorough investigation that would probably have to involve Federal authorities. It was the slaughter of the Clarkes that had opened a small window into this murderous business, and the tentacles that stemmed from it reached across Australia.

Incredibly, just 16 days after Vassallo's briefing to Cabinet and the top rung of Commissioner Lewis's force, police raided a farm north of the Daintree River, between Cooktown and Cairns. They took possession of rifles and hunting knives, and arrested drug dealer Terrence John Sichter, 31, of Gold Hill, the same man mentioned on page 44 of Vassallo's report as a drug dealer who had dealt with William (Paul) Clarke.

Sichter protested his innocence and told them, as he had years earlier, he knew nothing of the Clarke murders. He was duly arrested and charged. Sichter entered no plea and was remanded in custody.

Vassallo was astonished. He believed that by charging Sichter, the Queensland police had successfully deterred any national agencies from further investigating the links between Clarke and other major figures in the drug trade in, at the very least, North Queensland and New South Wales.

The matter was now before the courts. The Queensland police had bolted the door.

Death of an Auditor

In the winter of 1985 the acerbic Brisbane *Sunday Mail* journalist Marion Smith wrote a four-sentence item in her weekly 'Exit Lines' column that, on the surface, appeared innocuous. The state had just celebrated Queensland Day on 6 June to coincide with the date Queen Victoria signed the Letters Patent in 1859, formally granting Queensland its separation from the colony of New South Wales.

Smith's piece was a tasty tidbit of gossip about the Queensland Day Committee.

> Well, didn't Queensland Day go off with a flourish? Which brought some relief to those in the public service bureaucracy responsible for approving expenses. Seems they retrospectively approved a swag of expenditure incurred earlier this year by one public servant on an overseas trip supposedly in relation to this year's Queensland Day activities. Nice to know it was all worthwhile.

The Queensland Day Committee had been formed by Bjelke-Petersen's Cabinet on 17 March 1980, as a way of recognising the historic moment and promoting Queensland achievement. Its secretary in the early days was Judith Callaghan, wife of the Premier's former media unit hot shot and advisor Allen Callaghan, who had left his press role in 1979 and entered the lofty ranks of the public service.

By 1985, Allen was Under Secretary of the Department of Arts, National Parks and Sport, as well as Chairman of the Queensland Film Corporation and a member of the Queensland Day Committee. His second wife, Judith, would become the committee's executive officer.

Smith's cheeky column earned a rebuttal from the Chair of the Queensland Day Committee, Sir David Longland, in the form of a letter to the newspaper three weeks later. The identity of the jet-setting public servant had remained unknown, until Sir David's letter.

'The Committee is most concerned with the unfounded innuendos in this item,' Sir David retorted. He said no public servant incurred expenditure on an overseas trip, and that the staff of the committee were on contract. 'The Executive Director, Mrs Judith Callaghan, is a consultant,' he continued. 'If the item purports to refer to her travel overseas in February, this was at her own expense, accompanying her husband who was on official business. Mrs Callaghan did not seek, or receive, expenses from the Committee even though she could have.'

He said the committee's accounts were all audited by the Auditor-General 'in accordance with normal Public Service procedures ... The Queensland Day Committee seeks a retraction of this item which reflects adversely on it and its hard-working staff,' Sir David stated.

This rebuke, in turn, caught the attention of Ross Goodhew, an accountant for the Department of the Auditor-General. He began an investigation, and discovered discrepancies. Goodhew found that about $40,000 had been transferred from the Queensland Film Corporation to the Queensland Day Committee.

'During my audits of the Queensland Film Corporation and Arts Department I thought long and hard about the potential political damage to the ... Bjelke-Petersen Government and the careers of Allen and Judith Callaghan,' Goodhew later recalled. 'After a lot of soul-searching I decided to pursue the Callaghans and anyone else involved to the fullest extent.'

He was given two days to complete the audit. It would ultimately take ten months. Goodhew conceded that it was Longland's brusque and dismissive letter, published in the *Sunday Mail* on 30 June, which triggered his investigation.

'In Longland's vigorous defence he said that Judith had met all her bills herself ... I found that letter most interesting when I discovered her bills were, in fact, either met by the QFC [Queensland Film Corporation] or the Queensland Tourist and Travel Corporation.

'That discovery led me to investigate transfers of money totalling $40,000 to the QDC [Queensland Day Committee] purely on the basis of letters of request from the QDC director [Judith] to the QFC director [Allen] and approved by the latter.

'With the help of auditor Pat Gallagher, I discovered the $40,000 had been deposited into passbook accounts accessed solely by Judith as signatory. I also found that Sir David Longland and other members of the QDC had no knowledge of these accounts.'

Goodhew needed to confirm that the money transferred from the QFC had hit the Premier's Department accounts. He assigned Hank Coblens, 32, then a Premier's Department auditor, to check. Coblens found no trace of the money.

Goodhew reported this to Auditor-General Vince Doyle, and it was decided that Coblens would conduct a thorough audit of the Queensland Day Committee. This was dangerous territory. This young and ambitious auditor was being asked to go through the books of the Premier's Department. Also, Allen Callaghan's reputation within the government was powerful. He was close to the Premier, whom he had always referred to as 'Chief'.

Hendricus (Hank) Coblens was highly regarded as an auditor, and had what would later be described as 'an extremely high and finely tuned sense of pride in his work'. He had recently been involved in the audit of the Dairymen's Organisation State Council report. He asked in writing for clarification of the legal basis for the Queensland Day Committee audit and that detailed instructions to him as auditor be fully documented 'in order that I can ensure that my actions, in such a sensitive situation, are totally in conformity with the directions from my senior officers'.

Coblens got to work. Despite being well regarded around the offices of the Auditor-General down in Edward Street, he had no real close friends among his colleagues. 'He was a very meticulous person, straight as an arrow,' says contemporary Pat Gallagher. 'He was married [to Mary] and lived out at Belmont. He wasn't one of the boys. You'd take ten blokes out west or to the islands up north [for the purposes of audits] and it was like a rugby league tour. Hank didn't fit into that culture.'

Another colleague says: 'People in the office were very, very impressed with him, both professionally and personally. He came from a very serious minded Dutch family. He was a perfectionist.'

Auditor-General Vince Doyle – who had only been in the position since December 1984 – later reported that sponsorship payments to the Queensland Day Committee from the Queensland Film Corporation funds 'had not been brought to account through the official accounts of the Premier's Department'.

Coblens interviewed Judith Callaghan and then compiled his evidence. On 2 October, he told Goodhew that he planned to present his findings to Judith Callaghan the next day. She duly protested her innocence. It was believed, too, that Coblens met with her husband Allen Callaghan later that same day. (Mary Coblens would later state that her husband got home late that evening and that he was angry and upset about something.)

On Friday 4 October, several co-workers noticed a change in Coblens' demeanour. He phoned Barrie Rollason, who had worked with him on the Queensland Dairymen's Organisation State Council audit along with Pat Gallagher.

Rollason was concerned for Coblens' welfare. He was with Gallagher when the call came through.

'What do we do?' Rollason asked.

'Hank might do himself in,' Gallagher said.

Rollason was shocked. He immediately called Vince Doyle, seeking advice. Doyle, in turn, phoned Police Commissioner Terry Lewis later that morning. Lewis, with personal assistant Inspector Greg Early, headed out to the police academy that morning on business then returned to his office. He noted in his diary: 'Vince Doyle, A.G., phoned re Hank

Coblens, auditor, missing and probably suicidal.'

Coblens telephoned his wife at about 1.30 p.m. that day, and then disappeared. The next morning, he was found dead in his white Mazda which was parked in Clay Gully Road at Victoria Point, west of the CBD and by the bay. He had suffered a single gunshot wound to the head from a .308 Parker-Hale Midland rifle.

He also left a note: 'Dear Mary, Sorry but I made a blunder. I'm too disgusted with myself. It's no one's fault but my own. Don't blame the people at work. It's really I who am flawed. I love you. Hank.'

Rumours went around the Auditor-General's office that Coblens had been threatened from 'high up' over the Callaghan audit. There was another story that he was last seen dumping documents into a street bin not far from the Executive Building in George Street.

Allen Callaghan says he can't remember meeting Coblens prior to the death of the auditor. 'I don't recall dealing with him directly,' Callaghan says. 'If I had contact with him, it would have been fairly brief. If I met Coblens – and I possibly did – it would have been a fairly brief meeting.'

Coblens was cremated at the Mount Thompson Memorial Gardens in Nursery Road, Holland Park. His plaque was inscribed simply and efficiently: *In Loving Memory / of Hendricus Coblens / Who Passed Away/ 5–10–85 / 32 Years.*

Good Knight

Police Commissioner Terence Murray Lewis, the little boy from Ipswich with a fractured family, the young man who had left school aged 12 and later, by force of will, earned himself a university degree, and the ambitious police constable who had become Commissioner less than 27 years after he was sworn into the force, was now of an age where he was thinking about his legacy.

Of course, he had to run the police force day to day, but his position was so elevated, his friends the cream of society, the rich and powerful, that it must have been a constantly difficult transition, from administrator dealing with police transfers, departmental paperwork and correspondence, to performing his ceremonial function which took him into Government House, Parliament House, art galleries, boardrooms and aboard yachts.

The highly organised Lewis, however, handled it with aplomb. His diaries expose a man constantly on the move, darting from place to place as dictated by his full appointment schedule. For any ordinary citizen, it would have been a punishing job. But he soldiered on, working through everything from a bout of winter influenza to family problems, year in, year out.

But by the end of 1985, he had his eye on life after the police force, and what he might leave behind. Plans for his new family home at 12 Garfield Drive, Bardon, were well advanced, and so too was his hugely ambitious decision to build a new Queensland Police Headquarters in Roma Street, around the corner from the old digs in Makerston Street. It seemed no coincidence that Lewis's plans for both buildings were unfolding at the same time. The house in Bardon would shelter Lewis and his wife Hazel comfortably for the rest of their lives, and for decades into the future Brisbane's population would look at the new headquarters building and know it was the brainchild of Commissioner Lewis.

This was the state of play as the end of 1985 neared. And come November, a man with a more than keen interest in ceremony and ritual, Lewis approached, as he did each year, the anniversary of his appointment as Police Commissioner. This particular anniversary would have about it a secret electric charge.

The month heralded the annual merry-go-round of Christmas parties for Lewis, as well as lunches and dinners with old friends. On Thursday 7 November, he invited several of them to 'luncheon' at police headquarters. '... with senior officers and Mr Justice Angelo Vasta; Hon. Don Lane; Ron Richards, Sun Newspapers; Ron McConnell, McConnell Holdings Ltd; Kevin Driscoll, National Homes; Barry Maxwell, Belfast Hotel; and Reg Tegg, Petrie Hotel'.

Still, after all these years, Lewis could not shake his dislike for former commissioner Ray Whitrod – or KoKo as they had called him behind his back – and fastidiously kept up to date with what Whitrod was doing in his life. Later that week he made a point of reading 'Mr R[ay] W. Whitrod's submission to "The Comm. Of Inquiry into Youth," 58 pages.'

On Sunday 10 November at five minutes to midnight, the phone rang up on Garfield Drive. Lewis recorded in his diary: 'Sir Edward Lyons phoned to say he had over 3 hours with Premier and discussed Knighthood ...'

The next evening, Commissioner Lewis and his wife Hazel entered the stately grounds of Government House, just across the way from Garfield Drive, and joined Governor Wally Campbell and Lady Campbell for dinner. There, in that old white mansion on the ridge, the Governor had a personal discussion with Commissioner Lewis. 'Sir Walter Campbell asked me if I would accept a Knight bachelor from the Queen in the N.Y. Honours List [and] of course I said yes.'

Of course the boy from Ipswich said yes.

On Thursday 14 November, Lewis agreed to be interviewed by *Courier-Mail* journalist Ken Blanch for a story to appear the following day. The article would be published on the anniversary of Inspector Lewis of Charleville's promotion to assistant commissioner under Ray Whitrod, with the headline: LEWIS STILL FIRMLY IN CONTROL.

Queensland Police Commissioner Terence Murray Lewis is just four months short of his 58th birthday. But yesterday, with a wry grin, he confessed that he sometimes felt 80. The events of the past year or so are a fair indication of why Terry Lewis is paid $1260 a week – only a round or two of drinks short of the $1338 a week his boss, Lands and Police Minister Bill Glasson, gets.

In that time, Mr Lewis's detectives managed to arrest the wrong man for a particularly sordid Gold Coast murder [Barry Mannix]; his police raided a 300-strong bikers' party at Dayboro in which a complainant policeman was later alleged to have participated; and a senior North Queensland investigator [Ross Dickson] left the force amid a welter of stories about suppressed investigations.

Mr Lewis's predecessor, Mr Ray Whitrod, threw in the towel after six years in the top chair; his predecessor, Mr Norm Bauer, held the office only briefly; and the Commissioner before him, Mr Frank Bischof, was there for 11 years. But with nine years behind him, Mr Lewis still has seven to go to reach retirement at 65.

Commissioner Lewis told Blanch that he was not daunted. He had drafted the 'purpose and aims' of the Queensland Police Department and ensured they were incorporated in the Police Manual. He said the purpose was 'to contribute to the well-being of persons in Queensland by protecting life and property, preserving order, preventing and detecting crime, and the apprehending and bringing to justice of offenders'.

In 1985, Lewis saw breaking and entering as 'the most prevalent and worrying offence' facing police. (This, despite ABCI officer Peter Vassallo briefing police and Cabinet on a burgeoning drug industry involving murder and generating millions of dollars in profits from huge marihuana plantations.)

The Commissioner also nominated other worrying crimes – credit card and cheque fraud, robbery, stealing and unlawful use of cars, and homicide. Lewis quoted house-breaking statistics – up 7.5 per cent from 30,000 to 32,000 in a year. Thankfully the clean-up rate had increased nearly 275 per cent from 2235 to 6119 cases.

Queensland's top cop said the break-ins were linked to drugs. 'Householders could help immensely by locking up when they go out,' he said. 'And when they are going away for an extended time, they should tell a neighbour and notify the local police. We have a special form just for that purpose now.'

It was a domestic warning that harked back to those issued by Lewis's former mentor, Commissioner Frank Bischof, in the late 1950s and 60s. With murder, violent crime and bank robberies on the Queensland crime plate, Bischof would make solemn proclamations about making sure you didn't leave your milk money outside as a temptation to thieves.

Blanch and Lewis went on to discuss the strength of the police force. 'Mr Lewis says penalty rates and overtime are a cost problem in his department, but he doesn't think his 4720 men and women police are misdeployed because of that,' the article stated. 'He denies Police Union suggestions that the State is seriously underpoliced at weekends because large numbers of police are rostered off, but says there are some areas – the rapidly-growing ones north and south of metropolitan Brisbane, for instance – where the demand for police service is very high "and we don't always have sufficient people to give immediate response".'

Lewis added that the force was always on the lookout for ways to improve the use of resources. Despite this, Commissioner Lewis said 'there will never be enough police to do all the work that has to be done'.

The practised Lewis ended the interview on a practical note. 'Police are there to help the public,' he said. 'But the more help they get from the public, the more useful they will be.' This was Lewis the public servant – the dry collector of facts and figures. But somewhere beyond that epaulette facade, there must have been an itch of excitement and satisfaction over his impending knighthood.

What very few people knew at that point was that the Commissioner had, according to future friend and academic at the University of

Queensland, Joseph Siracusa, filled in the application for his knighthood himself, and simply passed it on to the Premier. Who better to do it than the man himself? Lewis was nothing if not thorough.

Meanwhile, the Director of Prosecutions, Des Sturgess, released his report into child sexual abuse, prostitution and pornography. Perhaps it was the impending silly season. Perhaps the subject matter of the report was something people didn't want to acknowledge existed. Whatever it was, the report sank like a stone.

A Hairline Fracture

On Sunday 22 December, Commissioner Lewis, ever the workaholic, popped into the office at headquarters at 10 a.m., checked his correspondence and made a few phone calls before heading back up the hill to Garfield Drive. In the afternoon he treated himself to the September issue of *Police Chief* magazine.

That day, however, an article appeared on page one of the *Sunday Mail*, underneath a picture story about an intolerable heatwave that had descended upon Brisbane. The headline read: WARBURTON ASKS NEW QUESTIONS ON FUNDS TRANSFER.

The Queensland Day Committee affair was not going away, though much of the angst over the possible fraud was being played out behind closed doors.

The audit had been formally reported to the Premier's Department on Tuesday 3 December. That morning, Commissioner Lewis saw Premier Joh Bjelke-Petersen 'and thanked him for loyalty and support'. They also discussed that Lewis would 'stay until at least his [the Premier's] retirement; overseas travel, leave due 145 days; ministerial changes; travel State in 1986; see Sir Robert Sparkes; firm men needed in Mag. Courts re demonstration cases; E. Pratt for Supreme Court and my family occupying space on the 11th floor [of police headquarters] next year [during the building of his new house at 12 Garfield Drive, Bardon]'.

Lewis then saw Coordinator General Sir Sydney Schubert 're investigation by Aud-Gen. of possible misuse of Qld Day C'tee funds by Judith Callaghan'. The next day, Schubert arrived at Commissioner Lewis's office and met the two officers appointed to the Judith Callaghan case – Detective Inspector D. Plint and Detective Sergeant 1st Class J. Moczynacki.

The Callaghan affair was quietly unfolding alongside one of the highlights of Lewis's life – his knighthood. On Monday 9 December, Lewis wrote in his diary: '... letter arrived from Governor advising that Her Majesty the Queen has conferred on me the dignity of Knighthood'.

Bjelke-Petersen dismissed Judith Callaghan from the Queensland Day Committee on 19 December. In the *Sunday Mail*, however, Warburton demanded answers from the Premier with regards to the fraud case. He asked if Allen Callaghan was the head of the government agency under investigation into the dubious transfer of funds. 'Is Mr Callaghan the husband of Mrs Judith Callaghan, who was the coordinator of the Queensland Day Committee?' Warburton asked. 'Is the agency headed by Mr Callaghan the same agency which transferred funds totalling $35,000 in 1984–85 to the Queensland Day Committee? Did that $35,000 fall within the legislative guidelines of the agency involved?'

Bjelke-Petersen, at home on the family property in Bethany, Kingaroy, confirmed that 'a departmental head and his wife' were being investigated by the Auditor-General. He did not name names. 'He [Warburton] can shout to high heaven but I'm not going to muck it up to please him,' Sir Joh said. 'It's in the hands of the Auditor-General and the police. The auditors are looking for anything they can find.' The Premier reassured the public that there would be no government cover-up.

This was a major scandal that went to the very heart of the Premier's Department. It also involved a man who was intimately acquainted with the Premier, and had been for years. The matter was on its way to becoming emblematic of the public's growing perception of the government itself – that there was corruption at extremely high levels.

Lewis says he remembers Callaghan as a smart operator. 'I give him great credit,' he says. 'And what he was pinched for, unfortunately or fortunately – I think a lot of politicians and bloody senior public servants were doing exactly the same thing, taking their wife for bloody dinner and every bastard for dinner – I think he was a bit, he must have fallen out with somebody because ... I got a phone call [from] ... the Auditor-General. I'm not sure if it was Doyle, but whoever it was ... Syd [Schubert] said, "I want to come and see you urgently. Joh has told me, directed me or whatever, told me ..."

'So they both rolled up and said: "Oh, the Premier knows we're here and this is it, we want ... Callaghan has been touching the funds ... we want something done now. So I got in touch with, I don't know, whoever the assistant commissioner was for Crime, and I said, "Get a couple of men from the CIB and get onto it." That was my part in it.'

Lewis says he never received any direction to go lightly on Callaghan. 'It wasn't to let him go, it was to check whether all the transactions were false ... but it wasn't so you can't do anything. He felt sorry for them obviously,' Lewis recalls. 'Yeah, I think he [Sir Joh] asked me to double check that ... all of the, well, not that all of the charges were right, but that he wasn't being charged with anything he shouldn't have been charged with, if you like.

'He [Bjelke-Petersen] wouldn't have been happy to see him [Callaghan] in trouble, put it that way.'

Lewis says Callaghan had enormous power when it came to the government. He had been a strong advisor to the Premier. 'I would be surprised if he [Sir Joh] didn't accept most of it [Callaghan's advice],'

Lewis recalls. 'Particularly dealings with the public. He would have been a very powerful man in his time there.'

Warburton continued his attack on Bjelke-Petersen over the scandal. On Monday 23 December, the *Courier-Mail* published even more demands from the Leader of the Opposition. He asked if the Auditor-General was investigating the Queensland Film Corporation. 'I'm simply asking the Premier and Treasurer of this State straightforward questions which he should be able to answer regardless of any investigations that are being carried out,' Warburton said. He also asked Tourism, National Parks, Sport and Arts Minister Peter McKechnie – who cut short his holiday and rushed back to Brisbane to attend to the crisis – if he had fulfilled his ministerial responsibilities with regard to the Queensland Film Corporation.

McKechnie confirmed that the corporation was being investigated. He unsuccessfully tried to hose down the gathering drama. 'It is normal for the Auditor-General to have officers in government departments from time to time throughout the year,' he said. 'There is an auditor in my department at the moment.'

Warburton went for the Premier, too, saying that in his role as Treasurer, Sir Joh was responsible for the debacle. 'We're not asking him to act as judge and jury,' Warburton added. 'We're merely asking him to disclose certain basic information. The allegations involve public funds – taxpayers' funds.'

The House Shaped Like a Piano

By late 1985 Jack Herbert and his wife Peggy had moved from their East Brisbane apartment, with its splendid views of the Brisbane River, first to a flat at South Bank, just across the river from the CBD near West End, and then to an extraordinary property at 29 Jordan Terrace, Bowen Hills, north of Fortitude Valley.

The new Herbert house was set back from the street and, unusually, its architecture was inspired by the curved housing of a grand piano. The two-storey house had a grand foyer and a sweeping internal staircase. The rooms were generous and the lounge and dining rooms were graced by a huge red-brick fireplace with a timber mantel. The upstairs bedrooms had French doors that opened onto a curved marble balcony, the black cast-iron railing intermittently decorated with circles. The shadow of the circles and railings looked like whole notes on sheets of music. Out back was an in-ground swimming pool.

The house sat on the prime hillock that is Bowen Hills, facing north, in the shadow of the Spanish-style landmark Our Lady of Victories Church. The church had a famous blue illuminated cross on its bell tower – a sort of eternal flame in memory of those who had fallen in World War I. (Because of the small parish, the church itself was handed over to Brisbane's Polish community in 1955.) Indeed, the church was so close to the Herberts' new mansion the blue crucifix shone on the swimming pool water at night.

Just as Commissioner Lewis was planning for his Robin Gibson designed home at 12 Garfield Drive that would comfortably see him and wife Hazel through to retirement and beyond, so too Herbert and wife Peggy seemed to be eyeing the permanence of stone and tiles for their final big home. In fact, Herbert had bought the home off two old mates – Geraldo Bellino and his associate Vic Conte.

'A friend of mine had driven past and seen a "For Sale" sign on it,' Herbert later wrote in his memoir, *The Bagman*. 'At the time Bellino and Conte owed me $20,000. They had fallen behind in their payments for protection. I was confident they would come up with the money eventually.

'All the same, when the chance came to buy the house I saw it as a good opportunity to get the $20,000 back ... Conte and Bellino wanted $160,000 for the house so I offered them $140,000 and told them I'd give them $40,000 on the side and $100,000 on the contract.

'I asked them to deduct another $20,000, which was the amount they owed me, but they said they were in financial difficulties and needed all the cash they could get from the house.'

Herbert, ever The Bagman, was not thrilled with the arrangement but he wanted the house. 'The agent was completely innocent and didn't know what was going on,' Herbert recalled. 'When she showed me around the house I pointed out a few faults – cracks here, there and everywhere – and offered $100,000.

'She said the offer was a bit low and she didn't think the vendors would accept. But later she rang to say they'd accepted $100,000, which surprised her but didn't surprise me, as I was going to slip them the extra $40,000.'

So Jack and Peggy got a fine inner-city home for a bargain, and The Bagman continued to take in about $17,000 a month from the Bellino syndicate to continue to protect illegal games, parlours and nightclubs. At the same time, Herbert was raking in about $23,000 a month from the Hapeta/Tilley enterprises. That was just shy of half a million dollars per annum from the two groups.

On moving into the house, Herbert installed some of his perennial necessities. In the large lounge room not far from the fireplace, he built a long bar where he could socialise with friends and do business. Behind the bar, close to floor level, he had a convenient cavity for bundles of illicit cash. He created another upstairs in one of the bathrooms.

Out the back of the house, he had a large hot tub put in, along with mirrors on a neighbouring wall. Jack liked to party, and here he could rest his weary bones in a warm, bubbling spa at the end of a long day. For the impoverished bobby from London, he had finally made it.

By this stage, Herbert believed The Joke was invulnerable. 'We had the Commissioner of Police on our side,' Herbert alleged in his memoir. 'We had a minister, Don Lane, who told us everything that happened in Cabinet. We had an assistant commissioner and someone in the Bureau of Criminal Intelligence. We believed no one could touch us.'

And the funny and extremely likeable Herbert had a clutch of good friends that who trusted. 'I had a lot of time for Jack, actually,' says one close friend. 'He came from nothing, make no bones about it. He was a top bloke. I'd trust him with anything. He was a rogue, sure. He had a great saying – everybody's corruptible, it's just the price. It's so true. It really is very true.' Everyone in the Herbert circle knew one thing – nothing mattered to Jack Herbert more than his family. 'He was the best family man I'd ever seen.'

But business was business. Police would come and go from Herbert's various houses and apartments over the years. 'He wasn't fussed with Lewis. He had to get along with him,' the friend says. 'Hazel [Lewis] had the best memory of anyone I have ever seen in my life. She could meet you this year at a Christmas party, and come back in a year's time and take up the conversation. I've never seen anything like it.

'I saw Lewis there [at Herbert's place] quite regularly. He was there more than once. More than twice. A lot more. [Lewis would] come over and run stuff by Jack.

'It was like an open door. Jack was a great party animal, he'd have them all there for parties and drinks. He'd have the head of the Drug Squad there. [He'd have] Tony Murphy. Murphy was there all the time. He was alright. Nice enough bloke. I never had any dealings with them business-wise, but socially he was a nice guy.'

While Herbert never explicitly outlined the machinery and function that constituted The Joke, he offered enough to trusted friends for a picture to emerge. 'He gave me bits and pieces, never the whole thing, never,' the friend says. 'You picked up bits and pieces and put two and two together and you certainly knew what was going on.

'There was a guy who was recruited into The Joke. We had a problem with our body corporate and the builder of the block of units lived there. Jack did his block. This guy rang the police and they sent a copper around. Jack recruited him while he was there interviewing him. It was like *Dad's Army*, it really was.

'Jack never involved anybody who was a friend, ever, in any of his evidence, books, ever, he never incriminated anyone.'

Herbert also started developing more elaborate ways to earn corrupt money, devising an ingenious system of laundering cash through the very SP bookmakers that were paying him protection money. Herbert would give the bookmakers cash sums in exchange for a winner's cheque. The bookie would then class the amount as a losing bet for taxation purposes. In a similar vein, Herbert would buy winning TAB tickets for the valid amount with a 10 per cent commission on top. In the mid-1980s Herbert successfully laundered over $200,000 using this system.

The wall cavities in the house on Jordan Terrace were soon stuffed to the gills with cash.

Mrs X

On Monday 30 December, Commissioner Lewis's day was largely taken up with press interviews in advance of the official announcement of his knighthood. At home in Garfield Drive early that evening, a *Courier-Mail* journalist and photographer interviewed Lewis and took a photograph of him and the soon-to-be Lady Hazel.

Lewis joked about how, given he was born on 29 February, he may have been the youngest Knight ever. 'I only get a birthday every four years, so I'm about 15 I guess,' he said. 'As far as I know, I am the first Queensland Police Commissioner in the force's 121 years to get this honour.

'I have no hesitation whatsoever in accepting the knighthood. I believe I have done a good job.'

He said he worked on average about 70 hours a week, and had stabilised the force during his tenure. Lewis added that the force's clean-up rate of 52 per cent was one of the best in Australia. 'I have got away from the desk,' he stated. 'I am the first bloke in 121 years to visit every police station in the State at least once.'

The following day, according to Lewis's diary, 'phone calls started at 5am re Knighthood'. He did more media interviews and noted: 'Received huge number telephone calls, telegrams and telex messages.'

On his last day in the office before his annual vacation pilgrimage to the Gold Coast, Police Minister Bill Glasson phoned him 're report on Callaghan investigation'. The Callaghan affair was a potential time bomb for the Bjelke-Petersen government, and it was in the full glare of the media given that Christmas and New Year were traditionally known as the 'silly season', when serious news stories were typically thin on the ground.

On Saturday 4 January, Lewis and his wife headed down to Surfers Paradise and a unit at Panorama Towers, a holiday high-rise that backed on to a canal. He joined fellow knight Sir Edward Lyons for drinks on Tuesday 7 January, then had dinner with friends John and Betty Meskell. The following evening he again met with Lyons as well as Jack and Peggy Herbert for drinks until 9 p.m.

A story on page three of the *Courier-Mail* that day would not have escaped Lewis's attention. The Auditor-General's report into the Queensland Film Corporation had been leaked to journalist Tony Koch. He reported that the auditor had discovered 'two apparent breaches' of the Film Industry Development Act. 'The fraud squad has been called in following an inspection of the accounts by the Auditor-General's Department.'

The Auditor-General, Vince Doyle, had earlier demanded from the Queensland Film Corporation the appropriate paperwork relating to the money transfers. Allen Callaghan had replied with a memo, stating the Queensland Day Committee was 'inter-departmental', set up by State Cabinet and controlled by the Premier's Department. Callaghan reminded the Auditor-General that Cabinet had asked all government departments to assist the committee 'with manpower and resources'.

The memo added: 'This has been done in a variety of ways with Cabinet's full knowledge and concurrence.'

Two days later Koch reported on another memo from Callaghan to the Auditor-General, this time dated 2 September. Callaghan accused the auditor of being 'zealous', and pointed out that most auditors 'paid department permanent heads the courtesy of discussing their final report before completion'.

It was a measure of the seriousness of the situation that the heavy-hitting National Party president, Sir Robert Sparkes, was then wheeled out to placate an increasingly sceptical Queensland community. 'The public can be reassured that there will be no cover-up,' Sparkes told the *Sunday Mail*. 'Even if they are the most senior public servants in Queensland, they will still face the appropriate action.' The government insisted on not identifying Judith Callaghan, and by referring to her as 'Mrs X', although it had been the worst kept secret around town for many months.

Meanwhile, public pressure had forced Justice Minister Neville Harper to do a backflip and order a coronial inquest into the death of state government auditor Hank Coblens, whose body had been found in his car at Victoria Point in the middle of his audit into the Queensland Day Committee. The news of Coblens' suicide took a week to hit the papers.

An article in the Brisbane *Telegraph* was headlined: SUICIDE BAFFLES POLICE. 'Detectives said a high-powered military rifle Coblens bought from a city gun shop on the day of his death was found beside his body.

'Cleveland police are trying to ascertain what he meant by the hand-written note, and in their inquiries they interviewed several senior Government figures.'

Harper initially saw no need for an inquest given that police had ruled the death a suicide, but in response to public and political pressure, he changed his mind. He said that although he agreed with the Coroner that there were no suspicious circumstances surrounding the death, an inquest needed to be held to allay the concerns of Coblens' family and the community at large.

Courier-Mail journalist Tony Koch reported that 'Government sources said investigations [into the Judith Callaghan fraud charges] were being hampered by the absence of some files concerning the Queensland Day Committee.'

The inquest was set down for March 1986, but prior to the formal hearings the press speculated about a mysterious 'missing briefcase' in relation to the case. In the Brisbane *Telegraph*, journalist Lane Calcutt wrote that a relative of the now notorious Mrs X [Judith Callaghan] 'questioned the whereabouts of a "brown leather" briefcase, which the relative claims contains vital files of the Queensland Day Committee.

'The relative said the briefcase and files were handed to an Auditor-General's Department officer [Coblens] who had investigated the committee. The relative claimed Mrs X had been told that the Auditor-General was not to be "embarrassed" over the affair.' Understandably, the relative wanted to know: What happened to the briefcase?

Lewis was back from holidays and in his office on Saturday 25 January, and was immediately phoned by journalists in relation to the 'Mrs X' investigation. He may have wished he was still on leave. Amid this turmoil, however, Lewis noted in his diary on Friday 31 January: 'Hon. Glasson phoned re moving him from Police and Hon. [Bill] Gunn becoming our Minister.'

Then, on Tuesday 4 February, two major events occurred. Firstly, Lewis was summoned to the Executive Building and the office of Bill Gunn, the new Police Minister and Lewis's fifth since he became commissioner in late 1976. William Angus Manson Gunn, then 64, was from a large family that had its seat in Laidley, west of Brisbane. In 1972 he was elected to state parliament as the member for Somerset which encompassed the Lockyer Valley. He had been seen for years as the successor to Bjelke-Petersen.

232

When the Premier offered Gunn the police portfolio, he didn't want it. He knew he was inheriting a 'can of worms'. He had also heard, for years, that there was corruption in the force, but he had no proof. Gunn's secretary Gwen Butler had previously worked for former Police Minister Max Hodges, the man who had brought in Whitrod to put a broom through the force in the 1970s. She warned Gunn of corruption in the ranks. Clearly, Bjelke-Petersen was also aware. His brief to Gunn was to clean up the force – a request that echoed back in time to 1970, when a fresh-faced Premier tasked Ray Whitrod with the same job.

Gunn's appointment posed a difficulty for Lewis. They had no relationship; Gunn was a straight-shooter and could not be sweet-talked. According to Lewis's diary on 4 February, they discussed 'crime income; illegal gambling; SP betting; prostitution (massage parlours serve useful purpose he believes); need for 500 more police; my using part of 11th floor ...'.

Lewis is adamant Gunn made the comment about massage parlours in the presence of himself, Don Braithwaite and Ron Redmond.

'... Gunn did say, when he became Minister, and we asked him ... that prostitution serves a useful purpose. That's what he said. And whether you agree with it or not it does protect ... most of the decent women in the community,' says Lewis. 'You could enforce all the law if you liked, but there'd be hardly anybody out of gaol. Like keep to the left on the footpath. You could go on and on ...'

The second major event of that day was the resignation of Allen Callaghan as Under Secretary of the Department of Arts, National Parks and Sport would not disclose why he had tendered his resignation. Minister Peter McKechnie refused to comment. At the same time, Fraud Squad police began interviewing Mrs X – Callaghan's wife, Judith.

Ultimately, Callaghan's letter of resignation was leaked to the press. He alleged that he quit because 'certain events involving my wife have made my position untenable and I consider it incumbent on me to act in the best interests of the public service'.

He then stressed to the press that there was no connection between his decision and the Auditor-General's investigation. He pointed the finger at government leaks that raised serious questions about public administration in Queensland. He hinted that he and his wife had been tried by media, not a court of law.

He then did what most thought was unthinkable – he had a go at his old boss and friend, Joh Bjelke-Petersen, saying that the Premier was living in fairyland if he wasn't aware of the leaks and the damage they were causing.

Nev Warburton said Callaghan's resignation only made the 'public funds affair' even more serious. 'I have said from the beginning that this issue had explosive political ramifications,' he said. 'I don't think anyone would disagree that Mr Callaghan's resignation falls into that category. It must be kept in mind that Mr Callaghan is not just another State Government employee. Apart from being one of Queensland's most senior public servants, he was also one of the Premier's closest advisors.'

This was a turning point for the government. Liberal Party State President John Moore said the Callaghan affair had 'shattered the National Party's aura of unity'.

Wheels turned swiftly. On Wednesday 5 February, Commissioner Lewis was telephoned by his old friend, former assistant commissioner Tony Murphy, who discussed 're daughter appln. to join Police and G[len] Hallahan emp[loyment] at SGIO [the State Government Insurance Office]'. (Incredibly, Hallahan, former detective and one of the original members of the fabled Rat Pack from the late 1950s and into the 1960s, had secured a position as a senior insurance fraud investigator with the financial institution.)

Lewis was also advised by Detective Inspector Plint that interviews with Judith Callaghan had been completed. His diary further recorded: '... $44,000 deficiency, she and Allen owe $300,000 with repayments of $3500 per month'.

On the Friday, Lewis noted: '... charge to be preferred against J. Callaghan'. She was due to appear in court on 25 February. That morning, Lewis also had a meeting with an old mate, Glendon Patrick Hallahan. Lewis's diary recorded: 'Conf[erence] with G. Hallahan, SGIO, and 5 Senior officers re liaison and cooperation.' More than a decade after he resigned from the force, Hallahan was back 'liaising' with the Police Commissioner. It had been a long time since they'd worked together in the Consorting Squad in the late 1950s, checking brothels and visiting the city's darker saloons looking for trouble. And it had been an age since they disarmed the crazed German gunman Gunther Bahnemann over in the bayside suburb of Lota in 1959, and been awarded the George Medal for Bravery for their efforts.

Lewis was back in the office on Saturday 8 February, where he read the Auditor-General's report into Allen Callaghan and the Queensland Film Corporation. The following Monday, Lewis phoned Callaghan 'and expressed sorrow at his present situation'. That same day, Lewis issued a press release about the matter, saying it would take the Fraud Squad several weeks to assess the Auditor-General's report into the Allen Callaghan affair. Meanwhile, the scandal had gone national. In Federal Parliament, Finance Minister Senator Peter Walsh was asked if he was aware of the 'alleged misappropriation of massive amounts of public funds by two close personal and political friends of the Premier'.

Walsh responded: '... it's a matter of history that the Premier of Queensland has surrounded himself for many years with close advisors who either are, or ought to be, in gaol.'

Collusion

Judith Callaghan, the now notorious 'Mrs X', was charged on 25 February with misappropriating $44,188.19 in government funds. She appeared in Brisbane Magistrates Court Number One.

Callaghan, 35, the former head of the Queensland Day Committee, said nothing during the brief hearing. She was remanded on bail to 6 June – ironically, Queensland Day. Two days later, her husband Allen was served a summons that he 'dishonestly applied to his own use and the use of other persons $17,362.31, the property of the Queensland Film Corporation'.

Opposition Leader Nev Warburton, who made hay against the government with the Callaghan affair, claimed there had been collusion between police and the Queensland government over the charging of Callaghan. He believed the 'rush' to lay charges was an attempt to stop the ALP from pressing the government on the matter.

Journalist Quentin Dempster had earlier reported in the Brisbane *Telegraph* that according to sources 'a prominent Queens Counsel alerted the Opposition Leader, Mr Warburton, to the significance of the hasty summons charge still to be served on … Mr Allen Callaghan'.

Callaghan's solicitor, Pat Nolan, also reportedly stated that it was 'most unusual' that Callaghan be charged without having been interviewed by police.

Dempster wrote: 'He [Warburton] said it appeared the Government was guilty of expediting criminal proceedings against Mr Callaghan in a calculated move to prevent further questions being raised over the public funds scandal.'

Only a couple of weeks later, on 18 March, the highly anticipated inquest into the death of Hendricus (Hank) Coblens, 32, state government auditor, went ahead in the Cleveland Magistrates Court, east of the CBD.

The body of Coblens had been discovered in his car in the Cleveland area, giving logic to holding the inquest in the nearest courthouse. But workmates of Coblens read something different into the assignation of the Cleveland courthouse. Some suggested the remote location, out of sight and mind of the major courts in Brisbane city, may have been selected to minimise attention to the case.

For all intents and purposes, it was a strange and sad purveying of a life that began in the Netherlands in 1953 and had shown so much promise in Brisbane, Queensland. Hank, along with his parents, father Hermanus, mother Jacoba, and older brother Nicolaas, had migrated to Australia in 1956 aboard the former luxury ocean liner and troop ship, the diesel-powered *Johan Van Oldenbarnevelt*.

The life and death of Coblens was discussed in the small and stuffy Cleveland courthouse – a rectangular-shaped, flat-roofed building in Passage Street. The Cleveland coroner, Mr P. Fitzpatrick SM, opened the inquest by quickly restricting publication of proceedings. The prohibition order was asked for by barrister D.R. Horton, who represented Coblens' closest family.

Before a packed media, Fitzpatrick granted the prohibition. Ruling under Section 30 of the Coroner's Act, he explained that the publication of evidence and facts not pertaining to the inquest interfered with the course of justice.

A lawyer for Brisbane's three free-to-air television stations argued there was a public interest in understanding the link between Coblens and Judith Callaghan – the object of Coblens' audit. However, Fitzpatrick stood firm, saying the barrister had yet to hear the evidence regarding a man facing charges of 'considerable magnitude' before the courts 'which has a far more direct connection with this inquest'. (This was Bevan Lloyd Whip, former executive officer for the Queensland Dairymen's Organisation, who was facing almost 200 charges of misappropriating more than $500,000, and whose outfit had also been audited by Coblens.)

In a case that was anticipated to last a single day, the first day evaporated in legal argument over what the public could and could not know. The next day, Coblens' co-workers from the Auditor-General's Department, including Ross Goodhew and Pat Gallagher, were called to give evidence. 'He was under pressure to do the right thing, to comply to save his job,' remembers Pat Gallagher. It was an area touched on during the inquest. Goodhew confirmed that it was well known among their colleagues that the Premier's Department was a sensitive one to audit.

Neither Judith nor Allen Callaghan were called as witnesses.

In the end, Mr Fitzpatrick concluded that an auditing mistake, allegedly made by Coblens in relation to the Queensland Dairymen's Organisation State Council, had 'weighed heavily' on the deceased. 'And,' Fitzpatrick concluded, 'in his state of sensitiveness and quest for perfection sadly brought about a conviction in his mind that he could not live with the situation and its consequences as he saw them.'

But was it enough to take his own life, in the middle of an extremely controversial audit involving the Premier's Department?

Coroner Fitzpatrick found there was no evidence of criminal action or negligence by any person, and that no person should be committed for trial on any charge. He duly closed the inquest.

Confidential

It took some months, but there was finally some public debate over Des Sturgess's report on child sexual abuse and other unsavoury topics, such as pornography and prostitution. It was just enough to stir the interest of the new Police Minister, Deputy Premier Bill Gunn. Minister for Justice and Attorney-General, Nev Harper, had sought comments on the report from Bill Glasson in the dying days of his Police Ministership. Now Harper was asking Gunn.

Gunn informed the Attorney-General that Police Commissioner Lewis had assigned two senior officers to go through the Sturgess Report, assess the contents that were relevant to the police department, and report back. The two men were Detective Inspectors B. Webb and R. Dargusch. They had completed their 'Strictly Confidential' report by the end of April 1986. They quickly examined, in the report, the allegation from Sturgess that men prominently involved in prostitution in south-east Queensland had not suffered much prosecution in recent years. The two detective inspectors identified those men as Hector Hapeta, Geraldo Bellino, Vittorio Conte and Geoff Crocker.

They listed the various charges on Hapeta's record, including possession of an unlicensed concealable firearm, drink driving and obscene language. 'It is obvious from the records that he is one of the principal controllers of prostitution in Brisbane and the Gold Coast,' the police report said. 'His associates are generally regarded as the human garbage of the community.'

Next on the list was Gerry Bellino. Their investigations revealed he had last been before the courts on 6 February 1978, charged with keeping a common gaming house. 'Bellino has been associated with numerous Night Clubs and Gambling Premises in Brisbane, and has also been associated with prostitution,' they concluded. 'He is the co-owner of the building at 142 Wickham Street, Fortitude Valley, with Vittorio Conte.' Conte was last before the courts in 1979.

The detective inspectors also identified Anne Marie Tilley. 'She first came under the notice of police on 8.2.72 when she appeared in the Minda Children's Court [in Sydney] charged with being Exposed to Moral Danger,' the report said. 'Since that time, she has incurred 27 convictions for Loiter for Prostitution in the State of New South Wales. She was last convicted at Brisbane Magistrates Court on the 9th November, 1984 for driving a motor vehicle while her blood alcohol content was .08. She is still actively engaged in prostitution in this State.'

The thorough report also listed 14 massage parlours and their respective owners. Here was proof that, more than a year before a *Four Corners* investigative report into the Queensland vice scene and its corrupt links with police, which would lead to a Royal Commission that would mention the likes of Hapeta, Bellino and Conte in its terms of reference, the main players were already known to Police Commissioner Lewis.

Reach for the Sky

In May 1986, Queenslanders awoke to a curious page-one story in the *Courier-Mail*. The headline read: BRISBANE TO GET ONE OF THE WORLD'S TALLEST SKYSCRAPERS.

Written by political reporter Peter Morley, the article outlined the proposal for a $400 million inner-city redevelopment, one of the tallest buildings in the world, which had been approved by the state government. In reality, a quixotic project was nothing new for Premier Sir Joh Bjelke-Petersen. His leadership was littered with them. And he famously measured the strength of the Queensland economy by counting the construction cranes hovering over the Brisbane CBD. But a downtown building that was within reach of the famous Sears Tower in Chicago at 443 metres and 110-storeys? This was Queensland – reach for the sky.

The report stated: 'The developer is Mr John Minuzzo whose Mainsel Investments group plans to complete the project within four years.'

Sir Joh said excitedly, 'It's a huge one.'

While the Premier was not ordinarily recognised as a sentimental person, he must have felt at least some sort of distant twinge at the prospect of the demolition of the old Canberra Temperance Hotel, which sat on the site of the prospective tower. For it was there, in Brisbane's famous 'dry' hotel, that Sir Joh and his new bride Florence had their wedding reception after being married in the Valley Presbyterian Church on Saturday 31 May 1952.

The Canberra had been officially opened in July 1929 by local businessman George Marchant, the 'soft drink king of Australia', who had made a fortune manufacturing hop beer, soft drinks and cordials, and patenting an extremely lucrative bottling machine. As part of the opening ceremony, Marchant said solemnly: 'I pray that the opening of these doors may be the opening of a way that will lead to the total abolition of liquor bars in all residential hotels. Alcohol has caused no end of misery to our young people, who are taken to hotels, and acquire the drinking habit, to the ruination of their health and the wrecking of their homes.'

The Canberra did extremely well for decades, despite its detractors, and was known as a city haven for country folk. But 57 years after its opening, and rebadged the Capital Hotel, there seemed to be some confusion in terms of the Premier's announcement that the site was set to house one of the planet's top-ten tall buildings.

The day after Bjelke-Petersen's news made the front page, Brisbane's *Telegraph* newspaper reported some bewilderment over this ambitious project. On the one hand, John Minuzzo, then 46, declared that the Capital would be demolished. At the hotel however, functions manager Robert Glover said the building was in the middle of $4 million worth of renovations, and that the demise of the establishment was news to him. Mr Glover said management knew nothing of the plans for the hotel to be sold and razed. He said it seemed 'strange' that the O'Brien's, who had owned the hotel for only eight months, would spend millions on a facelift if it was to be sold.

Mr Minuzzo stood firm: 'Mr O'Brien gave me an option to buy the hotel and may not have told his employees. The State Government has seen the option, it was attached to our application.' Shop tenants in the building were similarly left scratching their heads.

Gavin O'Brien, the proprietor of Drysdale Auto Books, fronting Edward Street, was forced to place an advertisement in the *Courier-Mail* to inform customers that he had a lease on his shop that extended until March 1988. He reportedly said he had not been told of any redevelopment. 'Our only information has come from what we read in the newspapers. If the hotel is supposed to be coming down in September, the tenants would have to have time to look for other premises, which takes time.'

Another tenant said he was similarly in the dark. Still, developers and the government said the new Central Place (the proposed name for the development) would go full-steam ahead, and any criticism of it was just 'sour grapes' from rival developers.

In fact, Minuzzo's name had been bandied about in parliament a year earlier in relation to a controversial development on the Gold Coast that had embroiled local government Minister Russ Hinze. During a debate over amendments to the *Local Government Act* in September 1985 – the government wanted to cut red tape for the approval of development projects – Minuzzo featured prominently.

Opposition Leader Nev Warburton had drawn attention to projects on the Gold Coast being developed by a group known as Oasis Holdings. He informed the House that the company was owned by developers Bruno and Rino Grollo. The projects included a $50 million hotel in Surfers Paradise and a $35 million shopping complex in West Burleigh. At the time, Warburton said the project manager for both developments was John Minuzzo. 'On my understanding,' Warburton had told parliament, 'John Minuzzo previously went by the name of Enzo Minuzzo. To say the least, he has had some difficult times before Melbourne courts in recent years.'

Warburton went on to inform parliament that Minuzzo, through the early 1980s, had appeared in court on three separate occasions charged with various offences, including the conspiracy to defraud operators in the sale of land and counts of bribery and conspiracy to breach the Criminal Act. 'I do not think I need to say a great deal more about the sort of people who are being attracted to the State of Queensland by the National Party Government,' Warburton said.

Now, as one of the world's tallest buildings was being touted in 1986, Warburton had another crack at the government in parliament. During Questions Without Notice on 2 September 1986, Warburton asked the Premier about a personal letter he had written to Mr Tony Nevins of Mainsel Investments Pty Ltd. Part of the letter read: 'I'm glad that you, Izzy and John are investing heavily in Queensland projects. That has been good to see.' It was signed 'Joh Bjelke-Petersen'.

Warburton addressed the Premier: 'Are the two persons referred to in that letter by their Christian names Mr Izzy Herzog and Mr John Minuzzo, who was previously associated with the Grollo brothers, Bruno and Rino, heading the company known as the Grollo Group?'

The Premier fired back: 'When will the Leader of the Opposition come up with something positive and do something constructive? He is always down in the gutter ... it is quite a job to keep people like the Leader of the Opposition out of the gutter.

'The two people referred to by the Leader of the Opposition have nothing to do with the Grollo brothers. Once again the Leader of the Opposition is on the wrong track. However, at the moment, I cannot help him any more than I have.'

Warburton wouldn't let it go: 'I refer to Mr Minuzzo and Mr Herzog, who I understand are still involved in the West Burleigh shopping complex application ... prior to his recent meetings with Mr Minuzzo regarding a major proposed Brisbane development [Central Place], had he previously had discussions with Minuzzo in 1984 or 1985 concerning a Gold Coast project, and was he aware at the time of those meetings of Mr Minuzzo's background and his appearances before Melbourne courts?'

'Negative yet again,' Bjelke-Petersen replied. '... the same tactics of trying to scrape up mud and dirt. The people he has referred to have come up to Queensland from Melbourne and are investing many hundreds of millions of dollars in this State. They are doing something constructive and very positive.'

The Lord Mayor Sallyanne Atkinson was troubled by a number of aspects of the project. The Premier's almost fanatical insistence that the building go ahead was one of the first instances of the state government usurping a role traditionally performed by council. 'How things were in the 1980s was that the state government ran the state and the Brisbane City Council ran Brisbane,' says Atkinson. 'There were no Cabinet ministers in Brisbane. They were all out in the country. It was total bliss.

'I went off and dealt with Russ Hinze, who did call me "girlie" and "pet". I put up with that because after the initial hiccups … I got on with Russ. It was a good working relationship.

'Until then, I regarded the Brisbane City Council as the planning authority. I was outraged that the state government would ride roughshod over us – there was a matter of principle involved.'

The issue soured her relationship with Premier Bjelke-Petersen. 'I was at a dinner at Lennons and I was at a table with [Coordinator General Sir] Syd Schubert and a couple of senior people, and Joh started attacking me about my stand on the world's tallest building,' Atkinson remembers. 'I'd sort of never seen that side of him before. We must have been at the top table, and then he got up and left. I remember turning to Syd Schubert and saying, "You should have protected me on that."

'It was quite out of character for Joh, who had always acted like the nice old country gentleman … to be really nasty.'

She also encountered developer John Minuzzo in her office in City Hall. 'He was like a character out of a movie. I can remember him coming into my office and virtually throwing himself on the floor and beating his little fists, saying, "I want this",' she says. 'He couldn't have it. You don't get everything you want in this life.'

Atkinson recalls: '[Liberal MP] Angus Innes rang me at home very early one morning and said, "You've got to stop it."'

She observes of the time: 'There was a bit of a culture around in Brisbane that we had to prove ourselves, that we were bigger and better than everybody else. The temptation to have the world's tallest building was there.'

Nobody could have known that not only would the saga of Central Place run for years, but would reach disastrously into the office of the Premier and wreak havoc.

A Tremor in the Valley

Anne Marie Tilley, brothel madam extraordinaire, had settled into an easy groove with her businesses flung across Brisbane, and was doing a roaring trade. Life was good. But she couldn't shake a premonition she was feeling, that perhaps life was too good.

Late one night, in one of the Fortitude Valley clubs, she bumped into Licensing Branch officer Nigel Powell. She knew Powell from around the traps. She was aware he'd been gathering information on her and her de facto husband Hector Hapeta for years, but no prosecutions had been forthcoming.

Nigel was straight. She had always considered him a bit of a 'dork'. Tilley knew he was smart, but what hope did he have when she and her empire were protected by the likes of men like Graeme Parker?

Powell, on this occasion, offered a simple question to Tilley that resonated with her for a long time afterwards. 'How do you keep all of this going?' Powell was referring to the highly lucrative empire she had helped create.

'I don't know. Go ask Harry Burgess,' Tilley replied.

Tilley says many of the corrupt police had begun to get too comfortable. 'I actually did complain to Jack [Herbert] once that they [the police] were down in the parlours too much,' she remembers. 'It was only a period of maybe a couple of weeks but they were coming in every night, standing around, drinking.

'I said, "You guys, give us a break. People aren't walking in because you're standing here."

'I asked Jack, "Can you tell them to lay off a bit, to go away?"

'He said, "I'll fix that."

'I think a couple of them [the police] didn't think they were invulnerable, but they were a little more intuitive than others. A couple of people, one of them, said to me: "This is going to blow up one day, hey?"

'I said, "Yeah, probably."'

'That was a couple of years before anything happened.'

It Was Madness

Within the government, questions were also being raised about Premier Joh Bjelke-Petersen's unique style of leadership. Cabinet ministers and backbenchers alike were seriously wondering if his increasingly dictatorial and arcane methods belonged in a modern Queensland. What might have appealed to a Country Party–style squattocracy in the 1960s – this no-frills, male-dominated way of doing business with a nod and a handshake – was now chafing against a contemporary, multicultural populace aching to move forward with the times.

Mike Ahern says Bjelke-Petersen stuck with the tried and true method that had seen him rise to the top and stay there – he made promises to all and sundry, and they owed him in return. 'He would promise them Cabinet positions and some of them were absolutely inappropriate ... the positions that they had,' Ahern recalls. 'But they were beholden to him. That was his power.

'In an ideal world you come into politics with an ideal plan. A zeal to do something. He didn't have that. He came in to be an operator, to show people that he could make decisions.'

Some of those decisions were ludicrous.

Ahern remembers the Premier granting a developer rights to build a resort in the vicinity of an oil refinery at Pinkenba, at the mouth of the Brisbane River. 'Around every power facility is what you call a "kill zone",' Ahern says. 'It's not known on the map as the kill zone but obviously you've got all that flammable carbohydrate around you and must have an exclusion zone there. And it's Crown Land or a reserve or some bloody thing ... and you don't let anyone build in there.'

On another occasion, Ahern was summoned to Caboolture for a major announcement by the Premier. A group of businessmen wanted to build an airport. They showed Joh the plans, and he immediately approved the proposal. 'They rolled it out in front of him [and said] we want to build this airport,' says Ahern. 'He had a look at it and he said, "Yes, I know exactly what you're doing." He approved it.

'The Queensland government had no right to approve an airport, that's a Federal Government matter, they had no money in a budget or anything like that and he didn't tell anyone. He didn't have any notes on a file, he didn't brief his secretary. He had no one with him. He just did it. So they came to me afterwards and they said, we spent $400,000 here on his say and [now] we're all embarrassed.

'It was madness. I mean ... absolute power, or what you perceived to be strength ... no tenders, no negotiations on infrastructure, no zoning issues, no studies on the environment to see whether they were appropriate things, whether there were endangered species ...'

It was no secret, either, that Deputy Premier Bill Gunn had waited patiently for years for the top job, and was getting restless. Bjelke-Petersen had in fact told Lewis that Gunn would take over as Premier when he retired from the position.

'Gunn got impatient,' recalls Lewis. 'I said [to Gunn] there's no way in the world I'd go round the state and sort of nominate or recommend him to be the Premier almost immediately.

'I got on well with my men, there's no two ways about that, and he knew Joh did, and he knew that the police vote in the country could be very useful because a lot of people were friendly with their local policemen [and] their local Sergeants or whatever, and they'd all talk together ... they thought Joh was a good bloke.'

Lewis says he doesn't know if the Premier fully appreciated Gunn's ambitions. 'I think he was a pretty trusting fellow old Joh, I think he would have thought, oh well, you know, Gunn knows he's going to get it,' says Lewis. 'You might think Joh was a bit naive and he may have been, too. I really don't think he thought Gunn would stab him in the back, I don't think that for a minute.'

Lewis says he didn't particularly trust Gunn. 'You can't just run and ring him [Bjelke-Petersen] up and say, look, Mr Premier, I think your Minister is a bit of a shit,' he says. 'But you can let him know in subtle ways, I guess. I did let him know somewhere along the line that Mr Gunn, you know, wanted to be the next Premier.'

The Slush Fund

Despite intimations that there had been a government conspiracy surrounding the highly damaging public funds affair involving the Premier's former press secretary and advisor Allen Callaghan and his wife Judith, or Mrs X as she became known, the latter's trial didn't get to court until August 1986.

In effect, the whole sorry affair had been lingering since December the previous year. And although allegations of corruption had been thrown against Bjelke-Petersen, the National Party and the Queensland police year after year, the Callaghan matter seemed to have finally united the public in their perception that there was something foul about the long-standing government.

Here was one of the government's most powerful officials, along with his wife, misappropriating public money for personal pleasure. And the court would hear that this was practically done with relative ease, given that the affected government committees had not been audited for many years. This was a story not just about personal greed, but also about government accountability. In this instance, the rumours were made solid with fact.

'It didn't do the government any good,' Allen Callaghan admits. 'I had a poverty-stricken upbringing. The cookie jar was too attractive.'

On Friday 22 August, Judith Callaghan arrived at the Brisbane

District Court in George Street with her husband. They passed the bronze statue of Themis, Greek Goddess of justice, and the waiting media, and proceeded upstairs to Court Seven.

The court heard that Judith had opened a Commonwealth Savings Bank Account on 25 May 1981, and called it the Queensland Day Dinner Account. She was its sole signatory. Subscriptions for the lavish annual Queensland Day Dinner were paid into that account, deposited by Judith's secretary Lisa Bryan. Bryan said Callaghan referred to that account as the 'slush fund'.

Another account – the Queensland Day Sponsorship Account – was opened on 13 August 1984. Again, Judith was the sole signatory. The Crown said Judith used the account to conceal sponsorships given to the Queensland Day Committee, one of which was from the Queensland Film Corporation, run by her husband Allen.

The court heard that Judith said records in relation to the sponsorships were contained in files that had been removed by Hank Coblens, the auditor found dead of a shotgun wound in October 1985. Coblens had begun auditing the Queensland Day Committee before his death. She told the court that she had given Coblens the documents as he was leaving her office after an interview on Thursday 3 October. (Judith Callaghan's office was a beautifully appointed space in the old Treasury Building. It had a marble fireplace and a large balcony that overlooked the Brisbane River. She had a keen interest in bronze sculptures.)

Coblens went missing the next day, his body found in his car in Victoria Point on Saturday 5 October. Judith said she did not work on that Friday, but returned to her office on Monday 7 October, and found a note from Coblens saying he had taken information required by him. She said she had given Coblens a transaction file – the only record relating to the sponsorship account.

Crown Prosecutor David Bullock said that that file had never been found. He told the court the maximum gaol sentence for Judith Callaghan's offence was ten years. She pleaded guilty.

On Wednesday 27 August Judith Callaghan was sentenced to 30 months in prison, with a recommendation she be paroled after three months. Judge McGuire ordered she be detained in the prison hospital for the duration of her sentence in Boggo Road Gaol; she suffered severe asthma.

The Judge gave her credit for pleading guilty and vowing to pay back the stolen money, but added: 'If offences of this sort are treated lightly by the court public confidence in the administration of the criminal justice system could be shaken.' He said her actions had, by association, smeared the names of fine men like Sir David Longland and Leo Hielscher. 'They have been betrayed by your perfidy,' he said.

Her husband Allen reportedly said outside the court after Judith's sentencing: 'She's been through hell in the last year.'

The *Courier-Mail* reported on Judith Callaghan's decline and fall. It wrote that a prison hospital bed in Boggo Road was a long way from 'the Fountain Room Restaurant, the most elegant and priciest of the Cultural Centre eateries where Callaghan, despite her salary of only $27,000 a year, lunched frequently'.

The newspaper described her office as 'a kind of salon, replete with fine paintings, huge bowls of flowers and polished antique tables; the kind of place attuned to the acquired tastes of an up-market personality with, it is said, a sense of history. Here Judith Callaghan could be at her often imperious best, besieged by the well-heeled or the well-connected.'

With Allen Callaghan's charges yet to be heard before the courts, there was an unusual by-product to the scandal. Quentin Dempster reported that the government appeared to have lost the loyalty of the public service in the wake of the affair, to the extent where 'confidential and highly damaging information is being posted, hand-delivered and telephoned to the Opposition and sections of the media'.

The Callaghan fiasco had opened a portal to disgruntled public servants. They also happened to be the keepers of government business – and secrets. 'What started as a trickle of information has turned into a steady flow,' wrote Dempster. 'The latest revelations included the intervention by the Primary Industries Minister, Mr Neil Turner, to order a $145,000 carry-on loan to drought-stricken grazier and National Party officer Mr Michael Behan against expert financial advice. And last week the Sports Minister, Mr McKechnie, was caught off-guard when Mr Warburton revealed through question time that a fraud inquiry was underway in his Sports Department. Apparently no one had told the Minister of this.'

An insider also leaked the size of the Bond Corporation's defamation settlement with the Premier over a 1983 television current affairs report. The sum looked like being about $400,000.

With an election looming, the Bjelke-Petersen regime had an image problem it had to fix, and fix quickly. For the ALP, they had been gifted a theme for their campaign – government corruption.

Meanwhile, stories started filtering out that Judith Callaghan was leading a privileged life in Boggo Road. The government immediately denied a newspaper report that two sick female prisoners had to be moved out of the hospital because Callaghan had allegedly demanded a ward to herself. The Brisbane *Telegraph* wrote: 'Jail sources said Callaghan's request for her own silk pyjamas to be brought to the jail was rejected and she was issued with prison night attire.' Furthermore, 'a transsexual prisoner delivering Callaghan's breakfast on her first morning in jail threw an orange at her when Callaghan demanded she be given juice in a tumbler'.

The Marble Man

In Far North Queensland, a local business was seeking state government assistance to take their dream one step further. The Vince Bellinos, both senior and junior, requested funding to help build a processing plant for their marble mine at Chillagoe, 200 kilometres west of Cairns.

Global Marble had, in just two years, exported quality marble around the world. The company's mine had been officially opened by Premier Joh Bjelke-Petersen. 'We have invested about $5 million to date,' Vince Junior told the *Courier-Mail* newspaper. 'Now we are seeking State Government help to set up a factory in the north or south of Queensland to get the marble to the final, finished stage.'

He said the processing factory would be located in either nearby Mareeba or in the Brisbane area. He projected that the plant would employ more than 150 people. Vince said: '... until this point we have only been discussing it over the phone with government officers.' He revealed that the Chillagoe marble had, in fact, been found by accident. In their spare time the Vince Bellinos, who ran the House on the Hill nightclub in Cairns, loved fossicking for stones. Italian relatives visiting them asked about some samples of white and pink crystallised rocks in their collection. Where had they found them?

The article read: 'The Bellinos retraced their steps to scrub country just outside Chillagoe ... Today, that rock-dotted scrub is the site of a mine which is producing thousands of tonnes of top-quality marble for export.'

The family hobby soon developed into a company, and within two years Vince Bellino, with his wife Raelene, had exported $1.5 million worth of marble to Italy for processing. Vince Senior, 53, who had worked with marble as a young builder in Italy, was the company's marketing manager. They claimed Chillagoe marble had been ranked some of the best in the world, and they had colloquially named a number of coloured marbles Pink Coral, Coral Rosa, Yellow Mango and White Koala.

'Different veins run into the quarry and we follow the veins,' Vince said. 'In Carrara [Italy] for 2000 years they have gone down hundreds of metres. We will keep following the marble and keep going down.

'We have had a lot of heartaches at this stage,' he added. 'We are still struggling as a small company, but we will make it. We keep together as a family and we stick it out.'

The Bluff

Down in Canberra, intelligence analyst Peter Vassallo, author of the Alpha Report, was still concerned for the safety of his mate Jim Slade, who had been shunted off to the 'punishment' station, Beenleigh, south of the Brisbane CBD. Slade was performing his duties, but his Operation Trek – an intensive investigation into the North Queensland drug trade – had proved to be almost too thorough, and had been shelved. It had also become clear, since the release of Vassallo's Alpha Report, that the two men were exchanging information.

This was anathema to the Queensland police hierarchy who would not tolerate outsiders sniffing around the Sunshine State.

Vassallo decided to test the waters. After his briefing of Bjelke-Petersen's Cabinet the year before, he had returned home to Canberra and verified within the bureau that there were no records of any criminal offences against any of the Bellino family. There were also no photographs.

Vassallo decided to ask one of the ABCI's Queensland representatives to contact the Queensland Bureau of Criminal Intelligence and ask for background material and photographs on Antonio, Geraldo and Vincenzo Bellino. It was a standard query. The ABCI wanted to update its records. It was something that was done all the time.

'So, I went to my mate – a lovely fellow and no question about him being straight up and down – and I just simply said to him, "Mate, will you do me a favour? Could you ring the [Queensland] BCI and let them know that we haven't got any criminal records on the Bellino brothers?"' Vassallo recalls.

His colleague in the Canberra office made the call. No less than 15 minutes later he called Vassallo into his office.

'What have you fucking done to me?' he asked Vassallo.

'Why?' Vassallo was curious.

'[The] Bellino brothers ... do you know who just rang me?'

'No.'

'Graeme Parker.'

Parker wanted to know who had been asking for the records and photographs of the Bellinos. The young officer replied it was Peter Vassallo of the Alpha project. Parker further allegedly said that if Vassallo needed any information like that, he should notify Parker directly.

Vassallo's co-worker was concerned by the response he had received from the top levels of the force. He asked his friend what was going on. 'I don't need this shit,' Vassallo recalls him saying.

The Big White House

By the mid-1980s Terry and Hazel Lewis were well underway with the construction of their new house in Garfield Drive. 'I was getting older and we thought, we really do love it here, what about we try and get a decent house built here?' Lewis recalls. 'It was an old wooden house and it always worried me with the kids. You think, you know, is it going to ever catch fire or anything?

'Anyway, I knew [architect] Robin Gibson very well, he was a lovely fellow ... and he said "Oh, I'll draw up a plan", so he did. We used to meet each other. He didn't even charge anything for it.' (Gibson, before his death in March 2014, said he had indeed designed the property at 12 Garfield Drive for the Lewises, but would have had to 'check my records' to see if he did or didn't receive any remuneration for the job.)

It was a substantial project. The old timber house was removed from the steep property site and the work started from scratch. Lewis managed to convince the government to allow him and Hazel to live in police headquarters in Makerston Street for the duration of the construction of the three-level house with heated pool and spa.

'I was [working] on the tenth floor and above that on the eleventh floor was an area set aside for a minister, which they never occupied,' remembers Lewis. 'I spoke to [Deputy Premier Bill] Gunn about it, and the Premier, too, I think. I said look, this place is empty upstairs, would there be any objection to Hazel and I living there for a little while because the kids were all doing other things, you know?

'I used to get a rent allowance ... about bloody five dollars a week or ten dollars a week ... and I said, no, stop that, which I suppose no other bugger would bother about. And Hazel and I moved in there. It was a little bit inconvenient but it was good.'

Those close to the workaholic Lewis quipped that he would now spend even more hours at his desk, given its proximity to his new living quarters. 'I said when I retire, we'll have enough money to buy a little unit down the coast, and if we rebuild on this site we'll have a house we can be safe in,' Lewis recalls. 'That was a time when the Premier started getting bodyguards. I said I didn't want a bodyguard ... even my driver, I didn't ask him to carry a firearm, although we did have a firearm in the glove box in case we ran across an armed robbery.'

Lewis says their investment property at 29 Garfield Drive was sold to finance the rebuilding of the house at number 12. He also secured a loan to pay for the new house, which he says cost about $450,000.

The big white house was the only display of extravagance for Lewis, in a lifetime of frugality and penny-pinching. He was a man of practical and inexpensive clothes and shoes, he drove no fancy cars, he consumed offal and cheap cuts of meat, and he and Hazel had a strict minimal limit on Christmas presents and birthday gifts.

Any socialising was largely done through Lewis's official capacity as Police Commissioner. After endless hours of official openings, functions and formal dinners, home had become a refuge. Now it was to be a grand home, seen for miles clinging to the ridge on Garfield Drive, with views all the way north to the Glasshouse Mountains.

Former Police Union president Ron Edington says he remembers the construction of the new house in Bardon. 'What happened, when they were building that bloody place up there opposite bloody Government House, Hazel would go around paying everyone from a bloody shoe box. She used to go around and hand the money out ... you know. I don't know where it was all coming from ...'

Sichter Goes to Trial

More than five years after the brutal shotgun deaths of Far North Queensland drug growers William (Paul) and Grayvyda Clarke, the man accused of their deaths – Terrence John Sichter – finally went to trial in July 1986. There had been a mistrial recorded three months earlier in Cairns, the judge declaring that certain evidence tendered was not relevant and prejudicial. This time, the case moved to the Supreme Court in Brisbane. Sichter had pleaded not guilty.

For years rumours had circulated about who really murdered the Clarkes, and they all pointed towards the New South Wales-based Mafia. Detective Jim Slade, in the course of his undercover Operation Trek investigations, had allegedly been told the killings were carried out by either Rocco Francesco Medici, 47, or his brother-in-law Guiseppe Loui Furina, 41, both Calabrians who resided in Melbourne's western suburbs.

The two men were in regular contact with growers like Clarke, and had been in Far North Queensland around the time of the murders on 24 May 1981. Medici organised the money, while Furina looked after the transportation of the Indian hemp into New South Wales and Victoria. Both men, in turn, were murdered, their bodies discovered bound in chains in the Murrumbidgee River south of Griffith, New South Wales, on 5 May 1984. They had been tortured prior to death.

The evidence against Sichter amounted to a variety of statements from criminals who indicated that Sichter had confessed to the murders while in prison, after his initial arrest.

At the trial, overseen by Justice Kelly, Sichter was represented by the legendary lawyer Col Bennett, the former ALP member for Kurilpa who had triggered the notorious National Hotel inquiry in 1963, and personally represented some of the biggest figures in Queensland criminal history, including the late prostitute and brothel madam Shirley Brifman.

The Crown alleged that Sichter, who was working on a property at Gatton in the Lockyer Valley prior to the murders, had driven north to Cairns in May 1981 to destroy Clarke because he had supposedly ripped him off in a drug deal.

Witness Barry Kenneth Fyfe, who was working with Sichter on a property owned by Clarke near the Pascoe River, in the vicinity of Idlewild Station near Portland Roads, North Queensland, said Sichter had bogged a supply truck and Fyfe said Clarke would be after him for it.

'One word out of him and I'll blow him away,' Sichter had allegedly said in response to Fyfe.

Fyfe said he was just joking.

'I'll still blow him away,' Sichter allegedly replied.

Fyfe lived on a property owned by his brother Donald, also on the Pascoe River, six kilometres from the Pascoe River Bridge. According to the ABCI's confidential Alpha Report, Barry Fyfe and an associate, Sylvester Perrett, were interviewed by detectives in late 1982 over drug matters. Both talked about the Clarke murders and volunteered suspects. Perrett claimed Robert 'Dave' Berrick was responsible (impossible, given Berrick was in Sydney at the time of the slayings). Fyfe nominated Terrence Sichter.

When Detective Sergeant Ross Beer took the stand he told the court he had been present when the charred bodies of the Clarkes were removed from the farmhouse in Pinnacle Road, Julatten, and was also in attendance when the remains were X-rayed at Mareeba Hospital. The bodies were riddled with hundreds of shotgun pellets.

Beer said he had travelled down to Brisbane and interviewed Sichter at the Inala police station, west of the CBD, on 18 December 1981. Sichter told him he had been in Brisbane when the Clarkes were killed. Sichter allegedly told Beer that in 1980 he had grown a marihuana crop and sold 18 kilograms of the drug to Clarke. He also said to Beer that some Italian men had ripped off a crop from a local grower at the time.

At the end of the first week of the trial, the Crown produced witness Matthew Kevin Ferris, 25, a motor mechanic from Sydney, who said he had lived in Cairns for several months in 1985. Ferris said he was arrested in September of that year on charges of possession and selling a dangerous drug, and was gaoled for 18 months. He told the court he was in the Cairns watch-house for a week and shared a cell with Sichter. He claims the pair talked about the death of the Clarkes.

'He [Sichter] said to me, "Yes, I got them", or "I fixed them", or something like that,' Ferris told the court. Ferris then admitted he told police about Sichter's comments.

The defence called Gatton farmer Colin Schafferius, of East Egypt Road, who owned a property next door to Sichter's. Schafferius said he worked on Sichter's property in Gatton on the weekend of 23 and 24 May 1981 – when the Clarkes were murdered – and saw him on several occasions.

Sichter had employed Schafferius to use a small bulldozer to repair the banks of a dam, and paid for the work on Monday 25 May. Sichter was given a receipt for the job. It appeared proof that Sichter was in

Gatton, and not 1794 kilometres away in Julatten when the murders were committed.

Although they took nearly 24 hours to reach a verdict, the jury ultimately found Sichter not guilty of the murders of William (Paul) and Grayvyda Clarke. He walked out of court on Saturday 2 August a free man, and claimed the whole thing had been a "police set-up".

'We will have to start from scratch,' Sichter said. His wife Janet added: 'We want to go home now and see our kids.'

Just three years later, Sichter left Gatton and set up camp at Chilli Beach, not far from his old stomping ground of the Portland Roads, on Cape York Peninsula. Sichter had grown marihuana for the Calabrians, escaped a double murder conviction and avowed that he was out of the drug scene and would make a go of his farm in Gatton.

On the night of Saturday 10 June 1989, Sichter was found dead of a single bullet wound to the head at his camp by his then girlfriend, Maria Camp. Acquaintance Robert 'Dave' Berrick says: 'He was off his face. He was playing Russian roulette. It was poetic justice.'

Masters

Investigative journalist Chris Masters had had an intense few months, researching the Italian Mafia and its Australian links for a *Four Corners* television report called 'The Family Business'.

The bespectacled Masters, whose face seems to carry the semi-squint of someone whose gaze is trained endlessly at the sun, was born in Grafton in northern New South Wales and finished his schooling in Sydney before joining the ABC. He is part of a brilliant and creative family. His mother, Olga, was an acclaimed novelist and short story writer, as well as having worked as a 'stringer' for small-town newspapers. His brother, Roy, is one of the country's best sports journalists.

Masters joined the prestigious team at *Four Corners* in 1983. His 1985 report 'French Connections', about the sinking of Greenpeace's *Rainbow Warrior* vessel in New Zealand, won him the Gold Walkley award.

As for 'The Family Business', it probed the links between the Italian Mafia and Australia, and in particular the disappearance of Griffith local Donald Mackay in 1977 and the death of a man linked to an Australian Mafia family who was assassinated while on holidays in Italy.

The story screened on 23 June 1986. Masters' source for the story was Peter Vassallo of the Australian Bureau of Criminal Intelligence in Canberra. Vassallo had been impressed by Masters and, in a quiet way, the Mafia story was a test. It proved Masters could be trusted. 'Chris didn't realise when I set him up with this story ... that it was a test for him that would lead him down a particular path and he'd get used to me,' says Vassallo. 'Because I knew the relationship had to be there. Jim [Slade] was always at arm's length, we only communicated by phone, we didn't see each other right? And often we spoke in code when we did speak.'

Masters was in Canberra after the story was broadcast, and met with Vassallo outside the offices of the ABC. Vassallo said he had another story for the investigative journalist.

What did it concern? Masters queried.

'Queensland,' Vassallo said.

Masters was sceptical. He knew many of his colleagues had ploughed the same field before: Allan Hall had done stuff; Andrew Olle; Kerry O'Brien had had a go. 'I felt too many people had already been there,' Masters reflects. It had been done to death.

'Not like this it hasn't,' Vassallo replied.

Most importantly, there was a man Masters needed to meet. Jim Slade of the Queensland police had a story to tell.

Soon after, Vassallo flew to Brisbane with Masters, and they met

Slade in a pub. 'He [Slade] looked more like a farmer than a cop,' says Masters. 'I remember when we got out of the car – we must have been going to have a counter lunch in a pub – Jim took his gun out and locked it in the boot of his car.

'I met his wife Christine also. I felt for her, for them both. I remember being struck by their predicament. It wasn't until I spoke to Jim that I found the moral energy to chase it. Jim's predicament made me angry.'

It was Saturday 27 September 1986. Jim Slade recalls: 'I said to Masters, I'd be part of anything that he wanted. But I said there was no way I'd get my photograph taken, stuff like that. We thought it was probably our best move, to do this.

'What I wanted was for him to have something that he'd be able to pin something on. I wanted to give him at least a statutory declaration.'

It was a beginning for Masters. Slade would talk about the bribes he had been offered from his superior in the Bureau of Criminal Intelligence, Senior Sergeant Alan Barnes, and how the money had allegedly come from Brisbane identity 'Uncle Gerry' Geraldo Bellino. He would explain to Masters the ins and outs of his exhaustive Operation Trek, and the Queensland police hierarchy's lack of interest in its findings.

Slade felt he had betrayed Barnes by talking about the bribes, but equally couldn't live any longer with the stress of the situation. Now he was prepared to tell all to Masters.

Masters gave Slade his word that their initial conversation was 'off the record', and that for the time being he would remain a 'secret, unattributable source'.

Masters would go on to write in a memoir: 'I could tell from the start this was a good story. The scent of institutionalised corruption gave it scale. The cri de coeur of the Slades gave it passion. I was angry at the notion that honesty could be so cunningly press-ganged into a career with the other side.'

(Bagman Jack Herbert would later admit to his biographer Tom Gilling that his ultimate downfall and the collapse of The Joke all went back 'to Slade'.)

Masters returned to Sydney later that day. He wrote in his diary: 'Fly back. Go to bed. Hear the phone. Dad tells me my mother died at 11.30.'

Naturally, Masters was depressed over his mother's death, as were all of Olga's children. She was a life force, and it was impossible to believe she was no longer there.

Masters would pick up the Queensland story in the New Year.

Sin Triangle

By late 1986, two things in Queensland remained a constant. The first was that Bjelke-Petersen would be Premier for another three years – his government increased its majority at the state election, held on 1 November, and the result handed him a seventh consecutive term, and the eleventh for the National Party since 1957.

The second was that the vice scene was bigger and more lucrative than ever, infecting cities and towns across the state, and especially in Brisbane and on the Gold Coast.

Around this time, the chief-of-staff of the *Courier-Mail*, Bob Gordon, was living with his parents in the Brisbane suburb of Wavell Heights, having recently returned to Queensland from Canberra. Gordon, a nuggetty former rugby player, and married with children, had accepted the position at the newspaper, but still hadn't finalised the full move from the Australian capital, where he'd worked for years on the *Canberra Times*. He felt he was an imposition on his parents, so he asked them if he could take up temporary residence at their holiday house at Broadbeach on the Gold Coast. Gordon decided he would commute for the time being.

A newspaperman through and through, Gordon's position meant he wouldn't leave work before around 8.30 p.m., when the first edition had been put to bed. This meant he was often driving through Fortitude Valley to get on to the Story Bridge in the evenings. He soon noticed hookers on all corners of the Valley.

'There was a house, a Queenslander, halfway down to the Valley, which was painted white – a lovely place – obviously had a lot of money spent on it, with a great big red light on the verandah. One night I drove down and there was a bloody queue of Japanese sailors in uniform.'

Back at work, Gordon asked political correspondent Peter Morley if prostitution had been legalised in Queensland since he'd been out of the state.

Morley burst into laughter. 'No, no, Bob,' he replied. 'There're no brothels in Queensland. Russ [Hinze] said there are no brothels in Queensland.'

On another day, Gordon hopped on the Queensland Newspapers bus for the quick trip from Campbell Street, Bowen Hills, into the CBD. It travelled south along St Paul's Terrace towards the city and, in Fortitude Valley, the bus route slipped past a peculiar-shaped building at the fiveways where St Paul's Terrace and Brunswick Street intersected. It was a stone's throw from the former Whiskey Au Go Go nightclub, where 15 people lost their lives after the building was torched in March 1973.

'As the bus went past what I later dubbed "Sin Triangle", all the girls in the bus looked out the window and up …'. Gordon asked a colleague what was going on.

'Oh, sometimes the girls up there flash their wares at everyone,' he was told.

While Gordon had been working in Canberra, back in Brisbane the Bellinos operated an illegal game upstairs, and a brothel – the Top of the Valley – had been in full swing for some time. Still, the brazenness of prostitution stunned Gordon. 'Two things came into my mind,' he recalls. 'One, obviously you know, how come this is so blatant and so tolerated? I didn't have any moral scruples about it, it was just kind of interesting from a journalist's point of view. But [secondly] down south, while I'd been there … there was a raid on a brothel … in Sydney, and when they checked the freehold of the title, it was owned by the local synagogue.'

The memory of that story lingered in Gordon's mind. He returned to the office and assigned a reporter to check on the title of Sin Triangle. 'I didn't want to know who was renting the place, I knew it was the underworld … but I wanted to know who owned the freehold on it,' says Gordon.

Dissatisfied with the reporter's results, he soon tapped on the shoulder of journalist Phil Dickie, who he had known briefly from Canberra when Dickie worked on the Australian National University student newspaper, *Woroni*. (To some, 'Woroni' had become Dickie's nickname around the office.) Dickie had also been a part-time copy boy at the *Canberra Times*. Gordon asked Dickie to go down and figure out where the main brothels were. At that stage the plan was to conduct company searches and publish a list of the respectable people who owned disrespectful houses.

Gordon says: 'He [Dickie] was obviously looking for something to keep his mind off his own … troubles [the young journalist had recently separated from his wife] … all that sort of domestic stuff. It plays havoc with young men.'

Dickie literally carried out the brief to the letter. He remembered that barrister and Director of Prosecutions, Des Sturgess, had written critically of the police Licensing Branch and their activities in his forgotten report of 1985. In it, Sturgess had concentrated on the Brisbane vice scene identities who controlled prostitution and illegal gambling. In the report he didn't identify the main players, but number-coded them.

Dickie's first task was to identify the brothels and massage parlours. Secondly, he had to try and find out who owned the various premises. 'I established, you know, quite easily – phone calls at that stage – that they were in fact brothels or escort agencies offering sex,' he says. 'And then I sort of worked through the rigmarole of the council, the Titles Office and the Corporate Affairs Office, which wasn't sort of nationalised at that stage … I quickly started to get the sense that there was something in this [story].'

Experienced crime reporter Ken Blanch, who'd been on the scene since the 1950s, and had known a string of Queensland police commissioners from Bischof through to Sir Terence Lewis, remembers the mild-mannered Dickie in the office at that time.

'Dickie came to me and said … "I'm to do a thorough investigation of Sin Triangle down the Valley – what will I do?"' says Blanch. 'I suggested that he go and find out who owned the buildings and start right from the ground up, and that's what he did.

'They were all shit scared as soon as he appeared on the scene and he knew who owned the buildings that the brothels were operating in – it happens to be illegal to allow your premises to be used as a brothel – and he had them on toast. They had to tell him that they knew what was going on there. Better to tell him than the coppers.

'He was lucky they didn't do him in, you know, very lucky. He was a very foolhardy young man.'

The editor of the *Courier-Mail*, David Smith, warned both Dickie and Gordon that if the story had 'holes' in it, they'd both be posted to Oodnadatta, the remote outpost in outback South Australia.

Front Page

The week before Dickie's story was published, Commissioner Lewis and his wife Hazel enjoyed a brief break down on their beloved Gold

Coast. On Sunday 4 January, the couple was given an aerial tour from Hope Island to Burleigh Heads aboard the Westpac Surf Lifesaving Association's surf patrol helicopter. A few days later they dined in the exclusive Margot's Restaurant – only opened for a couple of weeks – in the Gold Coast International Hotel, and deemed the meal 'excellent'.

There were the annual drinks with developer Eddie Kornhauser and a Magic Millions dinner at the Conrad International Hotel. There was also a luncheon with Queensland's Chief Justice, Sir Dormer (Bob) Andrews and his wife Lady Andrews. During his leave Lewis read *The Racing Game* by Marvin B. Scott, an analysis of the world of horse racing and those who work in the industry, and *The Complete Yes Minister,* the scripts based on the popular BBC television sitcom about the interaction between elected officials and the public service.

Dickie's painstaking front-page scoop was published on Monday 12 January 1987. It featured a small headshot of Des Sturgess, QC, and carried no by-line. The story opened: 'One year after the Sturgess Report lifted the lid on prostitution in Queensland, Brisbane's sex industry is thriving. In the metropolitan area alone, 21 clearly identifiable brothels are operating, well above the official police claim of the past three years that only 14 brothels are operating under the guise of massage parlours in Brisbane.

'When the confusing multitude of escort agencies is taken into account, some estimates put the number of prostitution outlets in Brisbane as high as 60.'

Dickie identified two distinct groups in control of the trade. The biggest group was that run by a man named Hector Hapeta, 44. His principal associate was his 31-year-old de facto, Anne Marie Tilley, Ann Marie Hall or Mary Hall. The second group had six brothels and controlled the World By Night strip club. It was also linked to the illegal casino at 142 Wickham Street. This other consortium, wrote Dickie, was linked to Geraldo Bellino, Vic Conte, Allan Holloway and Geoff Crocker.

The article continued: 'Sources within the industry described competition between the two groups as surprisingly harmonious but said independent operations and those trying to set up were sometimes subject to "action".'

Dickie quoted Sturgess's report, saying that police had sufficient powers to charge any property owners who knowingly allowed their premises to be used for the purposes of prostitution. 'No owner of any of these premises who had seen it in recent times could be unaware of the purposes for which it is being used,' Sturgess said. 'But ... the main offenders have, for years, enjoyed immunity from prosecution.'

Dickie asked the police department if any of the main players had been charged with prostitution, gaming or illegal liquor offences since the Sturgess Report had been released. The police media section said the release of such information would be a violation of privacy.

Chief-of-staff Bob Gordon says the Queensland Newspapers office was pretty nervous, as was editor David Smith. 'They probably didn't have as much confidence in me as they probably should have; I was the new bloke ... and of course they would have been getting heavy stuff from the Board.'

Deputy Premier and Police Minister Bill Gunn thundered the next day that there were no prostitutes in Brisbane massage parlours, full stop. He said there were only '13 or 14' massage parlours operating right across Queensland, compared to around 200 in Victoria. Gunn said the claim [in the Sturgess Report] that organised crime was behind Brisbane's brothels was 'only one man's opinion'.

(In the *Courier-Mail*'s classified advertisements published at the back of the newspaper that day, as Gunn was assuring the public that there were no prostitutes in the state's massage parlours, were a handful of ads for local brothels. They included Geoff Crocker's notorious Pinky's over at 625 Main Street, Kangaroo Point, and Hapeta and Tilley's Top of the Valley. Both included in their ad that staff were required.)

267

On the morning Dickie's story hit the streets, Lewis was at his desk in headquarters by 6.20 a.m. He attended to numerous meetings and phone calls and at the end of the day saw Assistant Commissioner Don Braithwaite 're plans for Personnel Section for 1987'.

There was no mention at all of the front-page story on the city's vice lords and the inaction of Licensing Branch police. There was nothing in his diaries on Tuesday or Wednesday, when he met with the Police History Committee, including his old mate, criminologist Dr Paul Wilson. Only on Thursday 15 January did the prostitution issue come onto the radar of the Commissioner. 'Phoned Hon. Gunn re media articles on prostitution.'

And that, it appeared, was the end of that.

Except that over in Highgate Hill in the city's inner-south, the former Licensing Branch undercover agent and police prosecutor, Nigel Powell, had also read the Dickie report in the *Courier-Mail*, and he recognised it as a small window into his own former life.

Powell had resigned from the police force, after being constantly harassed and labelled a 'dog', and then later blamed for leaking information to the press. The idea of corruption in the force and lack of police attention to the major vice players continued to eat away at Powell. Dickie's report fired him up.

Powell knew all the main players. He knew who was connected to whom, and he had his suspicions about a number of senior police he believed corrupt, particularly Harry Burgess. So Powell sat down at a typewriter and outlined what he knew about Brisbane's vice scene. He wanted to get it into the hands of the journalist who wrote the anonymous story in the newspaper.

Lewis says the Dickie article did not cause any great concern. 'We knew and everybody knew about the gambling joints,' Lewis says. 'There was never an official complaint about anything improper that happened there. You couldn't pinch them. To pinch them you had to get an agent in [the premises on] one or two occasions to show that you were running it, and after the game getting a cut of the winnings. Then you could apply for a warrant and go in and pinch them. Then they'd be fined $100.

'It didn't exercise my mind greatly, people playing games, the prostitution. And SP betting had always gone on. My interests were murder, rapes, armed robberies, road deaths.

'There's more prostitution now,' Lewis observes.

The Good Father

By early 1987 the former petty criminal, John Stopford, had settled happily on North Stradbroke Island and was starting a new life. The orphan had had enough of the mainland. He'd worked in the vice game, started his own escort service, blown all the money he made on high times, then become addicted to heroin.

He had a vast knowledge of the Brisbane vice scene, having first dipped his toe in its pool way back in the 1970s, when he took a job at the huge brothel, the Polynesian Playground. He'd been in and out of prison, and nearly lost his son, Jay, when his wife took the boy to Western Australia while he was briefly incarcerated. His wife had found someone else in the West, and it outwardly appeared that Stopford was set to return to society with nothing.

He did, however, have a mate who was living with a girlfriend at Sunnybank in the city's south, and in turn her parents had a caravan permanently sited at Amity Point. The parents agreed to let Stopford live in the caravan. He had no money but he took to village life. He even came across local flower farmer, former assistant commissioner of police, Tony Murphy. At the time Stopford thought that was a good thing. It made him feel more secure, that Murphy lived just around the corner. 'He wouldn't want anything happening in his front yard,' Stopford says of the former detective.

Stopford had heard all of the rumours of police corruption in the Queensland Police Force. But it was just that – rumour. 'I heard the odd thing,' he recalls. 'But at first I didn't believe it. At the time, it was just gossip. But as I ventured through … I surmised that this was possible. That it was a little bit bigger than Harry Burgess.

'I remember thinking at the time, if I've got my placings right, that is, how Ray Whitrod – the [allegations] he was bringing up – could well and truly be fair dinkum. I remember thinking about that myself. Whitrod got absolutely poleaxed.'

Meanwhile, Stopford settled into Amity Point and got involved with the newly formed social club in the village. They got together on Friday nights. It was so popular that Stopford soon convinced the club to hold a Sunday session as well. He formed some new friendships and soon sought, and got, custody of his son. Jay joined the local kindergarten and Stopford got a job working as bar manager for the social club. It seemed his worries were over. 'Back in those days it was God's country,' says Stopford. 'We moved to the old post office in Birch Street [at Amity], and we were very happy there.'

Shortly after coming out of prison Stopford had met Peter Cassuben, a local ABC reporter, and they had started talking about Brisbane's illegal gambling and prostitution scene. Cassuben had taped some of their conversations, which Stopford saw as some form of potential insurance, if anything ever went wrong. 'I gave him a bit of information about the vice scene, but his main thing at the time was more on the drugs thing,' he says. 'It was only when he realised, as I waffled through contacts … that this was a bit bigger than him …'

Later, Cassuben pointed his Sydney colleague Chris Masters to the tapes. Given what Masters was researching, he wanted to speak with Stopford also. 'Peter said Chris [Masters] was on a journey, an investigation into some of the stuff that I'd spoken about and thought was relevant, and he'd like to speak to me,' recalls Stopford. 'I wasn't aware of how big it was.'

The Powell Letter

Nigel Powell, the former Licensing Branch officer, had been a little rudderless since he'd resigned from the Queensland Police Force and left behind those long nights trawling through Fortitude Valley and piecing together the mosaic that was Brisbane crime and corruption. He'd tried repeatedly to bring the branch's attention to the wheeling and dealing of men like Hector Hapeta and others, and had received good information from informants on the streets. He was still confused, however, by the complete indifference displayed by his superiors.

'I still had the attitude that I wanted to do something about Tilley and Hapeta,' Powell later said. Upon reading Dickie's piece in the *Courier-Mail* that January, he decided to approach the newspaper. At the time he was living alone in a small cottage in Prospect Terrace, Highgate Hill. He was studying Arts full-time at the University of Queensland and just making ends meet. He sat down and typed a 12-page missive. His experience with the Queensland Police Force since 1979 all came down to this *j'accuse*.

Powell wrote that in the first half of 1980 it had become apparent to Sergeant Ron Lewis of the Licensing Branch that Hapeta and Tilley owned and ran the Top of the Valley massage parlour and some escort agencies, and were pulling in about $250,000 a year.

In the letter, Powell explained how at one point he suggested to his boss, Noel Dwyer, that he resign or be falsely sacked from the police force so he could penetrate an SP bookie outfit. Dwyer later told Powell he could not proceed as 'it would upset too many important people both upstairs and in politics'. (Dwyer later denied ever saying that.)

Powell went on to talk about strip clubs like the World By Night that operated without a liquor licence. 'Why did we not conduct a raid on the premises every night they were found operating?' Powell virtually asked himself in the letter.

He went on to say he had grave suspicions about his colleague, Sergeant Harry Burgess. There were also police on the Gold Coast that he had heard from sources were corrupt.

Powell conceded that he had no hard evidence of corruption, but said there was 'too much circumstantial evidence for any other reasoning'. He said there appeared to have been for years 'apparent favouritism' shown by police to the Bellino/Conte consortium and the Hapeta/Tilley group.

'This is not just Police inaction or ineptness,' he concluded. 'The Bellino name has been mentioned on a number of occasions in connection with illegal gaming on the floor of parliament. Indeed, the Premier himself has seen fit to open a marble mine at Chillagoe in which the Bellino family are open partners. I cannot believe that he would not have been aware of the name and its repute.'

Powell ended the document by pointing out that police and politics had to be 'as separate as possible'. He added: 'The extent of corruption, vice and organised crime is directly proportional to the degree of police and political involvement.' He couldn't have known how prescient that observation was.

After dropping off his letter to the offices of the *Courier-Mail* at Queensland Newspapers in Bowen Hills, Powell contacted an old colleague from his days as a police prosecutor, the lawyer and civil libertarian Terry O'Gorman. They met in O'Gorman's office in the city. 'I knew if I was going to get on board with this I had to have back-up,' says Powell. 'I had a good feeling he [O'Gorman] was trustworthy. We had an appointment late one night. He asked me if I knew *Four Corners* was in town.'

O'Gorman and Powell discussed cooperating with the media on the story. Powell says O'Gorman recommended he speak with the ABC team as the show was powerful and had a national presence. Chris Masters, too, was well respected across the country.

'So I said, yes, I would like to talk to *Four Corners*,' recalls Powell.

Confluence

Masters, who had returned to Queensland in January, was not just sniffing about Brisbane but was also following up some of the intelligence contained in officer Jim Slade's Operation Trek report on the drug trade in Far North Queensland. Masters took *Four Corners* to Cairns, then dropped into Rockhampton. They had someone they needed to talk to in Yeppoon – the former Sheriff of Mareeba, Ross Dickson. Having maintained his silence for a few years Dickson now felt safe enough to talk to the media. 'He had a small fish restaurant on the coast ... with the unforgettable name, "Sea Food and Eat It",' Masters later wrote.

'Ross Dickson was aproned and busy. Our conversation dived and plunged between the wrapping, the salting and the cash register. He was a great yarner. He knew the inner workings of the Queensland Police Force well and was prepared to give up some of its secrets.'

Masters had been on the road at this point with producer Shaun Hoyt. When they returned to Brisbane after speaking with Dickson, they were joined by *Four Corners* researcher and qualified lawyer Debbie Whitmont. Masters knew that it was better that he not work alone on the story, given its growing scale. Not only could the workload be shared, but he knew it was sensible to have a witness by your side should anything untoward happen. He learned, in the course of his investigation, that 'some of the police I was up against were prepared to arrest and charge me with a mythical offence'.

It was, in fact, a little more serious than that. Masters later learned that there had been a plan hatched to set him up with an underage boy. (They similarly tried the 'gay' card on journalist Phil Dickie. 'Of course I fucking go to the gay bars in the city – where do you want to get the information ... I talked to the taxi drivers, too. If someone calls me gay it doesn't matter to me. I know I'm not, the people it matters to know I'm not ... But yeah, they tried ...')

The *Four Corners* team settled into the Tower Mill Hotel on Wickham Terrace, up the hill from police headquarters in Makerston Street. The iconic hotel had been the flashpoint for tensions between Queensland police and protestors rallying against the arrival of the South African Springboks rugby team 16 years earlier. At the time, a younger Terry Lewis had been on the ground in front of the hotel, manning the barricades. The hotel would now be home to the *Four Corners* investigative team for months.

Terry O'Gorman soon put Masters and Powell together. 'Nigel was gold because he was the credible witness who could be believed,' says Masters. 'He was prepared to speak.'

Masters and his colleagues got down to work. 'There were witnesses to find and interview,' Masters later reflected. 'There were newspaper files to search. Land title and company searches would help prove the ownership of the brothels and illegal casinos.'

Masters paid a visit to the ABC's local film library, and came across the story by Allan Hall of *Nationwide* just five years earlier. He watched the admissions of former police officers Bob Campbell and Kingsley Fancourt. He noted that the only major reaction to the program had been a flurry of writs. One of these was in relation to police officer Neal Freier, who had been acquitted of corruption charges with Jack Herbert in the mid-1970s and been adversely mentioned by Bob Campbell during the program. On 5 September 1984, the ABC had sent Freier a letter admitting they had defamed him, offering an apology and paying $30,000 in damages. 'We now unreservedly accept that at no time had you been involved in corrupt practices either on your own account or for any other Senior Police Officer,' wrote ABC General Manager for Queensland, Charles Grahame, to Freier.

Following the program being aired Bob Campbell had fled the State, in fear for the life of his family, while Kingsley Fancourt was also threatened following the interview. 'There was a sobering lesson in all this,' Masters later wrote, reflecting on the implications of people getting caught in the crossfire of any media investigation. 'Not just for myself but for any potential whistleblower. In the days ahead I would telephone a succession of retired, battered policemen. I can remember well their words: "Forget it. Go away. You will only make it worse. Today's news is tomorrow's wrappings. The public don't care anyway."'

Threats from the Top

On Thursday 12 February 1987, Commissioner Lewis, in the course of a typically busy day, mentioned in his diary that apparently a team from the television current affairs program, *Four Corners*, were out and about 'muck-raking'.

Chris Masters hadn't been in Brisbane town that long and already he'd caught the eye of the Commissioner of Police. As Masters would later write in a memoir, *Inside Story*: 'There was no chance of keeping our work secret. We were approaching too many people. Someone was going to alert the opposition. Before long, it was clear they were watching us closely. We would talk with a policeman and the policeman would be immediately interviewed by superiors who wanted to know what we were up to. I got a bit nervous when I realised how close they were watching.'

Peter Vassallo, head of the Italian desk at the Australian Bureau of Criminal Intelligence (ABCI) in Canberra, had also attracted Lewis's attention. On 23 February Vassallo was interrogated by his own people for several hours over an allegation of impropriety against him, made by Commissioner Lewis. Vassallo was facing the loss of his job.

He says Commissioner Lewis had allegedly told his superiors at the ABCI that he had handed a Queensland BCI document to journalist Chris Masters, and that the author of that document – the Operation Trek report – was Jim Slade.

Vassallo says he was asked if he had ever travelled anywhere with Masters. He answered in the affirmative. He says he told his boss, director Robin Chalker, that his role on that day in Brisbane was to facilitate the meeting between Slade and Masters. Slade was Masters' informant, he told them.

(Robin Chalker says he has no recollection of the interrogation of Peter Vassallo, 'I can't remember the incident. That's not to say it didn't happen.')

Vassallo, technically a New South Wales police officer but on secondment to the ABCI, was referred to the state's integrity unit and was interviewed in Sydney. 'Until Chris Masters' story went to air, and from the time that Lewis made the open allegation against me, I suddenly realised that these blokes were now starting to panic,' Vassallo recalls. 'I said to Chris, I said to Jimmy, I said, "Cover your backs – they're coming for me, they've had a go at you, but I now think they've realised that there's more to come." And ... I said to Chris, "Look, you know, you need some protection, mate."'

Vassallo heard from other sources that if he continued doing what he was doing, he would end up 'with a bullet in him'. He assumed that word of the after-dark activities of the *Four Corners* crew – their filming of nightclubs in Fortitude Valley, for example – had been passed back to the upper levels of the Queensland Police Force. 'It had nothing to do with the cops; you're now focusing on the crooks,' he says. 'What's happening is the crooks are now complaining to the people they're paying ... they're demanding their protection.'

A Trip to the Zoo

Amity Point bar manager, John Stopford, saw no real harm in meeting with Sydney investigative journalist Chris Masters. He knew that Masters' *Four Corners* program was looking at the drug scene, and since kicking heroin himself, drugs had become something of a 'soapbox issue' for him. Why not have a yarn with a journalist?

What Stopford didn't know at that point was that the Queensland police still had their eye on him. Police had approached one of Stopford's neighbours on the beach at Amity and said they'd been ordered to come down hard on Stopford because he was a 'known drug dealer'.

The Stradbroke police station came under the authority of the Wynnum police district, and the head of the Wynnum CIB was Detective Sergeant Harry Burgess. In the end, Stopford was convinced to head to Sydney and talk with *Four Corners*. It was all expenses paid. He leapt at the chance of a couple of days in Sydney, and took his son.

'They paid for the limo to pick us up ... paid for the flights, motel room for two nights, $40 spending money a day,' recalls Stopford. 'They took me out to ABC headquarters. I met David Hill [the ABC's then managing director]. They took Jay and showed him the clock in the studio. He was rapt – they took us to Taronga Park Zoo.'

Masters had an unpleasant duty to perform at the zoo as he strolled around the animal enclosures with Stopford. It concerned the original tapes that reporter Peter Cassuben had made of his conversations with Stopford. Cassuben had passed them onto Masters, then Masters had passed them on to a friend in the Australian Federal Police. Somehow, news of the tapes' existence had gotten out, and the head of the AFP office in Brisbane then passed them on to the Queensland police, where they ended up in the possession of Assistant Commissioner Graeme Parker.

'He told me ... that the tapes had been passed on to somebody and now they were in the hands of the Queensland police,' says Stopford. 'I was very apprehensive from then on ... an uneasiness started to come to me.'

Stopford and son Jay returned to Amity Point. He said it was a difficult decision – to agree to appear on camera. He was still smarting over the tapes leak. 'I tend to remember Chris virtually begging me and saying, "I know we've done the wrong thing with these tapes, but would you like me to get in touch with Nigel [Powell]," or something like that …' Stopford recalls.

'We hadn't found a location safe enough at this stage to do the filming. I told him, "I don't think I can go through with this, mate."

'I did believe him. If I didn't believe in Chris Masters I would have pulled it then … I was in tears. "You've put me between a rock and a hard spot here." I had no one to talk to about it. I agreed [to be interviewed on camera] in the end. I'd come to realise that it was probably my only way out of this.'

Stopford wasn't used to telling all before a camera, and in turn to hundreds of thousands of viewers. 'They didn't want me to gloss over words,' says Stopford. 'They needed the truth. I said to them all along, I reckon Harry Burgess is your link, I think he is the weak pin. I think he's the one who will buckle first.'

Stopford says nerves set in between the time he was interviewed for the report, which would become known as 'The Moonlight State', and its public broadcasting. 'I was looking over my shoulder,' he says. 'I never stopped looking over my shoulder from the time in Sydney I was told that those tapes had gone [missing]. I knew that was like waving a red flag to a bull.'

Stopford was growing increasingly anxious. He decided to ring the officer he'd once informed to, and they met in a car park in front of the old Scurr Brothers hardware store at the Mount Gravatt Central shopping strip on Logan Road. Stopford told the officer he'd been speaking to the ABC in Sydney.

'At first he appeared disinterested in my problems, but once he learned I had spoken to the ABC … he began to take new interest,' Stopford recalled.

'He raised with me, not I with him, whether there had been any discussion with the ABC about a detective called Slade.'

A Constable Retires

Not only was the Commissioner, Sir Terence Lewis, contending with rumours that a *Four Corners* investigative crew was sniffing around North Queensland and the state's south-east, he also had some nasty leaks emanating from within his own department. A month earlier, on 9 February, one of Lewis's daughters, Laureen Ireland, 25, a police constable, was found medically unfit to continue serving in the force. As he recorded in his diary for that day: 'Laureen appeared before the Police Medical Board. Certified permanently unfit for any further duty in the Police Force.'

Laureen had been in the force for a total of six years and five months, including her probationary period. She was first posted to the Mitchelton police station in February 1981, had a stint in the Traffic Branch in Brisbane, joined Gold Coast Mobile Patrols in 1984, and had a year in the Gold Coast Juvenile Aid Bureau before serving in uniform at Southport. Between 1985 and 1986 she performed 101 arrests and issued 239 cautions. She had married Constable M.W. Ireland on 30 January 1982.

The Police Medical Board concluded that Constable Ireland suffered 'anxiety depression of such chronicity and severity that she is permanently unfit for any duties in the Police Force'. She was discharged from the force on 10 February, the release signed by her father. Laureen had dinner with her parents that night. Her superannuation payout totalled $142,199.64 after tax.

In early March, someone in the force released details of the payout to ALP parliamentary firebrand Tom Burns, and he rose in the House on Tuesday 10 March to probe Deputy Premier and Police Minister Bill Gunn on what appeared to be a generous payout for someone with less than seven years in the job.

While it must have been aggravating to Lewis that his own daughter's illness, and the superannuation figure, had been put under media scrutiny, it was also a headache out of the blue for Gunn. He had been forced to defend the police department over the *Courier-Mail* story on brothels and illegal gambling dens in January, and now this.

Burns revealed that many police officers told him they were 'outraged' at the size of the payout. 'It would seem to be far above what the ordinary working man would receive in similar circumstances,' Burns said.

Lewis was forced to comment, and he gave selective interviews to journalists about depression and its impact on everyday police officers. He refused to talk specifically about his daughter. Sir Terence said he would not talk about the matter as it was being 'canvassed in the political arena'. Similarly, the Queensland Police Union made itself unavailable for comment.

The *Courier-Mail* reported: 'The issue has divided police throughout Queensland.'

Lewis had always been a lightning rod for media stories by virtue of the nature of his position, but the tenor of the stories now circulating around the Commissioner had changed. There was a slipping of niceties. He was now fair game on matters big and small. Was the Ireland superannuation fiasco a case of nepotism? Or was the young woman simply entitled by law to her payout? Once upon a time, the questions wouldn't have even been raised. Had Dickie's front-page story in January made a slight tear in the age-old fabric of the police force and the trust in which it was held by the general community? Had there been an infinitesimal shift in this perception?

It was clear that the Queensland Police Force, at this point, was under siege. But as some police knew only too well, attack was always the best mode of defence. In early March, lawyers Robertson O'Gorman representing Lewis and Murphy in their defamation action against the ABC, issued a warning to the ABC's lawyers.

Dear Sirs,

We have been informed that your client through its 'Four Corners' programme may be screening a programme in the near future, the content of which in part may touch on the material published in the *Nationwide* programmes the subject of our clients' actions.

This letter is to give you notice that in the event that there is any further publication by your client of any material defamatory of our clients or either of them, then our clients will seek leave of the Court of the trial to introduce this letter on the issue of damages.

Yours faithfully, Robertson O'Gorman [lawyers]

Only the Opinion of One Man

It had been just over two months since *Courier-Mail* journalist Phil Dickie had published his story on Brisbane's tawdry vice scene and who was behind the mutli-million-dollar local industry, and still there had been nothing but denial from the Bjelke-Petersen government. In the interim, Dickie had sat down for talks with former Licensing Branch officer Nigel Powell, and Chris Masters had concluded much of his research for his *Four Corners* investigation into Queensland crime and corruption.

In parliament, the member for Logan and Opposition Police Spokesman, Wayne Goss, was not going to let the issue fade away. On Tuesday 31 March, he let fly during debate over a second reading of the National Crime Authority (State Provisions) Act Amendment Bill. The Bill sought to remove the Attorney-General from the Inter-Governmental Committee of the National Crime Authority (NCA) and replace him with the Police Minister. The amendment was introduced by Deputy Premier and Police Minister Bill Gunn.

'My concern and suspicion about this government move arises from the fact that ... the government has not given any reason for the change,' Goss said. 'The Minister has already shown his lack of commitment to fighting organised crime by his refusal just this year either to act on the findings of the Sturgess Report or to even acknowledge the validity of those findings.

'I refer in particular to ... two organised criminal groups [who] control prostitution in Brisbane in Queensland. Even more serious is the finding by Mr Sturgess that the main offenders have for years enjoyed immunity from prosecution.'

Goss was at pains to point out that these findings were not just allegations being made by the Opposition under the protection of parliamentary privilege. Sturgess was the government's own Director of Prosecutions whose inquiry had taken over a year to complete.

'However, Mr Gunn, the Police Minister, dismissed his own Government's report and the report of his Director of Prosecutions without any hesitation as "only the opinion of one man",' Goss continued. 'I ask honourable members: How can such a Minister be given responsibility for assisting the National Crime Authority in investigating organised crime anywhere, much less in Queensland?'

Goss said his 'sources' told him that the problem initially rested with the previous Attorney-General, Neville Harper, who declined to cooperate with the NCA on a specific issue but was persuaded that there was a need for the NCA to 'come into Queensland on a particular matter'.

Goss noted that 'the quite proper decision to cooperate, made by the previous Attorney-General, upset certain senior sections of the Queensland Police Force and they are determined to see that it does not happen again ... I believe that the attitude of the Government is exposed by its refusal to allow the Commissioner of Police to cooperate with, or to brief a joint committee of, the National Crime Authority.'

It was intriguing stuff from Goss who, in the wake of the Dickie article, was trying to hypothesise a conspiracy. His questions were simple enough: Exactly why did the Queensland Government want to keep the powerful NCA outside the gate? What did they have to hide?

Goss quoted directly from a report of the joint committee: '... the Committee was disappointed that it was unable to receive a briefing from the Queensland Commissioner of Police. As Queensland is an important link, such a meeting would have been valuable in completing the Committee's overview of matters relating to the fight against organised crime throughout Australia.'

Goss read further from the report: 'One theme which has been stressed by many of the representatives of the law enforcement agencies who have appeared before the Committee is the crucial need for a high level of coordination and cooperation between all agencies involved in the fight against organised crime.'

He said the government's refusal to allow Commissioner Lewis to appear before the committee was 'a shame and a disgrace'. 'The role of the police and, for that matter, that of the Police Minister, have become highly politicised,' said Goss.

It was a drum that the Opposition had been beating for years. In Queensland, the separation of powers was a myth. And since the late 1970s, Premier Bjelke-Petersen had increasingly used the services of his police force to enable his political will. The closeness between Bjelke-Petersen and Police Commissioner Lewis, too, had been raising eyebrows since Lewis's famous speech at the induction of new constables at the Queensland Police Academy in 1983. 'The people of Queensland and the police force owe the Premier a very deep gratitude,' Lewis had told the congregation. 'The free enterprise policy of the Bjelke-Petersen government has been responsible for Queensland's tremendous growth.

'Irrespective of whether some people agree with the politics, statements or stands, there is a universal respect, even admiration, for the total loyalty he and his colleagues show for what they believe is in the best interest of Queensland.'

To some, the Premier and the police had become indivisible.

Tick, Tick

After a hiatus of several weeks since Phil Dickie's first report on vice and corruption, the *Courier-Mail* – now under the new editorship of Greg Chamberlin – forged ahead with its investigation into Brisbane's seedy underworld. On Monday 13 April, the newspaper published another Dickie piece that this time looked into the city's illegal 'casinos'. He suggested that as many as six illegal casinos were operating in the city. 'The owners of both the former and present casinos are Geraldo Bellino, of St Lucia, and Vittorio Conte, of Bowen Hills,' the article said.

A further report appeared on Saturday 18 April, this time targeting the Hapeta and Tilley empire. 'Queensland's second largest organised crime syndicate has grown from nothing in the past eight years,' Dickie wrote. 'In the process it has changed the face of prostitution in Queensland, tipping the balance of returns away from prostitutes to brothel and escort agency operators.'

Dickie revealed that the *Courier-Mail* had put two questions to the Queensland police through its media section. Had any action been taken against Hapeta and Tilley in the past two years? (Assistant Commissioner (Crime) answered 'no'.) What did the department have to say about allegations of this police inactivity?

'Assistant Commissioner Parker ... asked for information on who was making the allegations,' Dickie wrote. 'When told this information could not be given, he responded ... "no comment".'

The pincer movement of Dickie and Chris Masters of *Four Corners* had started to have an impact. Commissioner Lewis's assistant Greg

Early recorded in his diary for Monday 20 April: 'Senior Sergeant Ron Pickering Holland Park rang re 4 Corners programme. Said that main informant was Nigel Powell an ex Licensing Branch man. He said his information was that the programme hosted by Chris Masters was aimed at a Royal Commission with Detective Senior Sergeant Burgess and Assistant Commissioner Parker in mind.'

Two days later Early wrote: 'Senior Sergeant Freestone rang from Rockhampton after COP [Commissioner of Police] had spoken to Minister re 4 Corners. Minister said would be stupid to talk to them.'

Vice madam Anne Marie Tilley wasn't overly concerned about *Four Corners*. She believed, erroneously, that the program's targets were Geraldo Bellino and Vittorio Conte. 'When they were sniffing around the casino, I was wrapped – [I thought] they're not looking at us,' she says. 'I thought they were just picking on the casinos.'

While rumours of police corruption had been floating around for decades, the culprits had always managed to evade the noose. This time, Dickie believed, he just might be able to nail them on an accumulation of facts. 'I think this was a system that was ripe to fall, it was supremely arrogant and over-confident. You know they'd weathered everything … [the Sturgess Report] had blown over them … that was inconvenient but it wasn't a catastrophe.

'I didn't want to … go back to the same game of, you know, here is someone telling what they know about corruption. And then getting crucified … you know?'

Dickie says Powell was a huge help with the second volley of stories in April. 'He also stopped me doing stupid stuff like, you know, parking across the road from places,' he says.

As his research progressed, Dickie admits he did sense danger. 'There was one night when I was feeling a bit sort of surrounded in the Valley, when I … rang my father in a bit of a state and dictated a will,' he says. There was a string of incidents. 'At that point in late April … you could palpably feel the tension on the streets rising.'

He says at one point he gave *Four Corners* producer Shaun Hoyt a quick tour of some of Brisbane's vice hot spots. 'I sort of showed them the lay of the land,' he says. 'I didn't see it as a rivalry from them. I was glad of a bit of intelligent company.'

Similarly, Peter Vassallo of the ABCI was more than cognisant of the dangers involved on the ground in Brisbane at the time. 'I mean these people [corrupt police] were preventing things from getting done,' he says. 'They were protecting an institutionalised situation. They were trying to discredit Jim [Slade], they were trying to discredit me, they were trying to discredit the [Alpha] report.

'Remember this is a group of people who, for years, issued writs and discredited. They either prevented a story from being told or ... you make them a laughing stock, you ridicule, it's ... [a] political tactic more than a law enforcement tactic. However, you have to understand that ... the law enforcement people who were trying to protect the situation clearly were the corrupt police. Only they knew how it could bite them on the arse. There was no politics in it at that point ...'

Vassallo, too, began to worry that Masters' story might never get to air. 'I had the great fear, I'll tell you personally now,' he says. 'Chris, Jim and I separately knew different parts of the story. And it was important from my perspective that that remained.'

Masters' work had by necessity gone from covert to overt, given that the *Four Corners* crew needed to film various clubs in Brisbane at night. They had become conspicuous, and the police were watching. 'I remember him [Masters] telling me he felt he was being followed. He had put on ... he had protective services ... hired private investigators to look after him while he slept and all that sort of shit. And I knew it wasn't paranoia, it was fucking real,' says Vassallo.

What nobody knew was that the head of the powerful Queensland Police Union, John 'Bluey' O'Gorman, brother to lawyer Terry O'Gorman and an old-style, no nonsense copper, was also helping Masters during the compilation of 'The Moonlight State'. O'Gorman provided Masters with a mud map of the characters involved in the story, namely, who knew who in and outside the police force. He felt his involvement was important, a way of providing 'balance' to the story. He had no doubts that what Masters was compiling was going to be explosive.

Meanwhile, The Bagman Jack Herbert had first become aware of the *Four Corners* investigative crew snooping around Brisbane in the first quarter of 1987. He and his wife Peggy were at home in their splendid two-storey, piano-shaped house in Jordan Terrace, Bowen Hills, when they noticed a camera crew outside, chatting to their neighbours.

A month later, his good friend and contact Allen Bulger was transferred out of the Licensing Branch. Herbert later said that it was this precise period when he felt 'we were all in danger'. He was gauging a lot of panic within The Joke. He claimed he hadn't seen Commissioner Lewis since February. (Lewis's diary would record that the Commissioner and his wife had drinks with the Herberts on Saturday 7 February.)

Herbert said he met Vic Conte near the New Farm library, and again at the Toombul Shopping Centre just north of the CBD, to discuss the *Four Corners* threat. The Bagman also had to get in touch with Hapeta and Tilley, '... but with camera crews snooping around I couldn't risk meeting Hapeta in person'. In the end he met up with Tilley and told her he didn't want Hapeta coming anywhere near him for a while.

Then Harry Burgess came around to Herbert's place in Jordan Terrace. 'He said he had $45,000 in a safe deposit box and wanted to know if he should close it down,' recalled Herbert. 'I could tell that Harry was starting to panic. He was up in Wynnum but I was still giving him money every month.

'He wanted to know if I'd heard anything from the Commissioner. I dare say he thought Terry must know more than the rest of us.'

Still in a state of agitation, Herbert then alleged he met Graeme Parker in the car park of the Alderley Arms Hotel in Samford Road in the city's inner north-west. 'It was dark and I'd just given him some money when we saw a yellow car drive past,' Herbert wrote in his memoir. 'Except for us, the car park was deserted. Parker said, "That's a *Four Corners* car. Let's go." He wanted to get away as quickly as possible.'

Herbert then met Allen Bulger in the car park of the Brothers Rugby Union Club at Albion just north of the CBD. He remembered that Bulger was 'scared out of his wits'.

With all the self-imposed radio silence, it was difficult to relay messages. Herbert said: 'None of us knew what was going on. We were all just hoping for the best. I met [police officer] Noel Kelly at a hardware store in Mount Gravatt and asked him to tell Graeme Parker about the camera crew filming my house so that Parker could tell the Commissioner and he could get a message back to me.'

As for journalist Chris Masters, he wasn't quite sure what sort of 'mess' he'd let himself in for with this Queensland story. He met with an official attached to the National Crime Authority. He was told to be careful. Later, an Australian Federal Police officer was attached to Masters. 'They formally put somebody on the case to look out for me,' he recalls. 'They were giving me real-time evidence of the Queensland police surveilling me. There was this plot to set me up.'

In the meantime, he and his colleagues had dug up an extraordinary piece of documentary evidence. The title deeds for Herbert's house in Jordan Terrace, Bowen Hills, revealed that in late 1985, Herbert had purchased the house from the two former owners – Geraldo Bellino and Vittorio Conte. The document proved a direct line between Bellino and his men and a former police officer who also happened to be good friends with the current Commissioner of Police, Sir Terence Lewis.

It was the bridge Masters had been looking for. 'Someone in the underworld told me about it,' Masters says. 'I asked Deb Whitmont to do a title search. At the time it took about two weeks. When it finally appeared in our hands, there was no greater joy than holding the smoking gun. We had a bit more evidence, but this was the key piece of evidence. It was indisputable.'

The Man Who Had Everything

High-profile public servant Allen Lindsay Callaghan, born and educated on the Gold Coast, and known as a history, political science and opera fan, railway buff and purveyor of fine clothes, went to trial for misappropriating public funds in early 1987. He appeared in the Brisbane District Court on Wednesday 22 April, the same law precinct that had seen his wife Judith sentenced to gaol for similarly stealing money as head of the Queensland Day Committee. He pleaded guilty to taking $43,574.06 for his own personal use between 1979 and 1985.

Callaghan, 46, of Siemon Street, Toowong, was accompanied in the court by his wife Judith (who had served only three months of her two-and-a-half-year sentence). She sat in the public gallery behind him.

The court heard that Callaghan had racked up $8860.11 in restaurant expenses which he claimed were for legitimate business. There was a bill for $800.70 from the Fountain Room restaurant for Art Gallery trustees, one from Stephanie's Restaurant in Melbourne, another for Cavills on the Gold Coast. The Crown said the meals were had, but not with the people listed on the expense claims. Callaghan also recorded $2898 worth of entries for Melbourne tailor Hendon. He purchased jewellery, antiques in Bahrain, and hired luxury vehicles for the wedding of one of his daughters. All were marked as Queensland Film Corporation expenses, according to the court. Crown Prosecutor David Bullock said it all added up to what 'could only be described as extravagance, luxury and self-indulgence'.

Callaghan's counsel, Bob Mulholland, QC, disagreed, saying Callaghan had a very demanding job and worked day and night. He said it couldn't be suggested that Callaghan accumulated such enormous restaurant expenses on his own, nor that it wasn't necessary for a man of his position to dress well.

Mulholland said Callaghan took full responsibility for the misappropriating of funds. He wished to blame nobody else. On 28 April, Callaghan was sentenced to four years' gaol with hard labour by Judge McCracken. There was no recommendation for early parole. The judge said he had found it difficult to arrive at an adequate sentence. 'Such conduct by an employee in a business or undertaking, when it amounts to the misappropriation of funds of the magnitude revealed here, would call for a significant penalty to be imposed,' Judge McCracken said. 'However, you were not just any employee when you embarked on your course of dishonesty. The members of the community expect that such office-holders will exhibit the highest standards of personal and professional probity in the administration of the affairs of such an office.'

Callaghan didn't flinch when the sentence was handed down. He simply nodded his head. Judith trembled in the public gallery. As he was about to be led away she grabbed his hand and kissed it, then stood crying.

Callaghan arrived by prison van at Boggo Road Gaol in a dazed state. His head and beard were shaved and he was issued prison clothing. He was initially housed in the gaol's old section. Prisoners soon recognised him from television news reports. He was the man who had everything. But now, inside his prison cell, all of his achievements, his reputation as a quick wit, his widely admired skill as a press officer and his contribution to Joh Bjelke-Petersen's long tenure as Queensland Premier, came to nothing.

Three days later, the Premier was the star guest at a Christian Outreach Centre 'businessmen's breakfast' at Brisbane's Royal on the

Park hotel, facing the Botanic Gardens on Alice Street. He received a framed quote that read: 'With God Anything is Possible'.

Bjelke-Petersen, in turn, offered his own little commandment. 'We're all sinners,' he told the crowd.

Eleventh Hour

At the eleventh hour the Queensland Police Department was still trying to pre-empt the upcoming *Four Corners* investigation and construct some sort of defensive narrative.

On Wednesday 6 May the *Courier-Mail* ran a suite of stories about the local vice scene, offering supposedly official police statistics on how the force had not just contained prostitution in Brisbane, but reduced it. As for illegal gambling, the head of the gaming squad, Detective Inspector Ross Beer – who had been named years before in state parliament by the late Kev Hooper as a man who frequented illegal games and drank there – declared that police had not found any evidence of it despite having suspect establishments under surveillance for the fortnight.

Beer, who would have to have been granted permission by Commissioner Lewis to speak with the media, said police had only witnessed legal card games. 'I've been in the job for a couple of weeks and before then I've had nothing to do with gambling,' Beer reportedly said. 'I can only say I've seen nothing in that time that you could call an illegal casino.'

Beer used the opportunity to defend himself against Hooper's old allegations, which included that he had once taken a meal up to Gerry Bellino when the latter was being treated in the Wesley Hospital. 'The allegations that I'm some sort of a friend to criminals is absolutely rubbish,' Beer said. 'Why would I have been interested in going to any of these alleged casinos? I'm not even a gambler.'

Another story in the newspaper that day denied that the Brisbane vice scene was run by two organised crime syndicates, as had been reported by journalist Phil Dickie. A week or so earlier the *Courier-Mail* team had organised for a series of questions to be sent to Police Minister Bill Gunn. Upon receiving them Gunn had been so disturbed that he demanded the Commissioner of Police answer them.

'Gunn didn't want the police to give the answers to us but he wanted the answers for himself,' Phil Dickie recalls. 'He didn't have a great relationship with Lewis then.'

When the answers to the questions were finally provided, on 5 May, some of them were clearly evasive. In the end, the *Courier-Mail* received a writ from Assistant Commissioner Graeme Parker. In its belated response the statement said dismissively that the term 'organised crime syndicate' was 'something of a modern catch phrase'. It said police had identified the names and addresses of the owners of 12 Brisbane massage parlours. 'There is some recurrence of two groups of names involved in the different parlours but the names are not limited to these two groups,' the statement continued. 'Police priority has been to contain the prostitution industry and an example of success in this aim is that, in 1977, 24 massage parlours were operating, now there are 12.'

The *Courier-Mail* article continued: 'The department ... did not respond specifically about why police had not used a 1980 precedent [of the successful conviction of an uninvolved real estate company for owning premises used for prostitution] against four syndicate leaders who owned and operated multiple prostitution outlets.'

The day before the *Four Corners* program was to go to air, the *Sunday Mail* ran a major front-page story pre-empting 'The Moonlight State' and what it contained. It said the program would examine the assets of 'some wealthy senior Queensland police and former officers'.

'[Chris] Masters yesterday said part of the Queensland investigation involved digging into company and Valuer-General's Office records in

Brisbane, Sydney and Melbourne and an attempt to find reasons why suspiciously large sums of cash were paid into certain bank accounts.'

Masters himself added: 'We concentrated on the system, rather than on individual police. We probably will air only five per cent of what we have. That might bring enormous relief to some.'

On the day the show was to go to air, Des Partridge featured a little quip in his popular 'Day by Day' column in the *Courier-Mail*. 'ABC-TV will be guaranteed at least one viewer for tonight's *Four Corners* program highlighting alleged police links with illegal prostitution and gambling rackets in sunny Queensland,' he wrote. Partridge wondered if the Police Commissioner, Sir Terence Lewis, would be tuning in.

A police media spokesman answered: 'You can put a week's pay on that one.'

A Moonlit Night

At 9 p.m. on Monday 11 May 1987, the ABC's *Four Corners* program went to air with its usual introduction of a stylised map of the world followed by a cavalcade of what appeared to be official-type documents before dissolving to reveal the show's host, journalist Andrew Olle.

The program opened with the image of a setting sun before moving indoors, to a strip club, where a topless dancer poured oil over her semi-naked body before a baying crowd of enthusiastic males. It was a fitting opening to Chris Masters' report, where he alluded to the fact that, despite some 'wholesome attempts to pretend otherwise' the Queensland Government had not managed to stop 'the devil' at the border.

Wide-ranging in its scope, the hour-long report featured Nigel Powell, John Stopford, and police and prostitutes willing to speak on the condition their words were spoken by actors. Masters told the nation of the workings of the two major Brisbane vice syndicates, of Hector Hapeta, Anne Marie Tilley, Geraldo Bellino and Vic Conte. He even went into history, showing footage of former police commissioner Frank Bischof, a clip from former commissioner Ray Whitrod's final press conference following his resignation in November 1976, and another conference with the newly crowned Commissioner Terry Lewis.

Stopford went on the record saying he had paid protection money to a serving Queensland policeman. Others said the vice industry could not exist without the involvement of corrupt police. Footage included a *Four Corners* camera crew drawn into a scuffle outside The Roxy nightclub in Fortitude Valley, and the camera being struck to the street.

The crucial evidence, the epicentre of 'The Moonlight State', was the link Masters had made between Bellino and Conte, and former Licensing Branch officer Jack Herbert. Bellino and Conte had sold their piano-shaped Bowen Hills property to Herbert. It was on the title deeds in black and white. In doing so, Masters had connected Brisbane's so-called underworld to the police.

On the night of the broadcast, Commissioner Sir Terence Lewis was up in Garfield Drive, Bardon. He says he has no recollection of watching 'The Moonlight State'.

'I made some mistakes,' says Lewis. 'Masters … wanted to interview me and I said to him … I said, "Look, Ian [Hatcher from the police media unit], find out … what he wants to talk to me about." It's a bit awkward if you go there as Commissioner and they want to talk to you about the rate of crime … and you haven't got it. But he [Masters] wouldn't … send us a few questions … then they [Hatcher's unit] said, "Oh well, all you'll do is give his program … not validity … give his program air, or whatever, if you go on it, it will attract some attention," and then I said, "Oh, don't bother."

'But then about one day before it came on they said, "Oh, [it] might be a good idea to go on." I said, "Look, it's a bit late now," but I should have gone on. I should have gone on.'

Lewis says he would have answered Masters' questions. 'They were obviously aimed at gambling, prostitution or the Bellinos or that, and I didn't know any of them,' he says. 'Never heard their names ... never met Hapeta, never met Bellino, never met Conte, and I think we could have at least given answers.'

(Lewis's personal assistant, Greg Early, would record in his diary for that night: 'Saw 4 Corners programme 9 – 10 pm. COP [Commissioner of Police] rang after 10 p.m. re programme.')

Over at Taringa in the city's inner west, Tony Fitzgerald, QC, viewed 'The Moonlight State'. His view of the program probably would have been similar to those of the bulk of the city's legal community. This had been tried before. Similar issues in the past had bubbled up to the surface and then dissipated. Queensland resembled a dictatorship; it was a one-party state. How could the curtain be torn back?

Still, 'The Moonlight State' was a powerful report. In Spring Hill, on the edge of the Brisbane CBD and a short walk to Fortitude Valley, both Anne Marie Tilley and Hector Hapeta were settling back with a drink, watching *Four Corners*. 'I was already drunk,' says Tilley. 'I was told about it the day before, the week before ... We were a little bit dumb in certain ways, people saying we'd be right. I saw [Commissioner] Lewis in an interview. I thought, shit, you're my boss? I thought, this is going to get very bad. Hec was the same when it all came to a shovelling halt.'

Former Licensing Branch officer Nigel Powell, who had been interviewed by Masters for the program, watched the show alone in his bungalow off Prospect Terrace, Highgate Hill. Powell, by coincidence, lived just three streets up the rise from the home of notorious tattooist, criminal and police informant Billy Phillips. It was also two streets away from the house in Dorchester Terrace where, in 1974, Barbara McCulkin, wife to criminal Billy 'The Mouse' McCulkin, and her two daughters vanished without a trace and were presumably murdered.

Powell was more than a little concerned. He had no idea what Masters had put in his investigative report. He studied the program on his tiny box television in his kitchenette. 'I didn't realise how good it was going to be,' says Powell. 'I'd made my decision to talk to Masters. I figured I'd be safer if I went public. If they went for me now I thought I'd be protected by the publicity. I didn't know if they knew where I lived. I watched it and waited.'

Courier-Mail journalist Phil Dickie had been covering a flood in Lismore in northern New South Wales, and returned to Brisbane in a Channel Nine News helicopter late that Monday. He made it down from the television station at Mount Coot-tha to the Bowen Hills office of Queensland Newspapers just in time to catch Masters' report.

'Oh, I thought it was a magnificent bit of, you know … current affairs,' says Dickie. He wrote later that its impact was 'devastating', particularly the Herbert connection.

'I'd looked at all their properties,' says Dickie. 'Because I wasn't immersed in Queensland police history it [the Herbert connection] didn't mean anything to me. So, you know, that's something that *Four Corners* uniquely brought into it, you know, there is this additional character … I didn't have that.'

John Stopford, the former escort agency operator and driver for escort king Geoff Crocker, was at home that night in Amity Point on North Stradbroke Island, rugged up in the town's former old post office that he was renting as a residence. 'I watched it alone,' Stopford recalls. 'I didn't sleep that well.'

His young son Jay was fast asleep. 'I had an intuition something was coming, but I suspected it in the way of the local sergeant,' Stopford says. 'I got a phone call from Brisbane, I'd like you to come down, or some crap like that.'

When 'The Moonlight State' finally went to air, Jack and Peggy Herbert, over in Jordan Terrace, Bowen Hills, were not particularly concerned about Masters' report. They of course knew it was coming.

Herbert had received a telegram from *Four Corners* a few days earlier, telling him about the program and informing him that he would be featured in it. The telegram referenced his house purchase off Bellino and Conte. It also asked him of his relationship with Commissioner Sir Terence Lewis.

'There was a reference to an anonymous policeman collecting $500 from a massage parlour,' Herbert recalled in his memoir. 'I felt that [reporter Chris] Masters was fishing. He didn't have enough to hurt us.

'When the program was over I told Peggy not to worry. "It'll blow over," I said. "It always does."'

ABCI intelligence officer Peter Vassallo was at home with his wife Kerrie in their townhouse in the Canberra suburb of Cook, just northwest of the heart of the capital. That afternoon, Vassallo had told key staff at the ABCI that the program going to air was imminent, and ensured that it was taped. But at home, leading up to the broadcast, he was uneasy. So was his wife. 'I watched it and kept going, "Fuck, fuck",' says Vassallo. 'Chris had put it together so well. I was beside myself with excitement.'

In Sydney, Masters went to producer Shaun Hoyt's house for dinner, and they watched the program together. His diary recorded that he was back at his home on Sydney's North Shore by 12.15 a.m.

Masters, however, was up at 5.45 a.m. the next day. 'Woken by my own blood pressure,' he recorded in his diary.

Manhunt

By the break of dawn the following day, single father John Stopford had been identified as a whistleblower. His target had been corrupt Queensland police, and he'd cleared his conscience on a national television program.

In the small, close-knit township of Amity Point, the locals didn't stick their noses into your business. Live and let live. But when there was a problem, they all pitched in together. Now one of their own, Stopford, had aired the dirty linen of some very dangerous people, and he was vulnerable in the old fibro post office in the heart of Amity, opposite a clutch of holiday cabins known collectively as the 'Fishing Village'.

On the morning of 12 May, in the wake of 'The Moonlight State', the caretaker of the 'Fishing Village', Ralph, took the short drive to Dunwich for supplies. He headed for 'The Chook House', a small building in Ballow Road that housed the 'Dunwich Buffalo Memorial Club', the only place you could buy takeaway alcohol in the area. Ralph hit Dunwich at about 10.30 a.m., just in time to see a police helicopter coming in to land on a local football oval. The chopper was greeted by the local sergeant in his four-wheel-drive police vehicle.

'Obviously, he [Ralph] saw "The Moonlight State" and as he's got into Dunwich he sees this helicopter coming in to land,' says Stopford. 'So Ralph rings his [teenage] daughter [at the Fishing Village]. I didn't have a phone. He told her, "Go and get John, hurry up. Go and get John."'

Ralph reported that the chopper had landed and the occupants had piled into the police vehicle and headed off in the direction of Amity Point. 'You reckon they might be coming for you?' Ralph asked his neighbour.

'I think so,' Stopford replied.

(What Stopford didn't know was that Commissioner Terry Lewis and other senior officers had already met that morning with Deputy Premier and Police Minister Bill Gunn. They discussed the *Four Corners* program and a possible inquiry. According to the diary of the Commissioner's personal assistant, Greg Early, an attempt would also be made to 'try and get a … statement from Stopford on Stradbroke Island …'.

Stopford's son, Jay, was at the local kindergarten in Dunwich and was imminently due back at Amity by bus. Stopford had fled his home and sheltered with a friend who lived on the edge of the village. The friend then drove back to the old post office and learned the police had been in Stopford's driveway. Now they were sitting in a vehicle off the Amity bus stop. 'She came back and told me,' says Stopford. 'I said, "Listen, we've got to get him [Jay] off that bus."'

'The bus had already left Dunwich. So we intercepted the bus, on what they call the Beehive Road, and we got him off ... we got him and then went up to a friend who was living at Flinders Beach [near Amity], and that's where we hid out. The chopper stayed until the afternoon, I think, and disappeared.'

Being such a small place, Stopford knew the local sergeant. They'd crossed paths several times at social events. 'I rang him and he said he was being pressured to grab hold of me – he didn't put it in those words – and bring me in for a police chat with one of the inspectors. He said he was being pressured and that it would be easier all round ... he'd make sure I was safe.

'I asked, "What's it in relation to?" And he said, "You know."'

'I got in touch with [lawyer] Terry O'Gorman that night. I snuck into a new friend's place – his parents owned the corner store – and rang from there.'

The Amity locals immediately protected Stopford and Jay. 'We would not have survived without the cooperation of the Amity community,' John Stopford reflects. 'They weren't a part of ... hiding me out or trying to pervert the course of justice, but I certainly wouldn't have been able to survive. I didn't comprehend ... I knew something would come, but I didn't comprehend that they would be so bloody brazen to fly into uncharted waters in a helicopter the morning after.

'Thank God Ralph had his brains about him and realised, this is a rare event. What's going on?'

Stopford says he did fear that someone from the Brisbane underworld would be sent to the island to deal with him. An associate told him that he had information that Stopford would 'wear it and wear it very quick'. He started to consider what he was going to do with Jay.

Stopford says: 'Through it all, I didn't give much consideration to that side of the seedy past. It was always the police I knew had more to lose than anybody ... I regretted going on the program in those early days. Probably for quite a while there.'

In Canberra, the day after the broadcast, Peter Vassallo went into the Australian Bureau of Criminal Intelligence office at London Circuit, as usual, and suddenly started suffering severe chest pains. 'Nobody in the bureau knew of my involvement with "The Moonlight State",' Vassallo recalls. 'I had treated the whole thing as a counter-intelligence operation.'

Months of stress had taken its toll. Vassallo was transferred to a hospital in Woden and ultimately cleared, but was granted three months' stress leave.

On Tuesday 12 May, the *Courier-Mail* reported that Deputy Premier and Police Minister Bill Gunn believed the integrity of the Queensland police had been seriously questioned by the *Four Corners* report. 'I am meeting senior officers of the police force today to discuss these very serious allegations,' Gunn said. 'We are interested in evidence. This is absolutely essential. We want to speak to anyone who has any information. I also believe *Four Corners* has a lot of material that was not broadcast. I would like to see all of that too.'

State Opposition Leader Nev Warburton said an independent judicial inquiry into the allegations needed to be held. The government could not brush off these allegations, he said.

On the same day, Gunn announced a commission of inquiry. He said, optimistically, that he still wasn't convinced that corruption was occurring. 'But a series of police ministers have had these types of allegations hanging over their heads,' said Gunn. 'They are not going to hang over mine. I am setting out to get something done.'

Gunn initially entertained an inquiry to be held by the Police Complaints Tribunal and its head, Judge Eric Pratt. However, after speaking with Commissioner Lewis and the Premier, he ruled out the idea. Gunn said Sir Terence had agreed with the idea of mounting an investigation. The Police Minister added that he was not embarrassed about having denied the existence of a problem for many years. 'It is not at all embarrassing,' Gunn said in his defence. 'It is a great move. You should be congratulating me.'

Up in Cairns, Vincenzo Bellino, 31, of Ponticello Street, Whitfield, issued a Supreme Court writ against the ABC for alleged defamation.

All the Premier had to say about 'The Moonlight State' was that there may be 'one or two policemen' who may have not been doing the right thing.

According to the diary of Greg Early, the Police Commissioner's personal assistant, on Thursday 14 May, he 'rang Detective Inspector Taylor (Special Branch) re debugging of COP [Commissioner of Police] office, AC Redmond and AC Parker and Licensing Branch as well ... spoke to AC Donoghue and Superintendent Errol Walker re custody of files from Records Section, notebooks and diaries from Licensing Branch, locks on doors, a safe and a room for his crew to use. [*Sunday Mail* journalist] Ric Allen rang with seven questions. Saw COP and drafted answers.'

The next day, according to Early's records, everyone was offering an opinion on the credibility of the *Four Corners* program. Some thought it was a 'non-event' and the ABC 'would end up with egg on its face ...'

Early said he telephoned Bill Gunn at his electoral office 'and he said the inquiry must go on so that the ABC can be discredited and that if it did not go on the ABC would have some credibility'. The diary entry for that day continues: '[Ross] Dickson does not know which way to go and he admitted to a friend last night that he has nothing. A couple of police have been a bit stupid and they'll have to pay.'

To Bethany

On Saturday 16 May 1987, having made no public comment in the five days since the broadcast of 'The Moonlight State', and the subsequent announcement by Police Minister Bill Gunn of an inquiry, Lewis had some urgent politicking to do.

He first visited Transport Minister Don Lane in Brisbane, and then telephoned the Premier at his property, Bethany, 210 kilometres north-west of Brisbane and just outside Kingaroy. 'I said [to Joh], "Look, can we come up? I want to just tell you something." So I went up [to Bethany].'

The splendid rural retreat, over 600 hectares first purchased by the Premier's grandfather, Hans Poulsen, featured an old Queenslander and a newer, brick residence, built by Sir Joh for his bride Florence after their marriage in 1952. The brick house was set back from the road and was veiled by trees. Lewis had some important information to impart to the Premier.

Conspiracy theories behind the announcement of the inquiry were flourishing. Lewis says, firstly, the whole thing was part of Bill Gunn's strategy to seize the premiership. He says at the time he was also feeling threatened by his own deputy, Ron Redmond, whom he believed was simultaneously eyeing the position of Police Commissioner.

Lewis adds that around this time he had heard a rumour that Gunn and Redmond had been at a function and Gunn, standing next to the Deputy Commissioner, declared to the room – here's your next police commissioner. (A witness to the event agrees that Gunn made the announcement.)

Meanwhile, a source that Lewis refuses to name, told him that Tony Fitzgerald, QC – the prominent lawyer whose name was being bandied around to potentially head the inquiry – had political leanings towards the Labor Party, and Lewis felt it his duty to inform Bjelke-Petersen. 'He [the source] rang me and said, look, he said … he's [from] a famous legal family, a very famous one, a lovely bloke … he said, "I know Fitzgerald personally … I know he's a red hot Labor supporter, I know he hates Joh and he [Joh] … is absolutely mad if he leaves him to run this commission. He'll get Joh",' Lewis recalls.

'So I got in the car, I went to Kingaroy, because they were having a Cabinet meeting at Roma the next day, and I went up and I said, "Look, Mr Premier, I can't tell you who said this but I was told …"'

'And at that stage I'm not sure if it went in this ear and out the other. He was thinking of bloody Canberra and he went to Roma the next day and Gunn put this submission through, whatever it was, and of course away it went from there.' (With the support of National Party President Robert Sparkes, Bjelke-Petersen had, earlier in the year, instigated a campaign to tackle the perceived socialism of the Hawke Labor government and win the Office of the Prime Minister. Known as the 'Joh for PM' campaign, the aim was to dismantle Medicare and, among other things, introduce a flat-tax system.)

'Joh lost track of things and Gunn was aware of that, he raised it when Joh was overseas, and then he'd just got back … and Joh's mind was on other things. It's a pity I couldn't tell him who it was. But whether it would have changed his mind, I don't know.'

Lewis also had his doubts about Bill Gunn. 'He didn't have the mind for thinking that a minister should have,' Lewis reflects. 'See … you've got to have trust and you've got to be able to talk to people which I had with [Tom] Newbery totally, even old [Russ] Hinze, I used to drive him nuts … and Glasson was alright but Glasson was, he was a nice fellow but not as strong as some men … but Gunn wasn't terribly trustworthy in that sense, I didn't think so.'

Lewis is adamant that during this period Bjelke-Petersen was distracted. 'He had that fixation about going to bloody Canberra,' Lewis says. 'I said to him a couple of times when we were talking about different things, "Oh, you know, Premier, Canberra's a different place to here. You wouldn't have a lot of friends there …"'

'It couldn't happen, even if he was God, well not quite God I suppose. But he wasn't, he didn't have an electorate. Then would the Party have him? And then if they had him, would they immediately make him Prime Minister? It just, it couldn't have happened. But he couldn't see that ... he was, in many ways, a smart man, but in other ways he wasn't ...'

Lewis says he could tell immediately that Bjelke-Petersen was distracted during that last-minute visit. 'I could see that he wasn't taking it in, because somebody said something, he said, "Oh, the plane's ready to take me to Roma",' recalls Lewis.

'I thought, oh, shit. He had the chance then to stop the Fitzgerald Inquiry and put some ... an unbiased person there ... if you're going to have a Royal Commission, you've got to pick an experienced ... a judge is the logical person. I've thought of it ever since, and after I went away I was ... on the way home I was disappointed ...'

No Complaints

It took just short of a week for Commissioner Lewis to finally offer some response to the allegations unleashed by the *Four Corners* investigation. While Lewis had been aware that Masters had been making queries throughout Queensland since early in the year, he hadn't seemed overly concerned about Masters' ultimate report. Similar reports had come and gone. This time, however, the disquiet was not going away.

Lewis sat down with his assistant Greg Early and they nutted out some answers to questions put to them by *Sunday Mail* journalist Ric Allen. The headline above the 'exclusive interview' banner read: LEWIS REPLIES.

'The Police Commissioner, Sir Terence Lewis, yesterday was full of praise for his officers after a week of criticism,' the story said. 'I'm proud of my policemen and women and their continuing efforts to fight crime,' he said. 'Neither I nor any of my senior officers believe the Queensland police force is corrupt. In the event of any judicial inquiry, I'll be happy to testify.'

Lewis was asked what sorts of controls did he have in place as Commissioner to prevent corruption. He answered that he had four deputies who were 'completely autonomous in receiving and having complaints investigated'. He added that there was also the safeguard of the Police Complaints Tribunal, run by Judge Eric Pratt. 'It is of note that since the inception of the tribunal in 1982, not one complaint of police corruption about an officer has been lodged,' Lewis said. 'It is amazing, to say the least, if a corrupt police officer can evade this net.'

Allen also went back into history, querying Lewis's rapid elevation from an Inspector in Charleville to Commissioner at the end of 1976, following the resignation of former commissioner Ray Whitrod.

His answers were curt. 'My promotion to my present rank was in 1976 and any questions about it were ten years ago,' Lewis responded. 'I do not recall what questions were then raised nor the answers which were then given. I did not seek that promotion.'

Lewis additionally offered a critique of 'The Moonlight State', calling it 'disgraceful'. He said 'knowing the calibre of some of the people interviewed', they lacked any form of credibility.

In the same edition of the *Sunday Mail*, columnist Quentin Dempster offered a warning about the forthcoming inquiry. 'It all comes down to the terms of reference,' he wrote. 'While the appointment of an open inquiry into organised crime and allegations of police corruption in Queensland will provide an historic challenge for a judge or senior lawyer, it will be the Government's riding instructions which will be the foundation stone.

'If public confidence in the police is to be restored, the Government, by its stated terms of reference, will have to give the inquiry leader substantial investigative powers and facilities.'

A week after his exclusive interview with Commissioner Lewis, Ric Allen reported that the police inquiry would be limited to allegations made in the previous five years. The buck would stop in 1982.

Deputy Premier Bill Gunn, who predicted the inquiry would last for four weeks, offered his rationale on the terms of reference. 'My legal advisor and myself are of the opinion that it's useless to pursue any action which may have occurred before the five-year deadline,' Gunn said. 'Anything going back over five years is useless. The trail is cold and a lot of the witnesses are gone and it's virtually impossible to get a judge to convict on such old evidence.'

Gunn rejected calls that the inquiry examine the era of former commissioner Frank Bischof. The Deputy Premier may have appeared firm in his stance, but there was a lot of discussion happening behind the scenes in relation to the 'shape' of the proposed inquiry. Gunn met with then Attorney-General Paul Clauson. They dined at Milano Restaurant at 78 Queen Street, Brisbane city, and privately discussed a raft of issues. 'Bill Gunn was not going to cop the same level of obfuscation that all the previous [police] ministers had with this,' says Clauson. 'He was going to get to the bottom of it.

'Bill and I went down there [to Milano's] and had dinner and we talked about what we should do at the next Cabinet meeting [in Roma]. He said, "You'll have to set it up, can you do this and do that?" We talked about the mechanics of it. He said, "I'm not going to put up with this situation by myself …".'

Opposition Justice Spokesman Wayne Goss described Gunn's terms of reference as 'defective'. 'I understand that most of the information of two witnesses who appeared on the *Four Corners* television interview predates June 1, 1982,' he said. 'That makes me very suspicious.'

Even members of the police force feared a 'whitewash'. 'If there are any corrupt policemen out there, they have got nothing to worry about,' one officer told the *Courier-Mail*. 'And that's a pity because it means police in Queensland will continue to have to put up with never-ending allegations that they are paid off.'

As the debate raged, Brisbane's once free-wheeling massage parlours and illegal casinos began quietly closing their doors. A storm was on its way, but nobody could predict with any certainty the dimensions of its ferocity.

Director of Prosecutions, Des Sturgess, may have had a better appreciation of the synaptic chart. He had heard the rumours that Judge Eric Pratt of the Police Complaints Tribunal might preside over a limited inquiry. He knew from experience that judges and corruption inquiries did not mix well. He went to see Chief Justice, Sir Dormer Andrews, and offered his opinion. Sturgess, on a mission, then met Neville Harper, the Minister for Lands and immediate-past Attorney-General. Harper and Sturgess could always speak candidly with each other. Harper was packing his papers for the impending country Cabinet meeting in Roma in western Queensland. Sturgess told him of his thoughts on the Pratt appointment, and his meeting with the Chief Justice. 'He asked me whom I'd recommend to take Pratt's place,' Sturgess later recalled. 'I told him [Gerald Tony] Fitzgerald.

'He hadn't heard of him. I assured him he'd stand up to any examination; he was a former Federal Court judge and I'd just finished briefing him in an appeal to the High Court.

'He [Harper] thanked me and said he'd put his name forward.'

Satisfied, Harper headed off to Roma, and Sturgess returned to his office in the State Law Building.

The Tiger's Tail

Almost 11 years to the day after Premier Joh Bjelke-Petersen had a personal discussion with then Inspector Terry Lewis in Cunnamulla in western Queensland following a country Cabinet meeting, he was back with his Cabinet in Roma, about 515 kilometres west–north–west of Brisbane.

After all those years, the issue that would now dominate discussion would be about Commissioner Lewis's police force, and whether it had engaged in corrupt practices. Joh flew out for Roma knowing full well Cabinet had to thrash out the finer details of the inquiry, announced by Deputy Premier and Police Minister Bill Gunn in the wake of 'The Moonlight State'.

The Premier and his Cabinet ministers stayed in the Overlander Heritage Motel on the Warrego Highway just out of town. The motel, only opened since 1984, had reputedly the best restaurant west of Toowoomba and its décor – early Australian settler-style – may have made several members of the Cabinet feel at home. The motel was built by Heyward Robertson and run by the Robertson family, including the head of the family, David, and Heyward's sister Amanda.

On the Sunday the VIPs arrived, a barbecue lunch was held. Attorney-General Paul Clauson observed some deep and prolonged discussion between Bjelke-Petersen and Transport Minister Don Lane. 'Lane was onto Joh because he was trying to control … if this was going to happen, and it's only my assumption, he [Lane] wanted to appoint someone who was going to be a stooge to run the commission of inquiry,' remembers Clauson.

'I can't remember who it was … some fellow who was at the Bar. There was a guy who was a QC, a reserve defence force advocate, who'd been a colonel or something in the army … that was a name that Don was putting forward … Gunn said to me that he wasn't going to be railroaded on any of this. Gunn was very adamant about that. That he wasn't going to be blind-sided. I said that's fair enough.'

In his memoir, *Trial and Error*, Lane recalled that shortly before he left Brisbane for Roma, he received a call from 'a city lawyer whom I had been acquainted with for several years' with news of the rumour that Tony Fitzgerald, QC, was going to head up the inquiry. 'He [the caller] claimed that Fitzgerald had recently given legal advice to the Labor Party, and advised that the Government should be cautious about appointing him,' Lane said.

'I remarked that I had never heard of him and that I did not wish to be embroiled in the issue. I did, however, take the time to telephone a senior member of Joh's personal staff and passed on the information.

'The staffer said a similar call had been received from the same source but she did not know if it was correct.' It was the precise message that Police Commissioner Sir Terence Lewis had passed on to the Premier face to face, during his rushed trip to Kingaroy the day before.

That Sunday evening, Joh got a message to Clauson and Gunn that he wanted to see them in the motel restaurant for a late dinner. 'What's all this about?' Clauson asked Gunn.

'Lane's been in Joh's ear, and there's no prizes for guessing what they're talking about. They're going to try and sink this inquiry.'

'What are we going to do?'

'Don't worry. Don't worry about it,' said Gunn. 'It's not on.'

The Overlander Heritage restaurant was already well known for the quality of its steak, and the Premier loved his steak. It was also renowned for its pianola. Often, Amanda Robertson would sing along to it before the meals were served. But there was no music on this night.

Heyward Robertson remembers the austerity of the Bjelke-Petersen government when it stayed at the motel. 'When dining with his entourage in the restaurant the meals for everyone were very spartan,' he says. 'We were instructed that everyone was to drink water or cordial as the meals were being paid for by the state government. They were allowed a piece of bread or toast and soup for the entrees, with the main course of chicken, fish or steak. There was to be no desserts or alcoholic drinks whatsoever.'

Amanda, who was working in the restaurant that night, said the meeting was 'very serious'. 'They were very conscious of their privacy at the dinner,' she says. 'Even though we only had three or four people per night on average at the restaurant at that time, a late dinner was best for privacy. Joh was very stressed. We were very conscious of the fact that he was stressed. You could tell he was under a lot of pressure.'

Gunn later recalled the late-night meal with the Premier. 'On our arrival at the motel's dining room, Sir Joh indicated to us to sit either side of him,' he said. 'Some of his staff were also at the table. He said words like, "I'm greatly concerned about this inquiry. I don't think it's a good idea at all."

'I explained that the allegations that had been made had been around for a long time, hanging over the heads of several police ministers.'

Bjelke-Petersen said to Gunn: 'You know Bill, you've got a tiger by the tail and it's going to bite you.'

'I'm not worried about that, Joh. It'll end up biting you, if anything,' Gunn replied.

'Well, I think you should knock it right out of the ring.'

'Now listen here, you have been talking to Lane for hours,' Gunn said. 'If you want him to be your police minister you can bloody do it tomorrow, because I am not going to tolerate that.'

'Oh, well, you know ...' the Premier said.

'Look, the subject's closed. It's finished. It's done. And that's all there is to it.'

'Oh well, you know best, but you'll be sorry about this,' the Premier warned his old colleague.

'No, if this doesn't go ahead I know who's going to be sorry.'

Gunn said the conversation was strained, and some of the Premier's staff had left the table. Clauson remembers the atmosphere in the room: 'He [Bjelke-Petersen] wasn't wound up or furious or anything like that, it was almost like a father saying to a son, you know, if you get a motorbike it can be dangerous riding it. It was in that context.

'I don't think he was happy about it, but generally politicians aren't happy about holding inquiries. Let's not beat around the bush here. No one likes an inquiry, particularly when you are the incumbent government, and you're setting one up and you don't know where it's going to lead.'

At the Cabinet meeting on Monday, the possibility of getting Judge Eric Pratt to head the inquiry was mentioned. Gunn produced a letter from Chief Justice Andrews, recommending the government steer clear of a judge for inquiry commissioner. Clauson remembers the meeting: 'There were some very nervous nellies around the table that day.'

Gunn pulled out a piece of paper and asked the room what they thought about Tony Fitzgerald, QC. 'I said he was very well regarded and would be very capable of running the inquiry,' Clauson recalls. 'Gunn said, "Good, go and ring him."'

Gunn handed Clauson the sheet of paper which had Fitzgerald's telephone number on it. 'I went out and rang him from a public phone box near the Catholic church,' says Clauson. 'There were people hanging around the bloody phone box … I rang Fitzgerald and asked him whether he'd be prepared to head the inquiry.

'He said, "Yes".'

During the stay at the Overlander Heritage Motel, the Premier's Cabinet colleagues witnessed something extraordinary. Between official business they saw Sir Joh Bjelke-Petersen on his hands and knees assisting World War II hero, David Robertson, lay some tiles around the motel verandah. The Premier explained to Robertson that he always felt a measure of relaxation by doing some form of manual labour. It was indicative of the pressure Sir Joh was under.

One former Cabinet minister says the Fitzgerald Inquiry probably came about by accident. He says both Bjelke-Petersen and Gunn confused the definitions of an 'inquiry' and a 'Royal Commission'.

'Joh succumbed to an investigation, but he didn't know the difference between investigation and inquiry, and some journalist said to him, "You mean an inquiry?", and he said, "Yes, yes, yes". He didn't know the difference ... suddenly, publicly, he was stuck on the inquiry.

'Gunn was one of the laziest ministers, but it was the only good decision he ever made ... there's no doubt that the commission was a mistake by Gunn, which Joh never forgave him for ... but he did a good thing, I think.'

Bjelke-Petersen was also adamant the wrong person had been chosen to head the commission. Joh told everyone that Fitzgerald was a 'Labor man'.

Former premier Mike Ahern remembers Gunn getting together with National Party President Bob Sparkes, to discuss the inquiry. 'Gunn was not a powerful character at all,' he recalls. 'Sparkes was the top guy and Sparkes put it all together. He got [Neville] Harper in and Harper was former Attorney General, a mate of his, and they identified this fellow called Tony Fitzgerald.

'And then Sparkes got on the phone to the ministers and said this is the time to sort all this out. I don't think they knew what they were doing. They hadn't thought it all through. They had just arrived on the day with Tony Fitzgerald and no one had heard about him before.'

Fitzgerald himself had conditionally accepted the position during the call to Clauson from the Roma telephone booth. The details had yet to be ironed out, but Fitzgerald was pleased with the distraction. He was successful but he was bored, he wanted to do something different.

Sir Joh's former right-hand man, Allen Callaghan, then in prison for fraud for less than a month, believes – like Lewis – that Gunn's broader strategy was to take over as Premier. 'Gunn believed Joh wasn't going to go and he'd never get his chance as Premier, that was my personal view,' Callaghan says. 'I think he thought they'd have a little inquiry down the Valley and that was it, but it got out of hand.'

Rapid Fire

The Premier and his Cabinet had returned to Brisbane from Roma by Tuesday 19 May, and there was a flurry of activity down at police headquarters in Makerston Street. Police Commissioner Terry Lewis's personal assistant, Greg Early, recorded in his diary that on that day he, Lewis and other senior officers had a meeting with Gunn in his office.

Early wrote that it had been decided a draft press statement would be written up in preparation for notices served on those affected in the massage parlour industry. The blitz wasn't restricted to Brisbane. All of Queensland would be hit. 'It was agreed that Minister [Gunn] would give COP [Commissioner of Police] a written direction as to the Government's policy to be followed. It was resolved not to worry about escorts [escort agencies]. Discussion was then had on legal aid for the senior officers and the Union.'

The next day Early wrote that he 'spoke to Ken Crooke [Press Secretary to Hon Premier] re a written direction from the Minister as none had been forthcoming'.

Gunn may have been avoiding the police department, but he was forging ahead with commission of inquiry business. The initial terms of reference, prepared by the Justice Department and published in the Queensland Government Gazette on the same day – 26 May 1987 – were initially limited to matters arising from allegations contained within the *Four Corners* report. The specific focus would be on Geraldo Bellino, Antonio Bellino, Vincenzo Bellino, Vittorio Conte, Hector Hapeta and their involvement with prostitution, unlawful gambling or the sale of illegal drugs.

The terms also asked if those men had 'directly or indirectly provided or attempted to provide any benefit or favour, whether financial or otherwise, to, for or on behalf of any member of the police force ...'

Premier Sir Joh Bjelke-Petersen, still on his quixotic Joh for PM campaign, happened to be in Disneyland in California on the day of the announcement and issuing of the terms of reference.

Former Attorney-General and minister for justice, Paul Clauson, says preparatory work on the terms of reference was kept 'fairly close'. 'We worked on that through my department with the Department of Premier and Cabinet,' Clauson recalls. 'When amendments or extensions were required, they were granted within reason.' While they liaised with Fitzgerald, he says Bjelke-Petersen was not involved.

The next day, Early recorded in his diary that the Department of Justice rang him 're getting the addresses of the three Belino [sic] brothers, Conte and Habita [sic]'.

He said he arranged for a Detective Inspector Scanlan to 'pick up the subpoenas at 5.20 pm from the chambers of Tony Fitzgerald, QC, on the 13th level of the MLC Centre and spoke to Stewart and Scanlan re service of the subpoenas'.

Early later spoke with 'Regional Superintendent [Kev] Dorries and Detective Inspector Churchill in Cairns with a view to serving a subpoena on Vincenzo Bellino who lived in Cairns or at his Chillagoe marble mine at 6.00 am the next morning'. The police jet, with a subpoena on board, left for Cairns that night.

Also on that day, Australian Prime Minister Bob Hawke announced a Federal election for July. A few days later Premier Joh Bjelke-Petersen officially abandoned his quest for the Lodge.

Amid all this high drama, former constable Dave Moore, the former children's television personality who had nearly brought the force to its knees in late 1984 following a sex scandal, was re-tried and sentenced to two and a half years' prison.

Moore was originally charged with conspiring with radio announcer Billy Hurrey to commit homosexual acts on boys under 17 years, between January 1982 and November 1984. He was also charged with sodomy, having permitted sodomy, and five charges of indecent dealing and attempted indecent dealing. He had pleaded not guilty to all charges.

In November 1986 Moore was found guilty of all charges and was sentenced to six years' imprisonment. However, in March 1987 Moore appealed the verdict. The Court of Criminal Appeal found that justice had miscarried in the November trial, and Moore was released from prison. A few months later, in June, Moore was re-tried and found guilty on two sex charges against a 16-year-old boy. He was sentenced to 30 months' gaol.

A tawdry chapter in the force's history had quietly closed. But another, of titanic proportions, was about to open.

Grubby Little Gambling Joints

Commissioner Terence Lewis remained flabbergasted by all the fuss and bother over the *Courier-Mail* stories, and the *Four Corners* investigation. Why would you call for a Royal Commission into some grubby little gambling joints that had been operating in the shadows of Fortitude Valley since time immemorial?

'Everybody knew, everybody including Dickie ... I mean, the number of people who told me that Dickie and other journalists used to go to 142 Wickham Street ... it was no secret thing if you're like from the public, the press, the police,' Lewis says. 'And contrary to what they thought or suggested in some of the articles, there was more to it than the police just rolling up to the gaming places ... and walking in and saying, "Hey, you're all pinched". They have to get in there, firstly, and then they have to prove who the keeper is. They have to prove he's getting money from the clients, and the same with the prostitution.'

Lewis says that at the time his force had a handle on the containment of vice. To prosecute prostitutes, he said, police would had to have 'gone in, taken their pants off and had sex with the female'.

'Instead of harassing them, for want of a better word, I suppose, [the police would] go around every so often … oh, I don't know how often, whether it was every fortnight or every whatever … and say, "It's your turn",' says Lewis.

'Strictly speaking, the girls could have just pleaded not guilty and it would have been up to the police … well, it was a shocking waste of police time and the court's time and everybody's time. As it was the government [who] were getting a licence from them … there's big fines every, say with every fortnight, so … everybody was happy to some considerable degree.'

He says to call the gambling joints 'casinos' was a farce. 'One was a little one mainly to look after Chinese, another little one was to look after Italians, and I think another one looked after the Greeks,' recalls Lewis. 'And it wasn't anybody being exploited, nobody. I've never heard anybody ever in the Lebanese [community] saying they were robbed there or they were forced to go there or they were threatened. It was the same with the SP bookies, you know.

'These were three areas that I really didn't see as our prime interest. My prime interests were murders, rape, armed robberies, serious home invasion, break-and-enters, the road toll, young missing persons and a whole heap of other things. These other three really hardly ever exercised my mind. And I thought I had a good fellow running it, particularly for the four years that Ron Redmond was there.

'I thought he had it by the throat because he'd come along to our morning conferences [or 'prayers' as they were known] at nine o'clock and say, "Oh, you know, things are going well. They are charging X number of girls from yesterday or last night". And it all looked good.'

Meanwhile, Geraldo Bellino, mentioned in the terms of reference of the inquiry, issued a statement through his lawyer, Noel Barbi, that he welcomed the forthcoming inquiry so he could clear his and his family's name. 'I have sat back and been the subject of innuendo, inference and suggestions,' Bellino said of the 'intolerable atmosphere' that he'd been subjected to since the terms were published.

'It is the unhappy situation in this country that the media are permitted to make baseless and unfounded allegations without the benefit of facts. I emphatically deny that I have been in any way involved in any bribery or corruption of any police officer in this state or anywhere else. Much has been made of the fact that I have not been prosecuted and the inferences that this is because of my being responsible for the bribery and corruption of police officers.

'It may occur to any thinking person that I might also not have committed any offences. I say the latter is the truth.'

As the possibilities of a Royal Commission were being canvassed, government members were being quizzed back in their own electorates about the inquiry and the extent of corruption. Mike Ahern, the member for Landsborough on the Sunshine Coast, told a local newspaper that he was pleased that there appeared to be no corruption in his neck of the woods.

But, after that quote was published, Ahern says he got an urgent phone call from a senior Sunshine Coast police officer who he knew well. The officer asked Ahern not to repeat that there was no corruption in the region. 'He said there was a [local] sergeant here, whose … duty on a Friday afternoon was to go around the brothels and the other places that were being tolerated and collect the money.

'At three o'clock in the afternoon he'd poke it in an envelope through the wall up at [12 Garfield Drive], the home of Commissioner Lewis. He said that was his duty, that he took a police car, he drove around the whole Sunshine Coast and did the collections, and then at three o'clock it was his duty to drop the envelope through the wall up there. So he said, don't be misled into thinking it wasn't going on here.'

The Police Wife

It may have been one of those publishing coincidences, or it may not have, but the July issue of *Vedette*, the journal of the Queensland Police Department, featured a cover story on Lady Hazel Lewis, wife of the Commissioner. The cover photograph for issue number 116 was a warm and moving shot of Lady Lewis crouching down beside Rachel Baguley, age three, the daughter of Constable First Class Fred Baguley, serving at remote Torren Creek, 1503 kilometres north-west of Brisbane and 293 kilometres south-west of Townsville.

Little Rachel, a trifle grumpy in the picture, was showing Lady Lewis, replete in a strand of pearls, her pet chick. The headline of the issue read: KEEPING IN TOUCH.

Inside, Lady Lewis opened up on life as the wife of the Police Commissioner, and family life in general. She told the journal that travelling with her husband throughout Queensland gave her the opportunity to meet with the wives of police officers. 'I like to see their living conditions and find out if there is any way I can help to make their homes more comfortable, such as following up requests for repair work,' she said. 'I like to ensure they have a good stove and the other things that are important to a housewife.'

She said wives who accompanied their husbands on transfer into the country were the 'unsung heroes' of the Department. 'I have found that most police wives take great pride in taking care of their homes, police stations and grounds. You can tell a lot about the people by the way they maintain their home.'

In the end, said Lady Lewis, the most important contribution a police wife could make was to create for their men 'a warm and loving relationship'. She offered her experience of 35 years' marriage to Sir Terence. 'Police officers today, regardless of their rank or station, frequently have to deal with awkward, difficult and heart-rending situations,' said Lady Lewis. 'Having that warm, loving relationship to come home to helps them to be good policemen and to carry out their duties.'

She said she was aware of 'friction' between young couples when wives placed more importance on their careers than their husband's. She said women married policemen knowing a transfer could be imminent. 'They [the wives] must decide whose career is the most important, and usually it is the husband's,' philosophised Lady Lewis. 'In most cases, a wife plans to work a set number of years before starting a family. The husband's life-time career must be considered.'

Her counsel would probably be needed more than ever in the coming months as Tony Fitzgerald made ready to start his public hearings in earnest on Monday 27 July.

In a state that had, for decades, been plagued with rumours about both political and police corruption to the point where it had become a running gag, passed from one generation to the next, there was a curious optimism about Fitzgerald's inquiry. For weeks, between the announcement of the inquiry and the advent of formal hearings, the press had at last given its full attention to crime and corruption in Queensland. The inquiry gave it focus. And the reports acted as titillating shorts to the main feature.

On the Saturday before the first witness was called, reporter Phil Dickie revealed that there had been an attempt to bug the offices of the commission of inquiry. 'There is evidence that an attempt was made to tamper with the commission's telephone system, although my advice is that it seems it was not breached,' Tony Fitzgerald said. He added that there was 'a very real possibility that those with something to hide will seek to create a controversy about the safety of witnesses in the hope that ordinary decent people will be frightened into silence'.

Fitzgerald warned the media not to be used as an 'unwitting tool' in such a scenario. It was also revealed that Deputy Premier Bill Gunn had met secretly and privately with Fitzgerald to avoid any chance of listening devices.

The Bagman Takes Flight

After Chris Masters had connected Jack Herbert to Gerry Bellino and Vic Conte via the Jordan Terrace property he'd purchased from them, Herbert wasted no time in offloading the house for a loss to a business friend. He claimed he received a message through the grapevine from Lewis: 'The message was that I leave the country,' he said in his memoir.

Two weeks before the inquiry began substantive hearings, Herbert and his wife Peggy went to Hamilton Island in North Queensland for a break. Coincidentally, his old friend, Sydney businessman and yachtsman Jack Rooklyn, was also staying on the island.

'So what are your plans?' Rooklyn asked Herbert.

He told his old boss he wasn't going to leave Queensland. 'He thought I was making a mistake,' Herbert later wrote. 'I decided that it was time to get out of Australia after all.'

Herbert flew to the United Kingdom via Honolulu. Feeling lonely, he soon sent for Peggy, who flew first-class to London just as the Fitzgerald Inquiry began its historic hearings.

Back in Brisbane, former assistant commissioner Tony Murphy arranged to come into police headquarters in the city and view a sensitive file that was filled with ghosts. For some reason, Murphy urgently needed to see the 'Brifman suicide file'. (Lewis says he allowed Murphy to see the paperwork, and that it didn't strike him as an unusual request.)

Shirley Margaret Brifman, prostitute and madam, had been dead for 15 years. She had blown the whistle on corrupt police and in lengthy records of interview with police, had revealed her close friendship with Murphy. Her corpse was discovered by her children in their witness protection flat in Clayfield, Brisbane, only weeks before she was to appear in court as chief witness against Murphy in his perjury trial stemming from evidence he gave at the National

Hotel inquiry in the early 1960s. No coronial inquest was ever held into Brifman's death.

So why, as the Fitzgerald Inquiry was being set up, did Murphy need to head into the city and see Brifman's old file?

'Well ... I wrote it in my diary apparently that Murphy came in and asked if he could look at the file,' says Lewis. 'I thought it'd be so he'd be going before the inquiry. And he'd want to refresh his bloody memory or whatever it was.

'I don't think I'd ever read the file. Never, ever.'

The First Witness

After some preliminary hearings that stuttered through early June, Commissioner Tony Fitzgerald's commission of inquiry began in earnest at about 10.15 a.m. on Monday 27 July, in Courtroom 29 on the fourth floor of the District Court in George Street. It was a typically mild winter's Brisbane day. Commissioner Lewis, in a regular suit and striped tie, arrived at the courts trailing a phalanx of staff from the police media relations unit. It was a crowded courtroom.

Sydney Morning Herald journalist Evan Whitton observed: 'The carpet is burnt orange; the high walls are in a striated dark brown wood. Mr Fitzgerald sits at a high-backed orange chair at a bench above those named in the terms of reference and the hordes of lawyers who must be looking forward to gainful employ.'

Journalists were forced to observe from the public gallery – 'a loft above the well of the court', as Whitton described it – due to the large numbers of legal representatives in the court proper.

Commissioner Fitzgerald informed the commission that the terms of reference had been extended back to ten years.

Gary Crooke, QC, the senior counsel assisting the inquiry, opened proceedings on an ominous note. 'Mr Commissioner,' he said, 'we are embarking upon a task of considerable magnitude.' He then called his first witness, Sir Terence Lewis, to the stand. After Lewis was sworn in, Crooke asked: 'Sir Terence, could you favour the commission, if you would, by perhaps dealing with a potted history of the Queensland Police Force? Where do we see its beginnings?'

'Certainly,' Lewis said with his impeccable, old-school manners. 'Mr Commissioner, may I refer to notes?'

'By all means,' Fitzgerald responded.

Lewis proceeded to give a lengthy account of the force's history. It was a position Lewis was comfortable with. He enjoyed the detail of history and his countless memos and diary entries over the years betrayed a man who was at ease the more he was surrounded by accumulated data. He kept every slip of paper. He notated the most minor of incidents. The keeping of records was an integral part of his daily existence. It was he, too, who had instigated the Queensland Police Museum. He could have talked for hours on the history of the force.

As Evan Whitton noted of Lewis's history lesson: 'Mr Fitzgerald chewed absently on his spectacles through this tedious dissertation and did not trouble to ask Sir Terence how he reconciled his demand for more troops with his assertion that the Queensland force appeared already to be the most efficient in the Western world – that the clear-up rate (of alleged offenders arrested) was a little better than 50 per cent against, say, New South Wale's 23.95 per cent, and Scotland Yard's 17 per cent.'

But Lewis was soon drawn to more contemporaneous, and contentious, matters. In his evidence, he told the inquiry that Premier Joh Bjelke-Petersen and five police ministers had instructed that prostitution be 'tolerated'. Lewis said the direction of government and various ministers was that SP betting should be constantly monitored as it deprived the government of revenue, but that prostitution and massage parlours – while needing attention – were not a high priority if they were being conducted 'in a tolerable manner'.

Lewis was further questioned about chains of command – who would be in control of monitoring prostitution and illegal casinos? Was there anything formal in place in relation to police accepting gifts?

After lunch, Lewis reiterated the unwritten policy on prostitution that had been passed on to him verbally via ministers Tom Newbery, Ron Camm, Russ Hinze, Bill Glasson and Bill Gunn: '… uniformly the policy as to prostitution has been put on the basis that prostitution was to be contained and controlled rather than that there be any major resource allocation to its elimination,' Lewis told a packed Courtroom 29.

He cited a report dated 23 May 1974, that listed for the first time all the massage parlours in Brisbane, compiled by Inspector Osborne for senior officer Norm Gulbransen. He said the report was received by Gulbransen on 3 June 1974 and filed away. (Incredibly, Lewis was trying to not only lay blame on the Whitrod administration for the prolificacy of massage parlours, but indicated there had been a precedent in police doing nothing about prostitution.)

Lewis claimed that he had received instructions, from both the Premier and the Minister, to take action to endeavour to close all massage parlours through the state and where possible to prosecute the proprietors and owners of the buildings if they didn't close.

Crooke asked Lewis if this initiative came before or after the screening of 'The Moonlight State' on 11 May. 'It might sound funny but I don't remember, but I assume it was after,' Lewis said. 'I'm nearly certain it would be after.'

Lewis's revelations were always going to be a sensation, given it was the first real day of evidence before the commission of inquiry. Still, for the Commissioner of Police to lay blame for the sin of prostitution, and its attendant vices, at the feet of not only the righteous Lutheran, Sir Joh Bjelke-Petersen, but five of his National Party ministers as well, was a political bombshell.

Opposition Leader Nev Warburton wasted no time in condemning the government. 'The first day of the Fitzgerald investigation has shown the National Party Government to be a righteous fraud,' he trumpeted. 'No doubt many ministers will tonight be sticking pins in their Bill Gunn dolls.'

Lewis was back in the stand the next day.

Bob Mulholland, for the Australian Broadcasting Corporation, ran through a number of press stories over the years relating to brothels and prostitution in Brisbane. He quoted former police minister Tom Newbery in a story in 1979 detailing a clamp-down on massage parlours. Another story in the *Courier-Mail*, on 9 August 1979, reported that seven massage parlours had been closed following successful police raids.

A newspaper report on 24 April 1983 proclaimed: ALL OUT WAR ON VICE. It said police minister Bill Glasson had ordered the closure of all illegal gambling casinos, massage parlours and brothels in Brisbane in an attempt to clear up police corruption. Then on 13 January 1987, Police Minister Bill Gunn was famously quoted as saying there was no evidence of prostitution in Brisbane.

Mulholland also discussed the Lucas inquiry in 1977 and the Sturgess Report of 1985. 'And again part of that inquiry by Mr Sturgess involved the operation of prostitution, did it not?' Mulholland asked Lewis.

'Yes, he touched on that in it,' the Police Commissioner replied.

'You say he touched upon it – it was an important part of his inquiry, was it not?'

'I assume so,' Lewis said. 'I haven't read the report.'

It was not a wise answer from Lewis, and it would come back to haunt him. Why had the Commissioner of Police failed to read the report of one of the most important investigations of the previous decade? In that report, Sturgess had questioned why those who owned and ran the city's brothels and illegal gambling joints had not been prosecuted to the full extent of the law.

Commissioner Fitzgerald, however, kept the friction to a minimum in the early stages. '... there should not be any basis for a suggestion that Sir Terence is being accorded some special privilege,' Fitzgerald told the packed courtroom. 'He is not, but he has come here in the first instance ... to provide a necessary basis for dealing with more detailed matters as the commission progresses, and I think there has to be good faith on all sides. He is available and he will be brought back if he is required.'

Mulholland asked Lewis about the three Bellino brothers, Hector Hapeta and Vic Conte. 'Mr Commissioner, to the best of my knowledge, I have never met any one of them, neither have I had anything to do with any of them,' Lewis responded coolly.

Throughout that first week, the commission wrestled with the argument of the containment of prostitution. Where had this notion come from? And what, by definition, did containment actually mean?

Deputy Commissioner Ron Redmond was called to give evidence on the topic. He said massage parlours weren't prosecuted because that was consistent with the state government's containment policy on prostitution. He said he had overheard Police Minister Gunn tell Lewis that prostitution served a 'useful purpose'.

'I do not dissent from the containment policy because it seems realistic,' Redmond said. 'Police have to have knowledge of lurid acts or evidence of touching of private parts ... It is my belief police have to get to the brink of committing the [sexual] act to get evidence. I believe no officer should have to do this.'

The following Monday, Commissioner Lewis was recalled and further examined. Lewis said in a statement: 'In 1978, consideration was given to a transfer for widening the responsibility for the policing of massage parlours. On 7 April 1978 in a discussion I had with the Premier, and later Mr [Ron] Camm, I was advised that policing of massage parlours should be left to the Licensing Branch, and on 2 October 1978, Mr Camm telephoned me and informed me that the

Premier had mentioned that the Assistant Commissioner, Crime, was not to be placed over the Licensing Branch.'

This was, of course, harking back to the time when former top cop Tony Murphy was trying to bring the Licensing Branch under his control during the beginning of the great purge of the branch under Alec Jeppesen.

Lewis spent a total of six hours in the witness box. Tony Fitzgerald said to the courtroom: 'We want to find the truth, but we don't want to spend our lives doing it.'

As drama, the first week of the inquiry did not disappoint. As one *Sunday Mail* columnist wrote: 'Oh-oh! The Fitzgerald Inquiry, described last week as the "most important thing to happen in Queensland in 100 years", has already, in the space of one short week, given a jolly good shake to the foundations of government in this state.'

What the inaugural week also proved, was that it was absolutely inevitable that the hand of the inquiry would, at some point, be reaching back into the dark past of the Queensland Police Force.

Bulwarking

As the inquiry found its feet there were typewriters across the city clacking in overdrive as various parties prepared lengthy statements in advance of what might emerge in evidence before Commissioner Tony Fitzgerald.

Over at 32 Naretha Street, Carindale, not far from the Belmont Hills Reserve, south-east of the CBD, former assistant commissioner Tony Murphy – now splitting his time between the mainland and Amity Point – prepared a large document that touched on some of the more contentious moments in the history of the Queensland Police Force stretching back to the 1960s.

Murphy was spending less and less time at his flower farm on North Stradbroke Island, and had started an insurance-related investigation business – Queensland Retired Police Investigations. His multifaceted treatise not only aimed at underlining his innocence in all matters corrupt, but at skewering the enemies he'd attracted in his career. Another apparent thematic purpose in his writings was to display to the commission of inquiry that he had, in fact, actively fought the good fight against the illegal casino operators mentioned in the terms of reference.

One of the first things Murphy cited in his statement, for example, was his arrest of gaming-house keeper Luciano Scognamiglio in 1967. Scognamiglio had famously tried to put straight Licensing Branch undercover operative Kingsley Fancourt on the kickback payroll in 1974. Fancourt had also secretly taped Scognamiglio offering the bribe and naming his links with police officers like Jack Herbert and Tony Murphy during a conversation at the illegal casino at 142 Wickham Street, Fortitude Valley.

In his document Murphy also attempted to rewrite history. He argued that his name was never mentioned by Scognamiglio on the secret tapes, and 'is … even if it were to have been said, quite innocuous'.

'This verbal statement attributed to SCOGNAMIGLIO to the effect that he [SCOGNAMIGLIO] was friendly with me was not I am told identifiable on the tape recording produced in Court and so patiently listened to by the Bench,' wrote Murphy. 'THIS ALLEGED REMARK BY SCOGNAMIGLIO was proved to be a substantive part of the grounds called on by the ABC when *Nationwide* put to air a series of defamatory broadcasts in March 1982.'

Murphy's ultimate contention, however, was a conspiracy of such grandness and complexity that it beggared belief. It was Murphy's view that Chris Masters' pivotal and damning *Four Corners* program, which triggered the inquiry, was 'designed as a desperate tactical manoeuvre by the ABC to destroy the credibility of MR LEWIS and myself prior to the matter of our 1982 defamation suits being taken to trial'.

Logically then, the Fitzgerald Inquiry, which resulted from 'The Moonlight State', was also a part of that conspiracy on behalf of the ABC to get Murphy and Lewis before their legal matter got into a court. This was despite the fact that the case against Campbell, Fancourt and *Nationwide* had yet to see the inside of a courtroom in almost five and a half years.

Commissioner Lewis's statement, on the other hand, was more straightforward but also more expansive. It was both a testimony to his glowing achievements since he joined the force and was sworn in as a constable on 17 January 1949, and an answer to his critics over many decades. Lewis's literary life raft had some touching moments.

He recorded that during a particularly damaging flood in the Charleville region – where he had been posted by former commissioner Ray Whitrod [Murphy was sent to Longreach], Lewis underlined his dedication to duty: 'I worked 33 days straight without a day off.'

He devoted just one sentence to him securing the top job over Whitrod, failing to mention the Machiavellian nature of the appointment and the involvement of Premier Joh Bjelke-Petersen in Whitrod's demise. 'I was appointed Commissioner of Police and took up that position on 29th November 1976,' Lewis blandly recalled.

Also with an eye on the terms of reference of the Fitzgerald Inquiry, Lewis's statement included an in-built historical excuse in relation to the prosecution, or lack thereof, of massage parlours and prostitutes. He said on taking up the position of Commissioner of Police under Minister Tom Newbery, it was the latter's responsibility to heavily advise Lewis given the former inspector third class did not have 'any previous administrative contact with Cabinet'.

He said Newbery's advice was by and large given 'verbally', and traversed government policy. Some of that advice included: reducing the road toll; lowering the serious crime rate; halting the police resignation rate; and to improve the general morale of the force. 'The Honourable Minister also touched on police buildings, housing, transport and equipment generally and also on the aspects of SP betting, illegal gambling and prostitution,' Lewis wrote.

'He [Newbery] stated that the Government wanted constant attention given to SP betting and illegal gambling as they deprived the Government of revenue, whereas with prostitution "it has been around for a long time and would be very difficult to eliminate". He said police should give massage parlours attention but if they were being conducted in a tolerable manner they should not receive a high priority considering all the other serious matters requiring police attention.'

Lewis explained that this policy – clearly a government request – had been maintained for the past ten years. He then went on, page after page, about his achievements in the job, and his philosophy on effective policing. Furthermore, he provided an exhaustive number of attachments to his statement. Some laid blame on Ray Whitrod and his trusted men. Others skipped through almost every controversy Lewis had encountered as Commissioner. He also tried to put out fires before they'd even started. 'Australian Royal Commission of Inquiry into Drugs – John Edward Milligan claiming association with me, A. Murphy and G. Hallihan [sic], in wrongdoings in connection with illegal drugs,' the statement said. 'The Commission found the allegations were baseless and untrue.'

And another: '1983/84 Paul John Breslin – claiming that he was a friend of mine and had been loaned a police vehicle and that there was considerable homosexual behaviour between cadets and Probationaries at the Queensland Police Academy. All of this and a lot of other information circulated by Breslin was false.'

And more still: 'In early 1986, Mr Abe Saffron purchased two hotels in Queensland and Mr Merv Stubbins, Chairman of the Licensing Commission, said that there was nothing before the commission to indicate that Mr Saffron was not a fit and proper person to own the properties. I had a confidential conversation with the Honourable N.J. Harper, MLA, Minister for Justice and Attorney-General, and in March 1986 he recommended to the Governor in Council that the Licensing Commission's stamp of approval be rescinded.'

Commissioner Lewis had kept one of Sydney's career criminals from infecting Queensland. He also denied knowing any of the men named in the inquiry's terms of reference. He said he did not know of 'any member of the Police Force' who was guilty of 'misconduct, neglect or violation of duty' when it came to policing such premises.

His clause 1(c) stated: 'I have not received any benefit or favour, whether financial or otherwise, either directly or indirectly, from those same five persons for neglecting to enforce the laws in respect to any such premises.'

All in all, it was a curious document, a potpourri of self-defence, pre-emptive attack, personal aggrandisement, history lesson, a blizzard of statistics and an insurance policy. It had, too, in its structure and busyness, and with its mistakes in the spelling of the surnames of people like former police minister Tom Newbery and former Rat Packer and detective, Glen Hallahan, an air of desperation about it.

The Company Director

Sicilian-born Geraldo Bellino, adagio dancer and author of the musical *Sharon, Oh Sharon*, appeared before the Fitzgerald Inquiry on 18 August, neatly dressed with his fulsome moustache clipped. He gave his occupation as company director. Bellino, 45, told the packed court he had run seven illegal casinos in Brisbane, four during the inquiry's terms of reference that dated back to 1977.

He had only a single conviction for keeping a common gaming house in 1978, following a massive raid by the Licensing Branch after

Bellino had missed an illegal protection payment to police. Bellino gave evidence that he had earned a living off running illegal games since 1974. He said he had gone into partnership with one-time waiter, Vittorio Conte, in 142 Wickham Street. 'I think there was some manilla at times, some games of chances, crown and anchor, baccarat, whatever people required,' he told the inquiry.

The casino was open from 7 p.m. Monday to Saturday. Downstairs was a 'health studio', Bubbles Bath House. Bellino and Conte ended up buying the building at 142 Wickham Street in 1982, having previously leased it. He said the illegal casino was 'more of a club' – food and alcohol were served free of charge to patrons. 'We had no membership; we just knew the people who came frequently,' Bellino said.

The company director later estimated that he earned about $1 million a year from his illegal casinos. He described it as a 'highly profitable exercise'. He said the only policeman he recalled seeing at 142 Wickham Street was retired officer Nigel Powell, who had appeared in the *Four Corners* program, 'The Moonlight State'.

Bellino outlined how he owned the World By Night and The Beat nightclubs. He flatly denied being involved in the prostitution industry. His frank evidence was the talk of the town, and yet another rupture for the government. The press began to ask – how could Bellino have been running illegal casinos since the 1970s, by and large free of prosecution? Where were the police? And why had successive police ministers denied that illegal gaming existed in Brisbane?

One commentator reflected: 'The inquiry is now four weeks old and so far the "show" rarely has failed to entertain with some spectacular revelations, elements of humour and occasional drama. Bellino had at one point shouted at Ralph Devlin, junior counsel assisting the commission, and then at Commissioner Fitzgerald. He later apologised.'

As for Vittorio Conte, he seemed to be the source of much mirth. 'Mr Conte appears as cool as a cucumber as he tells of hiring crystal glasses for parties held at the illegal casinos to boost business,' the column reflected. 'He obviously likes to air his sense of humour, but one of his better lines was unintended. When asked how many police he would see in a night, he said as many as 15 would come to his World By Night strip club looking for "criminals".'

Despite the jollity, the evidence of Bellino and Conte had prompted some very big questions.

Journalist Quentin Dempster, in his weekly column in the *Sunday Mail*, correctly assessed the gravity of the situation. 'Pressure is growing for Sir Joh Bjelke-Petersen and some of his Ministers to take the stand at the Fitzgerald Inquiry into organised crime and police corruption,' he wrote in late August. Dempster said it wasn't until the investigative work of Phil Dickie and Chris Masters that the government started to take notice. Previously, they had not 'demonstrated any concern about the potential growth of organised crime and police corruption through these illegal activities'.

He posed the question: Why did Cabinet ministers consistently accept police department advice on these matters year after year?

'Maybe it was because of the perceived immense power and influence of the Police Commissioner, who everyone knew had been hand-picked for the job by the Premier after the Whitrod years,' Dempster wrote. 'To countermand the Commissioner would be tantamount to crossing Joh, perhaps. And which junior Minister with any political nous would be silly enough to do that?'

Meanwhile, Commissioner Fitzgerald reminded police officers that those wishing to be granted an indemnity from prosecution in exchange for evidence before the inquiry had until Monday 7 September to step forward.

One of the first to do so was Senior Sergeant Harry Burgess.

Early Days

For the first six weeks of the inquiry, lawyers, politicians, police, the press and the public would have been forgiven for thinking they had a damp squib unfolding in the District Court. Lewis's seemingly endless explanation about how the Queensland Police Force worked set a dreary tone, like a dud note derailing a symphony from the outset.

It was, however, a tactic from Fitzgerald and his team. It provided context; a base on which to build. Presumably it would have given Commissioner Lewis a measure of confidence. One inquiry source says the almost 'pedantic' opening to the inquiry was deliberate, and that patterns of malfeasance then emerged on top of that context.

Terry Lewis was less sanguine about the opening weeks of the inquiry. 'We were able to answer some of their crap and Fitzgerald got very shitty and Gunn ... I'm not saying I'm precisely right, Gunn got in touch with me and said that Fitzgerald had complained about police having access to police records,' Lewis remembers. 'And I said, "That's not my fault" and Gunn said ... "You weren't to give your legal people any police records," something like that.'

Lewis says he immediately rang the Premier. 'Joh would have said words to the effect, "Now, you keep whatever your legal people want ... they're entitled to [have access to it]."'

The problem was that police counsel were raising issues at the inquiry before they'd been run by Fitzgerald and his staff.

'I believed we were going quite well because whatever was coming out of the inquiry we were able to give reasonable answers to it,' Lewis says of the early days of the commission. 'Cedric Hampson [QC, who represented the Police Commissioner and other senior police] phoned me ... and said, look, Fitzgerald had been in touch with him and asked him where was he getting this information from?

'Hampson had been involved in a number of royal commissions ... and I said, they were just our files. He said he didn't want anything brought up by anyone unless he'd been advised about it. But that was most improper. Anyhow ... we were not to supply anything to Cedric that hadn't been supplied to the Commission. And up till then they had the right to demand anything which they did and they got it. We couldn't bloody hypothesise what they might want.'

Lewis believes there were darker forces at work. 'And that really got them upset and that's when they got ... Fitzgerald had to get rid of me,' Lewis says. 'His target was Joh, that was his target, but then to get Joh they knew they'd have to get me because I would answer most of their queries.

'I mean Joh wasn't a bloody crook no matter what they might say about Joh. But one big deal was ... Sir Leslie Thiess repaired his tractors or something. Well strike a light, if that's corruption I'll walk from here to Bourke backwards. I mean, mates do that for each other. The other one was that somebody came in and gave him ... $100,000 or something? And Joh gave it to somebody to take up and to put into the funds of the National Party up at Spring Hill.

'If he'd wanted to be, he could have been a very, very rich man in those days. But I never heard one person say that Joh was getting a quid.'

Journalist Phil Dickie saw, in those early weeks, the emergence of Fitzgerald as a master tactician. 'I think he was conscious that there'd been a string of inquiries ... [where] there was some interesting stories and scuttlebutt coming out of them but not a lot of anything else. He didn't necessarily feel bound by the conventional wisdoms about how to do things. For that reason I think ... he was very clever. And I think ... all of his stuff was fairly carefully thought out. He seemed to get off to a totally slow start, an unproductive start ... [but he] let these buggers set themselves up and, you know, it worked beautifully.'

Dickie says from the outset Fitzgerald was interested in the big picture. 'He didn't lose sight of the main game,' Dickie reflects. 'Like the main game ... is not to get a pile of convictions at the end ... [but] to look at the society and its functioning and say we could do this a lot better.'

A Build-up of Conscience

Harry Reginald Burgess, 44, was within months of celebrating 25 silver years in the Queensland Police Force when he resigned on Friday 28 August 1987. He had taken one of Commissioner Tony Fitzgerald's indemnities. He was set to talk.

One of the first things he did on secretly taking the indemnity was to ring his old flame, the brothel madam Anne Marie Tilley, de facto wife to Hector Hapeta. Tilley met up with Burgess at a designated rendezvous point and sat with Burgess in his car. 'I got down there. He was shaking in the car,' says Tilley. 'He told me he loved me. I said, "Come on son, get over it … you haven't called me down here for this great, romantic thing."

'He goes, "No. I'll tell you what I've done. I've rolled."

'I said, "I don't think I should talk to you anymore."

'[Burgess said,] "They don't know I'm doing this so I want you to get as much together as you can and take off, run away."

'Then he … told me what he'd done, who he'd been speaking to, what cars they had.

'I believed him. I went home.

'Hector says, "What's wrong?"

'I said, "It's fucked, it's gone, it's finished."

'He goes, "No, no, no, no, no."

'I said, "That's it."

'He started to sweat. He sat in his chair. He said, "You've got to be fucking kidding me?"

'I said, "No, I'm not kidding you."

'"Just like that?"

'I said, "It's finished."'

Burgess stepped into the witness box on 31 August 1987. He came to the commission hearings alone, clutching a brown leather briefcase, and made no verbal contact with anybody before being called to take the stand. A security guard armed with a revolver sat one metre from the inquiry's new star witness.

Burgess duly sang, though some of the notes were indistinct. Still, he was the first connection between the police and Queensland's criminal underworld. In addition, he dropped former Licensing Branch officer Jack Reginald Herbert into the thick of it.

Burgess's revelations were sensational. He said he had accepted bribes of $500 cash a month from Assistant Commissioner (Crime) Graeme Parker between 1982 and 1985, and another $500 monthly payment from former Licensing Branch inspector Noel Dwyer. Herbert, he told the commission, gave him about $200 every six weeks.

He also admitted to having – along with other officers who he named – free sex with prostitutes while serving in the Licensing Branch from 1979 to 1985. Burgess also claimed he'd attended meetings with Geraldo Bellino and Vic Conte at the various homes of Jack Herbert where illegal gambling was discussed, and that he himself had visited Herbert at his home once in 1984. He told the inquiry he had come forward 'mostly as the result of a built-up conscience'.

Burgess went into detail about his contact with the Hapeta/Tilley consortium, saying he knew as early as 1981 that the pair was involved in prostitution, including a brothel at the Top of the Valley and a handful of escort agencies. He told the inquiry that in 1981 an unsuccessful raid had been mounted against the consortium. Tilley had been tipped off by someone in the branch. At this stage both Parker and Dwyer were in charge of Licensing.

Burgess admitted that he had a 'trusting relationship' with Tilley.

As for Hapeta, Burgess had interviewed him at the branch office. Hapeta denied living off the earnings of Tilley.

'A few days later I was in Inspector Dwyer's office and he told me it was alright in relation to the breaches on Hapeta and not to proceed,' Burgess said in evidence. 'He [Dwyer] handed me $1000 in \$50 bills – just folded over money ... around that time he gave me the responsibility of Tilley's agencies. He told me I was to do the work on them, to look after them.'

Burgess stated that Tilley had told him that Hebert was collecting protection money off her. Herbert's business, he understood, was 'whatever premises were of interest to Hapeta or to Bellino and Conte'.

Burgess said he last heard from Herbert when the inquiry was announced. 'He rang me at Wynnum CIB to say hooray ...' Burgess continued. 'He said he was going away. The conversation was along the lines of "I'm taking a holiday and going away".

'I said "a long way away" and he said, "Yes, I'm going to see Mummy." That indicated to me he was leaving the country and going back to England.'

Burgess was back before the commission the following day. He told a stunned courtroom that two crime groups involved with Brisbane's massage parlours and escort agencies were 'conservatively pulling in around \$500,000 each a month, and that one of the groups had been paying police around \$10,000 a month for protection'.

Burgess identified the groups as the Hapeta/Tilley consortium, and another consisting of Geraldo Bellino, Vic Conte, Geoffrey Crocker and Allan Holloway. He was asked about the initial bribe from Noel Dwyer back in 1981 by Bob Mulholland, QC, who appeared for the Australian Broadcasting Corporation. 'After the first payment from Mr Dwyer, you were the person placed in charge of Hapeta?' Mulholland queried.

'Placed in charge is the wrong term,' Burgess answered. 'I was his liaison officer.'

Graeme Parker denied any wrongdoing. 'There's no truth in it at all,' he said in response to Burgess's testimony. 'I'm flabbergasted with what's happened. The next move will be up to the solicitors.'

Similarly, Noel Dwyer was incensed. 'If it wasn't so serious it would be laughable,' he said. 'I strenuously deny it ... I think I did a good job with the facilities I had.'

Tilley Bolts

As for Anne Marie Tilley, brothel madam, who had found Queensland so welcoming and so conducive to business way back in 1978 when she and partner Hector opened their first parlour – the Top Hat – she made a snap decision.

'I just packed a bag and drove,' Tilley says. 'I had the Celica and traded it in for an old station wagon. I took off. I didn't want to be pulled in to have to answer questions. I was the same old Sydney girl – "I won't dob."

'Hec said I'm not going to answer that because it might "incinerate" me. We went over "incriminate" 100,000 times.'

While Hapeta stayed put in Brisbane, Tilley headed for her old stomping ground of Sydney. She had recently been going through her fourth IVF treatment. A few weeks after taking flight, she found out she was pregnant.

'I went and saw some criminals down in Sydney,' recalls Tilley. 'I went and got a little flat up near Randwick. I had very little cash. I just survived. Did a couple of other things while I was away to make money.'

Tilley went into labour as she was negotiating the sale of a small parlour she owned in the city's notorious vice strip of Kings Cross. The money from the sale kept her going. Her baby was born in the Royal Hospital for Women in inner-suburban Paddington. It was where Tilley had also been born.

'I got out of there just in time, too,' she says of her stay in hospital. 'Another crim I know in Sydney, he came up there with his wife to see me. He said: "We think it's the cops, they're very straight cops. Have you done that little [blood screening] test on her heel yet?"

'Yes. I was out.'

Pie in the Sky

It had been more than a year since Premier Joh Bjelke-Petersen had confidently announced his plans for the construction of the world's tallest building – just down at the corner of Edward and Ann streets – that would put Brisbane on par with some of the planet's great cosmopolitan cities.

But the Goliath of a project kept hitting obstacles. The contentious site – home to the Capital Hotel, once the splendid Canberra Temperance Hotel – was not yielding to Joh Bjelke-Petersen nor the project developer John Minuzzo. Tenants in the Capital were a sticking point.

One of them, chiropractor Dr David Reason, had launched several actions in the Queensland Supreme Court against Minuzzo's company, Mainsel Investments Pty Ltd. The actions came after a court order earlier in the year after Mainsel gave undertakings not to interfere in Dr Reason's premises. He had a lease that extended to October 1987. Mainsel also agreed not to make undue noise or interfere with access to Dr Reason's rooms. They also had to restore to working order toilets, fire alarms and a lift.

Dr Reason's actions stemmed from the undertakings not being met. He was asking that Minuzzo be jailed for contempt. As director of Mainsel, the action contended, Minuzzo had 'caused, permitted or procured' the company to breach the earlier undertakings ordered in the Supreme Court.

Dr Reason also sought an injunction against the demolition of the Capital Hotel. (Incredibly, according to one source, Bjelke-Petersen personally approached Dr Reason to convince him to give up his lease in the building.) The case was heard before Mr Justice Dowsett.

Minuzzo, it turned out, had gone overseas on business despite the court hearings. 'I really think Mr Minuzzo should make some attempts to come back,' Justice Dowsett told the court.

'We will try, your honour,' said Minuzzo's lawyer, Richard Chesterman, QC.

As the case dragged on, Justice Dowsett began to lose patience over Minuzzo's continued non-attendance. The judge described the property developer's actions as 'a great discourtesy to the court'.

A few hundred metres south along George Street, the ALP member for Wolston, Bob Gibbs, was also criticising Minuzzo, this man who had the ear of the Premier. 'I wish to raise a matter that is of concern to all Queenslanders,' Gibbs told the House. 'I refer specifically to the continual habit of the Premier of this state to associate with people of dubious character.'

Gibbs cited an article about Minuzzo's past in the *Times on Sunday*. He also reminded the chamber of various deals Minuzzo had been involved with in Victoria in the 1970s and 1980s, much as Nev Warburton had done the previous year. 'He now faces the very real possibility of being charged with the serious offence of contempt of court over the premises that he is leasing to a Mr David Reason, who refuses to leave the premises,' reiterated Gibbs. 'This is another clear case of shonky business operators coming to Brisbane. They seem to have the incredible ability to be able to obtain the listening ear of the Premier of this state.

'I say very clearly in this House today that members of the public have indicated that they are not in favour of this development. The state government should immediately cancel any negotiations that it has with Mr Minuzzo.'

Justice Dowsett fined Mainsel Investments $125,000 for failing to comply with various undertakings in relation to the site for the world's tallest building, and ordered that the company be restrained from further demolition of the building that might affect the running of Dr Reason's business until his lease expired at the end of October.

'The defendant [Mainsel] acted in a high-handed and irresponsible way which bespoke a complete disregard of the court, the undertaking given to the court and Mr Reason's rights,' said Justice Dowsett. 'I have no doubt that [Mainsel's] motivation in its conduct has been a desire to press on with the development ...'

When Minuzzo finally returned from overseas, his legal counsel apologised to the court. Justice Dowsett told the court he would have gaoled Minuzzo in the matter of contempt if he had not received that apology, and gave him a 14-day suspended gaol sentence.

Still, the project was alive, and it was confirmed not long after that a Korean company, Youchang Constructions, were in the final stages of negotiating financing for the ambitious project. Minuzzo told the press that excavations for the tower would probably commence in October.

There may have been much hullaballoo about the controversial building in court and in parliament, but one person was conspicuous in his lack of contribution to the debate – the project's early champion, Premier Joh Bjelke-Petersen.

The Blonde Behind the Screen

During the famously ineffective National Hotel inquiry into police misconduct in 1963 and 1964, the notorious prostitute and brothel madam Shirley Margaret Brifman was called by Justice Gibbs to give evidence. The appearance of the vivacious Brifman set the hearings alight – she appeared in court dressed in a stunning white frock and wore a hat. Brifman immediately went about perjuring herself, denying she was a working girl, although she had been paying off two members of the so-called Rat Pack – Tony Murphy and Glen Hallahan – since the late 1950s.

Twenty-three years later, brothel madam and prostitute Katherine James, 31, dressed in white and wearing a blonde wig, caused a similar sensation when she took the stand. A special wooden screen had been erected in front of the witness box to shield her identity. She went to and from the box guarded by police. James, who had been granted indemnity from prosecution, gave evidence before Tony Fitzgerald's commission of inquiry on Wednesday 2 September, 1987. She told the inquiry that brothel owners Hector Hapeta and Anne Marie Tilley told her they paid police about $10,000 a month for protection.

James alleged that the former detective sergeant, Harry Burgess, usually picked up the money, and had earned the nickname 'Harry the Bagman'. She fingered other police, telling the commission she had personally seen former deputy commissioner Syd Atkinson and former CIB chief Tony Murphy at an illegal game above Pinocchio's Restaurant in the city, run by Gerry Bellino, in the early 1970s. 'Sippy' Atkinson, she alleged, was in there three to four times a week drinking and chatting to Bellino.

Lawyers for Atkinson and Murphy responded immediately, issuing a statement: 'The accusations are completely false. They are denied and evidence will be brought before the commission in due course to demonstrate the falsity of these allegations.'

She also claimed in evidence that she'd had a sexual relationship with Bellino when she worked as a dealer at the game upstairs from Pinocchio's. (Bellino denied having ever met James.) Sensationally, James added that it was 'policy' at Hapeta and Tilley brothels to give free sex to police. She herself had had sex with at least six police officers. Police showed no interest in making arrests or looking for drugs in the massage parlours, she said.

'They'd come and see girls stoned off their heads ... there was no interest at all,' James told the inquiry.

In addition, as both a prostitute and brothel manager, James gave an insight into the immensity of the trade through the late 1970s and into the 1980s. Hapeta and Tilley, she calculated, were earning about $75,000 each week. In one of their brothels she managed in New Farm, James said, there were at least 300 to 400 regular clients a week.

The next day, James returned to the witness box and revealed that she had been threatened prior to making the decision to give her testimony before the commission. She said former Licensing Branch detective Neville Ross had visited her after the inquiry was announced and told her not to talk to investigators. If she did, her male partner would be 'jeopardised'.

In addition, she said she had also been warned by escort agency operator Geoff Crocker, who she alleged had confronted her at the hotel where she worked in the city a week before she was due to give evidence. 'He sat looking at me for ten or 15 minutes,' James said. 'Then he came up and ordered a meal.' He asked her how she was and she replied – 'fine'.

Then he allegedly said: 'Enjoy it while you can, babe.'

Crocker, who was a regular attendee at the inquiry hearings, later denied he had made any threats. He told investigators he'd been having a drink and a meal at the Melbourne Hotel when he noticed that Katherine James was working behind the servery counter. 'I didn't even know she was going to be a witness, for God's sake, until that day she opened her mouth behind the screen and I knew who she was straightaway ...'

James went on to titillate the public gallery and the slew of legal eagles alike with stories of wild, gangster-themed parties and Melbourne Cup Day celebrations at Pinky's brothel in Kangaroo Point, attended by several police.

It had been an extraordinary week at the inquiry. In its editorial, the *Sunday Mail* wasted no time in condemning the state's force. 'According to both witnesses this week, the police were virtually running the brothels with the syndicates, keeping out new competition ... if this is the case – the evidence so far suggests it is – then the situation was allowed to develop by the Queensland Government's curious morality.'

James also revealed why she had decided to blow the whistle – she wanted to highlight the exploitation of prostitutes. 'I really think it's time something was done not only about the managers but also the police involved,' she declared.

Katherine James had been a star witness. There were more to follow.

You Will Dingo, Joh

Down at the southern end of George Street – a ten-minute walk from the District Courts Section of the Law Courts Building – the Bjelke-Petersen government was feeling the heat of the inquiry revelations in Parliament House.

The Opposition Justice Spokesman and member for Logan, Wayne Goss, zeroed in on the Premier during Questions On Notice on 10 September. Without referring to any specific allegations aired before Fitzgerald, Goss asked that in view of the cost of the inquiry – reportedly $2 million – was the Premier 'prepared to give evidence ... in relation to any policy discussions in which he had been involved, including a reported direction from him in 1978 that the Licensing squad have exclusive jurisdiction over massage parlours?'.

Goss also wanted to know if former police ministers who held their portfolios during the period of the inquiry's terms of reference would also give evidence about such matters.

The Premier agreed that members of the legal profession were 'making an awful lot of money out of this inquiry ... The cost might be $3 million or $4 million at least,' he said. 'They are going to have a good time, including the honourable members and the members of his own profession. I guess that is the system.'

Goss pressed Sir Joh: 'Are you giving evidence?'

'Why don't the members of the Opposition go there?' the Premier retorted. 'They would know a lot about massage parlours. They are all experts in that area.'

It was a facile response, but Bjelke-Petersen went on to champion the Queensland Police Force, despite the recent revelations of protection money paid to them and sex romps in Brisbane brothels. 'In defence of the police force – it plays a very important part in the government of this state and in the activities of the community,' Sir Joh said. 'It consists of very respectable and good men. I support the work that the police carry out in very difficult circumstances.'

Goss did not let go. He urged the Premier to answer his question, then took another tack. '... is it fair to the public,' Goss asked, 'and in particular to the police force, that, whereas the police are compelled to undergo a difficult and embarrassing inquiry and to account for their actions over the last ten years, the Premier and ministers for police during the same period ... have declined to answer for their acts or omissions in directing the police force?'

The Premier immediately obfuscated: 'Everyone knows that the honourable member is trying to make capital out of nothing.'

'You will dingo, Joh,' barked the Deputy Opposition Leader Tom Burns. 'You won't go. You won't go before the inquiry,' Burns taunted.

'I will have the honourable member in court,' the Premier responded, 'and he can say all that he likes then.'

But beneath the patient exterior, the Premier was deeply concerned at the revelations coming out of Courtroom 29. In his memoir, *Don't You Worry About That!*, Bjelke-Petersen admitted he was shocked when stories of widespread bribery and other corruption in the force began to emerge following the Fitzgerald Inquiry. He was forced to speculate on potentially how long it had been occurring and after acknowledging his own stint as police minister at one time, reflected on how the knowledge of any police corruption over the years had simply not come to the attention of any ministers over the years, 'those wide-awake, highly responsible men' who would surely have seized on any evidence if they had opportunity.

As he wrote in his memoir: 'People have said to me, "How is it you didn't know about it?" My answer has been that I did not live in the Police Department.

'The police were never my sole responsibility.'

Parker Pressure

Following the evidence of former Licensing Branch officer Harry Burgess to the commission in relation to his own corruption and that of senior officers Graeme Parker and Noel Dwyer, Parker had fallen ill with a form of viral pneumonia and gone on leave. Many of his colleagues were deeply concerned for his health.

What nobody knew outside the Parker family, however, was that the Assistant Commissioner had gathered with his family on Father's Day – 6 September – and told his seven children of his history of corruption. 'I told them the complete story and what options were open to me,' he later said.

His brother-in-law then telephoned counsel assisting the inquiry, Gary Crooke, to discuss indemnity for Parker. 'After Burgess gave evidence, I came to realise that the matters had the opportunity of going further,' Parker said. 'I felt that I was involved. I felt that I was the target of the media. I had to consider my conscience. I had to consider the effect what I was going to say would have on my family.' Parker knew there was a very real chance he might go to gaol for his crimes.

Commissioner Lewis's personal assistant, Greg Early, recalls the period in his unpublished memoir. In his diary on Sunday 13 September, Early received a phone call at 7.45 a.m. from Police Union boss Senior Sergeant Col Chant 'regarding AC Parker'. Early wrote in his diary: 'Said Dr English had rung him and was very concerned. Said a lot of pressure was being put on Parker/his family to have him interviewed. An "Insp Powell" is involved ... Mr Crooke and others have put Powell in charge of Parker's safety and also a lot of pressure being put on him to retire and go and give Queen's evidence. If he does it will implicate other senior police and members of the National Party ... I said I had no knowledge but would try and find out simply that no harm was likely to be done to anyone.'

Early went out to Parker's residence at Newmarket and found nobody home except one of Parker's children, who directed him to a shop in Alderley. He eventually tracked down Parker's wife who 'volunteered that Graeme had spoken to Mr [Gary] Crooke [of the Commission of Inquiry] for four hours (may have been eight) the prev. week and she was concerned that he was not in a fit state to do this'. Early alleges Parker's wife said her husband had double pneumonia and had gone close to a mental breakdown.

Lewis's personal assistant then 'Rang Col Chant and told him that things were in order and that no help needed. Did not tell him of contact with Mr Crooke.' As was to be expected, Early made a decision to fully inform Commissioner Lewis about the situation. He went to Garfield Drive to speak with his boss. He writes: 'My recollection is that I told ... Sir Terence ... about Parker having spoken to Gary Crooke and that Mrs Parker was going to see Crooke.'

In response, Lewis allegedly told Early, 'The Minister will probably suspend me now.'

A naive Greg Early replied, 'What would he want to do that for?'

Early wrote in his memoir: 'I put in a report or a statutory declaration as to what he said particularly and at one stage, according to what Lewis told me at the Ferny Grove dump one day where we met up by accident, I was on the witness list to give evidence for the prosecution. At this "meeting" he referred to me having been taken off the witness list and that he was going to insist on me being put back on – not sure if for prosecution or defence.'

The pressure on both Parker and Lewis was building by the hour and the situation wasn't helped by the appearance of Seregeant Colin

William Maxwell Dillon before the inquiry the following week. Dillon, a Torres Strait islander, had joined the force in 1965. It was a career path he longed for.

Just before Christmas 1982, 'Dirty Harry' Burgess pulled Dillon aside as he was leaving the office and asked him if he'd like to make some easy money. All he had to do was turn a blind eye to certain activities in relation to brothels and prostitution.

Burgess retracted the offer a week later.

Then, closer to Christmas, Dillon went in to work and found in his locker a bottle of Chivas Regal Royal Salute whisky, packaged in a velvet drawstring pouch.

'Did you get your Christmas present?' Burgess later asked.

At the inquiry, Dillon produced the unopened bottle and it was tendered as an exhibit. On Thursday 17 September, he made an impassioned plea to his fellow officers: 'I would like [other police] now, at this point in time in our policing history, to stand up, boldly step forward and speak out what they know of any crime or corruption within this state that is presently, and that has for a great number of years, eroded our great police force like a cancerous growth.

'Do your part in helping to remove this cancer so that we can get on the road to restoring the good public image that we once had, and that we can restore the faith in the public we serve, and I ask, I implore, all members of the public, the decent members of the public, please do not write us off,' said Dillon through tears. 'We are there.'

Dillon received a round of applause from the public gallery.

Bless Me Father, For I Have Sinned

Not long after Early's visit to the Commissioner's house, Lewis received another visitor at his newly built three-level home at 12 Garfield Drive. A clearly befuddled Graeme Parker, Assistant Commissioner and the

State's third-highest ranking police officer, came to the door in his pyjamas. He had driven to Paddington from his home at 60 Alderson Street, Newmarket.

'He came early, very early in the morning to see me and … he was very, very ill,' Lewis recalls. 'He was in his pyjamas. And he was really crook … and I told him that he should go and see a specialist and get treatment. He was just rambling about nothing … it was a no visit if you like. A visit with no visit, and I think I might have rung his wife and said he should go and see a doctor.'

Parker had recently suffered a bout of pneumonia and had relapsed. Just a fortnight after the damning evidence against him from corrupt cop Harry Burgess, a disoriented Parker was now turning up unannounced at the home of his boss. Parker was about to crack – he was readmitted to hospital on 16 September – and soon after resigned from the force and admitted corruption to inquiry investigators.

Over at police headquarters, Early recorded in his diary that he was visited by Allan Morrish, Parker's personal assistant, who was concerned about papers in Parker's safe. Early wrote: 'He said he and Parker had a key … I asked him if he felt there was enough justification to check the safe and he said "yes". I saw Dep Com [Ron] Redmond and told him of the visit and of my rec. to check the safe and transfer the contents to AC McMahon in fairness to him and particularly in view of uncertainty about Parker's return to duty, his state of health and also that we had knowledge of him speaking to Mr Crooke and had changed his solicitor in recent days. Mr Redmond agreed … Told COP [Commissioner of Police] of safe matter and leaks inq. To office of Dep Com and saw receipt for safe contents.'

What nobody knew was that on the Wednesday evening Parker indicated to commission staff that he was prepared to roll over in exchange for indemnity. A secret bedside sitting of the inquiry was arranged in the Mater Hospital where Parker offered a minimal amount of sworn evidence. He gave it directly to Commissioner Tony

Fitzgerald from his hospital bed. The transcript of the evidence read in part: 'Is it the case that you have admitted to the Commission that you were involved in corruption as a police officer?'

'Yes,' Parker said.

The disgraced now former assistant commissioner agreed to give evidence before the inquiry when he was in better health. He also named other police involved in corruption.

Lewis recalls that one of his daughters, Lanna, was on nursing duty at the Mater Hospital when Parker rolled over to the inquiry. 'She said he was really ill, he nearly died,' remembers Lewis. 'And it would have been very easy for any of those nurses to let him die because he was really crook. And while he was crook they talked to him of course, Fitzgerald himself went over and talked to him and others. And supposedly, I haven't got any evidence of this, but somebody might – Parker might tell you – he asked for a priest. And they put a bogus one in and he confessed his sins to the bogus priest.

'Parker [was a] very, very bright fellow and I liked him. He was a real worker. How he got involved with Herbert ... I don't know, I don't know.'

The news of Parker's resignation hit like a thunderclap. On Wednesday 18 September, Early wrote in his diary: 'Saw Dep Com and AC McMahon re locks on Parker's doors and arranged for them to be changed ...'

Early would go on to write in his unpublished memoir that on 18 September Lewis, Deputy Commissioner Ron Redmond and the five remaining Assistant Commissioners (Braithwaite, McMahon, Hilker, Donoghue and probably Walker) met in the small conference room to discuss Parker's resignation and to select a replacement for him. 'I was told by the Commissioner after the meeting that I was the selected replacement for Parker,' Early wrote.

Parker was, to date, the commission's biggest scalp, and it immediately adjourned for two weeks to sort through and analyse huge volumes of information it had received.

In the meantime, Labor's Justice Spokesman Wayne Goss went on the attack, calling for Commissioner Lewis to stand aside for the duration of the Fitzgerald Inquiry.

'I am making no suggestion of any improper conduct on the part of Sir Terence,' Goss was quoted in the *Courier-Mail* on Saturday 19 September. 'But clearly he must accept some of the responsibility, in an administrative sense, for the conduct of senior officers who have been promoted on his recommendation.'

Bjelke-Petersen immediately stood up for his embattled Police Commissioner. 'I always support people until something has been proved otherwise.'

Police Minister Bill Gunn called Goss's comments 'ludicrous'.

By the next day, the ground had shifted slightly. In a page-one story in the *Sunday Mail* under the headline – LEWIS MUST GO IT ALONE – Gunn said the Commissioner would have to decide for himself whether he stepped aside or not. 'I think he's got to make up his own mind,' Gunn reportedly said. 'He may or may not decide to do that. I'm not going to pressure him, it's up to him.'

Opposition Leader Nev Warburton demanded that all police resignations be cleared by the Fitzgerald Inquiry before superannuation payments were made.

Opinionated columnist Quentin Dempster weighed into the debate. 'Does the Government stick with Sir Terence Lewis and leave the police force in turmoil for the months it will take to complete the inquiry?' he asked. 'Or does it stand him aside to stop further erosion of the public confidence in the police, and indeed the morale in the force itself?'

Those questions would be answered the following morning, when Commissioner Lewis made his usual trek to the office of the Police Minister, Bill Gunn, for their Monday briefing.

Stand Down

The next day, Lewis was driven from Garfield Drive to headquarters. His personal assistant, Greg Early, writes: 'On Monday morning, 21 September, 1987, I saw the Commissioner at about 7.30 a.m. as was my usual practice. I have recorded in diary 6/067 "Saw COP [Commissioner of Police] and he said he would not be standing down voluntarily".'

Lewis then headed for Gunn's office in the Executive Building in George Street. 'The next thing is, Gunn gets ... obviously he had it lined up because there [were] media people everywhere on the Monday morning,' recalls Lewis, '... so I went in and he said, "Look, I want you to stand aside" or "I'm directing you to stand aside" or whatever.

'I said, "No, I won't do that, I want to hear that from the Premier." So I went up with him to the Premier and I sat outside, of course, while he went in and saw the Premier.'

Gunn later said in an interview that Lewis brought one of his daughters with him. '... she started to do all the talking,' Gunn alleged. '[Lewis] demanded to see Joh. Well, I said, "I don't care about that, but you don't see anybody without me being present."'

Gunn said he phoned the Premier and escorted Lewis and his daughter to Bjelke-Petersen's office. 'It was only one floor up in the lift [but] it was one of the longest journeys you could take,' Gunn recalled.

Lewis remembers that he was made to wait for about ten or 15 minutes. 'Then I went in and the Premier said, oh, words to the effect that Gunn has said that Parker is going to give evidence implicating you in corruption. He's asked that you be stood aside ... he's the Minister ...

'I said he's wrong and I won't do it ... I said I wanted it in writing, so he gave it to me in writing.

'Gunn said that [Ian] Callinan [QC, senior counsel for the state government] had told him that Parker was going to implicate me in corruption. Gunn ... told Joh that. [But] Parker didn't implicate me in

352

corruption … like that got me stood aside. And of course once I was stood aside they had open season.'

Gunn had a slightly different version of events. 'I guess that the best form of defence is attack and Joh knew that … from when he came in the door, Joh attacked him,' said Gunn. 'He [Lewis] said, "I've done a lot in this state for the government," and by God, Joh said, "We've done a lot for you, too, and I'm standing by my Minister" – he really told him off.'

Gunn said he let Lewis make his own way to the lift. 'It was a quick exit,' Gunn added.

Lewis was offended at the haste of the directive, after so many years of loyalty to the Premier. '[It was] to take effect that same day,' he remembers. 'No chance to go and tidy up your office or … I had stuff everywhere. Well, not everywhere, it was all neat and tidy but I had 11 years of stuff there. It was the next day that [the] Fitzgerald mob came in and went through my office for several days.'

Greg Early says Lewis had returned to his office by 9.40 a.m. 'and said he had been directed by the Minister and Premier to step down as COP.'

Lewis gathered his men to tell them the news. 'I had to go back to the office … I got all of my men together and told them,' Lewis recalls. 'I tried to get … my personal clothing and that to take home. Of course, in retrospect, I should have tried to clear the bloody office, but it would have been impossible.'

Early wrote in his diary: 'Packed some items from COP's safe into cartons for him. Not known what they were except he said 2 were his tax files and a folder re his son's Tony's problems; also he said he put some coins into an airways bag. He put some personal items into this bag and showed me what was official and what was his in his office and shelves, in his storeroom and in his ante room. COP left some folders in his safe and at that stage all I knew was that they were conf[idential]. deptl files.'

Later that morning, Lewis wrote a letter to Gunn regarding the Deputy Premier's verbal request that he 'stand down' from his position. It had always been Lewis's way. To make sense of circumstances around him, he put pen to paper. His argument was clean and logical.

Dear Mr Gunn,

This morning you requested me to 'stand down' from the office of Commissioner of Police for a limited period because of evidence which had been given to the Fitzgerald Inquiry.

I replied that I had done my job during thirty-nine years in the Police Force to the best of my ability, that I was not guilty of any wrongdoing and to 'stand down' merely because some sections of the community thought I should, would do considerable harm to the Police Force.

I replied that as matters stood I would not voluntarily stand down.

Lewis said he had failed thus far to put before Gunn the circumstances, which he believed would be grounds for him standing down. Suppose, he hypothesised, the admittedly corrupt Graeme Parker fingered Lewis as one of his partners in crime. That, Lewis said, would be reason to vacate his position on full pay until the allegations had been tested.

Lewis went on:

As I understand the matter it is unlikely that a report from this inquiry will be available for many months yet. This morning, of course, you did not advise me of any serious definite allegation made against me by any significant witness but spoke only in generalities.

If you know of any serious allegations made against me by a person of significance I should of course appreciate receiving full details of it at your earliest convenience.

Lewis was fighting for his life, for his status and for his future. His letter was followed by another from Gunn.

Dear Sir Terence,

I refer to our meeting of even date at which matters concerning the Fitzgerald Commission of Inquiry were discussed.

In view of the developments which have occurred in recent days, I believe that the superintendence of the Police Force of Queensland can only be adequately secured if you stand aside until such time as the matters before the Commission are resolved.

Consequently I direct you to stand aside as Commissioner of Police as from midnight tonight and approve that you be granted special leave on full pay not debited to any leave account until these matters are resolved.

This action is not taken lightly but is, I consider, to be in the best interests of the public and the Police Force of Queensland,

Lewis replied directly, saying that in his letter he had set out circumstances in which he might stand down. 'These circumstances have not occurred and your letter under reply purports to direct me to stand aside.'

(Lewis says: 'I had a friend who was a lawyer and I went to him and he wrote a letter answering that to Gunn ...')

It was an astonishing rebuttal of the Deputy Premier. Lewis was arguing that, in essence he would only stand aside if the circumstances were agreeable to him. Also, to suggest that Gunn's written directive 'purports' – or appears, possibly falsely – to direct him, was perhaps indicative of Lewis's desperation given the situation.

He ended the letter: 'While I do not accept that this direction is a valid one I propose to comply with it to prevent the Queensland Police Force and the Office of Commissioner being involved in controversy.'

Given Lewis didn't see the order as 'a valid one', his letter hinted at potential legal action in the future.

That afternoon, Ron Redmond, who had given evidence before the Fitzgerald Inquiry just a couple of months earlier, was anointed Acting Commissioner of Police. According to Lewis, Redmond told him to leave 'the numerous files, reports, books, and innumerable items accumulated over many years in my office and storage room and they would be safe until I returned'. (The locks to both areas would be changed the next day.)

Lewis says he probably telephoned his wife Hazel with the dramatic news. 'And then I got Gordon to drive me home that evening and of course the media were outside my place as you can imagine,' Lewis says. 'To wake up in the morning and not to have to go to work and the media sat outside the place for days and days and days ... and even my family coming to visit, they'd want to try and interview them and we got phone calls from Sydney you know they [the journalists] were bloody drunk ...'

Lewis says he was in a state of shock. 'And it was later, much later that Joh ... gave me that statement saying that Gunn had come to him and obviously told him an untruth because Parker hadn't given them any indisputable evidence that I was corrupt,' Lewis says.

'Well, Gunn bluffed the Premier. He did bluff him that's for sure, Gunn did. I mean, Gunn was doing anything and everything prior to that to become the Premier.'

Lewis claims Gunn was trying to get rid of him. He believed that in his role as Police Commissioner he was seen as protecting the Premier, '... in the sense that if the Premier wanted anything from our files, or if the Minister did, they got them. But if Lewis wasn't there well the Premier wouldn't be getting them, only Gunn would be getting them.'

That night, Lewis spoke to the media outside his home on Garfield Drive. He said he had no comment to make, then added: 'It's a decision that's been made, my friends. Naturally we will abide by that decision.'

The *Courier-Mail* reported that Lewis was accompanied by several men, and that police media advisor Ian Hatcher had 'arrived with a blue overnight bag ... minutes before the Commissioner and entered the house with him'.

The next day, Tuesday 22 September, Early commenced duty at 7.25 a.m.: 'Seen by Act Com Redmond. Told we must run things as previously and that he would like my complete loyalty in exchange for his. I assured him of this and also from my staff. When all staff came in ... he repeated most of his prev. remarks to us all ...'

It was reported that Lewis would have to be replaced as current chairman of the Australian Bureau of Criminal Intelligence in Canberra – a position rotated annually among the nation's police commissioners. This had become a national story, given that Graeme Parker had been Queensland's liaison officer with the National Crime Authority. What data had Parker had access to?

The crucial issue of the day, however, would be the contents of Sir Terence's files, and in particular those in his office safe. Early says he was called into Redmond's office at around 12.15 p.m. and asked by Detective Inspector Jim O'Sullivan of the Commission of Inquiry staff, 'What was in the Commr's safe?'

Early replied the safe contained 'some folders and confidential papers'.

O'Sullivan then asked to see the files, and directed Early to make an inventory before transferring the contents into Redmond's safe.

'He asked specifically for a report on what was there yesterday, what was taken yesterday and what is left. I went with Act Com and O'Sullivan to the safe in my office, got the GM key and went into COP's room; put on the lights and opened the COP's safe with the combination kept in my identification card wallet.

'I took out the contents and placed them on the table ... I showed Dep Com Redmond that the safe and box at the bottom were empty and left the door open.' The inventory was completed and Lewis's papers bundled and tied with a white ribbon.

Early had an afternoon appointment at the Police College. 'Before leaving the Det Insp asked me re a private filing system the COP had in his office,' Early writes. 'I assured him I had no knowledge of this system nor of any inventory to the contents of the Com's safe. I said I felt he had no files whatsoever apart from the papers he had taken.'

O'Sullivan asked Early to report on the question: 'Does the Commr have a private filing system – files of correspondence – where is it and what does it contain?'

It was obviously a major blow for Lewis. In less than two months since the start of the inquiry's substantive hearings, the force had lost an assistant commissioner, dozens of other officers had resigned, and now Lewis had been temporarily locked out of the game, courtesy of this 'special leave'.

Just as his friend, former detective Tony Murphy, found life outside of the rigid strictures of the force difficult on his retirement in late 1982, so too would Lewis resent the abrupt change. He could still maintain his almost monastic dedication to his diary, and mount detailed arguments against his being stood aside, in his office in Garfield Drive, but gone was the ambassadorial side of the job, the meeting and greeting of officials, the endless lazy Susan of lunches and dinners, theatre and community events.

While he was still on full pay, he remained, by the nature of suspension itself, implicated in wrongdoing. And he was there in full view in his large, white, three-storey house on the hill, in the shadow of the old Paddington water tower.

Protecting Garfield Drive

The day after Lewis was suspended he reportedly moved to transfer the joint ownership of 12 Garfield Drive solely into the name of Lady Hazel Lewis.

The *Courier-Mail* reported that the application to release his name from the mortgage was received at the Queensland Titles Office at 11.39 a.m. on Tuesday 22 September. 'News of the move was leaked from the office an hour later,' the report stated. The documents were shown on the ABC's *7.30 Report* that night.

The report added: 'Sir Terence was not available for comment later. But his wife, Hazel, said the public display of the documents was an infringement on her family's private life.'

'That's private family business they're delving into,' she reportedly said. 'It isn't right.'

Lady Lewis said her husband had had a quiet first day of his special leave, and that he 'hosed the garden and played with our grand-daughter'. She quipped: 'Goodness gracious. I wonder what they'll want to know about us next.'

Lewis says the idea for transferring full ownership of the house to his wife had been suggested by his son, Tony. 'I don't know what I was feeling really,' he says. 'We'd worked all our bloody life for the house, all of our life, it was in both names and I think ... [I] went out with one of our sons ... Tony said, "Oh, why not just put it in Mum's name?"'

'And I thought ... it's alright to say you knew the criminal law, I mean, but civil law is another story. And I thought with this inquiry the way it started to go, I'd be better off putting the house in Hazel's name and the legal people can't get it. But that was a ... silly move really.'

He says he believed at the time that it was a way of protecting the home for his wife and children. 'It gave an impression that – "What's Lewis worried about?"' he says. 'And I hadn't been, you know ... I wasn't, I suppose, seriously ill, but I did have a problem with this bloody thing that I ended up getting operated on. It had annoyed me for twenty [years], and it was a worrying thing because you go in and you lose your breath. And I thought, oh yeah, I might have a heart attack or something and the pressure of this inquiry might bring it on.'

As the media continued to keep their vigil outside Garfield Drive, down in Courtroom 29, Tony Fitzgerald issued a firm statement about the suspended commissioner. He neither confirmed nor denied that inquiry staff had searched Lewis's office at police headquarters. 'However, you may take it that I propose to perform the task for which I have been appointed and for that purpose to exercise as necessary the powers invested in me, irrespective of who is involved,' Fitzgerald declared.

He added that as long as he was inquiry chairman Lewis would not be prejudged or unfairly treated by the inquiry. 'However, I doubt whether he would expect favoured treatment and he will not receive it,' Fitzgerald said. 'He certainly will not be exempted from investigation in the course of the inquiry to whatever extent is appropriate.'

Lewis says the whole situation was tough on his family, especially Lady Lewis.

'Oh … she went from being somebody, if you like … Hazel was just fantastic,' Lewis says. 'Like she'd, when she was able to do so she used to come around the state with me and every function she'd go to relating to police. And [she] would go and talk to all the groups at the Academy all for free. They never got, none of them got paid for it, they did it off their own bat.

'And to go from that and us having a car and a driver, working really hard but enjoying doing that, she became … it's hard to comprehend or understand how heartbreaking it was … what happened to our family.'

The Shark

Noel Francis Dwyer, former head of the Licensing Branch and named by Harry Burgess as corrupt, appeared as an indemnified witness before the inquiry in early November. He had initially expressed shock and dismay when named at the inquiry by Burgess, and denied the allegations. Like Graeme Parker, however, he had a dramatic change of heart. His evidence was wholly damning to Commissioner Lewis.

He told the inquiry he had received up to $30,000 in bribes during his time in the Licensing Branch between January 1980 and September 1982. He hid the cash in the wall of his garage at home, and used some of the money to build a wooden boat.

Dwyer alleged that in late 1979 Lewis had personally told him that he was to be promoted to inspector and that the commissioner had 'a place in mind for me'. Two days later, Dwyer was visited by Jack 'The Bagman' Herbert who said he had heard about the promotion. 'Herbert said he and the Commissioner were "great mates",' Dwyer said in evidence. 'The Commissioner wanted to know if I'd take on the Licensing Branch. I said to him [Herbert] – why didn't the Commissioner tell me?

'Herbert said, "I'm supposed to see you first."

'I asked him why and he said, "There's a couple of Jokes going on in the Valley".'

Dwyer began accepting cash bribes from Herbert as soon as he took on the Licensing Branch job. Dwyer in turn paid sums to Burgess and Parker. On one occasion, according to Dwyer, Herbert slipped him $800 and said: 'Sorry it's not more. The Commissioner is like a shark, he takes the big bite.' (Herbert would later deny he ever said this.) Dwyer said Herbert often referred to Lewis as 'the shark'.

'Herbert was more or less his [Lewis's] emissary,' Dwyer told the commission. 'He [Herbert] did say on one occasion he'd "fix the Commissioner up" – or pay him – and they'd meet later at a function and greet each other as though they hadn't met for a long time. I was confident, sure in my own mind that the Commissioner was being paid by Herbert. I believed Herbert fully.'

In a record of interview with his biographer Tom Gilling, Herbert would later say: 'Noel Dwyer, he was a fellow we got appointed. So I used to see the Commissioner and say we need so and so in this section, we need so and so in that section. So he used to just put them in where I wanted him to. He'd do anything because I was giving him ten grand a month. Anything at all ...'

Herbert alleged that Lewis regularly dropped around to his various homes to pick up the money. 'He used to come round home every month and sat at the bar,' said Herbert. 'I used to say to Peggy – take Hazel into the kitchen – and I'd go to the bar and give it [the money] to him and he'd put it away ... and you know, have a drink.'

Dwyer's unwritten instruction was to protect certain SP bookmakers and 'not to go heavy' on massage parlours and escort agencies run by Hector Hapeta and Vic Conte. They met often at Herbert's home and in car parks. Dwyer said Peggy Herbert would telephone him at the office using the code 'Mrs Eaton'.

'I succumbed to the temptation because I was weak and greedy,' Dwyer admitted. He said he had served in the force for 30 years before he took his first bribe. Back in the 1960s when he was serving in Mackay, he said he had heard the term 'Rat Pack', and that its alleged members were believed to be Lewis, Tony Murphy and Glen Hallahan. 'It was a derogatory term,' Dwyer told the inquiry, 'I didn't think much of it at the time at all.'

Parker Gives Evidence

The ailing Graeme Parker, 54, immediately followed Noel Dwyer in the witness box.

Lewis recalls: 'They brought him over in an ambulance, on a stretcher ... in the court he was terrible, I mean he'd go for a short time and was gasping for breath ...'

As the *Courier-Mail* reported: 'He left his sickbed to appear at the inquiry and looked pale and drawn. He fondled a small silver crucifix and at first mumbled his replies. His voice grew stronger as he progressed.'

Dwyer admitted he'd taken more than $100,000 in bribes when he took over as inspector in charge of Licensing in September 1982, and the payments continued from there. Prior to his appointment as head of Licensing, Parker said he had had a conversation with then detective sergeant Harry Burgess. 'He [Burgess] said that "shortly you'll get a call from a friend of yours you haven't seen for a long time."'

'I get a phone call from Jack Herbert. I hadn't seen him for many years. He introduced himself. He said he wanted to see me. He told me where he lived and I went and saw him. He went on to tell me that a system had been in place for quite a long time and that there was some pocket money in it for me.

'He gave me $2000. He told me that it related to areas of not over-policing gambling and prostitution and that there were six big SP bookies wanting protection.'

Similar to Dwyer, Parker said he kept in touch with Herbert often through Peggy Herbert, who phoned as 'Mrs Eaton'.

He said Herbert was meticulous with the payments. 'There'd be a number of bundles on the dining room table – four or five envelopes,' Parker told the inquiry. All were initialled, and given to Licensing Branch officer Harry Burgess, Allen Bulger, Neville Ross and a couple of others. 'I'd give an envelope to Bulger and the remainder I'd give to Burgess who would distribute them to other people,' Parker added.

His payments from Herbert ranged from $2000 to $6000 a month, with a boost during the Christmas period. More extraordinary evidence was to come. He said Herbert had told him that he was 'great friends' with Commissioner Lewis and he was also a 'business partner' of Transport Minister Don 'Shady' Lane. 'He [Herbert] told me that he had to pay half of what he got to the top and higher and that he had to pay a portion of proceeds to Don Lane for any massage parlour or escort agency that opened in his electorate,' Parker told the inquiry.

'He [Herbert] told me that Don Lane was involved in the business and that it had mushroomed. He gave me the impression that he and Don Lane were very, very close friends.

'Don Lane had been to see him [Herbert] to see if he could arrange for Herbert's two sons to be placed on the electoral roll in Bowen Hills, because the election was very close and he needed the votes. One lived in Sydney and the other at Dutton Park [in Brisbane].'

Herbert would go on to tell his biographer: 'Don Lane was a Cabinet minister, we wanted to know what he said in Cabinet. Don Lane would invite me down to Parliament House for dinner (and) he used to come over and see us.'

Parker said Commissioner Lewis also referred to Lane as 'Big Don'. He admitted he had never seen Lewis or Lane with Herbert. (A long-time associate of Jack Herbert, who regularly socialised with The Bagman and saw police come and go from Herbert's various homes, says Herbert often hinted at the money 'hierarchy' behind The Joke. 'Don Lane got the biggest share,' the source says. 'Jack told me that in a roundabout way. I worked out that Don Lane was the top, he was the total organiser and everyone answered to him.')

Parker was asked by Gary Crooke who was receiving money 'at the top or higher', as Herbert had indicated to him. 'He [Herbert] would hand me the money and he would say he had to see Terry a couple of nights later or "The Boss" was coming over to see him on a social visit,' Parker told the inquiry. 'He implied he was looking after the Commissioner. On one occasion, his [Herbert's] wife was going out and he said she was on her way to see Hazel [Lewis].'

Parker said he had had a discussion with Sir Terence after Burgess gave his evidence about Dwyer and himself to the inquiry. '... I spoke to the Commissioner, and he said "Big Don suggested that Herbert should leave the country",' Parker said.

Lane's lawyer said the evidence was merely hearsay and that his client vigorously denied the allegations by Parker.

Lewis says Parker spoke to him after giving evidence and said 'that he doesn't know what he said or what he did'. He remains incensed by the commission's treatment of Parker, and the activities of the Licensing Branch as a whole. 'Well, they knew the Licensing Branch would be ... well obviously they must have known that some of the bastards were doing what they were doing,' Lewis says.

'And Herbert probably told them that they were shagging and getting a quid and doing that. And ... and some of the challenges, well even now ... there were no real detectives rolled over, there were just these bloody bums that did little or nothing.

'Parker was a very, very, very ill man and they brought him to the inquiry ... [Parker came] to see me later, much, much later, and ... said how they misused him and tried to get him to come in and give evidence against me. But he ... at the hospital he would have admitted anything.'

Parker, a Queen's Police Medal winner for distinguished service, used his appearance before the inquiry to ask his fellow Queenslanders for forgiveness. 'I'd like to say I held a position of trust in the Licensing Branch and as Assistant Commissioner (Crime) and I betrayed that trust and I'd like to apologise to all Queenslanders and to all Queensland constables,' he said.

Over in London, Jack Herbert, in hiding, was furious at the testimony of Burgess, Dwyer and Parker. His son John, who worked for Qantas, had been bringing to London photocopies of inquiry transcripts for Herbert to pore over. He said he never called Commissioner Lewis 'a shark'. He denied Lane was taking any money from massage parlours in Fortitude Valley. 'I was incensed by what Burgess and Dwyer and Parker were saying about me,' Herbert said in his memoir. 'That's when I made up my mind to go back [to Australia].'

Meanwhile, suspended Police Commissioner Terry Lewis claims he was offered an indemnity from prosecution by the commission. He says it was offered by counsel assisting the commission, Gary Crooke.

'Well, they wanted me to give it against [Premier Sir] Joh, that was obviously the point and I said … no good offering me one because I haven't got any evidence to give,' Lewis says.

'And if I'd been a smartarse, I suppose, I could have said yes, I could give evidence against [some]one, like they thought up evidence against me … who would you like me to give it against?'

Lewis says he has no regrets over declining the alleged offer. 'How could you go and give false evidence and say I was a crook and I knew these people were crooks?' Lewis adds. 'At least nobody can say that I said I was a bloody crook and I know they rubbished me ever since, one way or another.

'It killed Hazel and buggered out my life.'

A former senior inquiry staff member says Crooke would not have been offering indemnities to Lewis. 'There's often a miscue between the speaker and the person spoken to,' the staffer says. 'I can imagine Gary saying something like – if you're prepared to really come out and tell us the whole story and implicate everybody, I'll ask the Commissioner whether there's any possibility of …

'Now if you want to hear that as an offer of an indemnity, you can. So conversations like that could have easily happened. I just … don't think it would have gone very far with Gary with that.

'I wouldn't say he's [Lewis] telling lies but I'd certainly say he's probably misunderstood the conversation, if any conversation took place.'

Exorcising the Demon

When Sir Joh Bjelke-Petersen reluctantly announced, after his failed bid for the Australian Prime Ministership, that he would retire as Queensland Premier on 8 August 1988, he pulled the trigger on his demise. After months of damning evidence about crooked Queensland police, protection money, prostitutes, sex parties, drugs and violence, the state's polite veil had been torn back. The picture of Sir Joh and his followers upholding the wholesome, hayseed image of a decent, old-fashioned Queensland, and the filthy reality of Fitzgerald's findings, was starting to blur.

By nominating his departing date so far in advance, it gave his colleagues and the public pause to think – do we want almost another full year of this?

In early November, after Joh's proclamation, the media was already discussing the 'post-Joh era', and surveys pointed towards Health Minister Mike Ahern as the preferred Premier over Deputy Premier and Police Minister Bill Gunn.

Bjelke-Petersen resented this debate over his political corpse. He struck back. At the National Party's annual state conference in Townsville in the first week of November, he criticised National Party president Sir Robert Sparkes and even hinted that his Premiership might extend beyond the agreed date the following year.

'You will have no one – truly – that would have the input I have,' Sir Joh said of his own leadership abilities. 'I would have access to every television station. That is a question you people will have to look at.' He added: 'The Party is coming apart very quickly.'

The Premier had every reason to be worried. A Morgan Gallup Poll in the *Bulletin* magazine put his electoral support at just 23 per cent. The Party's internal war between Sparkes and Bjelke-Petersen wasn't helping.

The *Courier-Mail*'s political editor, Peter Morley, wrote of the Townsville conference: 'There should be no misunderstanding about this conference – the State's two heavyweight knights may have always enjoyed a love–hate relationship, but this time they are locked in a death struggle. Each is determined that the other has to go for the Party's sake.' He concluded that the once rock solid Nationals were 'coming apart at the seams'.

As the conference convened – at Sir Leslie Thiess's Breakwater Casino – back at the Fitzgerald Inquiry in Brisbane, Transport Minister Don Lane was accused of taking bribes. He denied 'in the strongest possible terms the hearsay assertions of wrongdoing made against me.'

On Thursday 5 November, the anticipated heavyweight fight between Sparkes and the Premier did not materialise. Instead, Bjelke-Petersen fell ill – he claimed he was suffering laryngitis – and flew back to his Kingaroy property, Bethany. 'I will leave you alone this time,' he told Sir Robert.

In the Premier's absence, the Party did something astonishing. It decided to embrace the late 20th century, eschewing, according to one newspaper report, its 'fundamentalist cloak'. It moved to legalise prostitution, urged the government to legalise condom vending machines and pledged its support for AIDS education to school children. It also agreed to sex education during school hours. It was an astonishing philosophical turnaround for the National Party.

Peter Morley wrote: 'Highlighting the fact that there is no fight without Joh, the organisation shredded some of its fundamentalist policies. It was a cleansing process where delegates, encouraged by his 8-8-88 retirement commitment, showed signs of responding to community views – not Sir Joh's.'

When the conference disbanded, Sparkes revealed that his relationship with the Premier had completely broken down. 'It would appear that adequate communication with Joh is not possible at this point in time,' he told reporters.

Predictably, the Premier rejected the reforms called for at the Townsville conference as 'hoo-ha'.

Journalist Quentin Dempster described the National Party's hypocrisy as 'monumental'. 'This mob is so desperate to stay in power that it will do anything,' he wrote. 'It is even prepared to turn decent.'

A Child Goes Missing

As the Fitzgerald Inquiry continued to roll on smoothly, its daily revelations sending shockwaves throughout Queensland, an unpredictable incident also stunned commission staff and the media. The young son of John Stopford, one of the key figures who gave an interview to Chris Masters for his 'Moonlight State' report, had suddenly disappeared.

The boy, Jay, aged five, was reported missing on Thursday 12 November, when he failed to board the bus from his school in Dunwich to his home at Amity Point on North Stradbroke Island. Police believed he may have been abducted by his mother, Stopford's former de facto wife Wendy Ann Dillon, also known as Wendy Butler, based on descriptions of a woman seen with Jay around the time he vanished.

Stopford contacted his lawyer, Terry O'Gorman, who in turn went straight to the Supreme Court where custody of the child was granted to Stopford. Was the disappearance connected to the underworld? Or were the police behind the disappearance? Stopford had blown the whistle on corrupt police to *Four Corners*, and after the show had gone to air Queensland police had sent a helicopter to the island to bring Stopford in. Now his child was gone.

The matter was mentioned by Tony Fitzgerald who didn't think the abduction was linked to the hearings, but still felt the boy needed to be returned to his father. '… nothing has been brought to the attention of the Commission which indicates that there is any connection between the Commission and any events which have occurred involving Mr Stopford's son,' Fitzgerald said. 'There is no reason to doubt that ordinary law enforcement resources are sufficient and committed to the task of investigating what has occurred, and there is nothing to indicate that it is a matter in which the Commission should become involved.'

By chance, Stopford was talking to a person staying in the caravan park at Amity Point who knew Jay's mother and had recently seen her entering a housing commission property not far from Sydney's Long Bay prison complex at Malabar, south of Randwick in the city's east.

O'Gorman in turn phoned Nigel Powell, who had also appeared on the *Four Corners* program, and asked him if he would accompany Stopford to Sydney to find the child. 'My memory is that Wendy took him [Jay] out of school there and was with a couple of other guys at the time,' Powell recalls. 'The inference was that they were police. She was put up to it. That was the story I got.'

Powell agreed to help Stopford. 'John turned up in this old Falcon with a mate,' he says. 'We drove all the way through to Sydney. Neither John nor his mate had a driver's licence and I said I'd get behind the wheel when we got on the outskirts of Sydney. Within two minutes of entering the Sydney metropolitan area we were pulled over by police.'

They were allowed to continue on their way and they eventually found the supposed flat of Wendy's near Long Bay prison. Powell had a look around, leaving Stopford in the car. 'There was some kid's stuff there in the flat, I could see that through the window,' he says. 'Early the next morning we went to the Federal Police offices near Redfern. They were reluctant to get involved. I told them we had a court order and that this was in their jurisdiction. Eventually they came with us and got Jay. I didn't want to linger. I didn't want any problems. We drove straight for the Queensland border.'

The incident made Stopford even more paranoid about his decision to appear on 'The Moonlight State'. Had he doomed his child?

Stopford says he was later told that his former wife had been offered 'inducements' from outside parties to come to Queensland and take Jay. 'I've never been given the full story,' he says. 'I've always believed that the majority of the reason she did it was outside sources. That was the puzzle in my head.'

The Backbencher

Even in his political death throes, Premier Joh Bjelke-Petersen was still vigorously pushing for the construction of the world's tallest building in the heart of Brisbane. For a year he'd been adamant that the building would go ahead, despite the waning public interest in it and the indifference of his Party colleagues. What was it about this $800 million, 400-metre high phantasm that had so attracted the Premier's obsessive attention? His desire to push the project through Cabinet seemed incongruous with his political fortunes of the moment.

It was his backbenchers, however, who put paid to approval coasting through before the end of parliament that year. Special modified legislation for the 'superhighrise' was put on the table but would not be debated until the following year. Some backbenchers said they hoped to attach so many conditions to the building that it would never get off the ground.

Bjelke-Petersen, however, stood firm, and told parliament the project could not be stopped because $25 million had already been committed to it. 'The Government would be up for very heavy damages if you even attempted to stop it,' the Premier warned. 'In other words, it can't be stopped. It has started. It will proceed.' He insisted there was 'no alternative'.

It was Joh at his most arrogant and bullish, and it enraged backbenchers. The development had not even been approved by Brisbane City Council. It was subject to a Special Act of Parliament that had not even been formally tabled. The building's developer, John Minuzzo, reportedly gave the government an undertaking on funding for the building. He said he was still waiting for a response from the Foreign Investment Review Board in relation to Korean involvement in the project.

What the public didn't know was that during a fiery Party meeting over the Central Place project, backbencher and National Party member for Springwood, Huan Fraser, stood and confronted the Premier. Fraser had been born in Wyandra, about 820 kilometres west of Brisbane, and raised on the family's property, Claverton Park, on a tributary of the Warrego River. He had worked as a jackaroo and on the family estate before he was elected to the Paroo Shire Council in 1979. Fraser, with his wife Wendy and children, moved to Daisy Hill, south of Brisbane, in 1981. He was elected deputy mayor of Logan City, then ran for the newly created seat of Springwood at the 1986 election and won. According to a parliamentary colleague, he was a canny businessman and had made good money building spec homes for the Taiwanese community in the Logan area. 'They liked white bricks, tiled rooves, gold taps. He built to their liking.'

One day Fraser was approached by a Korean business contact who wanted to discuss the world's tallest building project in the city. 'You back the old guy [Premier Sir Joh Bjelke-Petersen] on this,' he told Fraser. 'It's a bloody good payout for him if it [the Central Place project] gets through. The old bloke's got nothing.'

Fraser, a lifelong National Party member, was incensed. At the Party room meeting, according to a senior government source who was present that day, Fraser ripped into the Premier. 'You know, he thought Joh was crooked and he wouldn't cop it,' the source says. 'He told me, "This is not right. This is corruption." He got up in the Party room meeting and did it. He said, "I know there is a bloody big pay-off to you coming as a result of this. You're a corrupt old bastard and I'm not going to cop it."'

Fraser didn't present any back-up evidence. There was mention that the Korean developers of the project had a nest egg worth more than $20 million in a foreign bank account for Bjelke-Petersen if the Central Place project was passed through Cabinet.

In addition, according to Mike Ahern's biography, *Lock, Stock and Barrel*, by Paul Reynolds, Fraser had also seen three letters – two from February 1986 and one dated March 1987 – that appeared to reveal that the Bjelke-Petersen government had committed to leasing 21 floors of Central Place for the public service. They also showed that developer John Minuzzo would be granted $5 million to outfit the floors.

Were these arrangements correct? Fraser asked the Premier.

'Bjelke-Petersen tersely replied that Fraser did not know what he was talking about and moved to close the meeting,' Ahern's biography stated. 'Fraser's response was that, if he did not obtain an answer, he would leave the meeting and "ask the question outside".

'All in the room knew that Tony Koch state roundsman for the *Courier-Mail* was waiting outside the room.'

A senior government member present at the meeting says everyone was gobsmacked, including Joh. 'The whole room – you could cut the air,' he says. 'Joh never said another word. Russ Hinze got up and said, "Mr Premier, I'll take over now if you don't mind."

'Joh went out and we waited until he caught the lift, we were listening, and when he did there was silence. I didn't know what to do. Hinze said, "Why don't we all go and have a cup of tea?" And that's what we did.'

Later, Bill Gunn apparently suggested that Fraser get hold of the actual letters before the meeting reconvened. 'Whether Gunn actually obtained them or read them, or was simply made aware of their contents, is unclear, but he verified Fraser's story and told Fraser that this "would soon blow over",' the book said.

The source says everyone realised the enormity of what had been said and what the ramifications of it were. 'Joh had to have the strong support of the Executive Council who would proclaim the special legislation for the building project,' he says. 'Joh had a plan to get his proposal through Cabinet and into Executive Council to proclaim it as a special project under the Coordinator-General's Act.

'Joh never went back to another meeting of the Party. The place was in turmoil. He made a desperate attempt to get it through because there was a payment. He was putting to the Party room a corrupt deal and involving all of us.'

On 13 November, Deputy Opposition Leader Tom Burns asked the Premier a Question Without Notice. It was related to the 'continuing saga of the world's tallest building and the twice-daily meetings that have been held to resolve the differences between the Premier and his Party members on this issue'.

Burns added: 'I refer also to the latest edition of *Australian Business*, which claims that Minuzzo's financial partner in the Central Place development, Youchang, is a very shadowy company about which little is known. I ask: Will he explain to the House whether Youchang is a Korean or Singaporean registered company, as there is considerable doubt about this? Will he explain why Youchang's Australian representative knows nothing about the financing arrangements for Minuzzo's Central Place?'

'The government is dealing with that question at this very moment,' the Premier said.

Within hours of parliament adjourning, the Premier launched his plans to sack five 'disloyal' ministers, including Bill Gunn, Mike Ahern, Brian Austin, Peter McKechnie and Geoff Muntz. Was Bjelke-Petersen trying to head off any immediate challenge to his leadership? Or was the removal of the ministers related to the rejection of the world's tallest building project, and a possible fast-track method to expedite it?

The senior government source says: 'The sackings were all related to that [Central Place] situation. He had to reshape the Cabinet to get that particular thing through. If he didn't, the government was not likely to accept the Executive Council minute. It was a bombshell. Everyone knew. It was a matter of high criminality.'

Ahern's biography said: '... [Joh] needed Cabinet colleagues who would not make trouble for him over the issue.' This, Ahern suggested, was the reason Bjelke-Petersen then went to the Governor. If Ahern is correct, this explains why Bjelke-Petersen, without warning, commenced the process of the unnecessary and hitherto inexplicable Cabinet reshuffle which was to bring him undone.

Huan Fraser told *Lock, Stock and Barrel* author Paul Reynolds: 'I had just given Mike [Ahern] the ammunition.' (Fraser died in 2010, but his family confirmed the rendition of events in Reynold's book.)

Former Attorney-General Paul Clauson says he doesn't remember the Fraser incident, but the building project did concern many people in and outside of government. '… the project caused a lot of dissension with the troops at the time,' he says. 'Joh was pulling it on with [Brisbane Lord Mayor] Sallyanne [Atkinson] and we members in the Brisbane … seats were very unhappy about the idea of pushing against the Brisbane Town Plan with a ministerial override as I seem to recall.

'It wasn't so much the concept as the way it was being promoted and potentially executed that was the concern.'

On Sunday 22 November, Transport Minister and former police officer, Don 'Shady' Lane, said he received a phone call from a senior staffer for the Premier, 'advising me that Joh intended to sack several of his ministers, including Ahern'.

Lane was straight on the phone to Mike Ahern. 'Lane would end up being a grub as far as I'm concerned, too,' says Lewis, who was fiercely loyal to the Premier. 'A disloyal, ungrateful so and so … Joh didn't particularly want him in Cabinet either, but anyhow. Just briefly, I think Joh or somebody must have said to Lane that they were … going to get rid of three ministers for something. Ahern and whoever. And bloody Lane that night rang Ahern [and] warned him.'

Reshuffle

The next morning, Cabinet met as usual at 10 a.m. There was no mention of any sackings. After the meeting, Bjelke-Petersen headed to Government House and informed the Governor, Wally Campbell, that he was set on forming a new administration. Five serving ministers would be absent from the revised make-up.

Campbell recommended he request each minister to resign their commission. Each was summoned to the Premier's office around 10 a.m. the following day. All refused to resign. According to Don Lane's memoir, Brian Austin told the Premier he could 'get fucked'.

Austin, the member for Nicklin, was on his way from Buderim to Brisbane that morning when he got a call at around 6.30 a.m. 'I was told Joh was going to sack me,' Austin says. 'That was the first I'd heard of it. Joh hadn't even called me. He told me I was being sacked because of my closeness to [Sir Robert] Sparkes. I think he said he was putting together a Cabinet he could work with.'

Lane beseeched the Premier in Austin's defence. Both Lane and Austin had defected from the Liberal Party to the National Party in the 1983 split and had made a considerable 'sacrifice' for Bjelke-Petersen.

'Joh responded with the statement that some ministers, including Brian, had lined up with Sparkes against him and that if I didn't watch out he would sack me too,' Lane recalled.

Mike Ahern was also called into Bjelke-Petersen's office.

'Mike, I want your resignation,' the Premier said.

'What's the reason?' Ahern asked.

'I don't have to give you a reason.'

'I want one if you want my resignation,' Ahern said.

'No.'

'If you sack me, keep an eye on the television,' Ahern responded. 'In 15 minutes I'm going to go down and hold a press conference, and I'm going to challenge you.'

Ahern told him that if he got the sack, the National Party would not be happy.

'I am the National Party,' Joh replied.

Later that day, the Premier went back to Government House and told Campbell he now only had three ministers he wanted removed – Ahern, Austin and Peter McKechnie. The press said

Bjelke-Petersen had 'signed his own political death warrant'.

'He has lost the confidence of the National Party … and the business community,' commented Peter Morley of the *Courier-Mail*. 'The goodwill he had built up over 20 years has been replaced by a clamour for his removal.'

Ahern announced his intention to contest the leadership of the Party. He intimated that the mass sackings were related to the ongoing Fitzgerald Inquiry. While Joh had changed his mind about sacking Police Minister Bill Gunn, the Premier had offered that Gunn change his portfolio. Gunn refused. Ahern wanted to prevent the inquiry being prematurely closed down.

Bjelke-Petersen, however, had no intention of stepping down.

'Why should I resign?' he said. 'Why should I go it alone? … I have been elected as Premier. I have done a very, very good job.

'I just want to, in the last period of my time until August [1988], I want to make sure this government is a good one and that it is loyal and that it is doing and operating without outside interference, which is one of the problems we have today. As I said, I have no intentions of resigning under any circumstances.'

In the meantime, the gossip around parliament was that late-night meetings were being held in Bjelke-Petersen's suite at Parliament House. Some were going to 2 a.m.

'The building was abuzz with it,' says Mike Ahern. 'My driver said there's something going on. He said Sir Edward Lyons, [suspended police commissioner] Terry Lewis and Beryl Young were up there with Joh.'

On Thursday 26 November, a parliamentary Party meeting was held at 10 a.m. The Premier was dispatched as leader of the Party and Mike Ahern was installed as new leader over Bill Gunn and Russ Hinze. Bjelke-Petersen only got eight votes.

According to Bjelke-Petersen's recollection of the moment, he said he received a visit in his office from Health Minister Ivan Gibbs after the leadership ballot. He remembered that Gibbs was upset. 'I'm terribly sorry to have to tell you, Joh, but the boys have all decided to dump you and support Ahern.'

Bjelke-Petersen was shocked. 'Ivan, surely you don't mean what you're saying,' he responded. How could this happen?

'Well, Joh, there was so much excitement and cheering and clapping at Ahern's meeting that we all got carried away with it and voted to support him,' Gibbs supposedly said. 'There were no speeches – we just got swept off our feet.'

In his biography Joh recalled: 'By the end of the week it was obvious to me that the end had come but I stayed on for a few more days. Each day Ahern would say he was about to become Premier, but I kept sitting there in the chair, like a kind of ghost, haunting him.'

Joh continued to taunt, refusing to resign his commissions as Premier and Executive Council member. He said he wanted to discuss his future with his family on the weekend before making any decisions on announcing his retirement. He proceeded to barricade himself in his office in the Executive Building in George Street. It was as if the overwhelming decision by National Party politicians to allow Ahern to take over the Premiership hadn't happened.

On the night of Friday 27 November, Russ Hinze's press secretary, Russell Grenning, was present outside the Premier's locked office door with Hinze. 'It was bizarre ... Russ went ... and banged on the door,' Grenning recalled. 'Joh wouldn't open the door and Russ was bending down, talking to him through the keyhole with tears running down his face, saying, "Joh, come out mate, it's all over."'

The wily political fox was not out of the game yet. Bjelke-Petersen did indeed go home to Bethany that weekend and talk with his family. They urged him to 'leave the whole ugly business behind'.

Meanwhile, ALP State Secretary Peter Beattie was on official business in Canberra when he got a call from a 'businessman that had links with several political parties'.

The businessman told Beattie that despite Bjelke-Petersen's apparently hopeless position, there was a chess move left open to him. Bjelke-Petersen could recall parliament, then have his few remaining partners cross the floor of the house and join the Labor and Liberal parties. It could be 'a mortal wound' to Ahern's new leadership.

Beattie did a quick calculation and didn't believe this arrangement would deliver the magic number 45 in the legislature. According to Beattie's recollections in his memoir *In the Arena*, the businessman told him: 'If Mike Ahern gets in, you're out for a million years.'

Wrestling with his conscience, Beattie phoned Bjelke-Petersen and told him point blank – he wanted 'an equitable and fair electoral redistribution' before even considering putting this possible move before the Labor Party.

'I slept little that night,' Beattie wrote. 'Every molecule of my flesh crawled at the thought of doing anything to help Bjelke-Petersen. There was so much for which he had to answer.'

Back in Brisbane, Beattie was still uncomfortable about the whole deal. He arranged to meet 'Top Level' Ted Lyons in his office in the T&G Building in the city. It was a place that for years had been the weekly meeting spot for Lyons and Terry Lewis, where they enjoyed a drink and talked politics.

'I've urged Joh not to resign,' Lyons told Beattie.

'Sir Edward, he's been run out,' Beattie replied.

Lyons explained that a parliamentary solution was possible. 'Sir Edward,' Beattie said, 'we're not in the business of propping up Joh.'

Lyons urged Beattie to see Joh in person and they met in the 'rarely traversed corners' of Bethany outside Kingaroy. 'In the afternoon we met in a field,' Beattie remembered. 'Joh Bjelke-Petersen sat in the back seat of my car, and I sat in the front. His eyes were slightly bloodshot from strain and fatigue, but otherwise he presented more or less the same aspect as usual. He was relaxed. It was not an act.'

In exchange for the ALP's support, Sir Joh said he would give the Party more facilities and staff, and drop the outstanding eight defamation actions he had against members of the Party. He was non-committal about a fair distribution.

'My heart sank,' Beattie said. 'I knew that it was over.'

Bjelke-Petersen returned to his Bethany homestead, and Beattie to Brisbane. At one point, it was later revealed that Bjelke-Petersen telephoned Buckingham Palace in London and sought the intervention of the Queen.

It didn't happen, and Sir Joh had no cards left to play.

That Sunday, Bjelke-Petersen also had words with new National Party leader Mike Ahern. The message was simple. Resign as Premier, or miss out on a generous retirement package. 'The time for playing games is over,' Ahern said.

'On the Monday morning [his pilot] Beryl Young flew in to take Flo and me down to Brisbane,' Bjelke-Petersen recalled. 'I sat up the front with Beryl, and Flo sat in the jump-seat between us, and on the way down to Brisbane we talked about what I should do.

'Both of them agreed I should wash my hands of it all.

'Before we landed in Brisbane, I told them I would do as they suggested – I would resign as Premier.'

Citizen Joh

On the afternoon of Tuesday 1 December, Sir Joh Bjelke-Petersen visited Government House in Paddington for the last time and submitted his resignation. He had been Premier of Queensland for a little over 19 years.

'The National Party of today is not the Party I took to the election last year,' Sir Joh said in his resignation speech that day at around 5 p.m. 'The policies of the National Party are no longer those on which I went to the people. Therefore I do not wish to lead this government any longer ... I've decided to resign as Premier and retire from parliament, effective immediately.'

'Goodbye and God bless,' the old man said.

It was an extraordinary end to a long career. 'For more than 19 years he was centre stage and for almost all of that time, he dominated it,' the *Courier-Mail* wrote in its editorial. 'Until the last he kept his audience in suspense. And, when he went, it was the old Joh Queenslanders have come to know – aggressive and unrepentant ...'

That night, Bjelke-Petersen and his family shared a meal at Denisons Restaurant in the Sheraton Hotel in the city – a building he had once officially opened as Premier. Before the food arrived, he said grace. 'This is what I look upon as a new phase,' he told a reporter. 'It's really and truly exciting.'

(The restaurant, however, had earlier received a bomb threat. While patrons' bags were searched, members of the public were encouraged not to sit near the Bjelke-Petersen clan.)

Sir Joh may have been out of the top job but it didn't diminish his presence in the media spotlight. The day after he resigned, he was back in the news, and this time over a pet project that, whether in office or out of it, he simply could not let go – the world's tallest building in Brisbane.

Former local government minister, Russ Hinze, suggested in state parliament that the 107-storey Central Place project was to be scrapped. 'I have very grave doubts that you're going to see the tallest building in Queensland,' Hinze remarked. Outside of parliament, he further said the project was 'absolutely dead'. He added, however, that there was nothing to prevent developer John Minuzzo and his company Mainsel Developments Pty Ltd from constructing a major building on the site in the Brisbane CBD.

The former premier immediately countered, saying that a Cabinet team, which had included Mike Ahern, had given approval for the world's tallest building. 'The Government must honour its word and its pledge and its undertaking, otherwise its reputation goes. If Governments are honest and have any integrity, they will honour the pledges of previous premiers,' Sir Joh told the *Couier-Mail*.

'I'm not interested other than there's a billion dollars' worth of jobs and materials,' he added.

Premier Ahern told Bjelke-Petersen to keep out of state government affairs. 'The Queensland Government will decide about the world's tallest building, not Citizen Joh,' Ahern said.

In the end, the issue of the controversial project made it all the way to the Supreme Court, where Justice Paul de Jersey ruled that as the law stood, it would be unlawful to construct.

Justice de Jersey remembers it as 'the most interesting civil case I've ever had'. He adds: 'It was also interesting because … there was a real urgency about a decision in the case for some reason or other.'

The Mouse Pack

Six months after the start of the Fitzgerald Inquiry, it was time to take a deep breath and assess its impact. For an investigation that was pencilled in for only six weeks of hearings, by Christmas of 1987 it was already shaping up as a culturally and politically transformative juggernaut. It had seen off the longest serving Premier in Queensland's history, it had stood down its longest serving police commissioner. It had gone a long way towards deconstructing generational corruption that had infected virtually every corner of society. Queensland was facing the prospect of having to reinvent itself.

Newspapers reported that the inquiry had been a heavy blow to the police force, with suicides among the ranks, imploded marriages and careers in tatters. Commissioner Tony Fitzgerald warned that those against his inquiry were behind a nasty propaganda campaign to discredit his hearings.

The *Courier-Mail* wrote: 'He [Fitzgerald] says stories have been spread around the force urging officers to stick together, because police can only rely on each other; not to help the inquiry because it is ruining police morale; and not to dob in mates or their career could be finished.

'Mr Fitzgerald has warned police not to be fooled by their corrupt colleagues.'

The article alleged that some police officers felt their colleagues were not getting a fair go at the inquiry. Many police objected strongly to prostitutes giving evidence, because they held grudges against the police. 'The officers behind this propaganda are known in the force as the "Mouse Pack". According to police sources, these officers are juniors to the more celebrated "Rat Pack".

The first six months had naturally been a destabilising period for the force as a whole. Week after week, the daily diet of police scandals in the media rolled out like some salacious, serialised penny dreadful. And officers across the board – corrupt or not – waited for their 'notice of allegations' – that slip of paper on commission of inquiry letterhead that informed them that they were soon to be named in evidence, and they best attend the hearings.

The family of former assistant commissioner, Tony Murphy, said it was a terrible time. 'Every morning he'd have to go and get the [news] papers – "I'm in it again." It was a horrible feeling to have things said about you that weren't true,' they said. 'On the news every night. We were all waiting for him to be called. His solicitor got a bit cranky with Tony. He kept saying, "I want to give evidence." He wanted to set things right and he never had that opportunity.'

Police morale hit rock bottom. 'For those who have been innocently named, it may be more than 12 months before their names can be cleared,' the *Courier-Mail* attested. 'But for others who have been quite rightly named, the biggest worry for them is: how much have they got on me?

'For the rest of the force, they are wondering who they can trust. "It's very disheartening," said one junior officer. "The policemen who you were told to look up to, you now realise are bad, bad people. A lot of them used to be the success stories of the police force, the people young officers modelled themselves on.

'"Well, nobody believes in success stories anymore."'

Another senior officer lamented: 'While I've been out risking my life doing my job, I discover some of these bastards around me have been sitting around getting paid off. They deserve all they get.'

As for Lewis, he says he had several discussions with Don Lane about the progress of the inquiry. 'I spoke to Lane a few times and said, "Look, for goodness sake, tell the Premier or somebody to … exercise some control over the inquiry,"' says Lewis. 'Because at that stage they were just going to go on forever, which they did … I thought he [Lane] might have some way that he could say, not stop it or interfere with them, but just to keep it within some sort of manageable … territory.'

Hunting the Predators

Kym Goldup, a fifth-generation Gold Coaster, could have done anything with her life. When she first graduated from the University of Queensland she considered becoming a forensic scientist. Instead, she joined the Queensland police and by March 1983 was sworn in as a constable. After a month at the city station in the Brisbane CBD, she served another month in the Traffic Branch before being seconded to Mobile Patrols on the Gold Coast – her home turf.

Early in her career, Goldup expressed a fascination with sexual offences, and acquitted a course with the Rape Squad. With her academic background, she was considered the perfect fit for the Juvenile Aid Bureau (JAB), founded by former commissioner Frank Bischof and headed up for a number of years by Terry Lewis. She started working for the Gold Coast branch of the JAB in 1984, investigating cases of incest. It was here that she got her first real insight into paedophilia. 'I didn't know at the time but there was a group of detectives in Juvenile Aid who were investigating things to do with paedophiles and the Brett's Boys [male brothel in Brisbane] thing,' Goldup recalls.

In 1987, she would have a year that would define the rest of her career. To begin with, a close friend, Senior Constable Ashley Paul Anderson, 29, died from horrific injuries in a motor vehicle accident at around 5.30 a.m. on Friday 26 June. Anderson, grandson to former deputy commissioner Fred Palethorpe, was driving a patrol car along the Nerang–Broadbeach Road when it collided head-on with a Toyota four-wheel-drive. Anderson's passenger, Constable Ewan Findlater, 20, survived, as did the driver of the other vehicle.

Just one month later, Goldup was the only female officer on a Tactical Response Group raid on a house in Walter Street, Virginia, in Brisbane's northern suburbs. Police were hunting Paul James Mullin, a criminal wanted for a string of armed robberies, and it was suspected he was holed up in the house. Senior Constable Peter Kidd and Detective Constable Stephen Grant, both 29, stormed the back entrance to the house, hoping to catch Mullin asleep. They reached a bedroom near the front of the house when gunfire rang out. Mullin fired through the bedroom door with a .233 calibre Ruger Mini-14 firearm, striking Kidd. The police officer continued forward, and was hit with four more bullets that penetrated his bullet-proof vest. Grant was also hit.

Another police officer killed Mullin instantly with a blast from a shotgun. Kidd later died in hospital. The murder of Kidd and the death of Mullin had a huge psychological impact on Goldup.

Nevertheless, in late 1987, after Commissioner Lewis had been officially stood down following revelations at the Fitzgerald Inquiry, Goldup was transferred to the Sex Offenders unit. There, she teamed up with Garnett Dickson, brother of former police officer Ross Dickson, who had proved such a headache for Lewis through the mid-1980s.

In Brisbane, despite the almost daily allegations of a vastly corrupt police force coming out of Tony Fitzgerald's commission of inquiry, over on the south side of the river excitement was building for the impending World Exposition. It was due to open its doors on the last day of April, and wash the city with a modern cosmopolitanism.

The event would attract dignitaries and tourists from around the world, but it was also set to lure predators. 'Expo 88 was coming around and we got some information from somebody in Juvenile Aid, I forget who it was,' says Goldup. 'They called us up and said they had received some information that a group of paedophiles were moving up [to Brisbane], or had moved up, for Expo, and that they were all street performers in the lunch and night-time parades. We decided to go about our business.'

It was, in fact, this specific investigation by Goldup and Dickson, and undercover operative Bob Sawtell, that formed the Paedophile Unit within the Sexual Offenders Squad. 'Because of the information that was received, something had to be done,' recalls Goldup. 'At this stage, when we received this information, we were still working in the old [police] building on the corner of Makerston Street and North Quay, and they said there was not enough room in the Sex Offenders office for us to conduct this paedophile work, so they were going to move us into another office ... we thought that was fantastic. But [then] they actually moved us into the stationery closet of the Major Crime Squad.'

Without resources, not even a computer, the unit went to work in earnest on the paedophile allegations. The primary target was a group that went under the name of BLAZE (Boy Lovers And Zucchini Eaters). BLAZE was begun in 1980 by 'paedophile identity' Emu Nugent, and was originally called 'The Australian Paedophile Support Group'. It published a newsletter and had members throughout Australia and overseas. Nugent had been a primary school teacher in Western Australia in the late 1960s and then moved on to become

Activities Director for the Children's Activities Time Society, then a coordinator and storyteller for the Jolly Jumbuck Story Caravan, a community arts project. He changed his name to 'Emu' so he would have 'a talking point with children', according to a confidential police report.

Nugent was also editor of Australia's first paedophile newsletter – 'Rockspider', prison slang for child molester. The mailing address for BLAZE was in Strawberry Hills, Sydney. 'It was a group of them who came up to work at Expo, and they were trying to open a chapter [of BLAZE] here in Queensland,' says Goldup. 'That's why we called it Operation Firefighter, because we were trying to put out the blaze.'

The police unit began to make serious headway. For the first time in history, they managed to embed an informant – Sawtell – in a paedophile ring. He lived and mixed with paedophiles, and confidentially recorded conversations. One of the men who crossed the police radar was a public servant who worked, of all places, for the Police Complaints Tribunal. They discovered this man had access to the personal information of every police officer in the force. 'One of the things that came out with the undercover operation was that they had people in pretty much every area of government and society, so that if anything went wrong they could easily stop it,' reflects Goldup. 'They had all of these plants, these people who were involved in it.'

Intelligence was coming through, too, of the involvement of extremely senior figures in the Queensland judicial system. Goldup noted, however, that her superiors were not showing any level of enthusiasm for the unit's groundbreaking work. All the unit's data and investigation notes – given no computer was provided – were kept in a four-drawer file safe. Goldup was nonplussed at the indifference of her superiors to the unit's work. 'They weren't taking us seriously,' she says. The closer she, Dickson and the rest of the unit got to high-profile targets, the colder the place became.

The issue of paedophilia had for decades been a burr for the Queensland Police. It was an activity that the public largely didn't want to acknowledge existed. And for investigators, it was difficult to separate fact from fiction. Rumours of subterranean paedophile networks comprising high-profile people – judges, lawyers, politicians, media and sports celebrities – were not simply confined to a city like Brisbane or a state like Queensland.

Still, the paedophile Clarence Osborne and his death in the late 1970s had opened a window into this crime that stretched back to the 1950s. The huge volume of files, paperwork and photographs found in his possession would have, at the very least, been fertile material for investigators serious about understanding paedophilia in Brisbane and potentially the people associated with it.

Curiously, no major investigation was ordered into the Osborne case. And it became clear in the early 1980s that the upper end of the police hierarchy were aware of the activities of one of their own officers, Dave Moore, and the likes of radio personality Bill Hurrey and businessman Paul Breslin had come across their radar.

Yet the question always lingered – for a crime as abhorrent as this, why didn't police and the government take the issue more seriously?

Big Daddy

Just prior to the reopening of the Fitzgerald Inquiry on 1 February 1988, after a Christmas and New Year recess, it was reported that former premier Sir Joh Bjelke-Petersen, would be summoned to appear in Courtroom 29. The topic he would be quizzed over would be the appointment of Inspector Terence Lewis of Charleville to Assistant Commissioner, then Commissioner, in late 1976. Similarly, the disgraced public servant and Joh confidant, Allen Callaghan, was also expected to be interrogated about the subject.

It was fact that businessman and Bjelke-Petersen advisor, 'Top Level' Ted Lyons, had already been subpoenaed to appear before Fitzgerald. And with suspended Police Commissioner Lewis also due for a second round in the witness box, it seemed that Bjelke-Petersen's old 'kitchen cabinet' was being rounded up to offer what they knew about police, and possibly political, corruption. The New Year hearings of the inquiry disappointed nobody.

On 2 February, just weeks before Lewis's sixtieth birthday, the bodyguard of Brisbane Chinatown identity and kung-fu master, Malcolm Sue, gave evidence that Commissioner Lewis had been given a 'Christmas present' of cash in an envelope by his boss. The bodyguard, who had been granted an indemnity from prosecution, went by the name of 'Mr Brown' at the hearings. The exchange of money, he said, happened at a dinner in 1982.

'I saw Sue putting money into an envelope prior to the dinner,' Brown told the inquiry. 'I could see the colour of the money through the envelope. He [Sue] said, "Merry Christmas, Terry." There was not a lot of surprise, just subdued laughter.' Brown said Sue referred to Lewis as 'Big Daddy'. He also named Sue as the head of a criminal network that engaged in everything from drugs, gambling and prostitution to extortion, arson and even murder.

Brown told the inquiry that he had seen both former National Party ministers Russ Hinze and Don Lane at a brothel owned by Sue in Brunswick Street, New Farm, in inner-Brisbane, with a Mr Liu. 'Mr Liu pointed out the girls inside and said take your pick,' Brown said in evidence. 'He [Mr Liu] said he was friendly with the [former] premier [Joh Bjelke-Petersen].' Brown added that he had seen former racing and police minister Russ Hinze at illegal gambling joints.

Sir James Killen, the former Federal minister, was in Courtroom 29 as legal representative for Hinze. It was an interesting act of symmetry for Killen. As a young lawyer and freshly elected politician in the early 1960s, Killen – who had been friends for years with former detective

Tony Murphy and with Lewis going right back to the 1950s – was responsible for leaking confidential immigration documents on former National Hotel doorman John Komlosy to Murphy in the lead-up to the National Hotel inquiry in 1963 and 64. That action had resulted in Komlosy's credibility as a witness at the inquiry being savaged and ultimately dismissed.

Thanks to Killen, Komlosy's life was destroyed and his family threatened. He fled back to Europe, penniless, before Justice Harry Gibbs brought down his findings. (In short, there was no evidence of police misconduct.) Now, here Killen was again, in the biggest probe into police corruption since the National Hotel whitewash, defending a National Party minister rumoured to have been manifestly corrupt.

Killen – described as being in a 'black mood' – savaged Brown during the hearings. The questioning was so heated that at one point Fitzgerald invited Killen into his office for a private discussion 'behind closed doors'.

The new Premier, Mike Ahern, was disturbed enough to announce that he was seeking legal advice on the naming of public figures at the inquiry based on 'hearsay evidence'. 'The Government is loath to interfere in any way with the proceedings of the commission, but this is a very difficult issue and one which I will take advice from Mr [Ian] Callinan [legal representative for the government at the inquiry].'

The allegations of Brown naturally incensed Russ Hinze. He immediately wrote to 48 National Party members of parliament requesting they discuss the Fitzgerald Inquiry and appealing for 'justice'. Hinze also wrote to the Party's management committee seeking their support.

My name has been smeared in the media right across Australia as the result of totally false allegations made in the Fitzgerald Inquiry ... I am confident that my legal representatives will do what has to be done to disprove those allegations in the inquiry.

But, I am equally concerned about the political side of what has been happening. It is now 60 days since I was stood down as a minister and I do not want it to continue. What I am seeking is reinstatement to my former position on the basis that I have not, in fact, done anything wrong.

Hinze implied that Mr Brown's evidence was part of a larger conspiracy to politically damage him. He said he knew the name of the figure behind the 'set-up', and was prepared to name him in parliament.

While Hinze may have been aggrieved at the slurring of his good name, and sought the support of political partners, Tony Fitzgerald read Hinze's move in an entirely different way. On 4 February he attacked both Hinze and Killen, asserting that Mr Brown's evidence was not hearsay, but direct evidence of identification. Fitzgerald said of Hinze's statements: 'It appears to imply that the present witness [Brown] is part of a conspiracy to damage him [Hinze] by perjured evidence ... at least, that seems the least scandalous of the possible implications.'

Fitzgerald warned that the inquiry would not be subject to political interference. Deputy Premier and Police Minister Bill Gunn said he was 'disturbed' by Hinze's attempts to have inquiry deliberations debated in state parliament. 'It's just not on,' he said. 'Quite clearly it's been ruled in previous sittings that the matter is sub judice until the final Fitzgerald report, and I recall Mr Hinze himself supported this stand, but evidently now wants the rule changed.'

Meanwhile, Premier Ahern finally decided to cease funding the suspended commissioner Lewis's legal representation. Opposition Leader Nev Warburton said it was 'about time'.

Up on Garfield Drive, Sir Terence again did not respond to media requests for a comment, and had his wife, Lady Hazel, do the talking. 'All I can tell you is that if this is true and we are told he will have to pay his own legal expenses Terry will be very disappointed. I suppose we'll have to work something out.'

The Bagman Bagged

The very sociable Jack 'The Bagman' Herbert was feeling confined and homesick in his bolthole at Kingston upon Thames, south-west of central London. The ancient market town, where several Saxon kings were crowned, was by February 1988 experiencing the full thrust of winter. Herbert and his wife Peggy, stuck in a one-bedroom flat, pined for sunny Queensland.

The couple had been living in the Kingston flat for over six months under the names of Mr and Mrs Niven. To other residents in the five-flat converted home, they were just Jack and Peggy, the friendly Australians on an extended holiday.

On the morning of 9 February, the Herberts were up early. They intended to take a bus into Australia House in London to read the newspapers from back home. While Peggy cooked breakfast, Herbert was preparing a defence against the allegations of Graeme Parker and Harry Burgess. He was gazing out the kitchen window that overlooked Manor Gate Road when he noticed two men on the footpath. Suspicious, he hurried to the bedroom window that overlooked a rear courtyard. He observed two more men staring up at the Herberts' flat.

'They're wallopers,' he said to Peggy.

Herbert recalled in his memoir, *The Bagman*, that the next minute there was some heavy rapping on the flat door. 'Open the door or we'll break it down!' a voice said. 'At the same moment the only door to the flat burst open,' Herbert wrote. 'Four male detectives and a plain-clothes policewoman rushed up the narrow staircase.

'One of the men was shouting at us not to move. They had brought several large plastic bags which they started filling with anything they could lay their hands on: books, slips of paper and numerous documents which had been sent over from Australia.'

Officer in charge, Detective Chief Inspector Philip Connolly, told the pair they were to be arrested. It didn't occur to Herbert that they might also want to take Peggy into custody. Herbert alleged that Connolly said both would be released on bail, and he apologised for his actions 'to a fellow policeman'.

The Herberts were driven in separate vehicles to Cannon Row police station in Whitehall. Four decades earlier, Herbert had worked out of that very same station. The couple were fingerprinted and photographed, then locked in facing cells. That night, Herbert jotted notes in preparation for their bail application. As for Peggy, she wrote a letter to their daughter Anne, admitting that they both felt like 'stunned mullets' but were 'keeping their chins up'.

Early the next morning, the pair was taken to the Bow Street Magistrates Court. Herbert was introduced to his legal counsel, solicitor Michael Fisher, and gave him his notes from the night before. The notes explained that he was willing to return to Australia of his own free will and that court extradition proceedings were not necessary.

When they were taken to the court, police opposed bail. The Herberts were charged with conspiring to pervert the course of justice and both entered no pleas.

One of the arresting police, Detective Chief Inspector Connolly, told the magistrate that the charges were serious and could attract severe gaol time, and that he understood that Herbert was wanted for questioning before the current Fitzgerald Inquiry into police corruption in Brisbane, Queensland. 'They travelled to this country and since arriving have lived under a false identity,' Connolly stressed. 'When arrested at their Kingston home they had on them 1000 pounds and American and Japanese currency.' He urged their remand in custody given the possibility they might interfere with Fitzgerald Inquiry witnesses.

Defence solicitor Fisher told the court that upon arrest Jack Herbert had offered to go directly to the airport and return voluntarily to Australia. He said Jack and Peggy had 'nothing to hide'. There was also a touching note to Fisher's plea for bail. If the magistrate decided to remand them in custody, he hypothesised, the couple would be potentially separated for months. 'They have been married for 38 years and they love each other dearly,' Fisher noted.

To the incredulity of officials back in Australia, bail was granted at $150,000 with a $12,000 surety to be lodged with their solicitor. The surety was provided by Herbert's brother Bill.

In the court, the Herberts, both 63, appeared delighted when bail was granted. Magistrate William Robins ruled that they could remain in their small flat in Kingston upon Thames on the condition that they report daily to the Kingston police station. They were also required to surrender their passports and travel documents.

Queensland Police Minister Bill Gunn was aghast, saying he could not dismiss the reality that the Herberts might skip bail. The Herberts were ordered to return to court on 23 March, to begin extradition proceedings. The extradition would then be in the hands of the Australian Federal Police. Soon after, a squad of senior Queensland police flew to London to expedite the extradition.

A close friend of Herbert's was in London 'when all hell broke loose'. 'I saw him in London,' he says. 'I used to send him all the stuff here in the mail. I was over there when they were locked up. They could never force them to come back.

'Jack was asking – what do I do? Live in exile or face the music and go back? They couldn't get Peggy either, she was married to a British resident. [But they had] two boys and a girl and grandchildren here [in Australia] – he came back because of that.'

Herbert said after their release the couple returned to their flat 'and spent a few miserable hours contemplating our predicament'.

The Past is Never Dead

For nine months Queenslanders had been both thrilled and horrified by the revelations coming out of the Fitzgerald Inquiry. It had it all – sex, drugs, a criminal underworld, late-night meetings in car parks, graft, murder, pay-offs, booze and gambling. Its cast of players included corrupt police, brothel owners, prostitutes, drug addicts and thugs.

In early March 1988, however, a whole new ensemble was about to enter the witness box – men who could potentially lay down a breadcrumb trail back to the 1950s and 60s to the source of Queensland's generational police corruption.

The history lesson was opened by retired Scotland Yard commander Terence John O'Connell. He had been brought to Brisbane in 1975 with a fellow officer to conduct an independent investigation into police corruption. O'Connell had interviewed hundreds of police, prostitutes and members of the public 'alleging corruption', and collected an enormous amount of data, all carefully notated on index cards.

By the time Whitrod had been overthrown as commissioner in late 1976, O'Connell's report had not been completed. He ultimately delivered it to Police Minister Tom Newbery in 1977, in the early weeks of Terry Lewis's commissionership. O'Connell learned that 'corruption and sectarianism' was rife in the force, but omitted these findings from his report. At the inquiry, he was asked why he had failed to include those conclusions in his report.

'I thought it incumbent on me to assist the new Queensland Police Commissioner, Terry Lewis, and the Queensland Government and not rock the boat,' he told Fitzgerald. 'If I mentioned corruption, it would have destroyed the new commissioner who was trying to put the police force back on its feet. I may have been wrong in hindsight. I could have put a lot of things in the report but I didn't.'

O'Connell socialised with Lewis when he was in Brisbane handing over his report in 1977, and subsequently caught up with Commissioner Lewis when the latter travelled to the United Kingdom on business. On one visit they went to a show together in London's West End.

During his 1975 sojourn in Brisbane, O'Connell said he was approached by detective Tony Murphy at a party, and that Murphy aggressively asked: 'What's all this razzamatazz? Why are you interviewing all these officers?'

O'Connell replied that he was 'doing his job'.

Another former police officer took the stand and carried the court all the way back to the 1950s and his memories of the Rat Pack. Louis James (Jim) Voight, who had joined the force in 1943, said he always suspected that Frank Bischof [police commissioner from 1958 to 1969] was corrupt and that he got some of his young men to do his 'legwork'.

Gary Crooke, QC, asked for the identity of the men. 'A. Murphy, Lewis, Hallahan – people like that,' Voight responded. He explained that before 1957 an inspector in charge of a district would collect corrupt payments in exchange for turning a blind eye to SP betting and illegal hotel trading. He said some of the money found its way into 'the Premier's fund', or the serving Labor Party at the time. Voight said he believed there was little he could do about corruption, because there was nobody he could offer suspicions or even evidence to, without being 'ridiculed'.

Former Police Union president and detective, Ron Edington, offered a contrary view. He said Lewis, Murphy and Hallahan were victims of 'corridor assassins' because of their commitment to excellence in police work. Others, he said, were simply jealous of the hard-working trio.

As observers had hoped, Ray Whitrod finally returned to Brisbane – the landscape of the worst years of his professional and personal life – to give evidence. Before making his appearance in Courtroom 29 Whitrod had spoken out, saying the inquiry terms of reference should go back further, beyond 1 January 1977, to retrieve in their net some crimes that still haunted Queensland and to beat a trail back to the source of the endemic corruption that was now being uncovered. He told the media the inquiry should at the very least take on the atrocious Whiskey Au Go Go nightclub fire at St Paul's Terrace, Fortitude Valley, in early 1973, in which 15 people perished. It still stood as Australia's worst mass murder.

Whitrod said that while he believed John Andrew Stuart and James Finch were not innocent of the crime, he believed there were unexplained stories surrounding the case that warranted investigation. 'When they first set up the inquiry, they must have thought that 1977 was a clear point to start because that was when Terry Lewis became Commissioner,' Whitrod had earlier told the *Courier-Mail*. 'But things do not occur overnight in the Queensland justice system. There are historical roots to the problems being seen now. The seeds of some of the practices by police were already well in operation well before 1977. Some of them go back 30 years.'

Now Whitrod had returned to Brisbane to appear before the Fitzgerald Inquiry. The frail 72-year-old reiterated that Bjelke-Petersen's Cabinet knew of allegations that Terry Lewis had been a 'bagman' for Frank Bischof when they promoted him in late 1976. Whitrod had famously resigned when Lewis was elevated to assistant commissioner. He recalled his clashes with Premier Bjelke-Petersen over inquiries into the bashing of a female street march protestor in Brisbane, and a raid on a commune of hippies in Cedar Bay, Far North Queensland, both during 1976.

'I was ordered by the Premier not to make inquiries into police activities north of Cairns,' he told Fitzgerald. 'It seemed to strike directly at my authority to run the police force.' Whitrod explained that his situation was untenable. 'The Premier had effectively taken away control of the police force from me by that [Lewis's] appointment,' Whitrod continued. 'He could communicate directly with assistant commissioner Lewis and countermand any instructions I might give. And so I could remain as a sort of "front man" for any sort of activities which might develop ... my reputation could be a shield for whatever might develop and in fact did develop later on.'

Both Whitrod and Voight admitted in evidence that they had no proof that Lewis, Murphy and Hallahan were corrupt. Whitrod did recall, however, that in his almost seven years as Police Commissioner he dealt personally with Premier Joh Bjelke-Petersen on just three occasions. By contrast, Lewis would have more than ten times that contact within his first year in the top job. When Whitrod left the witness box, he offered suspended commissioner Lewis a cheery wave, then walked out of the courtroom. Lewis himself smiled at the gesture.

In the same week that Whitrod and many figures from the past offered their recollections to the inquiry, Tony Fitzgerald made a gesture of openness and transparency that was, in its truest sense, Whitrodian – he began releasing extracts from the fastidious diaries of suspended commissioner Lewis.

Dear Diary

The previous October, having been suspended for less than a fortnight, Commissioner Lewis gave yet another exclusive story to *Sunday Mail* reporter Ric Allen. Sir Terence assured the people of Queensland that he had been fully cooperative with the Fitzgerald commission of inquiry and had nothing to hide. 'I have given all of my official diaries as well as my personal diaries to Fitzgerald,' he said.

Allen reported that government sources close to Premier Sir Joh Bjelke-Petersen were 'furious' that Lewis had allowed the diaries to be studied by the commission. He, and many hundreds of other people, may have shared the same reaction when the Fitzgerald Inquiry began making public Lewis's handwritten diaries, noting his years as Commissioner and the innumerable meetings he had with ministers, businessmen and women, celebrities, friends, royalty, charities and family.

As the diaries became public property, and on the eve of the Ahern government deciding whether to allow Lewis to take his superannuation payout of more than $1 million, Lewis decided to give an 'exclusive interview', once again, to the Brisbane *Sunday Mail*.

The bold headline read: LEWIS TELLS: MY FAMILY ANGUISH. Lewis said the trauma of the inquiry 'was taking its toll'. He said of the potential of Cabinet to block 'the golden handshake': 'It's in the hands of Cabinet but I must say that I've been suspended now for nearly six months and no one knows how long this inquiry will continue.

'Let's face facts: I could be dead before it finishes so I do have to think about Hazel and the family.'

Both Sir Terence and Lady Lewis said they were suffering deep depression. 'Please tell of the long hours and hard work Terry has put in during his 39 years in the force,' pleaded Lady Hazel. 'He did so many good things during his service and many other people have collected their superannuation.'

In hindsight, Lewis says the gesture of offering his diaries to the commission was regrettable. 'I've made a number of mistakes ... and one of them was giving them my diaries ... I never thought they would ... I had a considerable respect for the legal profession ... never ever thinking the rotten bastards would ... never return them to me, but more importantly would release them publicly.'

Lewis says as Commissioner he was not legislatively required to keep official diaries, but following the habit of a lifetime he continued diarising his life anyway. 'So I got these old ones and used them, but they weren't just an official diary about my work, I put my family things in it,' Lewis reflects. 'I wasn't going to keep two lots of diaries and if Hazel was sick or something that was in, all that stuff was in my diaries.

'Of course, what did Fitzgerald do? Release my diaries, told me the day before he was going to release my diaries to the media and the public the next day. And I objected, of course, and said they were diaries that had my own, a lot of my personal ... oh, he said, if overnight you want to go through them all and ... it was impossible. Absolutely physically and mentally impossible. And point out to them you know what it was that was so sensitive that they couldn't release it.'

Lewis believes the content of the diaries, too, was used in part to 'build up a story' for Jack Herbert. 'See, I used to put in the diaries that, you know, I saw Herbert and had a drink with him,' says Lewis. 'He used to ring up quite often and say ... he only lived over at those big units ... so it was only a stone's throw away and I couldn't go over all the ... but I'd go over about every three months or four months or six months and have a drink with him. And ... I'm sure he invited us to his place for dinner once and we invited him over to our place once. And they would be in my diary.

'They really, really, really you know it's ... it's annoyed me greatly the way that I was railroaded by Fitzgerald.'

Lewis says he also gave the commission the 'little notebooks' he kept at his bedside at 12 Garfield Drive, and numerous appointment books. He says his assistant Greg Early's shorthand notebooks were also turned over to be transcribed.

'That's hurt me ever since that one, still does, still does,' says Lewis. 'I don't know how many, there could have been a number of people putting them [the diaries] on computers, everything in the computer, so they could backtrack and check everything. And it helped them a little bit, well, a lot, for them to be able to say, oh, Lewis saw Herbert on so and so.

'I mean, if I was getting a quid, well, I wouldn't be here, I would have been ... [if] trouble had raised its head, I knew all the countries that didn't have extradition ... [I] would have got the family and pissed off with my millions of dollars and lived happily ever after.'

Lewis's former loyal assistant, Greg Early, says: 'He wrote his private life into his diaries. He should have thrown them in the river.'

If the exclusive interview with the *Sunday Mail* was to elicit sympathy, or sway the Ahern government on the matter of Lewis's superannuation, it didn't work. A week earlier, on 29 February – the occasion of Lewis's sixtieth birthday – he had lodged his resignation as Police Commissioner.

On Monday 7 March Cabinet rejected it, refusing Lewis access to his monster super payout. The government said it wanted to hold the money until the conclusion of the inquiry. If Lewis attempted legal action to recover it, Premier Ahern made it clear that it would pass special legislation to freeze the funds.

Lewis refused to comment on the decision.

The Watcher

One of the commission of inquiry's permanent fixtures was former Licensing Branch officer Nigel Powell. He sat daily during the hearings in Courtroom 29 of the District Court and watched and listened attentively, gauging the mood of the room, assessing witnesses and lawyers. 'Initially the atmosphere was like a disturbed sea,' Powell recalls. 'You couldn't work out what was going to happen. Some lawyers avoided other lawyers. In the early days I bumped into [corrupt Licensing Branch head] Noel Dwyer. He just sidled up to me in his fatherly way and said, "What's all this about, Nigel? I don't understand this."

'Everything changed when news came through that Harry Burgess had rolled over.' Powell, who had appeared on 'The Moonlight State', says that until then he constantly asked himself – what if I got this all wrong? Other corrupt police followed, leading up to the appearance of Jack 'The Bagman' Herbert. 'At that stage, it was a case of – how far can this go?' says Powell. 'Was Lewis a total incompetent or was he in on it?'

Powell says he was astonished at Fitzgerald's stewardship of the inquiry. 'I watched him one day; he had two separate files in front of him, both about a foot and a half tall,' he says. 'At the same time there was some cross-examination going on. He was listening to what was going on and going through the first lot of files. He would then pop in with a question. He finished the first file, still asking incisive questions, and finished the second file as well. This was the level of his intellect.'

Powell says he was also astonished at the length and breadth of the corruption. 'I had no idea how big it was, no idea,' he reflects. 'When I was a police officer I was working with facts. You don't get the relationships if you don't have that background of the humanity of the situation. You don't understand.'

As the inquiry progressed, Powell suffered some health problems including several bouts of pneumonia. His blood pressure was high. He was stressed. A former fanatical runner, Powell, who had moved into a flat in Dunmore Terrace, Auchenflower, had taken up cycling after suffering an ankle injury during a run in the Gold Coast hinterland. He often pedalled along Coronation Drive and out to the University of Queensland campus where he was studying.

He felt compelled, however, to embed himself at the inquiry for as long as it took. His study took a backseat. 'I took the view through the inquiry that if I could be of some use, I couldn't later turn around, if the whole thing went pear-shaped, and say I didn't do my best,' he says. 'I wouldn't have been able to forgive myself.'

Out of the Cold, Into the Fire

In the bitter London winter, cooped up in his single-bedroom flat south-west of the capital, Jack Herbert feared that he had missed the Fitzgerald commission of inquiry's deadline for indemnity from prosecution. He made a phone call to his lawyer in Brisbane, Tony Bailey, who promised to check. Several days later, Bailey called and asked if Herbert was prepared to meet with barrister Bob Needham, who was assisting the inquiry. Within days, he was in discussion with Needham in person at the Kingston police station. Needham had brought with him an application for immunity for both Jack and Peggy. They signed the document.

As preparations were made to return the Herberts to Australia, Jack claimed he got a phone call from Geraldo Bellino. Bellino allegedly told Herbert he was mounting a 'big propaganda campaign' to discredit the evidence of Harry Burgess and others, and asked if he would talk to a University of Queensland academic called Joseph Siracusa.

Siracusa had been attached to some of Brisbane's commercial television stations to provide nightly analysis for revelations that were coming out of Courtroom 29. The American had also conducted several interviews with the main players in the drama, including the Bellinos, for a book he was writing called *Queensland on Trial*. Bellino allegedly told Herbert that Siracusa would pay him $30,000 for an interview. Herbert took careful notes of the telephone conversation.

Within days, the Herberts were taken in separate chauffeur-driven vehicles by Australian Federal Police to Oxford, 90 kilometres west of London. Initially Herbert couldn't understand why they weren't heading for Heathrow, but preparing to leave from RAF Abingdon, an airfield initially used as a training station for RAF Bomber Command, and later a major training hub during World War II. Herbert claimed he had been stationed there briefly during the war.

As it transpired, the problem of how to get the Herberts back to Brisbane had vexed Premier Mike Ahern. There were rumours that Jack Herbert might be a prime target for a hitman, either in Europe or on his return to Australia, so a commercial flight would have been potentially dangerous to the public. Ahern had a meeting with Prime Minister Bob Hawke in the lead-up to World Expo 88 in Brisbane, which was set to open its doors on 30 April. 'You know ... the community had I think come to accept that ... there's always a bit of police corruption around, what can you do?' Ahern reflects. 'But when this thing got more audacious and drugs became involved, there'd be no doubt that that fellow Herbert knew that. Because the stakes were getting higher and higher …

'Hawke said, "Well I've heard all about it," and he said, "Let's say we'll do it [fly him home in a Federal Government aircraft]. We can't put people on board a Qantas aircraft at risk in case there's a contract out on his life."'

Hawke told the Premier that there was an RAAF aircraft that did the rounds visiting Australian troops abroad and delivering supplies. Hawke suggested – let's put him on that. 'He said, "I'll send you a bill for $140,000",' remembers Ahern. 'He didn't.'

The Herberts landed at Amberley Air Force Base near Ipswich and police whisked him away to a safe house. A source says they were way down the back of the short-range jet airliner, a BAC 1-11, 'in the cheap seats'.

Herbert recorded that they arrived in Queensland around 7.30 a.m. on Thursday 17 March 1988. It was St Patrick's Day. For some reason he assumed he and his wife could return to their luxury unit in New Farm, not far from the Sydney Street Wharf. Instead, they were rushed to a safe house in a high-rise unit building on Lower River Terrace, South Brisbane.

It was soon leaked to the local press that Herbert was set to give evidence at the inquiry and turn Crown witness on the condition his wife Peggy be granted immunity from prosecution. 'Herbert has knowledge that could reveal the full picture of corruption in Queensland, going back to his first days in the Licensing Branch in 1959,' Courier-Mail commentator Nick Maher wrote. 'It is also understood that Herbert has handed over important documents to the inquiry which contain the names of several well-known Queenslanders.'

Suspended commissioner Terry Lewis didn't seem fazed, arguing in a television interview that he would fight to be reinstated given he had been stood down on 'flimsy' grounds.

With Herbert back in town, though, the level of intrigue surrounding the Fitzgerald Inquiry ramped up even further, if that was possible. The day after the Herberts landed on home soil, police raided the private homes of Geraldo Bellino and Vic Conte. While both men had admitted to running illegal casinos, they had denied any involvement in prostitution or paying off police for protection.

Bellino was disgusted at the police swoop on his home in St Lucia. 'I have tried to co-operate,' Bellino told the press. 'Then they come on this standover business like you wouldn't believe. They left without giving any receipts. I spoke to Vic Conte and the same thing happened to him.'

Rumours about what Herbert 'knew' reached fever pitch. The *Courier-Mail* speculated that The Bagman had already offered a 100-page statement, and that he had gifted the police thousands of sensitive documents from his personal files.

The frenzy continued. Deputy Opposition Leader Tom Burns demanded that the Suncorp insurance company's chief investigator, Glen Hallahan – he of the so-called Rat Pack – be stood down. He said Hallahan should be suspended until the conclusion of the inquiry.

Then came the numerous 'sightings' of the notorious Jack Herbert. One minute he was in Brisbane. The next, he popped up on the Sunshine Coast. A close friend of the Herberts says of that period: 'The witness protection stories would rock you to your foundations. We used to have to accidentally bump into each other to see each other, you know. He'd ring me up and say, "We'll be at the Balmoral Pub tomorrow night at 6 o'clock, can you run into us?"

'They had him out on a farm in Thornlands one night and the house belonged to one of the senior coppers. And the farmer started up his tractor at four o'clock in morning, and they all hit the floor.'

He said he once met the Herberts at a clandestine picnic 'and the guys guarding him left their guns behind so we had to go back and get their guns … on a picnic table. Oh look, honestly, it was hysterical.'

The big question was: When was Herbert going to appear as a witness at the inquiry?

Everyone, it seemed, was waiting for Jack.

A Boat Called Corruption

Premier Mike Ahern was on a steep learning curve, deposing Bjelke-Petersen and becoming Premier of Queensland in the midst of the state's most far-reaching Royal Commission into corrupt police and the past actions of government. He stood tall and fully supported the inquiry, and worked with its commissioner Tony Fitzgerald to ensure the inquiry juggernaut stayed on track.

As the evidence poured forth, Fitzgerald expressed his discomfort about the role of drugs in the saga. He told Ahern that prostitution and illegal gambling was just the shopfront for the bigger drug operations happening behind the scenes. Subsequently, the chairman of the National Crime Authority, Justice Stewart, requested a meeting with Ahern.

'Justice Stewart seemed to be a very, very outstanding individual to me,' says Ahern. 'And of course, if the chairman of the National Crime Authority wants to see the Premier of Queensland, that's what you do.'

Stewart flew to Brisbane with some of his staff and met Ahern in his office in the Executive Building on George Street. They spoke in private; Stewart came armed with a large stack of files, bound in red legal ribbon. 'In those days there was a requirement for NCA matters under investigation, specifically in the state where arrests and warrants were required, for the state to give approval and to share some of the costs,' Ahern recalls.

'He [Stewart] said he was aware of ... a major drug and money laundering situation on the Gold Coast and he said, "All the information is in here [in the files] ... I'm asking you officially, as

Chairman of the National Crime Authority and you as Premier of Queensland, for you to give me authority to proceed."' The two men then discussed a 'cost sharing agreement' in relation to any potential future operations.

'So he sat there and I picked up the file and I handed it back to him, unopened, and I said, "Well, I agree … You will have your authority and I will instruct my secretary what's required to issue you with the necessary authorities, and as Premier of the state, to enable you to get on with the job which you think you should do. The National Crime Authority is a respected institution and if you say this needs to be done then you will see that due process is all carried through and people will be charged and they will have their day in court."'

Ahern told Justice Stewart that he didn't want to look at the files because he might recognise some names, and if there was any sort of 'leak' in the future, it could never be traced back to him or anyone else in the government.

'He [Stewart] was gobsmacked, he was absolutely gobsmacked,' says Ahern. 'He said, "Well, the last time I came here for this project it was very different, your predecessor [Bjelke-Petersen] was sitting there and … I had to endure at least a half an hour of abuse as to why he would never, ever issue any powers to the Commonwealth to do anything in his state. I pleaded with him. I pointed out that this was a very serious criminal matter."'

Stewart told Ahern on that occasion that Joh had rung Terry Lewis and organised for a senior police officer to accompany NCA officials on business in Queensland. In the end a sergeant was assigned to accompany the NCA operatives to the Gold Coast.

During the investigation, figures linked to illegal activities were either not home or had fled overseas. Persons of interest had disappeared. Someone had already leaked confidential data and thwarted the NCA investigation. 'So the sergeant said [to the NCA agents], "Look I'm sorry about this, there appears to have been a leak", says Ahern, "why don't you come round to my place and I'll have Mum make you a nice cup of tea?"

'So, they went around onto the Isle of Capri and the sergeant introduced his wife in this beautiful home ... the car in the yard was the biggest four-wheel-drive you'd ever thought to buy, and then there was this huge boat. And it wasn't really the boat [that upset the visiting NCA agents], it was the name of the boat.

'*Corruption.*'

Dogs

Police officer Greg Deveney, the 'greenhorn' who found himself on transfer to the Gold Coast in the early 1980s and was appalled at the corruption he witnessed, took the stand at the Fitzgerald Inquiry on 26 April.

At the time of the inquiry he was a Detective Sergeant Second Class attached to the Juvenile Aid Bureau's Child Abuse Unit. He told the court how, when he reported the corrupt actions of various colleagues in Surfers Paradise, and refused to take or sanction graft, his fellow officers turned on him. They would bark when he walked through a room – 'woof, woof' – implying he was a dog, an officer who 'ran to the bosses'. He arrived at work one day to find dog excrement on his desk.

Deveney told Fitzgerald that the stress contributed to him catching pneumonia, and that he feared for the safety of his family. Deveney broke down on the stand and wept. He said for several months he 'camped' on the front landing of his home with a loaded weapon. He was terrified his enemies would burn down his house.

Deveney was being persecuted even before he made the decision to give evidence before the commission of inquiry. 'I'd been fighting these bastards my own way for ten years,' he says. 'I'd been vilified and attacked, pushed against the urinal, I couldn't even go and use the urinals at CIB headquarters unless I got pushed or bloody pissed on. I used to go down to [the] City Hall [toilets], yeah.'

After giving evidence on that day, an emotional Deveney took the short walk from the Law Courts, west along George Street, to the offices of the Juvenile Aid Bureau in police headquarters. 'You know, the day [I] gave evidence, now this is how quick it was. I walked out of the witness box, out of the courtroom, I walked straight back to the Juvenile Aid Bureau,' recalls Deveney. 'When I opened up the door of the CIB headquarters there was no one on the counter, it was like church. The next minute [an officer] was on the stairway. [He said,] "You fucking cunt!" and … gave me a spray.

'I shouted back to him, "If you don't think I told the truth, go down and give your version." They said, "You're like your old man [who was an honest cop] you fucking …", and they gave me a big gob full.

'I got up the lift and got out on the floor of the JAB and it was just quiet, you could hear a mouse. Anyway, I walked in, sat down at my desk and everybody … was pretending to be working. The next minute a sergeant came out and he gave me a mouthful and he told everybody who was in that bloody office – if bloody anybody was ever bloody friendly with me, that they'd be scabs and bloody everything else.

'They'd be dogs.'

The Rattled Pack

On the same day that Greg Deveney gave his evidence in Courtroom 29, a curious alignment of the stars occurred.

With suspended commissioner Terry Lewis in the public gallery, two of his great old mates arrived to deny allegations of corruption levelled against them. They were former assistant commissioner Tony

Murphy, and former deputy commissioner Syd 'Sippy' Atkinson. The day they chose to address the inquiry was also the first day of sittings before Deputy Commissioner Patsy Wolfe, whose appointment allowed Tony Fitzgerald time to work on his overall response to the inquiry's findings. It was day number 96 of the corruption hearings.

Atkinson, 60, was up first. Bald, wearing glasses and dressed in a grey suit, he was reportedly nervous in the witness box. He sought leave to cross-examine witnesses. 'I am guilty of no wrongdoing,' he said, his voice trembling, 'except for trusting those officers who entirely let me down, and I am astounded.'

Atkinson had joined the Queensland Police in 1945, and later as a senior detective was involved in cases like the Whiskey Au Go Go fire massacre and the infamous Cedar Bay raids in Far North Queensland in 1976, just prior to Ray Whitrod's resignation. In the late 1970s he was superintendent on the Gold Coast before returning to Brisbane and rising to Deputy Commissioner. He was awarded an OBE, and retired from the force in 1985.

Murphy, 59, was Murphy. As the *Courier-Mail* reported: 'A strongly-built man, with a shock of grey hair contrasting sharply with dark bushy eyebrows, he oozed confidence as he walked through the doors of the courtroom. There were no signs of nerves from Murphy, who strode to the front of the court and addressed Mrs Wolfe as "Madam Commissioner".'

Murphy claimed he could not afford to be legally represented or personally appear again at the inquiry because his current financial situation dictated that he had to still earn a living. Using a somewhat arcane, yet technically precise language, he told the inquiry: 'Certain evidence of a hearsay nature has already been given to this commission alleging or suggesting that I have in the past been involved in corruption and/or improper practices within the terms of reference of this inquiry. I wish to place on record that such allegations are not only untrue but can be demonstrably proved to be untrue.'

Murphy had weathered the National Hotel inquiry in 1963, the allegations of dead prostitute Shirley Brifman and perjury charges against him that stemmed from that in the early 1970s, and criticism of his work during the Costigan Royal Commission in the early 1980s prior to his retirement in late 1982. He wasn't going to have his name trashed in the latest commission.

Two of the three members of the infamous Rat Pack were present in court that day. The only one missing was Glen Patrick Hallahan. Barrister and former director of prosecutions, Des Sturgess, who had on occasion represented Hallahan in court cases in the past, as he did Lewis and Murphy, said he ended up 'feeling sympathy' for the notorious Hallahan. 'His name came up in the Fitzgerald Inquiry,' recalls Sturgess. 'One day he came to see me … he was very upset and he wasn't well either, he'd contracted cancer. He wanted to ask me if I could use any influence to get him called as a witness at Fitzgerald, to respond to these allegations.

'I said I'd speak to … I think Gary Crooke was still running the show then … I rang him up, whoever it was, and said Hallahan wants to give evidence. That's all I did.

'He [Hallahan] never gave evidence. He was never called.

'I think he telephoned me once after that, to say nothing had happened. I do recall I received a telephone call from him at home one day … I recall him being upset and he did tell me his cancer was at a very advanced state. It was obvious he was dying. That was the last I heard from Glen Hallahan.

'Fitzgerald never bothered to hear his side.' (In fact, the inquiry tendered a written submission from Hallahan on 7 February 1989.)

Journalist Phil Dickie recalls loitering outside Courtroom 29 one sitting day and seeing Lewis and Murphy talking at the end of a corridor. 'Murphy was poking his finger into Lewis's chest,' Dickie says. He had no idea what they might have been discussing.

Death Bed

In April, the former police chief of the Cairns region, Kevin Dorries, 56, was dying of cancer. The year before, Dorries had appeared before Fitzgerald and denied any involvement in corruption, although he was later named as having received corrupt payments. A decade earlier, Dorries had also appeared before the Williams' Royal Commission of Inquiry into Drugs and been forced to deny then that he had accepted corrupt money from drug dealers.

Suffering increasingly poor health, Dorries tried to retire from the police force and take advantage of a $275,000 superannuation payout. State Cabinet blocked Dorries' application. The government said it would decide on how to handle retirement applications from officers named in the inquiry. A short time before he died in late April, he supposedly had a meeting with Deputy Premier Bill Gunn, according to one of Gunn's relatives.

Dorries, by way of confession, wanted to share some documents with the man who had called the historic inquiry in the first place. He possessed some information so powerful it could almost instantly bring down the government. 'Bill went and spoke to Dorries in a motel room,' the family member says. 'He [Dorries] wanted to give up [intelligence he had] on a paedophile ring. Bill promised he would go after this. He was really keen on this. But Dorries died of cancer before Bill got around to it.'

There was a rumour, however, that former Anglican police chaplain Walter Ogle had been passed the documents on Dorries' death bed. Ogle was a well-known and highly regarded chaplain who did not shrink from making his views public. If he felt impelled to criticise the government of the day on a particular topic, he'd go out with both guns blazing. As police chaplain, however, he became privy to a lot of confidential information, and in the course of his work befriended many officers in a variety of different departments.

One of those departments was the Paedophile Task Force, headed up by Kym Goldup and Garnett Dickson. In a later commission of inquiry, evidence was given that Ogle 'was a frequent visitor to the small office occupied by the Paedophile Task Force and members of the task force shared confidences with him'.

As Dorries lay dying in hospital, it was appropriate that Ogle attend to his comfort. Prior to hearing Dorries' confession, the chaplain would later say that he was handed a series of manila envelopes which were part of a larger bundle of documents.

The envelopes, it transpired, contained a series of credit card vouchers retrieved from the Brett's Boys male brothel in Kelvin Grove, which was raided by police in late 1984 during the crisis over Constable Dave Moore. Some of the credit card vouchers were supposedly in the name of a serving National Party MP.

Later, claiming to have never opened the envelopes, Ogle entrusted the documents with friend and Brisbane gay identity and hotel proprietor, Neil McLucas. Ogle and McLucas were long-time friends.

'The story behind it is ... Walter had these documents and he was too afraid to leave them at home because he would have been raided,' recalls McLucas. 'I would have been a friend of Walter's for quite a number of years, and he said would you like to take these documents; he said they're rather important. He said if you keep them up at the hotel [The Sportsman Hotel, in Spring Hill] ... one day I'll pick them up from you, you know? And I said okay, fair enough.

'All I was told was they [the documents] could bring down the government. Now I don't know whether that was really true or not.'

McLucas did as requested, and stored the documents downstairs on a shelf. He says he never read them. They remained there for years. 'Well I did look after them, and in the end they were inadvertently thrown away. We had some metal shelves downstairs and boxes ... they were put in the boxes downstairs. And when it was cleaned out down there, because we wanted to do some renovations, the boxes were thrown out.'

He says Walter contacted him years later and wanted to retrieve the documents. 'I said, "Oh Walter I've got something awful to tell you ... they've been thrown out",' McLucas recalls. 'And I think he had a sigh of relief over that.'

If the missing documents were as rumoured – evidence implicating a serving National Party MP in a male brothel scandal – then another crisis had been averted. But in a corrupt system as vast as The Joke, and one that had been running for decades, rumour and innuendo appeared and disappeared like phantoms. What was true? What was deliberate skulduggery? Corruption had so saturated the society in which it thrived, that everything was under suspicion.

Tilley Nabbed

Anne Marie Tilley, described as the Fitzgerald Inquiry's 'most wanted woman', had been on the run since the commission had been formed a year earlier. She had once presided over – with de facto partner Hector Hapeta – an empire worth $15 million, their portfolio studded with dozens of properties.

While she was on the run she had given birth to her daughter Rachel. The pair had spent most of their time in Sydney's eastern suburbs. Then Tilley decided it was time to show Hector their little girl. The baby was six weeks old when Tilley risked sneaking back to Brisbane. 'I went to see him, but then he had a mistress, and that got a bit ... he had many, but that was okay too,' recalls Tilley. 'His missus got a bit dirty because I turned up on the doorstep. I went somewhere else to stay, then at another aunty's place. I moved around bit by bit.

'I used to ring Hec up from phone boxes. Everything was bugged – we found one bug in the baby monitor ... I heard his other mistress out in one bedroom, and I've got the baby in another bedroom.

We were in a little house in Holland Park. I'm sitting there and I hear her talking through the monitor. I asked, are you in the baby's room? She said, no. We found the bugs underneath the house – the monitor picked it up.'

Tilley was finally caught at Indooroopilly Shoppingtown, a mall in Brisbane's inner south-west. She says Hapeta's health insurance, in Tilley's name, had run out. So she went into the MBF office at Indooroopilly to rectify the problem. 'My name came up on their computers. Keep her there and ring police,' Tilley recalls. 'These two young coppers walked in with their little walkie-talkies. My brother-in-law was with me and I said, "Run away, run away now."

'The coppers said, "You've got to stay here."

'I said, "I don't think I have to. I don't think you can hold me".'

In the confusion, Tilley broke into a 'fast trot'. She remembers: 'Suddenly they were everywhere, headed by that little skinny fella, one of the guys in the inquiry. He was as happy as Larry. I was on the phone to my solicitor. I said, "Do I have to go with them?"

'He said, "Yep, you're fucked."

'"Tell us the story," they said.

'I thought, who else has given themselves up? They were after Lewis, I think. I said, "I can't actually say anything about Lewis," which I couldn't. I thought, I'm stuffed here.'

Lock, Stock and Barrel

In early July, just weeks away from the inquiry's first anniversary, Tony Fitzgerald announced that public sittings would officially end on 1 December, and that the Queensland government would receive his final report by 27 May 1989. He said the timing would enable the commission to report to the government within two years of its appointment.

The news was probably met with a measure of relief in some quarters. It had been an exhaustive, some might say almost interminable, year that had torn down the picture Queensland had of itself and rendered it in limbo. The inquiry's revelations had been so damaging to certain individuals and institutions that there was no time or space during the process to consider the inevitable big-picture questions that would have to be addressed.

What should be done about a government that, over decades, failed to address the rampant police corruption occurring within its view, an act that over time became recognised by corrupt police as a virtual sanction of illegal activities?

How would the government and the community address a police culture of corruption that had flowed through to the 1980s but still carried all the tenets of a brutish and myopic cabal straight from the 1950s?

How much repair was needed to the infinite arms of government that this behaviour ultimately infected? And what safeguards needed to be enshrined in law to prevent this from happening in the future? Given the vastness of the corruption, was that even reasonably possible?

Fitzgerald said he accepted the commission may have tried to do too much. 'The time has come to ignore much of the information which the commission has received and to draw just some of the threads together in a narrower pattern,' he said. 'The commission did not create the problems and given their nature and size and the aspects of public administration involved, it is scarcely surprising that they are difficult to resolve.'

On the same day that Fitzgerald pondered the future, Premier Mike Ahern boldly declared that the state government would implement the inquiry recommendations 'lock, stock and barrel'.

Ahern says there was constant and vigorous debate within Cabinet about the inquiry and its future. He made a conscious decision to steer a straight course, come what may. 'There was an overwhelming conviction, which I had talked [about] with my wife — I said to her, "I think if I get thrust into this I've just got to see it through. And I think we should [allow] the Commission … to do what [it] feels it should do and live with the consequences."

'I had discussions in Cabinet on that basis. I said if you do that I think the people will probably support you. But the issue then became fine-tuned when it looked as though ministers were going to go to gaol and even Bjelke[-Petersen] was under threat.'

As for Fitzgerald and his family, an officer assigned to guard them during that period says they 'had a very tough time'. 'You could tell he was exhausted … I think he saw the whole thing as his duty, and there were varying expectations of him, not just in Queensland but across Australia. It was all down to him.'

One of Fitzgerald's only outlets for relaxation was playing tennis at home with close friends, journalists Adrian McGregor and Hugh Lunn. 'He enjoyed that because he didn't have any hearings on the Friday. But apart from that, the whole family just suffered.'

A virtual police station was set up in the garage of the Fitzgerald family home. They had to be driven in police vehicles to go shopping. The children were taken to school by police. There were repeated bomb scares where neighbours were ordered to gather out the back of their homes until the threat was cleared. On many occasions local residents had to get to their homes through police barricades.

In a tradition that went back to the 1950s, the Fitzgeralds received threatening midnight phone calls. In addition, Fitzgerald had up to 200 staff working under him. In his work, he enjoyed the thrill of discovery, the thrill of the hunt, but was constantly cognisant that what was being revealed was potentially damaging to other lives. Also, the technology of the day couldn't keep up with the input of material. In the end, the commission staff relied on an old-fashioned, manually drawn 'spaghetti' A-to-B-to-C, diagram, a sort of join-the-dots representation of who knew whom.

There were also threats beyond the physical. Fitzgerald, as he progressed through the evidence, found subterranean forces constantly pushing and pulling at the inquiry. Politicians tried to shift the tide one way, civil libertarians the other – it was a maelstrom of competing forces – the press were in there, as was the Police Union.

Keeping this in mind, Fitzgerald also had to be aware that some evidence could put people's lives and reputations at risk.

'That was, in a sense, the most challenging part about it [the inquiry], that there was a constant awareness that at any given moment there were a number, nearly always more than one, trying to unsettle some part of what you were doing,' a commission source says. 'It was impossible to switch off, just literally impossible to switch off. And they're very bad habits for your mind to get into of course. Because what you do … in that sort of role, what tends to happen is you tend to play the tape over and over to see if you can find the flaw this time that you missed last time. And that was challenging [for everyone within the commission].'

Herbert in Hiding, with a Beach View

Meanwhile, the inquiry's yet to be sighted supergrass, Jack Herbert, was being moved around south-east Queensland and interviewed by commission staff in preparation for his star appearance. Officers tasked with protecting him were on a two weeks on, two weeks off roster. Herbert was kept mainly in units on the Gold Coast, between Burleigh Heads and Main Beach.

One officer charged with guarding Herbert during this time recalls: 'We'd find something with only two units per floor so we could alarm the area. He only ever saw Peggy on Saturdays and Sundays. We'd pick her up and she'd spend the weekend with him. She was staying in New Farm.'

He says while Herbert was in hiding, lawyers for the inquiry gave police questions to ask the supergrass. The aim was to illicit information from Herbert, to build a narrative and get him to trust his security detail. They, however, didn't see it as their job to interrogate Herbert – they were tasked with keeping him and his wife Peggy alive so they could make their appointment before the inquiry. 'We had a list of questions,' the source says. 'We agreed we'd come back and say – we got nothing out of him, he wouldn't say a thing.'

Herbert told biographer Tom Gilling about his time in witness protection. It had its comic moments. 'I had four chaps used to go out with us all the time, two cars,' he said. 'And we'd park and the other car would sit behind so nobody could interfere with that car. And these fellows were gung-ho, they'd do the job. They'd go over little culverts and come to you and they'd get their guns and look underneath the boot … and they'd say to Peggy and me in the back [seat], "Get out, get down, that's how people get murdered over in South America, a motor bike is coming by."'

As had been the case in his civilian life, Herbert loved his daily beer at precisely 5 p.m. 'Clearly he was a manipulator,' Herbert's guarding officer says. 'He was very proud. He used to visit a family over at Burbank. It was a friend, another Englishman. They'd beat their chests and say what self-made men they were. He had impeccable manners. He knew how to present. He said, "No matter how much I have to drink, when I get home I always hang up my pants and my jacket and line up my shoes".'

Herbert fed his captors fantastic stories about his exotic past. 'He reckons he was a quarter master in the RAF and that he stole parachutes to sell to the Italians during World War II,' the officer recalls. 'He told me there was nothing he could add to his evidence to the inquiry about Tony Murphy. He said he gave Murphy 20 pounds a month in the 1960s because he was a mate.'

The objective for the nearly six months he was in witness protection was to keep Herbert 'happy'. While he waited to make his big appearance in front of Fitzgerald, Herbert took photos and developed them himself. 'He also had a typewriter and did a bit of writing. We used to give him a fair bit of time to himself. But Jack would do what it took to look after Jack.

'He used to get upset. He hated Catholics. One of our officers was taken off the job because of it. We were walking on the Southport Spit [on the Gold Coast] when Jack just sat down. He said, "I'm not going any further. I'm not getting into the car. I don't want you near me." This other officer was a Catholic. We told him he was old enough to grow up. [But] that was the officer's last week on the job.'

He says everyone was a little frayed leading up to Herbert's appearance in Courtroom 29, not the least Herbert himself. 'Jack was a weak person, psychologically and physically,' the officer adds. 'I didn't mind old Peg. She struck me as a harmless lady.

'Jack often said to me, "If she wasn't so nice I'd divorce the bitch."'

The Vice Queen

For Anne Marie Tilley, the savvy girl from Sydney who had migrated north to Queensland seeking a life in the sun, and who'd struck gold with an empire of brothels, the dreary machinations of court proceedings were anathema to her.

Her stepfather had once been a driver for the legendary Sydney madam Tilly Devine, and filled her early childhood not with nursery rhymes, but tales of the mean streets of Sydney – the sly grog, the razor gangs, the murders. But court?

Her life, before the establishment of the inquiry and her flight south, had been a nocturnal miasma of booze and drugs and sex. Her day-to-day routine was more about paying off crooked coppers and sometimes playing cat and mouse with them, just for sport. Court bored Tilley witless.

She appeared in Courtroom 29 in late July. The hours in the witness box were, to her, relentless and dull. 'While you're sitting there in the inquiry, you say, "Yeah, alright", to get it over and done with,' she remembers. 'Every frickin day you had to be there. I knew I was going to get prison, so I just agreed with everything.'

To the surprise of many in the court, Tilley said she had been told by a senior Queensland police officer not to worry about the Fitzgerald Inquiry because 'Joh will stop it all'. Bjelke-Petersen repeatedly denied he had threatened to shut down Fitzgerald. Yet, despite her loathing for proceedings, Tilley revealed the dimensions of her and Hector's empire, which began with the Top Hat brothel in Brunswick Street in 1978, and grew to four massage parlours, 14 escort agencies, four sex shops and a nightclub, all within nine years.

In a loan application document from 1986, Hapeta said he had at least 150 girls working for him. Each brought in about $2000 a week. Tilley admitted that she paid Jack 'The Bagman' Herbert about $39,000 a month in protection money. In addition, she gave Harry Burgess $2000 per month. 'He said something like, "You'll have to look after me as well, I'm the man in the field",' Tilley said in evidence.

Although she found the whole proceeding tedious, commentators deemed her testimony a 'major breakthrough' for the inquiry. Tilley told the inquiry that she had seen Jack Herbert when the commission was announced and he had told her it wouldn't last, that it was a 'fly by night' thing. She alleged he told her to keep a low profile and to not answer any questions about the inquiry. 'He knew everything [happening in the police department], he just knew everything,' she said.

As Tilley wound up her evidence, it was revealed that her old flame, Hector Hapeta, who had once had so much cash at his disposal it was difficult to know what to spend it on, had gotten a new job in East Brisbane. He was working at the Mad Pom Shop, a bric-a-brac outlet that he in fact once owned. 'They used to work for me and now I work for them,' Hapeta said of the owners, surrounded by old pots, jumper leads and used squash racquets.

As for Tilley, she told reporters she would return to the skin trade. It was all she knew.

Calling Jack Reginald Herbert

The Bagman woke early on Wednesday 31 August 1988 as people were stirring over on the site of the World Exposition. Expo 88 was Queensland's showcase to the world, defying critics who had claimed through history that the state was a backwater, and that Brisbane, its capital, a mere 'country town'.

Simultaneously, on the north side, in Courtroom 29, Fitzgerald and his staff were steadily peeling back the bark of corruption and exposing the true state of the woodwork. In between the two shows – Expo and Fitzgerald – flowed, as it had done for millennia, the perambulating Brisbane River.

Spectators were also lining up outside the Brisbane District Court, with their cut lunches and tea flasks. That morning, Jack Herbert was taken from his safe house and into a car by his witness protection team. Police checked for bombs before the vehicle left for the city. Herbert was, as ever, impeccably dressed in a white shirt and pale brown suit, which he would describe as 'well cut'. He was transferred to another vehicle, in Kangaroo Point, which proceeded the short distance into the CBD and into the basement of the court building.

Permanently accompanied by bodyguards, Herbert and his flankers were then led by a court officer into a room behind the witness box. At 2.22 p.m., counsel assisting the commission, Gary Crooke, QC, said firmly: 'I call Jack Reginald Herbert.' As expected, the courtroom was packed. Crooke asked Herbert if he had been granted an indemnity. Herbert agreed. 'This is going to be a long road,' Crooke said presciently. 'We are going to start at the beginning.'

While the inquiry had already exposed a roll call of senior police – Harry Burgess, Graeme Parker, Noel Dwyer and Allen Bulger – it was supposed, by osmosis, that Herbert's testimony would provide the central narrative of Queensland's sorry story of police corruption. After all, he had been the architect of The Joke. He had run it like a business. It was hoped Herbert would make sense of this monumental saga of greed.

Looking out at the public gallery, Herbert saw some familiar faces. 'One person I couldn't help noticing that day was Terry Lewis,' Herbert reflected in his memoir *The Bagman*. 'We'd known each other for nearly 30 years and now it had come down to the two of us facing each other in court.

'I wondered what was going through his head. Terry was a man who liked to know everything about everyone,' Herbert recalled. 'Terry Lewis was as guilty as I was and we both knew it. But Terry always thought he was too clever to be caught. That was the difference between us. I knew when the game was up but Terry never did. He didn't realise that once the inquiry was underway it was beyond anyone's power to save him.'

Herbert spoke with clarity and precision, and proved he carried a memory as formidable as his old mates Lewis, Murphy and Hallahan. He said he had paid $40 to $50 a month to suspended commissioner Terry Lewis since the 1960s. Herbert said Lewis was often grateful, and quipped: 'Little fish are sweet'. It was the first direct evidence of corruption levelled at Terry Lewis since the inquiry began.

The Bagman admitted he had been 'deeply involved' in corruption for 29 years. He explained that the money to Lewis was initially for Lewis's friendship with Commissioner Frank Bischof. Lewis was then heading up the Juvenile Aid Bureau.

Continuing with his history lesson, Herbert said he formed a close friendship with Tony Murphy in the late 1950s and they drank together almost daily in the Treasury Hotel, opposite the old CIB headquarters at the corner of Elizabeth and George streets. 'When Murphy came to the Licensing Branch I was approached by Gordon Hooper [a detective at Licensing] who said, "What about giving money to Murphy?"

'Murphy and Lewis were the connection with Frank Bischof who had been paying Hooper to protect a game in South Brisbane. The game was run by Tony Robinson. Gerry Bellino was the lookout. I agreed we should include Murphy.'

Herbert said he had met Murphy in the police canteen on the latter's first day in Licensing and told him there was a 'Joke', or corrupt system, going in the office. He said he had money then and there for Murphy, who said back to him, 'Watch your arm.'

Herbert also alleged that Murphy asked him: "What about including Terry Lewis in The Joke?"

'We had a meeting and agreed that we would pay Lewis [because of his friendship with Bischof],' Herbert said. 'I recall [the] conversation getting around to payments of money with Murphy and Lewis.'

Lewis interjected, declaring in a statement to the inquiry that neither he nor his wife Hazel had been involved in any illegal activities with either Herbert or his wife Peggy.

The evidence of Herbert was electrifying, laying out the history of The Joke and how it worked. How true was it? It didn't seem to matter. As journalist Don Petersen commented: 'This is not just a star witness to endemic crime in high and low places. All avenues of inquiry seem to have led back to the man who took his first bribe as a lowly constable in 1959.'

The next day, Herbert outlined a special 'code' he had with Lewis in relation to the exchange of corrupt money. 'See you at No. 1' meant a meeting at the Crest International bar, down by City Hall and King George Square. No. 2 was the corner of Elizabeth and Albert streets. No. 3 was the bar at the Park Royal, overlooking the Botanic Gardens in Alice Street.

One commentator remarked that Herbert seemed to be enjoying the 'cleansing' he was undergoing in the box. But while it may have been cathartic for The Bagman, he was, at a rapid-fire rate, flushing careers and reputations down the sewer. His second day of evidence also included an allegation that Sydney businessman Jack Rooklyn, involved with the Bally poker machine company in the United States, paid Lewis $25,000 to pen an adverse report on the introduction of poker machines. He also fingered former Transport Minister and former police officer Don Lane, saying he had been involved in corruption since the 1960s.

It was enough, even at such an early stage in Herbert's evidence, for the Ahern government to make a move on Lewis. When Herbert's evidence to the inquiry made front-page news, Sir Terence received two letters at 12 Garfield Drive on 1 September. Both were from the office of Bill Gunn, Deputy Premier, Minister for Public Works, Main Roads and Expo, and Minister for Police.

Dear Sir Terence,

As you are aware, at yesterday's sitting of the Inquiry into Possible Illegal Activities and Associated Misconduct by Police [the Fitzgerald Inquiry], former Detective Sergeant Jack Reginald Herbert gave evidence that you corruptly received from him certain moneys over a period of some time.

In my opinion, this conduct of which he has given evidence constitutes misbehaviour within the meaning of Section 6 of the Police Act 1937–1987.

In the circumstances, the Executive Council, in exercise of the Royal Prerogative and all other powers thereunto enabling, and upon my recommendation has today suspended you, without pay, from the office of Commissioner of Police and as a member of the Queensland Police Force.

The second letter stated:

> I refer to my letter to you of 1 September 1988 ... In the
> circumstances, I now call upon you to show cause to me in writing
> within seven (7) days of the date of this letter why you should not
> be dismissed from the office of Commissioner of Police and as a
> member of the Queensland Police Force.

Naturally, Lewis, through his solicitors Nicol, Robinson & Kidd,
protested the suspension without pay. 'We have instructions that our
client has always discharged his functions as Commissioner of Police
of this State in the full terms of the oath of office,' they retorted.

Gunn wrote Lewis another letter dated 12 September 1988,
informing him that Cabinet had given 'careful consideration' to
his appeal.

> It is the decision of Cabinet that, as presently advised, having regard
> to the contents of your submissions, you not be dismissed but that
> your suspension without pay remain in force.
>
> You will have ample opportunity in the Inquiry to give
> evidence and to explain fully your position with respect to not only
> allegations of corruption which have been made against you but
> also your administration of the Department and the Police Force ...

On the same day Lewis himself then wrote to the Premier, Mike
Ahern, from his new three-storey house in Garfield Drive. In short,
he was seeking permission to seek employment. 'I have very limited
financial resources and I would be very grateful if this request could
receive urgent consideration,' Lewis wrote.

The former commissioner got a reply from the Premier's office on
28 September. It was addressed to Sir Terence Lewis, O.B.E., G.M.,
Q.P.M.

I refer to your letter of 21st September, 1988, seeking approval to your obtaining other employment during the period of your suspension from the position of Commissioner of Police.

Cabinet considered this matter this week and it was decided not to accede to your request at the present time.

Yours faithfully, Mike Ahern

The Money Map

Jack Herbert spent the fourth day of his evidence metaphorically rolling out a huge map of where corrupt money went and to whom. Of Terry Lewis, Herbert said the suspended commissioner received 'thousands of dollars in corruption payments', sourced from prostitution, SP bookmaking, illegal casinos and in-line machines, primarily from around Brisbane and the Gold Coast. He went into detail about his dealings with the Hapeta/Tilley group and the Bellino/Conte syndicate. He admitted that he and Lewis together organised senior police transfers that suited The Joke.

Herbert astonished the court once again when he said, with chilling accuracy, that he had paid Lewis a total of $611,650 in graft over a period of eight years. The supreme organiser, he revealed that The Joke was so well run that corrupt Licensing Branch police who left to work in another area of the department were paid a 'pension' of $1000 a month. Herbert proceeded to list, down to the dollar, all of the graft money he had paid out and to whom over the years.

The outfall from Herbert's damning evidence was swift. Lewis was immediately hit with a $665,000 tax bill courtesy of his old friend's graft allegations.

Lady Lewis, once again, was the one to express her astonishment to the press. She said tax officials had come to Garfield Drive and served them an assessment notice. 'It [the bill] is only because of Mr Herbert's allegations – it has nothing to do with his [Sir Terence's] working period at all,' she said, as the government was still deciding whether it would sack Lewis as commissioner.

Lady Lewis said Sir Terence wasn't expecting the tax bill because 'we've never received that sort of money. We've put in all our denials, as you know.' She added: 'That's all we've got to say at this stage. We've just got to seek advice on it all, goodness me.'

Given that Sir Terence was conducting his own defence at the inquiry, it was inevitable that he would cross swords directly with Herbert at some stage. It happened on 20 September.

Lewis cross-examined his old friend for about half an hour.

Lewis: Mr Herbert, could you try telling the truth for a change?

Herbert: I am telling the truth, sir.

Lewis: That is your view.

Lewis went on to ask Herbert to agree that he was one of the greatest liars to ever take to a witness box in Queensland. Herbert did not agree.

Lewis: Can you nominate anybody who you think would be better or worse?

Herbert: I would say you have done your fair share of it, sir.

Herbert later said that Lewis's new house up on Garfield Drive was in his observation the first real 'extravagance' displayed by his old friend. He assured the court that before the building of the Robin Gibson-designed three-level house, Lewis's previous houses were 'austere'.

Fitzgerald found it difficult to understand Herbert's 'cool' relationship with Lewis after a friendship of so many years, and, if Herbert was to be believed, one that must have involved a large degree of personal interaction. 'How can you have a distant relationship with a man you are paying half a million dollars in graft?' Fitzgerald queried. 'It's hardly a position where you had to be respectful because he was a commissioner or a knight or something?'

Herbert responded: 'I didn't ask him, "Terry, what are you doing with your money?" and he never asked me. I can only tell the truth. I didn't ask what he did with his money.'

In fact, Herbert confided in biographer Tom Gilling that he never had a genuine friendship with Lewis. Indeed, he said he disliked him. 'He's not my sort of man,' Herbert said. 'He didn't seem to have any compassion for anybody. I didn't like him, to be personal, and I thought he was really very foolish inviting us to his home, to parties, getting his driver to pick me up in his car … to take me to functions with him.

'When I got to his house there's all these bloody big-wigs … and I'd been charged, don't forget … [over the] Southport [Betting] matter. Everyone knew I was Jack Herbert and yet I was at a party with non-participants in our job … [Lewis said,] "Oh it will be alright, you'll be right."'

When it came to answering questions about his other old friend, Tony Murphy, Herbert was curiously forgetful and vague. Fitzgerald said there appeared to be 'an attempt to deflect questions away from this era', namely the period when the Rat Pack operated in the late 1950s and through the 1960s and 70s.

Herbert couldn't explain why he had Murphy's details in an address book he took with him when he fled to London.

Herbert said he had hardly seen Murphy since the former detective had moved to Amity Point on North Stradbroke Island at the end of 1982 to grow Geraldton Wax flowers. 'He buried himself on Stradbroke Island for two years after he left the police force,' says Herbert. (He certainly didn't tell the commission that he had visited the island with Murphy in the 1960s when Murphy and Barry Maxwell had purchased land at Amity Point.) Herbert simply said Murphy wasn't aware of his corruption.

Ian Callinan, QC, for the state government, put to Herbert: 'Murphy was an intelligent, astute policeman who well understood the way criminals and the corruption system operated and he knew you were involved in corruption and yet you solemnly tell this commission he didn't ask you about your corruption. He must have known what you were doing. It must have been apparent to anyone with Murphy's sophistication and knowledge that you were on the take again.'

'I can honestly say he never asked me,' Herbert replied.

Herbert had spent 13 days on the stand and given 56 hours of testimony. Fitzgerald was not entirely convinced Herbert had told all he knew. One of Herbert's close friends says he told the inquiry 'just enough'.

'Jack never involved anybody who was a friend, ever, in any of his evidence, books, ever, he never incriminated anyone,' the source says. 'But Murphy had been a really good friend. Murphy's kids were friends with his kids. Tony Murphy and Jack were close friends. In Jack's view, Lewis was a colleague they dealt with and they were wary of.'

As for Lewis, he believes Tony Murphy was never called before the inquiry for a specific reason. Lewis says: 'Herbert was picked up in London, he said whatever he said, they came back here and they had to change a whole heap of it. One would have thought as soon as Herbert landed at the airport they would bring him into the bloody inquiry to give something … [but] they kept him for nearly six months … so he had [time] to get a story right.

'This is all hypothesis, but Herbert had an indemnity to say whatever they wanted him to say. If he'd strayed from that … say they called Murphy in and somewhere along the line he'd made a mistake and they'd asked him what did he do in the Licensing [Branch] for the four years that he was there with Herbert? Didn't he know that Herbert was running The Joke?

'And if he'd said, "Oh, he could have been" or whatever, he could have destroyed Herbert's story, which would have then got me off the hook ... if they called Murphy it might have ruined their inquiry.'

Peggy

From the outside they appeared to be two well-dressed, middle-aged ladies having coffee and a cake together in one of Brisbane's older department stores. McDonnell & East, at 414 George Street, had once been the epicentre of the city's retail trading for much of the twentieth century. In 1965, it opened its award-winning Queensland Room Coffee Lounge.

It was here, in early 1987, that Lady Hazel Lewis allegedly met Peggy Herbert for a catch-up. Peggy told the Fitzgerald Inquiry in evidence on 4 October that at one of these meetings she gave graft money to the suspended commissioner's wife. She had first telephoned Hazel at police headquarters where the Lewis's lived, for a peppercorn rent, in the Police Minister's largely unused apartment. They were set to move into the new house at 12 Garfield Drive in April of 1987.

'How about coffee?' Peggy asked.

'We arranged to meet at McDonnell & East at ten or 11 o'clock,' Peggy told the inquiry. 'Jack had parcelled up the $7000 or $8000, which I put in a plastic bag and placed in my handbag.' She said her husband had told her: 'Give this to Hazel ... make sure you don't lose it.'

The two friends met and took their seats at a table in the coffee lounge. 'She [Lady Lewis] left her handbag on the floor,' Peggy continued. 'While she was away getting the coffee I dropped the packet of money into her handbag. She knew what it was. She knew why we were meeting there. When she came back with the coffee I said, "I put that in there for Terry."'

Peggy insisted that they didn't need to talk about the money. They both knew the intention of the meeting. 'I did have a little look around each time before I did it,' Peggy added. 'Hazel said to me, "Let's not meet here again, I've just seen someone I know."'

Peggy Herbert said the two of them met again for the same purpose at Jo-Jo's restaurant in the Queen Street Mall. She said her husband Jack had gone back into corruption in the 1970s because Lewis was by then Commissioner and he would protect both him and Peggy. She alleged her husband reassured her by saying: 'There's nothing to worry about. Terry's at the top. If anything is going on, he'll hear about it.'

Peggy also said her husband made it clear that when Lewis retired as commissioner the corrupt system would have to end because there would be nobody left to protect them. She went into detail about her family's 20-year relationship with the Lewises. They had socialised in later years and the Lewises had been invited to the wedding of their daughter Ann in 1975. They also went to the Lewis home in Garfield Drive for dinners and social gatherings.

The Herberts were also friendly with Tony Murphy's family, she added. 'Our families were friendly when our children were little,' she explained. 'Tony had a big tent at Tweed Heads and the kids would go down and stay with them. I've known him over 20 years, I suppose. I knew Mrs Murphy quite well and I knew Tony was in The Joke.'

When Lewis cross-examined Peggy, she said she remembered another incident from the late 1970s when she was working for in-line machine operator Tony Robinson Senior in the Brisbane CBD. She said she had passed an envelope full of what she assumed was cash directly to him in Lennons Hotel.

Lewis retorted: 'You have no direct knowledge of my involvement in corruption, do you?'

Peggy said she had delivered the envelope on the instructions of her husband.

Lewis denied the meeting ever took place. He also quizzed her about meeting Lady Lewis.

Lewis:	I suggest you have never given my wife any money.
Herbert:	That's not correct.
Lewis:	I put it to you that you are in fact weaving fact with fiction throughout your evidence to give it a touch of authenticity.
Herbert:	That's not correct.

Hazel Lewis would later recall meeting Peggy Herbert at McDonnell & East in a signed statement. She said the meeting had nothing to do with money. 'Peggy rang me in the unit in police headquarters and told me either over the phone or later at Mac & East that Jack was working on the house at Jordan Terrace and there was so much noise she wanted to go shopping and was I available for a cup of coffee,' Hazel Lewis said.

'I went to Mac & East, had a cup of coffee with Peggy and walked around looking at the store. I doubt we were there together for more than an hour. I don't recall exactly what we talked about but most likely it was about what they were doing to their house and how our new house at Garfield Drive was going.'

As for the Jo-Jo's restaurant meeting, Hazel confirmed she had met Peggy there for a coffee and a bite to eat. It was the last time she saw Peggy Herbert. Hazel Lewis said she next read about Jack and Peggy being overseas in the newspaper.

Hazel denied the allegations that she took money from Peggy. 'I have never put my handbag down and walked away from it, as many years ago I had my purse stolen whilst I was in a cafeteria,' she stated. 'It is always my practice to keep it under my arm or over my shoulder.

'Under no circumstances have I ever had any financial dealings or transactions with either of the Herberts. I have not been party to any arrangements with them or anyone else involving collection or payment of money and have never heard nor participated in any discussion of such a matter.'

From the prostitute and brothel madam Shirley Brifman through to Shirley's own daughter Mary Anne to the prostitutes Katherine James and Anne Marie Tilley, integral to the story of crime and corruption in Queensland were women. They earned the money that the men exploited. And when they wanted to bring down the whole charade, they did that too.

Retrospective Honesty

The Fitzgerald Inquiry had been running for well over a year, and after the early shock and awe of its revelations, enough time had passed for Queenslanders to digest an apparently dark past, and work out their place in it. A blame game had begun, and it was never more finely, and brutally, enunciated than on the floor of parliament in October 1988.

Wayne Goss, member for Logan and the Leader of the Opposition, felt it prudent to stab some forefingers across the parliamentary chamber. '… what one sees is the cancer of corruption across the whole fabric of public administration in this state … yet the present Premier has never once raised his voice or stood up against corruption as it occurred, grew and flourished in this state for years,' Goss accused.

After Ahern rose to a point of order, Goss continued: 'But the question I am asking, which was implicit in the initial statement, is: Where was Mr Ahern when the problems were taking root? I am not referring to all the grand claims that have been made about the Fitzgerald Inquiry once he became Premier and once the Fitzgerald Inquiry was already on foot, having been initiated not by himself … but Mr Gunn.

'There is no such thing as retrospective honesty. The test of honesty, and the test of the Premier, is what he does when he has a choice. The time to do something is when one hears things and sees things and decides to speak up, ask questions, stand for what one believes is right and honest – when there is a choice.'

Goss said the Opposition believed that Ahern could not avoid blame for the corruption identified by the inquiry. He said Ahern was the only National Party representative who had served through the full 19 years of the Bjelke-Petersen premiership. 'In all that time, is there evidence of Mike Ahern ever raising his voice against corruption in public, in the party room, in parliament or in Cabinet? No!' said Goss. 'Not once when this Premier had a choice did he ever speak out or stand up. There is not a single shred of evidence that he ever raised his voice, much less that he ever did anything about what was going on. The public record shows that Mr Ahern sat as a backbencher and later as a minister, blindfolded, gagged and with corks in both ears.'

Goss accused Ahern of using the Fitzgerald Inquiry for political purposes. 'Mr Ahern claims falsely that his government set up the Fitzgerald Inquiry. He is using Mr Fitzgerald for political purposes to hide the culpability of himself and other members of Cabinet for allowing that corruption to occur and to grow.'

Ahern had done his best following the ousting of Bjelke-Petersen. But the community, and the politicians who represented them, were now at pains to understand a systemic deception so huge that it might take years to unravel, let alone understand.

Cracking the Code

Suspended commissioner Sir Terence Lewis was recalled to the witness box of Courtroom 29 in mid-October, well over a year after his turn as the inquiry's first witness, and this time he hit some substantial turbulence.

Fitzgerald had begun his inquiry in a pedantically systematic way. He allowed Lewis to explain almost interminably the history of the Queensland Police Force and how it functioned. It was a deliberate ploy to establish context, with the view to exposing cracks inherent in the system itself. In this way, quietly, the inquiry moved from establishing sufficient evidence, to acknowledging there was a problem, to being able to offer solutions. As Patsy Wolfe oversaw proceedings as deputy, Fitzgerald started preparing his systemic responses.

By the time Lewis returned to the box, patience was wearing thin. He attempted to explain the now famous 'codes' that he had used to communicate with Jack Herbert. He simply explained that Herbert had been his informant.

It was news to the inquiry. Why hadn't he explained this before? It flew in the face of an earlier statement lodged by Lewis, in which he claimed he had little of consequence to ever discuss with Herbert.

Fitzgerald: Why didn't you disclose that you discussed illegal-
              ities with him?
Lewis: Obviously I've left a little bit out there.
Fitzgerald: Herbert's association with you is of the most vital
              and utmost importance to this inquiry.
Lewis: He's not the top of the list of the names given to me
              by Mr Crooke.

Two of Lewis's little pocketbooks, for 1980 and 1981, were tendered to the inquiry. In those pocketbooks were code systems using numbers to identify people and places. Lewis said as an informant, Herbert gave him information which he then passed on to 'whoever [police officers] was working in that area'. He said the information covered SP bookmaking and illegal gaming.

'Why did you need a code?' Fitzgerald asked.

'It seemed the way to go,' Lewis replied.

The first three codes in the lists were locations: A and E for the corner of Albert and Elizabeth streets in the city; P.R. for Park Royal Hotel; and C for the Crest Hotel. Lewis agreed with Fitzgerald that 'Your H.' And 'My H.' referred to his home at Garfield Drive and the other participant in the code. Other entries in the code included 'Toowoomba', 'Kingaroy', 'Jack R.', 'Tony R.' and 'Syd'.

Doug Drummond, QC, put it to Lewis that his explanation for the codes was 'simply untrue' and that he was clutching at straws.

Lewis denied the assertion.

Drummond: The first ever suggestion that Herbert has this new role of informant to you comes this afternoon after you had had that list that you wrote out in your own hand in 1980 and again in 1981 put before you for some hours.

Lewis: Yes.

Drummond: And you have been trying to think of some possible innocent explanation for why you would have a code like that for communicating about the matters listed on it with Herbert. Is that right?

Lewis: I looked for the explanation. I never – I had forgotten all about this matter and to try and bring it back to mind was not particularly easy.

Drummond: You had forgotten Herbert was your informant?

Lewis: No, no. I had forgotten about this code.

Lewis was later quizzed about the urgent transfer of half his ownership of the house up on Garfield Drive to his wife Hazel. It was put to him that he made the move with the knowledge that Graeme Parker had rolled over and he might lose the house if, in the end, he was declared bankrupt.

No. Lewis feared he might die. He said he had a sore neck. He felt it best to have the house just in the name of his wife, Lady Lewis.

'Oh, come on, Sir Terence,' said an exasperated Drummond. 'Are you really suggesting that a neck problem necessitated all that urgency?'

Lewis added that he had a sore shoulder and chest, too.

Journalist Don Petersen assessed Lewis's performance in the witness stand. The story was headlined: A FORGETTABLE DAY. 'Never has an Australian police chief been subjected to such a well-documented examination of his affairs,' Petersen wrote. 'And it is doubtful if one ever existed who could remember so little about those affairs.'

As Lewis continued to be dissected before the Fitzgerald Inquiry, the former Queensland policeman and children's television star, Dave Moore, was serving time at Numinbah prison farm at the back of the Gold Coast. Moore, 33, was serving two and a half years in gaol following his re-trial in June 1987 over sex offences against a boy.

In late 1984, Moore had been the trigger for one of the biggest scandals in Lewis's commissionership. Inquiry investigators had already been out to Numinbah Correctional Centre and questioned him. Lewis was once again asked why he had done nothing about Moore, who senior police had known was engaging in questionable behaviour as early as 1982. Lewis was accused of attempting to 'cover up' the scandal.

Former police minister Bill Glasson said in a statutory declaration to the commission that he grew to mistrust Lewis and his staff after being fed information on Moore at the time that was 'untrue'. 'I recall the commissioner scoffed at the idea that senior constable Moore was involved with [ABC radio announcer Bill] Hurrey,' said Glasson. (On 5 July 1986 Hurrey was found guilty of numerous charges, including permitting sodomy on himself and of indecent dealing with boys under 17 years of age, and sentenced to five years in prison. He was released having served less than half of his sentence.)

Doug 'Bulldog' Drummond had another go at Lewis at the inquiry. Drummond said Glasson had written to Lewis in November 1984 asking him why Moore had not been transferred after revelations about his sex life had emerged.

Lewis blamed Opposition Police Spokesman Wayne Goss for peddling misinformation. Lewis said there was no truth to the allegations against Moore.

Drummond: I would suggest your answers are quite untrue.

Lewis: They would not have been as far as I was aware at the time. There is no way in the world I would go and try and tell Mr Glasson a heap of rubbish about a thing like this.

Drummond: Isn't that just what you were doing?

Lewis: No, it is not.

Drummond: Weren't you trying to cover up the whole matter as best you could?

Lewis: Absolutely not. Why would I bother covering up for a senior constable?

Drummond: Because there had been complaints afoot about this man who you kept in a high-profile position for many years.

Drummond suggested that Moore meant a whole lot more to Lewis than 'just an anonymous face in the 5000 in the police force'.

Lewis said Moore did have more access to him as Commissioner than many other young police officers. He said he had visited the Channel Seven television station on Mount Coot-tha to watch Moore at work. How could Lewis not recall complaints about Moore?

'I certainly would not have allowed him to roam around free if there was any possibility that he got involved with offences with children,' Lewis said.

As a witness before the inquiry, Terry Lewis refused to crack. Despite some fierce cross-examination, the suspended commissioner didn't give an inch, and it frustrated Tony Fitzgerald, the barristers and the public gallery. It also jabbed at journalists observing the inquiry.

It had seemed that the entire sordid tale of the Rat Pack and bagman Jack Herbert had been thrust, at last, into sunlight. And still Lewis kept his nerve and contributed little, if anything, to the grand narrative. They may have pursued Lewis and Herbert with vigour, but had they missed the man who cast the biggest shadow over three decades of police corruption – Tony Murphy?

Journalist Quentin Dempster reflected the mood of the public in an acerbic column after Lewis's second stint as witness. For all the inquiry's triumphs – and some would prove to be epochal – had the big fish got away?

'Tony Murphy ...' Dempster wrote in early November, just a few weeks before Fitzgerald's proposed deadline for official witnesses to appear before the inquiry. 'His name appears like a drum beat through the thousands of pages of transcript of the Fitzgerald Inquiry. In almost every phase of Queensland police history over the past 35 years, the name of Anthony Murphy is there like a mysterious presence.

'By all accounts Murphy was a police mastermind, who knew everything and everybody on his patch. The mention of his name seems to have struck fear into the hearts of petty and big time criminals. The word around the corridors of the Fitzgerald Inquiry is that although evidence adverse to Murphy has been given it remains doubtful that his role in events over the past 35 years will ever be fully known.'

The 30-Year Shot

In late October, a forgotten face in the great panorama of Queensland police history and corruption popped up in a story in the *Sunday Mail*.

It was Gunther Bahnemann, the one-time 'crazed gunman' who had wreaked havoc in the Brisbane bayside suburb of Lota in 1959 and attempted to kill Detective Glen Patrick Hallahan, before being subdued and handcuffed by Hallahan and his partner Terry Lewis. While both police officers would receive the force's highest honour – the George Medal for bravery – Bahnemann had been charged with the attempted murder of Hallahan and imprisoned in Boggo Road Gaol.

For years, Bahnemann received a Christmas card from Lewis, even when he became Police Commissioner. And Bahnemann wasn't averse to writing to Lewis from his home in Far North Queensland, seeking help and advice on his fluctuating financial fortunes through the 1970s and into the 1980s. The *Sunday Mail* revealed that Bahnemann received his last Yuletide card from Lewis at the end of 1986.

It also portrayed a very angry Gunther Bahnemann who was determined to set the record straight. 'I hope to see the day they strip him [Lewis] and Hallahan and the others of their medals,' he said.

Bahnemann was adamant they did not deserve the honours. 'I won my medals in the war,' he said, referring to the Iron Cross First Class and Iron Cross Second Class he was awarded when he fought for the German army in World War II. 'They gave Hallahan and Lewis civilian versions of the Victoria Cross – for what? What was I supposed to be – a bloody Tiger tank?'

Bahnemann stressed that 'the police version of their heroics was false', and that he had been verballed. He said in prison he learned that former police commissioner Frank Bischof had a stake in brothels.

Referring to the incident with Lewis and Hallahan that resulted in his arrest he said: 'I was in Belgium and France, Poland, Norway, Holland and Luxembourg and when we cleaned up Europe we fought in Africa. If I wanted to kill anyone, in that small room, I couldn't have missed,' he said.

Bahnemann recalled that Lewis visited him in prison not long after he had published his first novel, *Hoodlum* – a story about bodgies running amok on the streets of Brisbane. 'One day in gaol, Terry Lewis came to visit me,' he said. 'I asked him why, and he said it was a social visit. I found that astonishing. This was after my book was such a success. I think even then he was worried about the pen being sharper than the sword.'

Bahnemann said, in light of the Fitzgerald Inquiry revelations, he was seeking ways to have his conviction quashed.

It never happened.

The Joh Show

With Expo 88 having left town, and with many Queenslanders actually suffering from depression since the world exposition evaporated, the appearance of former premier Sir Joh Bjelke-Petersen as a witness before the Fitzgerald Inquiry would perhaps provide the perfect salve.

It was, in the end, more a curious cameo appearance, but it did come with its fair share of interesting statistics. Joh entered the witness box on 1 December, precisely one year since he'd been dumped as premier by his beloved National Party. The day had also been deemed by Fitzgerald as the last for witness evidence, though it was clear 'The Citizen Joh Show', as the *Courier-Mail* dubbed it, would blow out that deadline.

Just as Terry Lewis was the first witness, Sir Joh would be one of the very last. It was fascinating how the fates of these two men were so entwined over decades. Lewis, for example, was in training as a police cadet up in the old red-brick police depot on Petrie Terrace in late 1948 when a young peanut farmer called Johannes Bjelke-Petersen from Kingaroy was first elected to the Queensland parliament. Both men had married within weeks of each other in the early 1950s. Both had risen to the top of their professions, and indeed Lewis had indicated to Bjelke-Petersen over the years that he would serve as Commissioner of Police until the Premier retired, when he too would leave the force and enjoy the spoils of a long and successful career. And, as it turned out, Lewis was stood aside as commissioner during the early months of the inquiry, while Bjelke-Petersen was ousted just months later. Their lives had been tethered to each other for almost 40 years.

As for Joh, he arrived in Courtroom 29 looking fit and tanned, and was flanked by a large group of bodyguards, possibly more than those who watched the back of supergrass Jack Herbert. Straight off the bat, Bjelke-Petersen said he had had suspicions there was corruption in the police force, but he never had any actual evidence.

Allegations of corruption, he told the inquiry, were the responsibility of his police ministers. They then relied on the police commissioner. For 11 years, that commissioner was Sir Terence Lewis. The former premier said he always believed Lewis and thought the police chief wouldn't dare lie to his ministers. 'If you're not prepared to take the word of your top officials, who do you go to?'

Doug Drummond, QC, asked Bjelke-Petersen about the notorious *Nationwide* television program in March 1982, when whistleblowers and former police officers Kingsley Fancourt and Bob Campbell risked their lives and alleged corruption at the highest levels of the Queensland Police Force. He reminded Joh of then Police Minister Russ Hinze's attack on Fancourt and Campbell, and his rejection of their allegations. Drummond said in view of history, the allegations now appeared 'not too far astray'.

Bjelke-Petersen politely replied: 'You place your faith and confidence in your top men [Lewis] and that is why [Hinze] came out strongly against the two men.

'You get into a very confused position if a minister's top officers are not to be believed. [Hinze] would not have thought that Lewis himself might have been involved. He would be above suspicion from the minister's point of view.'

The *Courier-Mail* noted that Bjelke-Petersen, in person before the inquiry, had lost his aura of invincibility. 'Whether by design or genuine confession, Sir Joh Bjelke-Petersen emerged towards day's end as a bit of a mushroom man, allegedly kept in a lofty but dark place and fed a diet of departmental or ministerial droppings,' it wrote. 'It did not quite square with his strong-man image, or with his conceded close links with individual members of what came almost to be in years gone by a private army.'

Quentin Dempster took a different view. 'That ruthless, pig-headed, vicious side of his character was on display and the lawyers, with conspicuous courtesy, led him into areas where he got both feet and both hands on the sticky paper,' said Dempster.

One usually hard-bitten southern journalist remarked, incredulously: 'And you've been living with this for 20 years?'

In further evidence, Sir Joh said anonymous donors regularly left large sums of money in his office when he was premier, but he said he never got involved in identifying the sources of the money. He said he couldn't explain one donation of $110,000 in cash. The money was donated to a company called Kaldeal Pty Ltd, which funded National Party candidates chosen by Bjelke-Petersen. In 1986, another $100,000 donation was handed to his secretary by a Singapore businessman.

Commissioner Tony Fitzgerald was confused.

Fiztgerald: What do you say, Sir Joh – that one of your secretaries would come in and say, 'We've just had somebody drop by and leave $50,000 cash but we don't know who it is?'

Bjelke-Petersen: Sir, honestly, you don't talk like that, really. Nobody comes in and says, 'I've got $50,000 ...' I have nothing to do with the funds. I do not collect it. I do not sit at the door waiting for people to come in.

Fiztgerald: Obviously you didn't have to.

In other evidence, Doug Drummond, QC, revealed that Citra Constructions Ltd donated $250,000 to the National Party and soon after was awarded a $2.5 million contract to build the Bundaberg Maternity Hospital. It was also granted rail electrification scheme government contracts worth $59 million.

This was the Queensland way of doing business. The former premier, however, saw little that was wrong with this model. He had not proven to be an explosive witness. Quite the contrary. He was just an old man who had always possessed a peculiar understanding of the Westminster system.

Bob Mulholland, for the Australian Broadcasting Corporation, asked if he accepted any responsibility for the level of corruption that had clearly thrived under his leadership. The former premier simply said, no.

One of the more hair-raising exchanges during the commission of inquiry was between barrister Michael Forde and Sir Joh Bjelke-Petersen. The former premier was asked whether he understood the concept of the separation of powers – the fact that in a democracy the various arms of government (legislative, executive, judicial) must be separate.

Forde began: 'On many occasions you expressed your support for the democratic processes of the Westminster system of government?'

'Sure,' Joh said.

'In fact,' Forde went on, 'when you received your knighthood, the report on you said that you had a strong belief in the concept of parliamentary democracy. Would that be correct?'

'Yes, the free enterprise system that we have inherited.'

'… in your understanding of the Westminster system, what to you are the most important aspects of it?' asked Forde.

'The right to – well, we know, say and do what we want to do within the law; the freedoms that we have enjoyed in every other respect; faith and beliefs and so on; and the election of government along the system that the Westminster system of course outlines,' Joh said.

'... you see, when I asked you about what you understood by the concept of the Westminster system, your view of it was very limited, I'd suggest?'

'No, it is not very limited,' Bjelke-Petersen fired back. 'I have had 41 years' involvement in the whole system and I was there for ten years in the Opposition. I am probably the only member of parliament who is still alive who has had ten years there at any time in the Opposition.'

'... can you distinguish between, say, the head of the Health Department and the Commissioner of Police as the head of the department under the Westminster system?'

'I can tell you the difference. There's a very big difference as far as actual work is concerned; responsibility is concerned. The health one is a very important one, but it's not one in which you have to maintain the law and order in a time and period of our history when there's a very strong attitude towards lawlessness, and the Police Commissioner has a very, very difficult role and an important one.'

Forde continued: 'This is probably the most important question I will ask you, so be very careful in listening to this.'

'I am careful all the time.'

'What do you understand by the doctrine of separation of powers under the Westminster system?'

'The Westminster system? The stock?'

'The doctrine of the separation of powers under the Westminster system.'

'No, I don't quite know what you're driving at. The document?'

'No, I'll say it again,' said Forde. 'What do you understand by the doctrine of the separation of powers under the Westminster system?'

'I don't know which doctrine you refer to,' Joh replied.

'There's only one doctrine of the separation of powers.'

'I believe in it very strongly, and despite what you may say, I believe that we do have a great responsibility to the people who elect us to government. And that's to maintain their freedom and their rights, and I did that – sought to do it – always.'

'I'm sure you're trying to be responsive to the question, but the question related to the doctrine of the separation of powers or the principles ...' said an exasperated Forde.

'Between the government and the – is it?'

'No, you tell me what you understand.'

'Well, the separation of the doctrine that you refer to, in relation to where the government stands, and the rest of the community stands, or where the rest of the instruments of government stand. Is that what – ?'

'No.'

'Well, you tell me,' Joh said, laughing. 'And I'll tell you whether you're right or not. Don't you know?'

'See, when you received your knighthood, one of the matters that was suggested in the preamble to why you got your knighthood was that you were a strong believer in historic traditions of parliamentary democracy, that you had implemented many improvements in the parliamentary process, and you had rendered extraordinary and important service to the Crown, etcetera. Now, for many years the Westminster system has functioned, and you repeatedly have said that you are a great believer in the Westminster system?'

'Yes.'

'The question is this: Do you have any comprehension at all of the three areas under the Westminster system which must be kept separate in order for parliamentary democracy to function?'

'Yes, I do.'

'Well, what are they?'

'Well, I think, the system of election; the system; the area of government itself, responsibility to the people ...'

Forde says he was given no brief prior to cross-examining Bjelke-Petersen. He was simply told to do his best. He says he was stunned at Bjelke-Petersen's ignorance of the doctrine. 'I was interested in the political system and the democratic process. Absolute power corrupts and that's what was going on in Queensland,' Forde says. 'I was more concerned with Joh's interference with the law enforcement side of things and with the judicial side. If you get your knighthood based upon your understanding and respect for the democratic process in the Westminster system, then it proves that he was a fraud, and knighthoods were often given on fraudulent grounds, particularly under his regime.'

He said Bjelke-Petersen's lack of understanding of even the basic tenets of the doctrine was breathtaking. 'I was completely surprised. The reaction was laughter,' he says. 'They had rooms with speakers so people not in the courtroom could hear testimony at the inquiry. There was this raucous laughter. I'm told people fell off their seats.'

Fitzgerald formally closed his hearings on 9 December and addressed the court. 'We have arrived at what is hopefully the conclusion of the public evidence at this inquiry, in what is, fortuitously, a season of festivity and goodwill,' he stated.

He said there were 'very real risks' associated with 'the period which is about to ensue, both leading up to the presentation of the commission's report and the time needed thereafter for its implementation'.

'An even greater risk is that the interval will be filled with attempts by those who fear or resent reform to reassert control, including propaganda aimed at diminishing support for what has occurred and whatever changes are proposed,' Fitzgerald added.

He adjourned the commission until 10.15 a.m. on Tuesday 7 February 1989. That night, Fitzgerald, Gary Crooke and another lawyer and their wives went out for a celebratory dinner at a restaurant in Brunswick Street, New Farm. One of Fitzgerald's security detail asked if they needed to be watched.

'They decided they'd be alright,' he remembers. 'That they didn't need protection on that night. I thought it was silly after they'd had that protection for all that time. Anyway, I spotted an Asian guy who was associated with the Bellinos. I was parked near the Village Twin cinemas. I noticed this Asian bloke. He stood outside the restaurant looking at them. He spent about ten minutes outside.

'I told them later, and I think they thought I was being dramatic.'

The Opera

In the wake of the conclusion of hearings before the Fitzgerald Inquiry, the afterburn that followed in the vacuum between the end of evidence and the publication of the commissioner's report and the enactment of his implementations was, as Fitzgerald had partly predicted, tumultuous.

In late December former Rat Pack stalwart Glen Hallahan was reinstated as a chief investigator at the state government's insurance arm, Suncorp, following his suspension after allegations made against him at the Fitzgerald Inquiry. Suncorp said Hallahan had been reappointed after independent investigations proved that the allegations against him had 'no basis'. Suncorp prized Hallahan's work and needed him back.

Premier Mike Ahern however, had other ideas. He responded angrily, telling Suncorp the decision to re-employ Hallahan was unacceptable and had to be overturned immediately. Suncorp chief executive Bernard Rowley could not wait until the Fitzgerald report was handed down in June the following year to get Hallahan back on the books. Ahern was livid. 'I have spoken to Mr Rowley and told him that the appointment is absolutely, totally, completely not on.'

Meanwhile, it was reported that Lady Hazel Lewis, wife of the suspended police commissioner, was on unemployment benefits and looking for a job. She applied regularly at the Woolworths supermarket just down the hill on Latrobe Terrace in Paddington.

Former transport minister Don 'Shady' Lane also resigned from politics. Having admitted before Fitzgerald he had misused his ministerial expenses and mis-stated expenses in his tax returns, he said in his letter of resignation that the campaign of vilification against him was so overwhelming it had become too stressful on his family.

A *Courier-Mail* editorial bid Lane farewell: 'No longer a member of the National Party, no longer an impost on the public purse, no longer subject to calls for him to do the right thing and go. It has been a long goodbye.'

Lane had joined the Queensland police in 1951, and on his way through the ranks he befriended the likes of Terry Lewis, Glen Hallahan and Jack Herbert. He was one of 89 police represented before the National Hotel inquiry in 1963, and joined the Special Branch in 1967. In June 1971 Lane became a Liberal MP, winning the inner-city seat of Merthyr, before controversially joining the National Party in 1983. He was the long-time Minister for Transport.

As Herbert attested, Lane was The Joke's direct link to Cabinet. After Graeme Parker's evidence before Fitzgerald in late 1987, Lane was stood down as minister. He appeared before the commission of inquiry the following year, and denied he received any corrupt monies. (Ultimately, he was charged with misappropriating funds and gaoled.)

On a lighter note, former Licensing Branch officer Nigel Powell, who had done much to ignite the inquiry in the first place, and journalist Margaret Simons, who the commission had employed to help write the actual Fitzgerald Report, penned a comedic work, both for their own amusement and, one would think, as a pressure release.

It was titled *Fitzgerald Inquiry – The Opera*. It starred the 'Four Little Rats' – characters called Murphy, Hallahan, Lane and Lewis, as well as Buttons, the Minister for Police, Mother Russ, Father Joh and a man called Fitzgerald. Act one, scene one, featured the 'rats'.

Four little rats from school are we,
Fresh we come from the academy,
Filled to the brim with alcohol free,
Four little rats from school.

Everything is a source of fun,
Nobody's safe for we care for none,
Life is a rort that's just begun,
Four little rats from school.

It ended with the entire cast on stage, singing 'We all live in Courtroom 29', to the tune of the Beatles' 'Yellow Submarine'.

Homilies

The General Instruction of the Roman Missal – the document that guides the celebration of the Catholic Mass – gives several definitions of the 'homily' and how it applies to the priest and the congregation. It states: 'The Homily is part of the liturgy and is strongly recommended, for it is necessary for the nurturing of the Christian life. It should be an exposition of some aspect of the readings from Sacred Scripture or another text ... and should take into account both the mystery being celebrated and the particular needs of the listeners.'

During the inquiry hearings, chairman Tony Fitzgerald occasionally opened proceedings with comments or statements of explanation in relation to the hearings. They were dubbed 'the homilies' by the media. They appeared in the first few months of the inquiry and popped up throughout the extent of public hearings.

The Fitzgerald homilies were wide-ranging, sometimes clarifying the commission's stance on various points of law, through to chastising the media for inaccurate reporting. Others were warnings against attempts to derail the inquiry through gossip and criticism aimed at deliberately publicly devaluing the work and importance of the commission. In September 1987, chairman Fitzgerald had some words of observation about the culture of the police 'brotherhood'.

'It is impossible to concede how an honest policeman could rationally believe the acceptance of a situation that involves corruption by any of his colleagues benefits either himself or his force or is justified by his shared interest and burdens with any who are corrupt merely because like him they are policemen,' said Fitzgerald. 'If honest police officers believe these fictions it is because they are the victims of the propaganda and deceptions of those who benefit by them.'

He corrected the record when it came to public rumours that the inquiry was being deliberately strung out to line the pockets of the lawyers involved. 'It is necessary to try and understand the enormous amount of work involved, the volume of papers to be assembled and sifted, the investigations to be pursued, the checks to be made, and the physical effort needed in converting information into proofs of evidence, all of which are being attempted at the same time as the public sittings are continuing virtually non-stop,' proclaimed Fitzgerald.

'The gossip columnists have already started, and no doubt if there is insufficient scandal otherwise, others will join in, with the innuendo that the inquiry is being prolonged for the benefit of the lawyers, including perhaps especially myself.'

In June 1988, when the inquiry received further media criticism, Fitzgerald cut loose. 'This inquiry is not a competition between a bunch of lovable rogues and a group of narrow-minded prudes intent on imposing puritanical moral strictures upon a reluctant public,' he thundered. 'The commission personnel, including the decent police officers who have risked their careers and the scorn of colleagues, are just ordinary, somewhat tired Queenslanders who temporarily represent the society of which they form a part.

'The demi-monde with which the inquiry is concerned is not a jolly place peopled by happy-go-lucky fun lovers sampling the pleasures provided for them by generous benefactors. It is a world of greed, violence, corruption and exploitation, where the weak and immature are preyed upon even to the extent of the indescribable evil of the peddling of addictive drugs by which youthful lives are destroyed.

'The connection between so-called victimless offences and organised crime is well recognised …'

The homilies were feared by some and relished by others. In the end, they provided a unique insight into the thinking of the commission of inquiry as it marched towards Tony Fitzgerald's final report.

The Hitman

In January 1989, Fitzgerald Inquiry investigators brought in a no-nonsense fraud specialist to probe the finances of Sir Joh Bjelke-Petersen following the evidence the former premier had given the year before. John Huey had had a problematic relationship with the Lewis administration. Considered a straight-shooter and a superlative investigator, Huey had been an acolyte of former commissioner Ray Whitrod. Through the late 1970s, with Whitrod gone, Lewis grew increasingly suspicious of Huey. He suspected Huey was one of the famous Committee of Eight – honest officers who were trying to remove Lewis and his team.

In 1984 Huey further earned the ire of his boss when he investigated claims that police were involved in cattle duffing around Charters Towers in North Queensland. The inquiry was triggered by a complaint from then Detective Constable Gordon Hurrell, who believed a senior sergeant and a retired superintendent had repeatedly breached the Stock Act. Hurrell was subsequently ordered to transfer to Brisbane.

Huey, then based in Townsville, went about his investigation and believed he had enough evidence to lay 20 charges against the two men allegedly involved in the cattle duffing. Opposition Police Spokesman Wayne Goss tabled Huey's report in state parliament. When the matter was referred to the Police Complaints Tribunal, presided over by Justice Eric Pratt, the Opposition questioned why Commissioner Lewis had stopped the investigation and ordered that no charges be proffered. Instead, the tribunal investigation had come down against Huey. It recommended that disciplinary charges be laid against him for supposedly failing to adequately supervise Hurrell's role in the investigation, and for perpetrating 'fallacious rumours'. He was demoted from Inspector Grade 2 to Inspector Grade 3.

'He's the only officer I ever demoted,' recalls Lewis. 'I should have sacked the bastard … I was too kind. He went up north and caused a lot of chaos. He refused to do this and do that. But I should have sacked him because naturally he hated me intensely from there on.'

When the Fitzgerald Inquiry started, Huey was serving in Rockhampton while his wife Hilary, also an outstanding detective, remained at their home in Brisbane and worked out of the Fraud Squad. Huey remembered getting a call from Deputy Commissioner Ron Redmond when Terry Lewis was stood down as commissioner. 'He said he would bring me straight back to Brisbane as he didn't agree that Hilary and I had been split up,' Huey later recalled. 'He said he wanted me back in charge of the Fraud Squad.'

Huey made headway in cleaning up the 'mess' the squad had become, then out of the blue got a curious phone call. 'Suddenly one Friday afternoon I got a message to report to Mr Robert Needham, QC at the Fitzgerald Inquiry straightaway,' said Huey. 'I walked down North Quay in the rain to the Fitzgerald Inquiry office and met Mr Needham. He told me the inquiry was concerned about corrupt involvement of police in stolen car rackets and that I was to form and head a task force of initially six detectives to investigate it.'

Huey got to work, and ultimately uncovered a multi-million-dollar operation. His task force recovered more than 250 vehicles, including government and council cars. More than 81 people, 14 of them police officers, were charged for their corrupt involvement.

It was a major success for Huey, and it clearly impressed the Fitzgerald Inquiry staff. He was again called in to meet with Needham and Bob Mulholland, QC, and was asked to look into the former premier's finances. Huey and his partner, Brian Hay, first jetted to Sydney to interview a business partner of Sir Joh's – they had been involved in mining kaolin clay near Kingaroy – and to view the company books.

'Later the books were produced and as far as I knew there was nothing of interest in them,' said Huey. 'But it was obvious that Sir Joh knew we were investigating him. Soon after I became aware that a former police prosecutor named Bob Butler had been employed by Sir Joh at a reported $1000 per week to dig up everything they could find on me – obviously to use against the investigation and me.'

Nevertheless, Huey continued with his investigation. He was soon on his way to Singapore. This time, he needed to interview businessman Robert Sng, managing director of the company Historic Holdings, who had controversially been awarded the tender to construct a hotel precinct in the Brisbane CBD after handing over $100,000 during the period when the development decision was being considered by the government. Indeed, Sng had been developing properties in Queensland for a number of years, having also constructed a canal estate at Raby Bay in Cleveland.

A week before Sir Joh's historic resignation the Premier had phoned Sng seeking future employment. Shortly after being dismissed from the Party, it was Sng who accompanied the former premier on a week's rest and recreation in Hong Kong.

In Singapore, Sng agreed to talk to Huey. 'He was quite open in his admissions,' Huey later recalled. 'After submitting his tender [for the hotel precinct] he had been approached by a woman named Ann Garms who conducted a theatre restaurant in Brisbane. She told him that if he wanted to win the tender, he would have to give Sir Joh $200,000 cash. Sng didn't have this amount of ready cash, so he contacted another Singapore Chinese … this chap flew to Brisbane with the cash.

'They booked a room in the tower block of the Sheraton Hotel where they counted out … $100,000 on the bed.'

Huey said they then wrapped the cash in brown paper and proceeded to the Executive Building on George Street. It was 17 September 1986. It was later reported that Garms was interested in promoting education within the hospitality industry. There had been ovations that Sng might have been able to assist in conjunction with a TAFE college.

'Ann Garms joined them and they were ushered into Sir Joh's office,' Huey continued. 'They handed the parcel to Sir Joh. I asked Mr Sng what Sir Joh said when he received the brown paper parcel and Sng said, "All he said was, thank you, thank you, thank you." They left.'

According to Huey, Bjelke-Petersen gave an oral submission in parliament about the building tender the next day and the contract was granted to Sng's company.

'Back in Brisbane we interviewed Mrs Ann Garms in the presence of her barrister … [and she] from memory admitted what had happened,' said Huey. 'All that remained was to prepare the brief of evidence to charge Sir Joh with perjury and official corruption.'

Bjelke-Petersen had in fact told the Fitzgerald Inquiry earlier that he had never received the cash in person, but that it was handed to a secretary. Both his private secretaries denied they were present.

Huey, the Hitman, had done his job and returned to normal duties, but his role in trying to bring down the National Party's spiritual father would not be so readily forgotten. A massive anti-Huey media campaign haunted him, playing out in the press and on television news. Sir Joh labelled Huey a 'Labor hitman' out to get him. The pressure of this intense media exposure took its toll on the honest Huey, and in the end he resigned from the force. The Joh job was his last as a police officer.

Scoop

For decades the members of the so-called Rat Pack – Lewis, Murphy and Hallahan – had their contacts within the Fourth Estate. Brisbane in the 1950s and 60s was a small town for newspaper reporters, particularly police roundsmen. You either got on with the police and they fed you stories, or you challenged the status quo and were shut out.

Murphy and Hallahan were particularly good at calling in favours with reporters they knew and planting stories that either patted the Queensland Police Force on the back, distorted the truth, or provided a timely, diversionary smoke-screen when the heat was on.

In February 1989, the *Courier-Mail* began publishing an extended exclusive interview with suspended police commissioner Sir Terence Lewis.

It was curious timing.

Firstly, the government was still in limbo about what to do with Lewis. Should he be sacked and his superannuation of about $1 million be denied him? Or should he be allowed to resign and take the money? Fitzgerald's hearings had ended, and some of the inquiry's legal eagles were engaged in looking at what charges would be laid against whom. Doug Drummond was looking carefully and closely at what charges could be laid at Lewis's feet. And it was still five months until the release of Fitzgerald's final report.

Might a big, sympathetic read on Lewis, away from the drama and turmoil of the Fitzgerald Inquiry's daily revelations of crime and corruption, cast the Commissioner in a more favourable light?

The deal with Lewis and Queensland Newspapers was brokered by University of Queensland historian and Fitzgerald Inquiry media analyst, Dr Joseph Siracusa. Siracusa had been researching a book called *Queensland on Trial*, and had interviewed many of the major players in the Fitzgerald drama, including Geraldo Bellino and Russell Hinze. And he had become, in some strange way, a literary agent for Lewis.

Siracusa arranged a lunch with Lewis and Ron Richards, the editorial manager of Queensland Newspapers and one of Lewis's old friends, at a pub in Ferny Grove, north-west of the city. Another Lewis confidant, Barry Maxwell, formerly of the Belfast Hotel in Queen Street, the city, was licensee of the pub.

In the end, Siracusa scored $30,000 for the interview, with payment to be made in two instalments and only after publication of the series. Two of the *Courier-Mail*'s most experienced writers – Ken Blanch and Peter Charlton – were assigned the task. 'Peter Charlton and I spent five days with him in a motel room up in Spring Hill and we ... jointly wrote five articles about him, we interviewed him on tape for five days,' remembers Blanch.

The series – 'The Lewis Years' – began publication in the *Courier-Mail* on Monday 6 February 1989. During the interviews Blanch and Charlton weren't averse to hitting Lewis with some tough questions, particularly Blanch, given he had known Lewis for many years and had had many dealings with him in his early years as a police reporter.

As the Fitzgerald Inquiry had yet to formally conclude, some queries stemmed from recent evidence heard before Tony Fitzgerald. 'These people and their activities, these people in the Licensing Branch. Their activities have brought your 39-year career unstuck?' Blanch probed.

'Well,' said Lewis, 'there's no doubt about that at all and I've tried to say and have said many times, I still believe that this Queensland police force is one of the best in the world ...'

Lewis grumbled at how his commissioner's diaries were released to the public during the course of the inquiry. He said even his wife Hazel hadn't read them. 'These [the diaries] were more of a personal sort of thing and I put some things in there that you'd never write if you thought anybody would ever see them and I'm absolutely dumbfounded I suppose when they were publicly released,' Lewis told the reporters.

Blanch continued to press Lewis. 'Taken all together, they paint a picture of you as, Peter used the word, "sinister" may be a bit strong, but a rather omnipresent powerbroker,' he said. 'What do you say about that?'

'All I can say about it … that they were not written up for anybody to ever read, except me.'

'But Terry,' Blanch pressed on, 'the point I'm making is that apart from whether or not they were ever intended to be read, they were read, and that's the picture that emerged.'

'Well, that might be in the view of some people, but, ah, I can only then go back to saying well, they'll have to judge me as they know me and I can't think there'd be very many people in the community who would have very many adverse comments to make.'

'Yeah,' said Blanch, 'the point I'm making is that you didn't see yourself that way?'

'Well, not in that, no,' Lewis responded.

Lewis talked about the large quantities of cash found in his safe, his friendships with Angelo Vasta, Eric Pratt and Don Lane, his lack of extravagance over the years, the family home on Garfield Drive, his opinion of various past and current government ministers, and his loathing for former friend Jack Herbert, who he believed had used Lewis's good name to feather his own nest.

'I believe that he's a person who decided to use me some years ago and he's had ample opportunity … over the years to do so or to contemplate doing so, I should say, and I believe that he's done so, as I said, to get himself off … a long series of unlawful activities over a period of … 29 or 30 years, and also to help his immediate family. And as has been admitted by him, he's had no hesitation over the years in fabricating evidence, concocting evidence against people whom he had no … nothing against them whatsoever,' Lewis said.

Blanch and Charlton finally asked him if he was tempted to tell his own story in a book.

'Well, perhaps a little bit,' Lewis responded. 'I could write some articles or perhaps write a book that might be of interest … I certainly was contacted by a person with experience in the compilation of material for perhaps writing a book … [but] whether we'll ever get around to doing that, I'm not sure yet.'

Lewis Sacked

At 9.30 a.m. on Wednesday 19 April 1989, the Governor Sir Walter 'Wally' Campbell approved a very special piece of legislation. The Bill specifically declared the position of Queensland Commissioner of Police vacant, and allowed former commissioner Terry Lewis to take home his entitlements, including accumulated annual leave – about $65,000.

Premier Mike Ahern then sent Lewis a letter.

I desire to inform you that the attached Bill passed through all stages in Parliament yesterday. The Bill has been assented to and the Act proclaimed today. As a consequence you no longer hold the position of Commissioner of Police.

Arrangements are being made to deal with your superannuation entitlements in the manner prescribed in the Bill. You should contact the Police Superannuation Board in this regard.

As I explained previously, having regard to all the circumstances the Government has decided that this course of action is fair to both yourself and the Government and is in the best interests of the Police Department.

It was over. Lewis was 61 years old.

He didn't offer comment immediately, but eventually gave a brief interview to the *Courier-Mail*. 'There have been times when I've wondered whether I should keep going,' he said, clearly implying suicide. 'I certainly didn't think I'd make it this far. I think I'm worse off now than I've ever been.

'I think I would find it very difficult to obtain permanent employment because of the uncertainty of matters at the moment.

'I just don't know what I'll do … see what happens.'

Lewis still feels acute bitterness towards Ahern and the way he was removed as police commissioner. '… of course you see why I don't like him [Ahern], he's the one who refused me permission … I'd been suspended on pay to start with,' says Lewis. 'Then suspended without pay and then I applied for permission to work. And he refused that you know, bloody awful.

'Then what else? Oh, and then he brought the legislation in, they wanted me to resign or do something. And I said no, I won't, so they brought legislation in to remove me from office.

'Which [was] all before I was convicted of anything and of course you've got no appeal against an Act of Parliament. And I was always under the impression that you're not supposed to bring an Act of Parliament in for one person. You're supposed to apply to the population. But anyhow he did it, and got away with it.'

With possible charges pending against Lewis, and Fitzgerald's report due in less than three months, Lewis stayed quiet. He did not believe he deserved to be charged with anything. He had done no wrong.

It had been a monumental waiting game, or as Quentin Dempster put it, Queensland history had been in 'suspended animation' anticipating the delivery of Fitzgerald's report. He added in his weekly column in the *Sunday Mail*: 'In his report, we can expect him to not only spell out the enormity of the problem but also how attitudes have contributed to a situation where organised crime and corrupt officials had this state by the throat.

'With the delivery of the report and associated prosecutions, Queensland is about to enter a historic phase. The history of what has passed is about to be re-written.'

Thus Times Do Shift

Before 9 a.m. on Monday morning, 3 July, hundreds of journalists filed into the Walter Burnett Building on the Royal National Association's Exhibition campus in Bowen Hills in the city's inner-north. The building, named after a former RNA president, was to act as a government budget-style lock-up for journalists to receive and skim the Fitzgerald Report before its official release at 2 p.m.

It was an interesting choice of site for the historic launch of the 630-page report. Here, since 1876, the state's rural and urban dwellers had come together once a year to celebrate the Queensland lifestyle. Here, horses and cattle were trucked into the heart of Brisbane and put on show. For ten days, the perfume of manure emanated from the show site. A part of the annual palette, too, were extravagant displays of fruit and vegetables – a reminder that in years past, the wealth of Queensland rested in its soil. This was a community that survived on the sweat of its farmers. The Ekka was everything that defined Queensland.

On this winter day, Fitzgerald's report would possibly redefine that original charter. The report itself had been printed at the offices of the government printer – GoPrint – at 371 Vulture Street, Woolloongabba, under heavy security. One GoPrint sales representative remembers the building being guarded inside and out. 'Once we took the copy in there was 24-hour security around the building,' he says. 'Each night, when they finished working on the report, it was locked in the safe under the supervision of officers from the Criminal Justice Commission.'

The release of the report would be a momentous day for some, and a dark one for others. 'If the city seems somewhat quieter as you travel to work today,' wrote the *Courier-Mail*'s Mike O'Connor, 'it will probably be because a good number of folk around town are holding their breath until 2 p.m. … when journalists … will be permitted to start filing stories.'

Don Petersen of the same newspaper was part of the scrummage at the Ekka. 'For about an hour before yesterday's release of the report on the most massive corruption inquiry in Queensland's history, police dogs checked out Brisbane's RNA showgrounds,' he said. 'The dogs were a precaution against the possibility of a bomb in the Walter Burnett building, where about 400 reporters were to be locked up for a preview of the Fitzgerald Report.

'Coloured marker pens working overtime, scribes from every State and even New Zealand ploughed through pages which will take weeks to digest thoroughly. But most of what they found was predictable: a blueprint for political, judicial, law-enforcement and even electoral reform not likely to be too palatable for those in power – no matter what they say publicly.'

Still, as a narrative, the report was written with consideration given to a general reader rather than lawmakers and government, which made it unique among Royal Commission reports.

'Wherever possible, this report makes no adverse or favourable findings about individuals,' Fitzgerald wrote. 'The most important thing about the evidence before this commission is not the truth or falsity of any particular allegation or the guilt or innocence of any individual ... [but] the pattern, nature and scope of the misconduct that has occurred and the lesson it contains for the future.'

Fitzgerald said, 'When misconduct has become institutionalised, guilt and innocence are not matters of black and white. The entire community must take some responsibility, both for the problem and for its solution.'

Petersen reviewed the report as 'an occasionally turgid and legalistic common sense guide to slow reform'.

Fitzgerald reserved specific advice in relation to the gerrymander. 'A government in our political system which achieves office by means other than free and fair elections lacks legitimate political authority over that system,' the report said. 'There is a vital need for the existing electoral boundaries to be examined by an open, independent inquiry as a first step in the rehabilitation of social cohesion, public accountability and respect for authority.'

This was a direct challenge to Premier Mike Ahern and his vow to implement Fitzgerald's recommendations 'lock, stock and barrel'.

Fitzgerald also had a lot to say about 'police culture' in Queensland, and indirectly paid homage to the many men and women who had tried to tell the truth about corruption over the decades and been rewarded with careers destroyed and families shattered.

'For a long time in the Queensland Police Force, speaking out achieved nothing but hardship, loneliness and fear. Those involved in misconduct were not punished. Those who reported it were,' Fitzgerald said. 'Lies, including perjury, are used, both by way of false denials and to attack those who are regarded as a threat.'

He said the force had been 'debilitated' by corruption. 'The situation is compounded by poor organisation and administration, inadequate resources, and insufficiently developed techniques and skills for the task of law enforcement in a modern, complex society,' Fitzgerald said. 'Particular responsibility and enthusiasm for the police culture is to be found amongst some members of an elite within the Force, including senior officers, union officials and those with special appointments and functions, particularly detectives and other non-uniformed police.

'Members of the elite have been the major beneficiaries of the culture which they promote and exploit. Many of those involved are cunning and ruthless, with an intuitive capacity to assess and take advantage of human weakness and motivation which has been honed by experience and an uninhibited willingness to misuse authority and to lie.

'Some of those who have exerted authority and influence in the Police Force in the last decade have practised and been protected by the police culture for up to 40 years.'

That day Premier Ahern kept to his word and promised 'swift implementation' of Fitzgerald's recommendations. He was uncertain as to whether the gerrymander issue would be resolved before the next state election, due in late 1989, and what the yet to be formed Electoral and Administrative Review Commission would have to say. 'By agreeing to implement all recommendations, the Ahern government today stands proud,' he said. 'The report is a marker and a warning to all governments in Queensland.

'Now I challenge other states and the Federal Government to bite the bullet on corruption as we have done.'

Ahern says, however, there was much jostling behind closed doors within the National Party at the time of the report's release. '[Party president Bob] Sparkes had said to me, "Don't give an undertaking to implement any of this because we'll have to have a good look at it",' says Ahern. 'So they were rounding up the numbers [against me], they were making no secret of it, I knew it was all happening.

'And so I went out and said "lock, stock and barrel" and that sort of locked everyone in. You know in life I think you get … things to do. I think you're born with things to do. You may not like them and you have other plans but … at the end of the day, summarily, you look back and say "Well, maybe that was what I was born to do. To do that."'

He quotes the seventeenth century poet Robert Herrick: 'Thus times do shift, each thing his turn does hold; New things succeed, as former things grow old.'

Deputy Premier Bill Gunn said on the day of the report's release that it had been 'full of praise for the National Party'.

'Certainly, I did well out of it,' Gunn said. 'It has well and truly acknowledged right through that we did what we said we would do.'

After journalists had laboured through the freshly printed report, queues gathered outside the state government printer's office before the public release that afternoon. The report had a first print run of 2000 copies. It sold for $20.

That evening out at the University of Queensland campus in St Lucia in the city's inner south-west, the former police commissioner, Sir Terence Lewis, sat in the office of historian and academic Dr Joseph Siracusa. Siracusa had acted as a media analyst during the inquiry and earlier arranged a series of interviews for Lewis with the *Courier-Mail*. He sat with Lewis reviewing several sections of the Fitzgerald Report and labelling them with post-it notes.

Lewis was in a gruff and dismissive mood when interviewed by journalists Phil Dickie and Peter Charlton that day. He declared once more that he was not corrupt and that his relationship with former premier Joh Bjelke-Petersen had never been 'improper'. Lewis reiterated he had not been an incompetent commissioner despite Fitzgerald's assessment. 'I can't go into this chapter and verse,' he told the journalists. 'I've had no time to read it.'

Lewis also disagreed with Fitzgerald's conclusions about police culture. 'What is police culture?' he asked. 'Tell me one profession that does not have an interest in itself.' Lewis said he should not be charged with anything, and said that if he were, he could not get a fair trial.

'Each question we put to Sir Terence was greeted with either anger, a blunt no or a rejection of an argument advanced by Fitzgerald,' Dickie and Charlton wrote.

Twelve days after the Fitzgerald Report hit the streets, so too did thousands of Queenslanders. Between 5000 and 12,000 citizens marched in a 'democracy rally' up George Street and into the Roma Street forum. They carried banners that read: THE FITZ REPORT IS DEMOCRACY; PEOPLE FIRST; RELEASE DOCUMENTS; and WAYNE GOSS & LABOR WILL ABOLISH ELECTORAL CORRUPTION.

The marchers were reportedly given a police escort. At the forum, Goss led a chant of 'Change, change, change ...'

There were no arrests.

Dear Sir Terence

Just eighteen days after the release of Fitzgerald's much-anticipated report, another letter was hand-delivered to 12 Garfield Drive, this time from the office of the Special Prosecutor, Doug Drummond, QC.

'Dear Sir Terence,' the letter opened, 'I anticipate I will take out two summonses in the near future, one charging you with 16 offences of official corruption and another charging you with two offences of perjury. Copies of the draft summonses which I expect to issue are enclosed.'

The perjury offences related to evidence Lewis gave before Fitzgerald, and alleged that Lewis falsely swore he had no idea what certain items in two small pocketbooks for 1980 and 1981 related to and what he had in mind when he wrote the items, and that he swore that he had never met Sydney businessman Jack Rooklyn in a private room at the Crest Hotel in Brisbane.

The corruption charges alleged that Lewis had corruptly agreed to receive monthly payments from Herbert for the protection of various people and their associates in relation to racing, gaming and prostitution between 1978 and 1987.

Drummond wrote: 'Should I receive no response to this correspondence by the time indicated, I will proceed on the basis that you decline the opportunity to be interviewed. Having regard to the material available to me, I have come to the view that there is a clear case for you to answer on these charges.'

Lewis returned fire with a letter from his solicitor Quentin George, declining the interview. George said the charges appeared to be based entirely on the evidence of Jack Herbert.

'Mr Herbert is under an indemnity from the Crown and it is widely reported that to guarantee his continued cooperation, an indemnity has not been offered to his wife, who was a party to his nefarious activities,' George wrote. 'Mr Herbert has a certain notoriety as a witness and has admitted under oath the commission of serious criminal offences, particularly fabricating evidence and perjury, which would be material to his veracity as a witness.' George said Herbert's evidence and that of his wife had to be 'fatally tarnished'. He said the perjury summonses against Lewis amounted to charges of having a defective memory.

Lewis said there was nothing more he could reveal and did not fear any 'new' evidence against him that hadn't come out in the Fitzgerald Inquiry. 'Unless they have found another liar as good as him [Herbert] I cannot imagine there being reason to fear,' he said. 'I have done everything that I can and I feel that it should be over.' Lewis offered that the commission was looking for 'someone or something' to justify the $26 million inquiry. 'I don't see how you could find me guilty of anything,' he added.

Just over a week later, Drummond unloaded a post–Fitzgerald fusillade. He issued summonses on 20 people who were either mentioned or gave evidence at the inquiry, including Lewis, Sydney identity Jack Rooklyn, Hector Hapeta, Anne Marie Tilley, Geraldo Bellino, Vittorio Conte, several police including Allen Bulger, and bookmakers Bruce Bowd, Paddy McIntyre, Stan Saunders and others. They collectively faced 92 charges and were expected to appear before Magistrate Brian Connors at the Brisbane Magistrates Court on 10 August. All of them appeared that morning in court except for McIntyre (a warrant was immediately issued for his arrest), and the gathering resembled a sort of abridged Fitzgerald Inquiry moment.

Journalist Joe Budd for the *Courier-Mail* witnessed the event. 'There were a few eligible faces missing from this reunion, none more so than Jack Herbert, the alleged common link between this most diverse of groups.'

The Special Prosecutor, Doug Drummond, QC, told the court that he expected the combined committal hearings to take three months. Lewis expressed visible frustration at hearing this news. He had spent the best part of two years sitting in courts and no doubt he might have wondered if the nightmare would ever end.

The defence lawyers didn't believe such a massive task would take just three months. Lewis's lawyer, Quentin George, remarked: 'We now look like we're facing a cost that would exceed the national debt and a time frame that could be two years.' He would prove to be remarkably prescient.

As for Lewis, he had few options but to bide his time and build a case for his defence.

Meanwhile, as the months ticked by, the state again faced an election. It would be a moment that drew a line in history and marked the end of the excessive 1980s. Having dumped Mike Ahern, the Nationals went into the campaign headed by Russell Cooper, the cattle-breeding member for Roma, and Premier of Queensland since late September. He faced off with Angus Innes, leader of the Liberals, and the ALP's formidable Wayne Goss, a thorn in the side of the government for years, especially when it came to matters of policing and corruption.

The Nationals, not heeding mistrals of change in Queensland, sailed their familiar course and campaigned on law and order and the sort of social conservatism that had served Sir Joh Bjelke-Petersen so well. On the back of a combination of Bjelke-Petersen's misguided bid to become Australian Prime Minister through 1987, the Fitzgerald Inquiry hearings and Fitzgerald's devastating report in mid-1989, nothing could save the government.

The election, held on 2 December 1989, was a landslide win for the Australian Labor Party, and it was Premier Wayne Goss who carried the torch for a fairer, more modern Queensland into the 1990s.

1990s

Silent No More

As the washout from the Fitzgerald Inquiry and its official report continued to ebb and flow into the New Year, one man kept shouting for justice. It was a voice that carried to the present from the 1950s. Glen Patrick Hallahan, member of the so-called Rat Pack, had been embroiled in allegations of police corruption since the last days of the 1950s, when he briefly partnered a young Terry Lewis, bringing law and order to the streets of Brisbane.

It was Hallahan, known to his peers as 'Silent' for his habit of speaking softly, who had been briefly stood down for allegedly demanding a kickback pay rise from a prostitute in 1959, an incident that led to then commissioner Frank 'Big Fella' Bischof padlocking the city's brothels.

Again, Hallahan was named extensively by whistleblowing prostitute Shirley Brifman as not only one of her lovers and the recipient of her financial largesse, but as being involved in all sorts of illegal schemes, from counterfeit money to taking a cut in the proceeds from bank robberies sanctioned by Hallahan himself. And it was Hallahan who left the force after he was caught taking money from a prostitute.

Later, he would feature in police interviews with drug dealer John Edward Milligan, who alleged that Hallahan was a silent partner in major heroin importation in the 1970s. Now, as a chief fraud investigator for the Suncorp insurance company, the physically ailing Hallahan was aggrieved enough to take his anger to the press.

In February 1990, he told the *Sunday Mail*'s police reporter Peter Hansen that he wanted to fight to clear the 'smears' from his name. He said his reputation had been crucified by lies and rumours that emanated out of the Fitzgerald Inquiry. 'Initially, all the suspicion against me was predicated by a provable false story that I was a member of the so-called Rat Pack,' Hallahan said. 'As far as I'm concerned, 1989 was the Year of the Smear. Two months ago I received a letter from [Special Prosecutor] Mr [Doug] Drummond clearing me.

'It is now my intention to take action against certain people for the way they have wronged me. They will have to substantiate their smears in a proper court of law.

'I will get to have my say.'

Hallahan was terminally ill, and his attempt to cleanse his reputation may have been related to some form of 'legacy' he might leave behind. Although he left the force under a cloud in the early 1970s, his legend had lived on, his name popping up in various Royal Commissions in connection to drugs, especially in relation to his former associate John Edward Milligan. As Hallahan slipped towards death, he must have felt it was worth one last shot to remind the Queensland public of his stellar record as a detective, and his passion for locking up bad guys.

But those days were long gone. Before his resignation from the force, Hallahan had, according to Brifman, 'hit the pot', namely marihuana. Another witness often saw Hallahan smoking joints with his criminal informant Billy Phillips. After the incident which prompted Hallahan's resignation – taking graft from a prostitute in Brisbane's New Farm Park – his taste for drugs appeared to increase.

Jack Herbert told biographer Tom Gilling: '[Hallahan] wanted something to knock him out because he was in a bad state, you know. It was when he got pinched [in the park] and he was really upset about it. I went down and saw him with Tony Murphy, to his little flat at

Kangaroo Point. [I] Tried to calm him down. I was amazed because I thought he'd be a stronger character … I really did.

'I felt sorry for the poor bastard, you know? Because he was a good style of fellow … it's a bloody shame … he was an utter vegetable when we went there to see him, truly.'

Hallahan's attempt to correct history was never going to make it into a courtroom. As for Herbert, following the Fitzgerald Inquiry, virtually all of his friendships with police ended. He later told his biographer that he was aggrieved that he no longer saw or spoke with Tony Murphy and Alan Barnes. He missed the comaraderie. He missed the company of men and the five o'clock beers. 'I wouldn't mind if they came round, some of them,' Herbert reflected. 'Burgess and those fellows … if they knocked on the door I'd say hello.'

He never got to find out how his close mates – Murphy, Lewis and others – felt about him ratting on them and airing dirty laundry that had accumulated for decades. He didn't think about it. Herbert was a survivor.

Farewell to Garfield Drive

For a child who grew up in the Depression and had known austerity, it must have been a difficult decision for Lewis to sell the family home at 12 Garfield Drive. Lewis had been raised in humble houses in Ipswich and then Hawthorne just east of the Brisbane CBD. He and Hazel had lived in modest homes early in their marriage, and had finally built a place that was not only safe for their family, but was a reflection of their status in the community. The new home on Garfield Drive had been extremely important to Lewis. He had worked all his life towards it.

Now, just a few years years after moving into the Robin Gibson designed house, they were selling to meet Lewis's hefty legal fees. In late April, the doors of their home were opened for public inspection.

Despite Lewis's hope that the sale might go off quietly, there was intense interest in the sacked police commissioner's residence. Security was posted at the front door and interested buyers had to sign a register and record their personal details – all cameras were confiscated.

The *Courier-Mail* described the mansion: '[Lewis's] ... collection of police hats from around the world was proudly displayed in a glass cabinet in the lavish downstairs entertaining and bar area which opens onto a pool at the back of the house.'

The furniture was described as a mix of antique and modern, and the report claimed it was good quality but not extravagantly expensive. 'A marble entry foyer leads to the dining and lounge areas on the middle level. The upper level has three bedrooms and Sir Terence's study.' The family's personal effects were left in the home during the inspection, 'and visitors were invited to look over the couple's bedroom and ensuite'.

The house was expected to fetch $1.25 million. The auction itself was slated in for 19 May, six days after the beginning of Lewis's trial on corruption charges. The house would, ultimately, be passed in at $500,000.

The Misgivings of Jim Slade

In the years after police officer Jim Slade was offered a bribe, when he went on to assist journalist Chris Masters in putting together the extraordinary *Four Corners* investigation, 'The Moonlight State', Slade felt torn. By cooperating with Masters, and by giving evidence before the Fitzgerald Inquiry, he had turned his back on the police force's iron-clad code of mateship.

Slade had loved being a copper, had loved working in intelligence, and everything evaporated when they tried to recruit him into The Joke. 'I just take people as being fair dinkum, and then I got my job as a police officer and I didn't even know about corruption, for Christ's sake,' he says. 'You see, there're two sides to me as well. I love the police culture, if the police culture could be rid of that [other] side. It hurt me no end to bloody give evidence at the Fitzgerald Inquiry. It fucking hurt, and even I think my passing comment, I think which showed my whole feeling, I said to Fitzgerald, "You know ... I really regret what I've done."'

At the same time he acknowledges someone needed to take a stand against corruption. 'It's destroyed [wife] Chris and my life. But look, we're very, very strong people. We've got on with it, we're happy now, we've been married 40 ... something years. Same wife, same husband.

'We're not bloody madly rich, but we get by. But I tell you I'm bloody pleased [about] what we did, and that was with Chris's permission that I did that. It was against every single thing that I wanted to do as a police officer. Even now ... I get really emotional about it, I can't fucking believe it, and I'm no fucking angel.' He says he curses himself for not having seen the corrupt system earlier and done something about it.

His wife Chris begs to differ, and says her husband had 'a bit of an idea' that something was going on. 'When Barnsey gave you that bribe and you didn't know what to do. Well, I mean, you knew you ... weren't going to keep it [the money], but you didn't know how to handle the situation, and you said that you couldn't trust [Graeme] Parker,' Chris remembers. 'You knew ... Parker was not okay, and you knew that Col Thompson probably wouldn't side with you, but probably wasn't corrupt. So you did know some stuff, didn't you? You knew some people were corrupt and knew it wasn't safe just to go and blab.'

Jim Slade says he was asked by Graeme Parker, the head of the Queensland Bureau of Criminal Intelligence, if he had spoken to journalist Chris Masters. He simply told the truth and said yes. 'I just came straight out with it,' Slade recalls. 'I thought if I tell him that I talked to him ... they might think twice if they pull the trigger, and I might be able to pull the trigger first.'

Slade remembers, early in his career, being in several meetings in the presence of former assistant commissioner Tony Murphy and former commissioner Terry Lewis. 'Do you know how, if you're in a meeting or a group, it doesn't take long for you, in your mind, to get [an idea of] the pecking order?' he says. 'I would have had to have been at, you know, at least ten or 15 of those [meetings] with Murphy and Lewis ... and every single time I was left in no doubt that the person making the rules and the final plan and the instruction was [coming from] Murphy.

'At no time did the commissioner of police, well that person with the title, commissioner of police, have anything to do with what Tony Murphy had in mind.'

Still, Slade regretted having to inform on his colleagues. 'After those guys [Barnes, Parker etc.] came into the Bureau of Criminal Intelligence, we lost our innocence,' Slade says. 'You know, like we were a squad ... we would get a bone and we wouldn't let the bloody thing go. But after they came in, the bones were selective, and some bones we had a bite at and the bones were taken away.'

And some bones, says Slade, were simply obstructions to the corrupt system.

Legal Argument

Lewis's trial opened on 13 May in the Brisbane District Court before Justice Anthony Healy, and if the punters were expecting the pyrotechnics of the Fitzgerald Inquiry, they were to be sorely disappointed. The previous October, Lewis had waived his right to a committal hearing, concerned that adverse publicity might impact on the trial jury. He was represented by the brilliant legal mind, John Jerrard, considered one of the best barristers practising in Brisbane. However, after nearly three weeks, lawyers were still tangled in a complicated legal argument that would mire proceedings from the outset. Lewis was not required to enter a plea.

The deadlock had not been broken by 30 June, and the trial was abandoned so points of law could be referred to a higher court. Crown Prosecutor Bob Mulholland, QC, was granted a nolle prosequi in order to seek a second ruling on eight blocks of evidence deemed inadmissible by Judge Healy. Mulholland said the Crown's case had been 'greatly truncated' because of Healy's ruling, whereas Jerrard, for Lewis, told Judge Healy: 'Your control of the trial is being removed from you and eventually the prosecution must win if only because they have the greater financial resources.'

The Criminal Law Association said the decision to test Healy's ruling was unfair to Lewis and a 'monstrous advantage to the Crown'. Special prosecutor Doug Drummond defended the move, saying the Crown had only two choices: either go on with the case against Lewis without being able to present important evidence to the jury; or take the issue to the Court of Criminal Appeal, which is what was decided.

Lewis's lawyers argued the trial had never really begun because the charges had not been read out in open court and Lewis had not entered a plea. It wasn't until late August that the Court of Criminal Appeal refused to even consider the appeal. One judge described it as 'incompetent'.

Still, it meant Lewis's trial proper would probably not get underway until well into 1991. The former commissioner was, once again, stuck in painful limbo.

The Fate of Deveney

Juvenile Aid Bureau officer Greg Deveney was labelled a 'dog' by his colleagues after he gave evidence at the Fitzgerald Inquiry. He had told of police taking protection money from Gold Coast brothel keepers and described the antics of some of his fellow detectives with prostitutes. No one wanted to come near him. So, when he was transferred to Goondiwindi, 358 kilometres south-west of Brisbane, he saw it as a potential break from the pressures of the city. He could make a fresh start. He could get on with the career he'd always wanted – being a police officer.

The reality, however, was quite different. As soon as Deveney arrived at his new post, his senior officer gave him a hard time. 'When I worked late shift, no one was allowed to work with me,' Deveney remembers. 'I was told the reason being that none of the other officers had any trust in me because of my statements at the Fitzgerald Inquiry and everything.'

His senior officer also had something else to say to Deveney. 'He said, "I've had 50 phone calls from officers in charge of stations [and] no one wants you in this place",' Deveney recalls. 'And he said, "Are you aware of the fact that as soon as I've had my share of you, you'll be transferred to somewhere else and they'll have their share of you, and you'll be transferred to somewhere else and they'll have their share of you, until you go."'

Deveney persevered, but matters only got worse. 'When things [were] going really bad I received a phone call from someone claiming to be from the Commissioner's office, and he said, "Greg, you don't know me ... but they are out to get you. And by that I mean they intend getting you in gaol",' recalls Deveney.

'Well ... I was on a late shift on the Saturday night and three-quarters of the way through my shift my knees started to shake and I couldn't stop them. And the next morning when I went home I sat up all night drinking. Shrelle [his wife] took me to my doctor and I went on sick leave the very next day. I was off work for 18 months ... and, you know, during that whole time we never got a visit from one person. I was hidden in our bedroom for 18 months, and every two weeks Shrelle went up to get my pay. Not once in that whole period was she given the cheque on her first visit. They'd say [to her], "Oh, the senior sergeant's not in." Shrelle said she could see the senior sergeant looking through the venetian blinds as she walked up the steps. Yeah, we had a shit of a time, eh.'

When Deveney eventually returned to work, he lasted only two shifts. 'I couldn't handle putting my uniform on, I was ashamed of the uniform,' he recalls. 'I had no respect for it, you know, I had completely lost it and I was lucky that at that time the department had started employing social workers. A woman from Brisbane had read a lot about me and saw what I was going through … no one had offered me any assistance whatsoever. She grabbed my file and she came out to Goondiwindi and she spent a day with us and she said, "I'm leaving this shit organisation as soon as I can but I'm getting you out medically unfit before I go."

'And she got me out.'

Deveney was warned, too, that he would never secure a government-related job outside of the police force for the rest of his working life.

That's precisely what happened.

The Non-Person

Historian Dr Joseph Siracusa continued to act as a sort of proxy agent for Lewis – he says he had stitched up Lewis's exclusivity for a proposed book for three years – and remained one of his greatest public champions. On 28 October, he published a feature on Lewis in the *Sunday Mail*, updating the public on where Lewis's mind might be at after his trial was delayed.

The headline read: LEWIS AS A NON-PERSON. It was at times a melancholy read that weighed heavily in favour of Lewis and his wife Hazel and alleged that Lewis, while awaiting trial had 'reluctantly mastered the art of becoming a non-person'.

Siracusa wrote that for a former workaholic who would normally have started work by 7 a.m., 'Sir Terence, 62 and tanned, now rolls out of bed between 7 and 7.30 a.m. with nowhere to go. He has a leisurely breakfast of eggs, one piece of toast and weak mugs of tea, followed by a read of the morning newspapers.'

Siracusa, in the kind of detail Lewis would have identified with, went on to list Sir Terence's luncheon and dinner menus. 'His wife Hazel admits his greatest difficulty is filling in the time,' the article continued. 'The problem is that in Sir Terence's two-bedroom apartment [a rental in Kelvin Grove; Garfield Drive had sold a few months earlier for $600,000], comfortable and cosy by most standards, there is not much to do.'

When asked point-blank what he was doing with his life, Lewis smiled and said: 'Keeping from going nutty.'

Siracusa asked if Lewis – a Catholic who attended weekly his favourite church, the giant red-brick edifice of St Brigid's at Red Hill – had forgiven his accusers. 'Well the majority of them I don't know,' Lewis replied. 'I haven't met them or seen them before in my life until they appeared in the inquiry.'

Siracusa wrote it was doubtful that Lewis would ever be able to forgive the state government for 'the way in which it hurled him into oblivion'. Lewis had become the 'forgotten man', he added. 'The police medals, Orders of the British Empire and Father of the Year titles mean nothing to a man facing trial,' Siracusa further opined.

Siracusa now says: 'He's a tragic character. He's an operator; I knew he [Lewis] was trying to play me, in the nicest sense of the word.'

Shut Down

By the end of 1990, specialist officer Kym Goldup of the Paedophile Task Force, and her colleague Garnett Dickson, had amassed an enormous amount of material relating to a local paedophile ring. They had managed to embed an undercover police officer into the local outfit – probably a first in Australian policing – and their investigations had included secretly taping paedophiles in conversation.

On one occasion, two local paedophiles identified by Goldup and Dickson went on a day trip to the Sunshine Coast. One of the men was a senior public servant attached to the Police Complaints Tribunal. Transcripts were made of their discussion in the car.

The small task force had also, at one point, performed surveillance on the home of a Supreme Court judge. Goldup's work had revealed extensive paedophile activity on the Gold Coast, where celebrities and senior business people were linked to a paedophile 'facilitator'. It was time to make some arrests.

'We tell the bosses just a couple of days before,' Goldup recalls. 'We've got the transcripts from the Sunshine Coast trip. We've got the original and one copy. One was Garney's [Dickson], one was mine. The bosses said they needed copies, and one for the Commissioner.

'Garney and I made the copies. It was quite a lengthy document … I said to Garney, "I'm going to code these." I put a little code in every single one of the copies. If any more copies turned up, I could go to the page where I'd put the code, and I'd know who's copy was copied.

'And a copy did turn up … it got into the hands of [the Police Complaints Tribunal staffer].'

Incredibly, news of the assigned police raid on the paedophile network was also leaked to the media. Goldup and Dickson discovered the story would break on the 6 p.m. television news. The raid had been organised to take place at 5 a.m. the following day. It was potentially disastrous for the task force, and could have meant the loss of two years' hard work.

'So, Garney and I pulled the raids [forward] and conducted them at 6 p.m. that night,' Goldup recalls. 'We executed the raids that we could … but there was a lot of stuff already gone.'

Goldup later learned that the leak came out of Parliament House, and the copy of the transcript was one that had been designated to the Police Commissioner's office.

'And then everything went to shit,' she says. 'It was awful. We were pretty much bastardised by the rest of the Sex Offenders Squad. We were labelled as lazy, that we didn't know what we were doing. A lot of people didn't know what we were doing. We couldn't tell them. [After that] we were just given … shitty jobs.'

Goldup was summoned to the office of a superior and told the police force was setting up a new child exploitation unit. She would not be joining its ranks, she was told.

The next day, she was ordered to surrender the Paedophile Task Force's file safe containing all of the unit's confidential data. 'They picked up the file safe and moved it to another office,' she recalled. 'It was always locked. The keys were hidden in my desk. They were in such a hurry to get that file safe out of there they forgot to ask me for the keys. It was moved to a little sort of internal back office in the Fraud Squad. Everything that we'd gathered was in there.

'There were certain things [files with well-known names] that were so sensitive they were never even held in that office. They were held at a place unknown.

'I felt really incompetent. It made me feel really incompetent, like I had done something wrong. It also said to me we had come just a little too close. I've always maintained that the only thing I am guilty of is probably doing my job too well.'

Goldup fell ill, and during a stay in hospital she was told she was to be transferred to North Queensland. In the end, she was shunted off to Bowen, 1130 kilometres north of Brisbane. She reflects: 'I'd gone from [being] one of Australia's leading paedophile investigators, to uniform in a little country town … all in the space of five months.'

Despite the rigours of the Fitzgerald Inquiry, the relentless publicity about the need for a clean and accountable police force, and the insistence on both police and government transparency and accountability, some basic tenets of police operations – flowing beneath everything like old subterranean tank streams – continued unblemished. For decades, investigations into paedophilia had remained firmly problematic – surrounded by rumours of deliberate police obfuscation – and that didn't change into the 1990s.

At Last, the Trial

On Monday 18 March 1991, Sir Terence Murray Lewis, 63, made his way from his rented two-bedroom apartment in Kelvin Grove, in the city's inner north-west, to the District Court complex in George Street. Most times Lewis caught the bus. On rare occasions, a friend dropped him into town.

Three and a half years after he was suspended as Queensland Police Commissioner courtesy of allegations made before the Fitzgerald Inquiry into police misconduct, and following an initial aborted trial the previous year, Lewis was finally having his day in court. Lewis says he had gone with a law firm that quoted him a 'global fee' of $250,000 for the trial and appeals. That figure later crept up to $450,000.

Former director of prosecutions, Des Sturgess, reflected: 'Nobody ever came to trial with a greater handicap than Lewis. The [Fitzgerald] Inquiry, in which he'd remained the central figure, had attracted enormous media coverage. For nearly two years the papers remained full of it.

'His sacking and disgrace received the warmest applause. It would have been difficult to find a single adult not a member of his family who continued to believe in his innocence. His goose was all but cooked and, however earnest the intentions of those busily preparing for the court proceedings, it would be less than honest to pretend that they were likely to produce anything other than a show trial.'

On the first day, the court, before Judge Healy, heard that at least 110 witnesses were expected to be called to give evidence, including Jack 'The Bagman' Herbert, his wife Peggy Herbert, former Queensland Treasurer Sir Llew Edwards, and former police officers Ron Redmond and Noel Kelly. Kelly had spent the early years of his police career in Mackay before shifting to Brisbane in the late 1970s, serving under Senior Sergeant Allen Bulger at the Wynnum CIB, where he began taking regular corrupt payments. He at first denied corruption and perjury before the Fitzgerald Inquiry, then gave evidence under indemnity about corruption. He was subsequently sentenced to five years gaol for perjury.

Lewis faced 15 counts of corruption. He pleaded not guilty.

On Monday 8 April Crown Prosecutor Bob Mulholland told the court that Lewis had confessed to Jack Herbert that corruption payments had been all that made being police commissioner worthwhile. Mulholland said Herbert would give evidence that Lewis often spoke of the job's long hours, and had told Herbert that the 'protection' payments he received virtually kept him in the position.

The jury was told Herbert was Lewis's accomplice and 'on his own admission a villain'. The *Courier-Mail* reported of day two of the trial: 'Herbert would say he received up to $23,000 a month from the Hapeta/Tilley organisation and up to $17,000 a month from the Bellino/Conte empire. Lewis, Herbert and corrupt Licensing Branch officers all allegedly received a cut of the money. Payments from Hapeta and Tilley were to ensure the protection of more than 20 brothels in Brisbane and five Brisbane and Gold Coast sex shops.'

Mulholland went on to say that Lewis promoted corrupt or corruptible police to key positions within the department. He also pointed out to the jurors that much of the evidence against Lewis was circumstantial.

Herbert went into the witness box on 15 April. He would tell the court that Lewis had been one of many recipients of graft payments that came out of the corruption system known as 'The Joke'. He said he paid Lewis $1500 a month from 1978 to protect in-line machines, and that the payments were often made to the commissioner at the famous Lennons Hotel.

Lewis's lawyer John Jerrard quizzed Herbert about these 'scarcely discreet' public meetings.

Jerrard:	He [Lewis] had a very high recognition factor and you say you met in public in the foyer of a hotel?
Herbert:	That's correct. I could hand him money and look around to see if anybody was looking at the same time and if they were, we would go on with some chit-chat.
Jerrard:	You met this well-known man in a crowded place in probably the most crowded street in Brisbane at probably the most popular hotel in Brisbane?
Herbert:	It would have happened, sir, that's all I can say.

Jerrard suggested the notion was an absurdity, which Herbert rejected. Lewis's counsel also questioned Herbert's highly dubious record as a court witness.

Jerrard:	You agree that in the past you have picked up the Bible in your right hand and sworn to tell the truth, the whole truth and nothing but the truth?
Herbert:	Yes.
Jerrard:	And you have sat in the witness box and said you were telling the truth in the past when you were not?
Herbert:	Yes.
Jerrard:	Do you agree that the oath you took [in this trial] does not bind your conscience now?
Herbert:	Well, it does now but on the occasions you mentioned before it did not. In the position I am in now, I'm telling the truth.

Herbert denied he had been an 'informant' for Lewis. He told the court they had been friends from the word go and there was no necessity for him to cultivate Lewis to make use of his position as commissioner.

When Jack Herbert finally left the box after 12 days of evidence, his wife Peggy filled the breach. She recounted that she had handed an envelope of cash to Lewis on one occasion at Lennons when her husband couldn't make the appointment, and recalled meeting Lady Hazel Lewis twice in early 1987 and handing over large sums of money. She told the court she did not remember the payment to Sir Terence until after she had discussed an indemnity deal with the Fitzgerald commission.

The trial heard details from corrupt police and brothel madams about the vast network of protection payments in Brisbane, the Gold Coast and Cairns in Far North Queensland. One of Lewis's charges related to him allegedly accepting a one-off payment of $25,000 from Rooklyn to assist in an adverse report on the introduction of poker machines in Queensland being submitted to state Cabinet. A former head waiter of the Crest Hotel told the court he had witnessed a meeting between Rooklyn and Lewis in the penthouse suite.

Harry Burgess gave evidence. So too did self-confessed corrupt cop Cal Farrah, former traffic superintendent for North Queensland. Farrah admitted to the Fitzgerald Inquiry that he had received corrupt payments from Vittorio Conte to protect an illegal casino in Cairns. Jim Slade offered his own recollections, as did Allen Bulger.

As the trial wore on, Lewis's penchant for diarising his life again featured heavily, as it had during the Fitzgerald hearings. Mulholland, in his epic nine-day final address in July, zeroed in on the cryptic codes in the two small pocketbooks. He said they were 'like a fingerprint on a weapon in a homicide case, pointing … to the guilt of the accused'.

The Crown alleged that the pocketbooks contained abbreviations for cities where SP bookies operated, illegal casinos in Brisbane and on the Gold Coast, the names of vice figures and corrupt police and meeting places. 'But this is not a case where the Crown relies on one fingerprint to prove its case – rather, Lewis's fingerprints cover the room,' Mulholland continued. 'The Crown case is unanswered and indeed, unanswerable.'

Lewis says of the pocketbooks: '... that was a great weapon for them, a great weapon ... Mulholland used that relentlessly, [implying] that there was a code between Herbert and me. And I woke up later, going through my diaries about Herbert, when he raised it ... [he] was going to be an informant, if you like, for want of a better word.'

Mulholland told the jury it was doubtful they could make a more important civic decision than the one to find Lewis guilty or not guilty. He reminded them that Lewis's diaries 'time and time again' supported Jack Herbert's evidence.

'There is a saying,' said Mulholland in his final address, 'the truth has a strength of its own no matter from what sullied source it emanates.'

John Jerrard, for Lewis, argued that the Herberts were living 'the life of Riley' in exchange for testifying against Terry Lewis. 'The whole horrible, stinking thing at the centre of this case is that Jack Herbert goes free because he accuses Terry Lewis,' said Jerrard. Herbert had been the middle-man throughout years of graft and corruption, yet had not suffered a stretch in prison. Jerrard criticised the Crown case for not calling the only other man who was in a position to tell whether Lewis was corrupt or not – Graeme Parker. Why had it not done so, instead boring jurors with irrelevant evidence and 'trash', when Parker had also been granted an indemnity?

Jerrard also denied that the lists in Lewis's pocketbooks were codes, likening them more to the Dead Sea Scrolls, 'surrounded in mystery'. If they were so important, also, why was the code never used on Herbert's evidence, and why did Herbert not have a copy of the lists?

On 30 July, while continuing his final address, Jerrard appeared to choke up with tears as he listed the achievements of his client. He apologised to the jury claiming it was the result of a 'very long trial'.

The next day, Judge Healy, in summing up, told the jury it would be dangerous to convict Lewis on the evidence of Herbert. He said the Crown had not produced any evidence which corroborated that of Jack and Peggy Herbert. Theirs was the only direct evidence that Lewis was corrupt. He added that Herbert had the 'strongest motive imaginable' to implicate Lewis.

He said to the jury: 'I direct you as a matter of law that there is no evidence which is capable of corroboration, that is, confirming or supporting Jack Herbert's evidence that the accused entered into the corrupt agreements in the indictment.' He said the same applied to Peggy Herbert. 'You may convict on the uncorroborated evidence of the Herberts but it would be dangerous to do so,' he concluded. 'You may find yourself in the position where you think Herbert may be telling the truth: that is not enough, it is only if you are satisfied of the guilt of the accused beyond reasonable doubt that you are entitled to consider a verdict of guilty.'

The jury deliberated for several days and nights. They returned with a verdict on Monday 5 August 1991.

Guilty on all counts.

Judge Healy sentenced Lewis, 63, to 14 years' prison and set no parole date. Lewis says upon hearing the verdict he felt 'absolute bloody despair'.

'To stand up and hear them say "guilty" on all charges and then ... in almost any trial of any consequence the judge will adjourn before sentencing,' says Lewis. 'It's to give you or your counsel ... a chance to say, "Oh, he wasn't a bad bloke, he did some good in his lifetime", or some bloody thing ... [but at my trial the jury] brought in the decision, Jerrard said a little bit, [and] the judge sentenced me forthwith ... within half an hour.'

Lewis says he felt his life and career had been for nought. 'You feel you've worked your whole life and what for? What's the use?' he says. 'You feel you'd be much better if you, firstly, had never been born, and secondly, if you could just get out of it now without damaging your family that you'd be better off dead. But you've got to keep fighting.'

Lewis says he accepted instructions not to give evidence himself, as the trial would be prolonged further and after sitting for nearly five months already it may have put the judge and jury offside.

An editorial in the *Courier-Mail* the next morning stated: 'Twelve good citizens and true were sternly warned by the trial judge, Judge Healy, that they were considering evidence from a discredited and highly suspect source in The Bagman, Jack Reginald Herbert, and that they could not safely return a verdict of guilty unless they were convinced of the authenticity of this evidence despite its unsavoury source. They chose to convict even in the light of this cautionary advice.

'With that verdict, a sterilising lance has cleaned out yet another boil on the body politick … The corpse now laid out for public inspection is not his, but that of politicised policing.'

Directly after the trial, Justice Healy was criticised by some members of the press, including *Sydney Morning Herald* journalist Evan Whitton, for 'concealing' evidence from the jury by not including crucial facts. But the trial transcript showed that Healy actually ruled very little evidence as inadmissible. Presiding over one of the most unenviable trials in Queensland legal history, Healy made demonstrable efforts to ensure Lewis got a fair trial in impossible circumstances.

One thing was certain. The jury had spoken.

As He Smiled, He Died

On Monday 17 June 1991 – two-thirds of the way through the trial of former commissioner of police Terry Lewis – a former Rat Packer went to his grave. Glendon Patrick Hallahan, just 59, passed away in the Wesley Hospital in Auchenflower in inner-western Brisbane, following decades of health problems.

Tony Murphy regularly visited Hallahan in the weeks up to his death. So too did former head of the Queensland Police Union, Ron Edington.

'Oh, he was frightened of death, he was trying to say the rosary,' says Edington. 'Tony Murphy told me this ... this might be an exaggeration on Tony's part, but he reckons that when Glen got to the part in the rosary [that mentions death], he knew he was dying [and] he smiled.' (The end of the Hail Mary goes: 'Pray for us sinners now, and at the hour of our death. Amen.')

Incredibly, the former lawyer, political firebrand and anti-corruption fighter, Col Bennett, was also in the Wesley around that time, visiting his ill wife Helen. It was Bennett, as the member for South Brisbane, who had kicked off the National Hotel inquiry all those years before, and earned the wrath of men like Murphy and Hallahan.

Edington had at one point been a secret informant of Bennett's and knew him and his family well. Murphy, on the other hand, detested the former politician. The feeling was mutual. Edington recalls they met in a corridor and Bennett asked Murphy what he was doing in the hospital. Murphy replied, 'Poor old Glen, he's on his last.'

Bennett said, 'That's terrible, I'll say a prayer for him, Tony.'

Murphy reportedly turned to Edington and said, 'Wasn't that beautiful of Col to say a prayer for him [Glen]?'

Edington replied, 'You know the prayer he's going to say? He's going to say prayers that he fucking dies ... that's human nature ... he [Bennett] would have gone home and ... been real happy to think that the cunt was dying because of what he tried to do to Col Bennett.' (It was rumoured that Hallahan wanted to hire a hitman to kill Bennett during the 1960s.)

Edington says he spent a lot of quiet time with Hallahan during his last days. He says Hallahan told him that Murphy got more money than anyone, he was the top man. Hallahan allegedly told Edington: 'Tony always protected himself, because he thought if any of these allegations are going to be made against me [Hallahan], this is what I'm gonna say.'

The *Sunday Mail*'s Peter Hansen wrote a huge story on the death of Hallahan. 'Glen Hallahan left the Police Force in 1972, but never ceased being a detective at heart,' the article said. 'He died a bitter man, still under clouds of suspicion and controversy that dogged him all his working life.'

The article went on to say that Hallahan was an 'ace crime catcher'. Hansen wondered whether his record of catching criminals and underworld personalities may have sown the seeds of his destruction as a policeman. 'How close was he to his underworld friends, his enemies in the Police Force asked? And did he go over the line?'

The article posed the question to Hallahan: Why had such a fine young detective attracted so much negative attention and criticism?

'Envy,' Hallahan had previously told the reporter.

Hallahan's wife, Heather, told the newspaper: 'I would like to say my husband did more that was constructive for Queensland than all his persecutors put together. One cannot be successful in this country and not be a target for the unsuccessful. I am of the opinion, money is not the root of all evil, envy is.'

An unnamed police colleague said that Hallahan 'had more integrity in his little finger than those who accused him have in their whole bodies ... altar boys don't solve major crimes'.

Hallahan was buried in Grave 75, Section LO5 of the Beenleigh Cemetery at Brigade Drive, Eagleby, on Wednesday 19 June.

Edington reflects: 'Hallahan's death was terrible ... I'm starting to believe in it [karma] because when you see these fellows that are dying, the way they die, is there a punishment?'

To Boggo Road

When Terry Lewis was found guilty and sentenced, his wife Hazel was not in the court. Nor were any of his family. They had no idea he was about to be convicted. 'I was hoping I wouldn't be convicted, that's your hope against hope, I suppose,' he remembers. 'But I thought, well, if worse comes to worst I'll probably have a week or something to tidy up at home [but] … no, there was nobody there [in court that day]. Nobody.'

Lewis was immediately handcuffed and taken downstairs in the court building where he was strip-searched then placed in a cell. His counsel, John Jerrard, and another lawyer, Rick Whitton, visited him shortly after and assured him they would appeal. Nobody had contacted Lady Hazel Lewis about the conviction and sentencing. Lewis says she heard about it for the first time on the radio news.

'Then, of course, I was handcuffed again and put in the van with the media waiting outside to try and get photos,' says Lewis. 'I was then taken over to the prison and as I was told, well that night, even though the prisoners had heard on the radio that I'd been convicted … when the van went into the courtyard of the old Boggo Road, there was cheers and clapping and oh … a real bloody uproar in the prison.

'The head of the prison … he just got me inside, and again you get stripped and searched and showered and put in a shocking old bloody tracksuit of some sort, and they didn't even have sandshoes to fit. They put me into … a little medical centre … not that they had doctors and that, but they put me in isolation, for want of a better word.'

According to Lewis he slept little that night, and found it hard to believe the jury's decision.

The next day, he recorded in his diary – the compulsive diarist initially kept random secret notes of his experiences, then was later officially granted use of a conventional diary – that he had been interviewed by a prison intelligence officer and was told, 'it would be a great achievement for some prisoners to get me; need to take care re attack at all times; putting glass in food a popular thing; also put glass in or slash clothing if sent to Prison laundry ... try to retain sanity until after appeal'.

Lewis says he must have been visited by wife Hazel and the children in the first couple of days of his incarceration. 'Every time that anybody came to visit you, you had to go in in front of ... any other prisoners that happened to be there ... and drop your pants and let them look up your backside,' Lewis recalls. 'You know, I was 60 years of bloody age or more ... I don't think they should have necessarily feared I was going to be bringing drugs into the prison. I think some of the warders enjoyed the fact that they had ... this high-profile prisoner.'

The prison arranged, through chaplain Father Walter Ogle, for members of Lewis's family to see him. 'Really, the main thought was for your family,' Lewis says. 'I thought what a ... after working all your life that you finished [up] here through the bloody lies of one person, helped by [a] completely manipulated system ... and Hazel would have nothing and the family would be sort of maligned for the rest of their lives.'

On 14 August Lewis learned that he had lost his police long service leave and annual recreational entitlements. He wrote in his prison diary: '... hard to imagine the feelings of disbelief, dismay, shock, depression and horror when you constantly realise that it is not a nightmare, that it is real.'

Wacol

Ten days after landing in Boggo Road, Lewis was transferred to Wacol medium-security prison. That day, Thursday 15 August, he arrived at his new lodgings in a prison van at 4.20 p.m. and was immediately taken to a secure six-bed hospital ward. 'Warned to be careful as there was a lot of mouthing off by prisoners whilst on pill-run as to what they would do to me,' he recorded in his diary.

Lewis remembers: 'They put me in what wasn't really a hospital but ... an area with about five or six beds in it and a little dispensary, I suppose you'd call it, in the front. And [the manager] did say that I could stay there indefinitely because it wasn't used as a hospital. If anybody got ... ill they were immediately sent up to the 24-hour place at either Moreton [Correctional Centre] or David Longman [Correctional Centre] or sent into the Princess Alexandra Hospital.

'Well, I really was almost, if you like, in ... solitary confinement ... that was my home but they did give me a job in the store, which was maybe a hundred yards away from where I was domiciled. And in a very short space of time I was given a ... which some of the warders didn't like ... [a] key to get into the store, and they didn't think that was right. So, I'd have my cereal breakfast and then I'd go up to the store immediately and spend the day there.'

Lewis encountered a variety of cell mates in his early days at Wacol. There were corrupt former Federal police gaoled for drug offences, and a young man who later hanged himself in prison.

Given his extraordinary organisational skills, Lewis was soon running the little store single-handedly. 'Well, you'd get abused by one or two every now and then,' Lewis remembers. 'I didn't do any exercise for ages and they let me go out in a little enclosed area between the store and where I was staying, and adjoining that was the detention units. Eventually they let me go outside to exercise and then some smartarse warder after a while said ... that wasn't allowed, and then that was stopped for about two months until I managed to get it reinstated.'

In his first month at Wacol, Lewis was shown some kindness by a prison official who brought him a radio. He bumped into Toowoomba SP bookmaker Bruce Bowd, gaoled for corruption courtesy of the Fitzgerald Inquiry, who told him that perjury charges against Lewis had been dropped in the District Court that morning. 'Bruce B. said that he had lost a $1000 bet when I was convicted,' Lewis wrote in his prison diary. '[He said] that I was convicted by the media and that Jack Herbert is the greatest liar he has ever met.'

On Friday 6 September, Lewis received a phone call from his old friend Tony Murphy who 'said that he heard that the Forewoman on my Jury was in the Sales Tax Dept. and was determined to get me'.

It was the beginning of Lewis's relentless campaign to clear his name, which would preoccupy his thinking through his entire incarceration.

Declining Royalty

In September 1991, as Lewis got used to life behind bars, former premier Sir Joh Bjelke-Petersen went on trial for perjury stemming from evidence he gave before the Fitzgerald Inquiry. The charge centred on Bjelke-Petersen's evidence in relation to a $100,000 donation given to him personally by Singapore businessman Robert Sng.

Bjelke-Petersen had told Fitzgerald that the money had come from a Hong Kong businessman, whom he had never previously met. He also said the $100,000 in a brown envelope was actually given to his secretary. At the inquiry, the former premier was asked if he knew whether Sng was conducting business in Queensland at the time. 'Not that I know of, no,' Bjelke-Petersen had replied.

Bjelke-Petersen swore that he had first met Sng in September 1986, when in reality the two had actually been in contact 23 times between late 1985 and late 1986. Sng had even travelled out to Bethany to catch up with the then Premier and his wife, Lady Flo. Approval for the new hotel precinct on the site of the the old Port Office in Edward Street was announced by Bjelke-Petersen at a National Party conference on 17 July 1986. Final approval was given by the government in late

November, two months after Sng supposedly made his generous donation in the premier's office.

If found guilty, Bjelke-Petersen faced up to 14 years in prison. The trial was presided over by District Court Chairman, Judge Helman.

On 24 September, prosecutor Nicholas Cowdery told the court that it could expect to hear evidence 'of some improper dealings, which are at the heart of official corruption'. He further alleged that Bjelke-Petersen had lied to the Fitzgerald commission in order to avoid a link between the cash donation and the Port Office development. He said the fact that the accused had been the Queensland Premier was important to the case.

The court heard that Sng made his donation to Bjelke-Petersen on 17 September and the money went into the account of a company controlled by Sir Edward Lyons called Kaldeal. The next day, Sng made an identical donation to National Party President Sir Robert Sparkes, that money going into Party accounts.

Robert Sng was called as a witness.

He said his company, Historic Holdings, had been facing the final hurdle of government approval and he felt he had to somehow show support for the National Party. Sng said a former solicitor of his had told him, as early as 1984, that if he was going into business in Queensland he needed to make a donation to the National Party, as it was normal practice.

Sng said he had met Sir Joh on several occasions and had once given the Premier an 'inexpensive Rolex' watch as a gift. He added that towards the end of 1987 he had received a call from Bjelke-Petersen's secretary asking if he could find a job for her boss. He said he telephoned mining support service company Hastings Deering in Hong Kong, and then he and Bjelke-Petersen flew there together to see about the job. The former premier was soon employed by Hastings Deering in Brisbane.

In his final address, Cowdery told the jury that common sense would reject the notion that Bjelke-Petersen, in his later years, was a befuddled old man and didn't know where he was or who he was talking to. He said the defence had produced witnesses who held up Sir Joh as a 'figure of declining royalty' who was pushed out for people to look at, then pulled back in. Cowdery told them that when Bjelke-Petersen gave evidence at the Fitzgerald Inquiry, he knew what he was saying.

The Crown attested that Bjelke-Petersen's activities were such that he would never forget Sng unless dementia took hold. You don't forget the man who gave you $100,000, or the man who gave you a job when you retired, or the man you flew to Hong Kong with to spend a week, Cowdery said.

Robert Greenwood, QC, for Bjelke-Petersen, told the court the 'one miserable charge of perjury' was only 'supported by half-baked evidence of so-called corruption to do with a donation from our friend Mr Robert Sng'. He said with a flourish that the only thing between the jury and a guilty verdict would be the 'last possible kick in the teeth' that Queensland could deliver for the long-time premier. Greenwood said whether you like him or not, Bjelke-Petersen had done a lot of good for Queensland.

The trial lasted four weeks and the jury deliberated for five days. They could not reach a verdict. It was later revealed that the jury foreman, Luke Shaw, was associated with the Young National Party of Australia and for a few months had been secretary of the Brisbane Central branch. Shaw, 20, a commerce student at the Queensland University of Technology, said his political affiliations had not prejudiced his duty as a juror, which he had conducted 'with all the respect, authority and seriousness due to it'.

(In 2005 Robert Sng broke a 14-year silence and told the *Courier-Mail* that he believed Bjelke-Petersen was only charged with perjury because he had a 'rotten memory'. 'He used to refer to me as Robin, Richard and some other names,' he said. 'He had a terrible memory for names.')

Nightmares

In early 1993, Lewis began recording his dreams in his prison diary. They ranged from trips back into his past, to violent acts, to his fear for the safety of his family. On Thursday 29 April 1993, he awoke at 2.50 a.m. and then at 5.45 a.m., having dreamed of 'those two master perjurers Jack and Peggy Herbert'.

On 4 May he recorded: 'Dream/nightmare re: proposed reinstatement as Commissioner of Police.'

On 8 May he was stung by media comments made by lawyer Terry O'Gorman in relation to himself and the notorious saga of policewoman Lorelle Saunders, which was once again being played out in court as the disgruntled officer, the first female detective in the Queensland Police Force, alleged that she had been set-up by police and wrongly imprisoned. The Saunders case had caused enormous damage to Lewis, and still it refused to go away.

'Terry O'Gorman's comments on *7.30 Report* and CJC [Criminal Justice Commission] asking him if rumour was right that I wanted to give them a lengthy statement i.e. "roll over"; did I want to speak to them here about Saunders; or would I like a day out in town to speak with them. He agreed that my refusal on all three is correct as I have no information that would be useful for a "roll over" and nothing favourable about Lorelle Saunders.'

He wrote on Tuesday 25 May of suffering 'plenty of nightmares. Not good start for day.' He recorded that two inmates were assaulted overnight, one in his sleep. 'Every day seems more depressing,' wrote the former police commissioner.

Lewis would later reflect on his mindset in prison: 'I was feeling more and more useless. I felt I'd been a fairly useful person all my life … and I think nearly everybody I had anything to do with felt I'd been pretty useful. But there were times you felt, you know, what's the use? It would be better if you were dead.'

He says he contemplated suicide: 'I realised what the consequences would be, and actually, you don't even make any attempt to do anything but you think, shit, what a useless life it is, and looking at 14 years is just … you think, oh, I'll probably be dead in that time anyhow … [suicide was] just a general thought. I think it must cross most people's mind, you know, you'd be better off dead, but you don't think, yeah, I'm going to go and get a gun or get a bit of rope and learn how to tie a knot with it.'

A few days later, on Saturday 29 May, Lewis's depression had not lifted. As winter approached, he was telephoned by his old mate on the Gold Coast, former police officer John Meskell, and bumped into one-time brothel king Hector Hapeta. Tony Murphy also phoned to keep Lewis updated on the Saunders case.

Lewis had more dreams: about his wife Hazel enrolling him in medical studies; about his grandparents, the Hanlons; and about visiting the Juvenile Aid Bureau, where he spent more than a decade of his career. He wrote in his diary that the future seemed dismal.

On Sunday 20 June, he wrote that a cell mate's brother had recently seen Jack Herbert at the Hilton Hotel in Cairns 'with two males, apparently bodyguards, Herbert had hand-held telephone'.

His dreams, too, were physically troubling him. 'Feel tremendous tension in head, maybe partly caused by dreams involving family members in dangerous, annoying or sorrowful situations,' Lewis wrote.

Still, he continued on with his ambition to prove his innocence: 'I need access to transcripts, newspapers, certain persons, etc., to compile my project regarding my innocence. There is also the most important aspect of trying to clear my name for the future of my wife, children and grandchildren.

'While I have an intense dislike of Herbert and feel that he does not deserve to live, I do not want him dead, as there may be the possibility of him contracting some serious lingering disease that would cause him to tell the truth prior to his demise. He is certainly the grand master of merging truth and lies for his own criminal purposes.'

Meanwhile, he had his own personal safety to consider. He says he was the target of several verbal threats. 'I don't know whether you're supposed to know this or not, but … there's always threats, they'll get you … they'll get you,' recalls Lewis. 'There was one big bloke, a prisoner, I don't know why they picked on him … but they'd waited till he walked in a room, threw a bag over the top of him and four of them raped him … and they said [to me] … if we get you down there, we'll rape you, we'll do this, we'll do everything.

'Well it wouldn't have achieved much, but I said … they'll want to get in quick because … I'll kill the first two that try. I mightn't get the rest [but] whoever does do it won't want to walk outside the prison because, I said, I still have a lot of friends out there.'

Memory Lane

Prisoner Lewis received a letter from the Criminal Justice Commission (CJC), dated 11 June 1993, in relation to an investigation it was conducting – more than 10 years after the event – into the case of policewoman Lorelle Saunders. The CJC investigation, headed by Judge Ronald H. Matthews, QC, was charged with examining the framing and imprisonment of Saunders in the early 1980s.

Saunders had been charged with serious offences in 1982, including attempting to procure murder, and had been in gaol on remand for more than ten months before the charges against her were thrown out. It was found a chief piece of evidence against her – a secret tape recording where she could be heard attempting to hire a hitman – had been fabricated.

Although there was no evidence implicating Lewis in any alleged set-up, the judge presiding over the case requested that Lewis respond to comments Saunders had made in relation to him. Lewis had already indicated, through his legal advisor John Jerrard, QC, that he would not appear before the inquiry as a witness.

Instead, Lewis was asked to answer a series of questions by statutory declaration. It would prove to be a trip down memory lane – the CJC providing him with a sequence of written preambles, and questions that followed.

Saunders alleged that Lewis and Murphy had, in the early 1970s, been critical of then Commissioner Ray Whitrod, and disagreed with the way he wished to treat juveniles. She said Lewis had ordered JAB (Juvenile Aid Bureau) officers to circumvent Whitrod's directions. Lewis was also critical of Whitrod's establishment of the elite Criminal Intelligence Unit. Was that true?

Lewis's response was direct and to the point. 'I was certainly critical of the Commissioner for his [juveniles] policy ... I do not recall criticising him for the existence of the Criminal Intelligence Unit,' Lewis responded. He said the scenario alleged by Saunders did not cause him to dislike her.

In another preamble, Saunders claimed that Lewis and Murphy had had a 'major disagreement' over arrangements for the JAB Christmas party. She said Murphy was angry with Lewis for holding it at the old National Hotel, scene of the contentious police corruption inquiry in 1963 and 1964. Was this true, and did he ever form the view that Sergeant Saunders thought he was corrupt?

Lewis was dismissive and could not recall an argument with Murphy over the venue. Furthermore, 'I never formed the view that Sergeant Saunders thought I was corrupt.'

Saunders further alleged that she often sat outside the home of criminal and drug dealer Billy Phillips in Vulture Street, West End, and picked up people for various offences. She claimed that Lewis and Murphy were, at the time, very angry with her about this. Was he in any way improperly protecting Phillips?

Lewis flatly denied it. 'I have not heard of this allegation being made against me previously,' he wrote. 'I had never heard of Sergeant Saunders' alleged activities outside the house of Mr Phillips in Vulture Street.'

Saunders further claimed that the Police Administration considered her 'highly dangerous due to her knowledge of certain corrupt officers'. Did he consider her highly dangerous, and did he act improperly in relation to this?

'... I did not consider Sergeant Saunders was "highly dangerous" to myself or to my administration,' Lewis responded.

'I do not wish to be offensive,' he added, 'but the truth is that the existence of Sergeant Saunders was of no interest, let alone a threat, to me until her arrest. After that, my only interest was that she was a Police Officer.'

In the end, Justice Matthews would find that Saunders was not 'set up' by corrupt police, and that he couldn't see any justification for awarding costs. 'Considerable resources over the years have been committed in respect of the matter and to pursue further action at this time would serve no good purpose,' Matthews said. 'In my opinion it would certainly be in the interests of all parties to get on with their lives and try and put the matter behind them.'

Saunders was dismissed from the Queensland Police Force in 1995, after police alleged she gave three false statements before the inquiry looking into her case.

Visitors

As the second anniversary of Lewis's imprisonment approached, it gave him pause to think, not only about his life but the impact of his incarceration on his wife Hazel and their five children. On Saturday 24 July, Lewis wrote in his diary that he found Sunday morning the most depressing day of the week because although he was visited by his family for two hours, he'd then have to face another week before he could see them again. He also believed that his imprisonment had a powerful, irreversible adverse impact on the lives of his children.

Lewis says: 'Apart from my work [in prison], if I could call it that, I had very, very little contact with anybody else. And then … they did agree, thank goodness, that when Hazel or the family came in to see me they could see me in the store.'

'I had [police officer] David Jefferies come to see me, [police officer] Don Braithwaite come to see me, [Queensland newspaper executive] Ron Richards came to see me … oh yeah, I had quite a few. Some in their own time, some on duty, some in uniform, you know …'

It was around this time that Lewis began to question his faith. 'Oh, I didn't lean over backwards towards it,' Lewis ponders. 'While I was in prison at Wacol they used to have a Mass every week … but I must confess … I've never been much impressed with religion ever since.'

For Lewis, gaol time led to the conclusion that there was no God. 'I just can't get my head around it,' he says. 'You know, if you kick the bucket you go somewhere, you're there forever. Where are they going to put them all? They talk about a loving and forgiving God. Well it just doesn't quite add up. I hope I'm wrong, but no, I've never been interested in going to Church since. And in fact … all of my family have given it up, the lot of them.'

Lewis lamented the loss of all of the money he had saved after so many decades of hard work. He dreamed of former commissioner Ray Whitrod and a nerve-gas apocalypse where 'all my family died, but I survived'.

Tony Murphy telephoned to inform him about former police officer Pat Glancy having an operation, and Lewis's former personal assistant, Assistant Commissioner Greg Early, also called to fill him in on news from the police force. For the rest of the time Lewis literally counted the days. 'Well I did count it by the day in the back of my diaries,' he says, 'and it just didn't seem as if it was ever going to end really.'

As spring arrived, Lewis recorded that he had lost interest 'in most things'. He dreamed of Prince Charles, of Sir Joh Bjelke-Petersen, of a crocodile on a bed with one of his children, of cutting off the heads of murderers with a shovel, spying in Nazi Germany, and of a tiger pulling his body apart.

He had an upcoming visit from Tony Murphy to look forward to, but the question of his innocence still nagged at him. He was worried about the perceived pressure from prison officials for him to offer an admission of guilt before his parole would be considered. How could he offer that when he was not guilty?

Lewis also began preparing an application for Special Circumstances Parole consideration. On Sunday 7 November, he telephoned his trial lawyer, John Jerrard, QC, and told him the application would have to concentrate on Hazel's health, as well as his and possibly [daughter] Laureen's, before focusing on prison conditions and potential risk.

Three days later, Graeme Parker called. He told Lewis he only vaguely remembered the Fitzgerald Inquiry because he had been so ill at the time.

Then, on Monday 29 November, Tony Murphy visited his old friend. Lewis recorded in his diary that they discussed police gossip and a sighting of Jack and Peggy Herbert on the Gold Coast.

While Lewis may have been consumed by his own troubles, he was not the only person who faced gaol time following the Fitzgerald Inquiry. Geraldo Bellino was a fellow inmate at Wacol, having been imprisoned for seven years in 1991. Vittorio Conte, having served his sentence, had been released from prison and was living in a halfway house for ex-prisoners in South Brisbane. He would go on to publish a book on gambling called *Vic Conte's Casino Buster*.

And there were also a number of police whose lives, like Lewis's, had veered off-track. Harry Burgess was working in a metal factory on

Brisbane's southside, while Graeme Parker had supposedly turned to God and had become a travelling salesman.

As for Lewis, he stewed with anger in the storeroom at Wacol. 'I was so angry at the people who I firmly believed had conspired to put me where I was,' he says.

Helping Hands

Despite his lingering depression, and dreams of attempting suicide only to be revived by doctors, Terry Lewis approached his second Christmas in prison with grim determination. On Christmas Eve he dreamed of 'planning torture for some persons; killing some people by chopping them up with a huge blade – like meat for stew'.

He was also worried about his wife Hazel. Lewis had always been a stickler for the small, personal ceremonies of life – birthdays, anniversaries, Christmas – and he may have felt his separation from his wife and family more deeply during the festive seasons. Once, he and Hazel would have enjoyed a whirlwind of Christmas parties, drinks, dinners and cocktails, pressing the flesh with dignitaries and old friends. Now, Lewis had only Reader's Digest condensed books for company.

He recorded in his diary that he was conscious of Hazel's feelings in relation to their lack of finance and the loss of their home up on Garfield Drive. Lewis also worried over their 'uncertain future'. The only thing that kept him going, he wrote, was a desire to see 'certain people punished someday for their lies'.

On Christmas Day he had 'turkey roll, ham and salad' for lunch. 'Present of soap for Hazel, shaving cream and aftershave for me for Christmas,' he noted. 'Washed shower curtain. Bed at 10.30pm.'

In the first week of the New Year, Tony Murphy again visited, this time with some encouraging news. 'Visit by A. Murphy re approach by

Mr D[es]. Sturgess, QC, regarding my trial being fatally flawed from the very opening address,' Lewis wrote.

Not long after, he received a follow-up call from Tony Murphy 're: him speaking to Des, whom I will note as D.Q.C. in the future. Not a word to be said to anyone, I will not even mention to Hazel.' It lifted Lewis's spirit to know that a lawyer of the eminence of Sturgess, the former director of prosecutions, would be willing to revise Lewis's trial. 'He wants a copy of the opening and for me to read through the transcript and note where I protested about the evidence being allowed and not relevant.'

That same day, 'Jerry [sic] Bellino called at door of Main Store, said "hello" and "when are you coming up to the Work Scheme?" I replied, "I have no idea".'

On 8 January 1994, the Managing Editor of Queensland Newspapers, Ron Richards, popped in to see Lewis. 'Discussed my being railroaded by Gunn; Fitzgerald; some media persons and Herbert,' Lewis wrote in his diary.

On the night before Australia Day, Lewis was visited in his dreams by 'Mr F. Bischof'.

By March, with little or no action in relation to the trial being re-examined by Sturgess, Lewis again fell into an aggravated state, worried that his lack of patience had led to 'a deterioration in manners'.

Murphy again visited Lewis on 11 March and they discussed a defamation writ Murphy had out against the *Sunday Sun* newspaper. According to Lewis's diary, Murphy assured him that if the writ was successful, he would contribute some money towards Lewis's legal assistance. Lewis was delighted. A leading lawyer believed his trial was flawed, and an old mate was prepared to help out.

However, just 48 hours later, his mood slipped. He wrote: 'Another part [of my mind] says that you have to continue until you complete a true presentation by way of a TV series and/or newspaper articles and a book of the manner in which the Fitzgerald Inquiry came into being through the ambitions of Gunn and Ahern; how it was conducted by Fitzgerald and his close group of money hungry prostitutes of the legal profession by way of manipulation of the government, the media and many of the witnesses through conspiracy, perjury and censorship of media, particularly for example, Dempster, ABC; Dickie, *Courier-Mail*; and Whitton, *Sun* newspapers.

'This has to be done in an endeavour to show my innocence, primarily for the sake of my family who have suffered so much, as well as for the history of the Queensland Police Force and for the citizens of Queensland generally.'

A week later, Lewis received a message via his family from Murphy. 'He [Murphy] phoned ... at 7am this morning and said that his legal advisor, Evatt, a QC from Sydney, has told him that he will not win his action unless he forgets his loyalty to me and puts and [sic] blame from him onto me. He is to say that I must have misled him over the years. He is not to criticise the High Court decision against me otherwise he will be "pissing against the wind". He is to say that his visits to me were purely "compassionate visits".

'He is not to have any further contact with me whilst court action being undertaken. He said that if he won and got some money he would give me some to pursue the matter with D.Q.C.'

Murphy won his defamation case against the defunct *Sun* newspapers after they published in late 1988 stories that supposedly linked him to the Whiskey Au Go Go firebombing in 1973. In its apology, the *Sun* said Murphy 'had absolutely nothing to do with the Whiskey Au Go Go murders either directly or indirectly'.

After the win, Murphy declared he would have a beer and perhaps go fishing. He phoned Lewis in prison to give him the news. A few days later he called to tell Lewis: '... D.Q.C. has been busy and has not yet read part of transcript; Heather Hallahan saw the two Herberts at Jupiter's [sic] Casino recently, both very well dressed'.

Murphy visited again in April. 'Saw D.Q.C., who has "flogged" ...

sections of [Crown lawyer in Lewis's trial, Bob] Mulholland's opening and he is prepared to speak to [another lawyer] for an opinion if we agree. Tony will have his son, solicitor, speak to his boss re handling matter and he will then contact [the other lawyer] and Tony will pay for that.'

For years, Murphy, like Lewis, remained bitter over the Fitzgerald Inquiry. Murphy's family say he was 'soured off' and that the whole experience had unfairly tarnished an extraordinary career. 'When he was getting all the bad publicity he was wondering what people were thinking of him, people who used to look up to him.'

It was ironic that Murphy had never been convicted for anything, they observed. 'With everything that happened he was never ... not once ... the media didn't like him. He sued them a few times,' they said.

Even so, Murphy stood by his mates. 'Dad was very loyal, even to Jack Herbert,' the family says. 'Even Dad sticking by him during his first court case [the Southport Betting Case]. He stuck by him and didn't give him the cold shoulder.

'You know, whether Dad knew Jack was up to mischief, being how he is, he was a man about town ... he [Herbert] was the most polite, entertaining guy you'd ever meet. He knew how to work a room and make everybody feel good. He was a master of that sort of relationship.'

Murphy's wife, Maureen, adds: 'We didn't have grand things ... We never had flash cars and expensive trips around the world. We didn't have any money.'

On the Move

In the early hours of Tuesday 14 June, Lewis dreamed of 'a three year old boy slashing my hands with a Stanley knife'.

After a breakfast of tea, toast, honey, jam and cheese, he was told to pack his belongings. He was being transferred to the Moreton

Correctional Centre. Throughout his life, Lewis had been a man who clung to routine. It gave him structure. It provided certainty. Without it, he lost his balance. His diaries revealed that even overseas trips in his role as commissioner – though itinerated – threw him off keel. He loathed the loneliness and pined for letters and phone calls from home throughout.

Now, he was being pulled out of his prison routine and it didn't please him. At 12.20 p.m. he was escorted to his new digs. He recorded that the new environment was intimidating, and that he was on edge. He was taken to a 'cottage' with several rooms, where two inmates recommended he take 'room 9', which had a bar heater on the wall and was closer to the toilets. The facility had two showers, a kitchen, a lounge area and a laundry. There was 'very, very old carpet' on the floor.

Later in the afternoon, Lewis met eight or nine of his fellow inmates – young white offenders in their twenties and thirties. Dinner was brought to the cottage in a hot box at 4.30 p.m. Lewis was in bed by 10 p.m. but didn't sleep for most of the night. He immediately disliked Moreton, citing that he had less freedom of movement, contact and conversation.

Working in the store, Lewis crossed paths with former Labor Opposition leader and fellow inmate Keith Wright, jailed for sex offences. Wright had been the ALP's great hope in the early 1980s, and had come within a whisker of dethroning Joh Bjelke-Petersen and the National Party in the 1983 state election. In 1993, however, he was found guilty of raping a teenage girl. The court found that Wright had 'systematically sexually abused' the girl over a three-year period from age 13. He was imprisoned for eight years. In gaol, the erudite Wright taught prisoners literacy skills.

Lewis noted that Wright seemed to have 'plenty of money' and that he had purchased $100 worth of foodstuffs and confectionaries. The two would later converse. Wright told Lewis that any book he might consider writing would be a 'blockbuster', and that the former police commissioner's enemies were actually within the National Party. Wright further made the observation that he thought the media had allowed Lewis to receive a fair trial.

He assured Lewis that he had befriended the 'heavies' in prison and had only two unwelcome incidents with inmates. Wright said, too, that Lewis had a significant number of supporters within the Queensland Police. Soon after, Wright – a former teacher and Baptist preacher – asked Lewis to attend his Church Fellowship meetings. Lewis declined.

On Sunday 10 July, wife Hazel and daughter Lanna came to visit. It was a cold and wet day. Later, Lewis's lawyer, Rick Whitton, encouraged him to record in his prison diaries his thoughts and feelings, saying it would be nearly impossible to accurately recreate them in later years. The suggestion seemed to trigger Lewis's melancholy. He noted that he had worked as hard as he possibly could for 37 years, which in turn had denied him quality time with his family. He wrote that he had had many plans for the future, one of which was the construction of the new house on Garfield Drive, which he and Hazel had hardly had time to enjoy when the Fitzgerald Inquiry was announced. His other dreams for the future had disappeared like a 'mirage'.

Lewis recorded in his diary that his blood pressure was tested in the prison hospital and the mention of the word 'politicians' shot it 'right up'. A nurse asked him about Sir Joh and he told her he was 'an outstanding Premier'. Another nurse said she had heard of many unlawful things done by Russ Hinze. Lewis refused to comment.

In August, Tony Murphy again visited and talked about his recent trip to the Seychelles, off the east coast of Africa, which was 'good but very expensive there – $500 per night for hotels, $48 for carton of beer, [a] millionaire's holiday there'.

On Saturday 20 August, the *Courier-Mail* published a report on the outcome of all court cases stemming from the Fitzgerald Inquiry that had been running for several years. It began: 'They were the men and women who changed Queensland. Some corrupted it with greed and betrayed public trust. Others, like heroes, cleansed the state with scrupulous integrity that helped Queenslanders regain lost faith in public officials.' The article described Police Commissioner Lewis as 'rotten to the core'.

Lewis fought back in his diary entry for that day, saying that it caused him 'terrible heartbreak' to read the frequent articles saying what a dreadful person he was, and that he was not in a position to defend himself. He hinted that his fight back was yet to come and that in time he would expose the 'conspiracy' that was the Fitzgerald Inquiry. He hoped Tony Murphy would help him out, given that his friend had a sharp mind, a great knowledge, and that he was 'tenacious'.

In late October, Lewis was again moved, this time to Palen Creek Correctional Centre near Rathdowney, south of Beaudesert. He had been downgraded to a low-security classification. The Queensland Corrective Services Commission Chairman, Professor Patrick Weller, told the press he didn't expect a prisoner like Lewis to be any threat to the public. 'Lewis is being treated exactly the same as any other prisoner,' he said.

Tilley, Civilian

Former brothel madam Anne Marie Tilley had pleaded guilty to two charges of official corruption and had been sentenced to five years in prison.

On her eventual release she opted to stay in Brisbane. She conceded that the Fitzgerald Inquiry 'basically' got to the core of the corruption. She said the 'Sydney connection' probably wasn't adequately explored. 'I wouldn't fuck with people in Sydney,' she says. 'They don't tell you. They don't threaten you. They just do it. I was glad it was all over.'

Local human rights advocate and lawyer Debbie Kilroy gave Tilley a job on her release from prison. 'I didn't have much choice,' says Tilley. 'My daughter was in foster care. Deb had helped my daughter. Deb was the only one I knew to ring. When I had to get parole, I needed a parole address. Deb said, "Put my address."'

Adjusting to life on the outside was a challenge. Tilley admits she found it difficult. She had only known one thing – prostitution. 'When Deb employed me, I knew nothing,' she recalls. 'Up until then, I'd never lived straight in my life.' She had to learn how to keep house, how to pay the electricity bill, how to start a bank account. 'I didn't want to go near anyone [after the inquiry],' she says. 'How could it just be Jack Herbert [who got away with it]? He was retired, sitting up in his [expensive] unit [in the city]. It's ridiculous.'

In the Joint with Hector

Anthony 'Tony' William Corrigan came from a good and respectable family in Melbourne. He was well educated and had a natural intelligence, particularly for numbers, but conventional suburban life never appealed to him. He preferred to be out on the streets, checking out the action, or on the move, 'having a look around' and travelling where the whim took him. As a youth he got into some minor trouble on the streets of the Victorian capital before he set out on his travels.

He did a stint in Sydney, where he worked as a strapper for the renowned trainer, Tommy Smith, before heading to Adelaide. He successfully studied accountancy, putting his talent for numbers to good use, before eventually returning to Sydney. He got married and started working for a large health food company then seriously damaged his back lifting palettes of goods in the warehouse. A not unreasonable compensation cheque came his way, and flush with cash he decided to move north, to Queensland. Life was looking good for Corrigan. He bought a house in Petrie, north of Brisbane, and after a few false starts he landed a senior position with the Black and White taxi company.

In the early 1980s, he was amused at how business was conducted in the country's northern state. 'There was a fuel roster in Queensland,' Corrigan recalls. 'In the Brisbane metro area, only one or two garages were allowed to be open on a weekend. Taxi companies were allowed to be open to deal with their members. If you wanted fuel off the roster you had to go to Carseldine, the taxi companies traded illegally. We made a fortune.

'Every Monday, the Department of Transport would come in and say they observed so and so buying petrol. We were facing 77 summons and fines of $10,000 for illegal trading.'

He soon learned there was a simple way to make all those problems go away. 'To keep going, each of the taxi companies put in about $1000 each,' says Corrigan. 'I remember writing cheques and charging it to spare parts. On behalf of all the taxi companies I took it to [Transport Minister] Don Lane's electoral office in Merthyr. I took it in a brown paper bag. I did it a couple of times.'

As soon as World Expo 88 came to town trading hours were opened up. '[Premier Sir] Joh had all the fines wiped. We were heavily supported in Cabinet by Don Lane and Joh Bjelke-Petersen. They cancelled them all.'

What Black and White didn't know was that Corrigan was siphoning off funds for his own personal use. He was soon living in a splendid house in Bridgeman Downs, north of the city. He bought some classy trotters and imported racing greyhounds. He had new cars. A boat. He was rolling in money. In all, he says he took about $1.86 million. It brought Black and White taxis to its knees.

Corrigan was subsequently charged with the fraud and pleaded guilty to 103 misappropriation charges. On 13 May 1993, he was sentenced to ten years in prison. It was there, in Borallon Correctional Centre, west of Brisbane, that he first met Hector Hapeta, star of the

Fitzgerald Inquiry and in prison on drugs charges. (Hepeta had been charged with heroin trafficking in 1998 and was also serving eight years after pleading guilty to six charges of official corruption stemming from Fitzgerald Inquiry findings.)

'He was just an affable bloke,' remembers Corrigan. 'He was interested in what you were doing. He didn't sort of suffer fools. He'd say hello to everybody. It's hard to have a bad word for him.'

The two yarned about their respective pasts. Hapeta told Corrigan how he got into crime. He was 16 years old and working on the wharves in New Zealand. On a day off, he drifted into a local pool hall and struck up a conversation with another man. Do you work? Hapeta asked him. No, the man replied, you don't have to work.

'He introduced Hector into crime,' recalls Corrigan. 'He met some girl and he was the first man charged in New Zealand with living off the earnings of a prostitute.'

Later in Sydney, Hapeta told Corrigan, he worked as a nightclub bouncer. 'His advice was to never pick on the little guy, and always give a person an honourable out, because with the little guy if you don't do that, you give him no option but to come back with a gun.'

Hapeta talked often about the time leading up to the Fitzgerald Inquiry and the inquiry itself. He allegedly told Corrigan that when the commission was announced he [Hapeta] and other crime figures discussed murdering The Bagman, Jack Herbert. 'They knew that if they killed Herbert, they'd be okay,' says Corrigan.

'Well, no one was going to kill him. No one had the intestinal fortitude to do it. They relied on [Sydney businessman and Mafia-connected] Jack Rooklyn. They thought Rooklyn would do the job.'

Corrigan also recalled an incident where Hapeta got involved in a fight over the city's illegal gambling casinos and trashed one of them in frustration. 'Hector was hopeless on the drink,' says Corrigan. 'He got upset because he wanted a share of the gambling. Hector got drunk and had a blue and destroyed the place.'

Days later, Hapeta was 'called in' by Jack Herbert and 'chastised like a school kid'. Hapeta said Herbert had to fine him for his poor behaviour. They permanently confiscated his motor boat.

'Hector laughed, he said it cost him a boat,' says Corrigan.

He said Hapeta 'did it easy' in gaol. 'He didn't cause any trouble in gaol. Everybody sort of looked after him. I used to cook his meals at Borallon. I got him down from about 170 kilograms to about 97 kilograms. We talked and walked and talked and walked. Talked shit most of the time. He wasn't a liar. He wouldn't tell you a lie. He simply wouldn't answer the question.'

Did Hapeta give up all he knew in relation to the Fitzgerald Inquiry?

'I don't think anybody did,' Corrigan says. 'Hector did indicate that Bellino paid the same [to the police]. Might have been other rorts, I have no idea. You're talking $80,000 to $100,000 a month ... there were that many coppers who were dirty and their names were never mentioned. Nobody's ever heard of them.'

Hapeta had little to do with Terry Lewis, although at one point they were both in Wacol at the same time.

'I think there was some respect for him [Lewis] because he never opened his mouth. It's hard to open your mouth and not implicate yourself,' says Corrigan. 'The minute you know something ... it's only a crime if two people know. They gave him credit because he didn't open his mouth.'

As for Hapeta, it was all fun while it lasted. 'Hector ran businesses for the coppers and they all made a quid,' Corrigan reflects. 'He wasn't a killer. It was hard not to like him.'

A String of Deaths

While Lewis was contemplating his own mortality – prisoners had advised him that the best way to bleed to death was to cut the flap of skin under your tongue – he would soon be rocked by a string of deaths on the outside.

His dreams remained vivid: 'Attempt to kill the Queen ... I fired five shots and Queen helped me to remove shells and reload revolver.' And life in gaol continued one slow week at a time. His lawyer Rick Whitton called, urging Lewis to come to a decision on legally fighting for his superannuation. Whitton suggested he forfeit it.

'Said I did not want to as I owed them nothing,' wrote Lewis. 'Rick said you cannot beat them as they do not have to prove guilt but I would have to justify innocence. How do you prove something that did not happen?'

On 1 December his old police mates John Meskell and Patrick Glancy dropped by. 'John brought four chocolates, three novels and four bottles of water,' recorded Lewis. 'Many sent their regards.'

Lewis's new duties at Palen Creek included washing and wiping up crockery and cutlery, sweeping all of the administration and the store area, unloading bread and milk on Mondays, Wednesdays and Fridays, refuelling vehicles, unloading cartons of soft drink, unloading fruit and vegetables, faxing purchase orders, answering the telephone, dividing loaves of bread into three portions and dividing sugar.

On New Year's Day, 1995, he awoke from a nightmare that included a 'male maniac chasing the Queen' and a 'big male cooking a number of human bodies and eating them'. In the coming weeks he would dream of Murphy, Glen Patrick Hallahan and crooked Sydney cop Fred Krahe.

In the third week of January, it was stormy and gloomy outside. Lewis could hear some of the younger inmates shouting out 'Good night for a murder.'

Come 12 March, Lewis received the news that former Transport Minister Don Lane, had died. He simply recorded in his diary: 'Don Lane, heart attack yesterday, dead.'

In 1990, before Lewis's trial, Lane had been sent to prison for

12 months after being found guilty of misappropriating public funds, the money spent on meals, hotels, car hire and wedding gifts for his staff and close contacts. At just 59, Lane dropped dead on his property at Warwick, 155 kilometres south-west of Brisbane.

Former premier Joh Bjelke-Petersen commented on Lane's death, painting his former transport minister as a victim: '... a minister takes his family out for dinner over the many years he was a minister and he goes to jail for it and, boy oh boy, talk about a one-sided, lopsided sort of system of justice,' Bjelke-Petersen said. He added, 'It had a very big effect on Don. He took that very, very hard.'

Lane's death may have spooked Lewis. While he claims that they never shared a close friendship, the late minister had certainly been a beneficial contact within Cabinet.

Then on Friday 28 April, Lewis heard the news he had not wanted to hear. He had lost his legal battle for his $1.4 million superannuation payout. Supreme Court Justice Brian Ambrose ruled that Lewis was not entitled to any of the money being held in trust, and ordered that he pay the Crown's costs.

'Hazel phoned. Rick Whitton advised her that all of my superannuation was forfeited. Nothing whatsoever allocated to Hazel,' he wrote. He felt acutely for his wife, and again questioned the existence or not of 'a loving and caring God'.

A week after that shock, Lewis, having had time to settle down and think, began to revise yet again the history that had delivered him into prison, and poverty. He wrote long screeds in his diary about the political ambitions of former deputy premier Bill Gunn being the catalyst for this entire 'macabre tragedy'. Lewis now believed that it was Gunn who had wanted him 'destroyed'. His broadening conspiracy also had Gunn, using his power as acting premier when Sir Joh was out of the country, to specifically appoint Fitzgerald to head a committee of inquiry. In addition, Lewis suspiciously queried the friendship between Gunn and his own former deputy, Ron Redmond.

Lewis held the greatest contempt for the 'prostitutes of the legal profession'. He wrote that they would do anything for money, ignored the traditional legal custom of impartiality and then manipulated the commission by encouraging the giving of evidence of hearsay, rumour, gossip, innuendo and blatant perjury. The media was also thrown into the mix, which he believed had been manipulated against him. It was an extraordinary conspiracy that Lewis had outlined.

To cap it all off, just days later he was again visited by Murphy who told him that he and his wife were off to Europe but were flying 'stand-by' because it was cheaper.

On Tuesday 27 June, Lewis received the news that a former officer he'd worked with in the 1950s, Syd Currie, had died. Currie used to prowl the city hotels looking for prostitutes. One he often came across was his own cousin, Shirley Margaret Brifman.

Then on Saturday 15 July, Lewis learned that his appeal lawyer, the flamboyant Shane Herbert, had died in intensive care at the Wesley Hospital from complications following a car crash. Lewis wrote of the news: 'Death of Shane Herbert, QC, apparent victim of drug overuse. He has no more worries or depression and world will soon forget him.'

It was also state election day, and while the renewed Coalition fought hard for an eight-seat swing, Labor under Wayne Goss triumphed with a majority of one seat.

Then on Sunday 13 August, Lewis got a message that the irascible Gunther Bahnemann, the 'crazed gunman' of Lota who, in the late 1950s, had been apprehended by Lewis and Glen Hallahan and charged with attempted murder, had passed away. Bahnemann had always protested his innocence, and claimed he had been verballed by police. But out of that incident, both Lewis and Hallahan were awarded the police force's highest honour for bravery, the George Medal.

Now the old soldier, who had fought for Rommel in World War II, was gone. The *Courier-Mail* reported: 'Few turned up to bid a hero farewell. Just 25 family members clustered in a tiny Cairns crematorium to say goodbye to a man who leaves behind a life story that reads like a movie script.'

The accumulation of deaths had an impact on Lewis. He wrote in his diary that he had begun to feel old. He complained that there was not enough work to keep him occupied. To compound his woes, Hazel was unwell, and he was helpless to relieve her worry and tension.

Age was also catching up with Tony Murphy. He was due for an operation on his eye. Still, Murphy indicated to Lewis he was hoping to be granted a meeting with Sir Joh Bjelke-Petersen, to discuss Lewis's imprisonment. A few months earlier, the former premier told the press that Lewis was 'only found to be corrupt', and that many people had committed worse crimes and been given far lesser sentences.

'Well I think they've been very tough on Terry Lewis, there's no doubt about it,' Bjelke-Petersen said. 'I guess the judge has his reasons for it but you can go and knock somebody on the head, you can stab them in the stomach and you'll only get a fraction of the penalty that they've given Lewis, 14 years, and then taking his superannuation from him.'

Lewis's old mate, criminologist Paul Wilson, also came into bat for him. 'I've talked to him by telephone on several occasions and despite what has happened to him he still expresses what I believe to be a genuine desire to serve the community in some meaningful capacity,' Wilson said.

The press began to speculate that Lewis was behind some sort of media campaign to see him released early from prison. One columnist in the *Courier-Mail* condemned him. 'Lewis turned himself into a rich man, not by hard work or particularly smart investments – but by being on the take while holding one of the highest positions of trust in the state,' the column said. 'He rewarded himself with a jetsetter's lifestyle. There's no evidence he put one cent of his take – which came from grubby gambling and protection for underworld scum – into anything more noble than his own pretentious desires.'

Police and Corrective Services Minister Paul Braddy attacked the apparent campaign to accelerate steps towards Lewis's release from prison. 'He has not served sufficient time to be eligible for consideration for such favourable treatment as a transfer to a community corrections hostel in Brisbane,' Braddy said emphatically.

Indeed, Lewis was directed in no uncertain terms by the Minister and corrections chief that, as he recorded in his diary: 'You are not to go public with the media. Not to speak to [journalists]. You will be in breach of regulations if you do and action will be taken against you. You can still speak to your family or friends who telephone you.'

Meanwhile, in early December, the Court of Disputed Returns threw out the election result in the seat of Mundingburra – it had been won by Labor's Ken Davies. It revealed that 22 overseas military personnel had been denied the opportunity to vote, and called for a by-election. The days inched along, and Lewis dreamed of being in a gun duel with Jack Herbert.

Hope

In early 1996, Terry Lewis, prisoner of Palen Creek, began sharpening his old political lobbying skills as the state by-election for the seat of Mundingburra approached. His diaries revealed that, with the help of Tony Murphy, he was attempting to reach out to former premier Bjelke-Petersen, and Nationals like Russell Cooper and the member for Toowong, Denver Beanland. Late the previous year, Murphy told Lewis he had made contact with Bjelke-Petersen and had left a message for Cooper. To date, he had yet to hear from the MP.

What did he hope to achieve? Could he sense a return to power of the Nationals? And if so, could his allegiance to the Nationals give his cause some future leverage and maybe even accelerate his release from prison?

While this political agitation increased, his dissatisfaction with the media, the Fitzgerald Inquiry and the legal fraternity never abated. He wrote that the relentless newspaper articles and editorials which contained 'straight out lies and assertions' were causing him great tension.

Lewis surmised that Fitzgerald and 'his money-hungry group' would never want to see him free of prison. He wrote that those involved knew of the manipulation, perjury, conspiracies and greed that surrounded the Fitzgerald Inquiry and flowed on to the office of the Special Prosecutor, then to his trial. He speculated that they would not want their nefarious activities disclosed to public attention or possible scrutiny.

Still, he continued to lobby, and took a phone call from Tony Murphy who informed Lewis he had yet to secure a signed statement from the premier about his predicament.

Lewis managed to get Joh on the phone for a personal discussion: '... said he is getting old and slowing down; very cold in Tasmania, recent snow; like me he detests Gunn and Ahern; if change of Government wants to attack the putrid way that Fitzgerald handled the Inquiry; Neil Turner has right attitude to Fitzgerald and CJC, give regards to Hazel'.

Lewis had always been a consummate tactician, and he was clearly sensing that his circumstances might change considerably if the National Party was victorious in the upcoming by-election. He noted in his diary that a friend saw former National Party education minister Val Bird, who said Terry had a lot of sympathy and if Nationals regained power something might be done in terms of Lewis's incarceration.

On Friday 12 January 1996, Lewis, as had been his habit as commissioner of police, phoned Bjelke-Petersen on the former premier's 85th birthday. Sir Joh told Lewis that he thought the Coalition should win in Mundingburra. He also told Lewis that politics put Lewis in prison and he was now a 'political prisoner'. Around this time, too,

Murphy phoned in to let Lewis know he 'spoke to Sir Joh on phone for 20 minutes last week'.

At this point, as Lewis calculated, he had spent 1630 days and nights in prison. He wondered about his mental health.

Incredibly, the Coalition's Frank Tanti took the Townsville seat of Mundingburra in the by-election, resulting in a hung parliament. Independent Liz Cunningham gave her support to the National/ Liberal Coalition, and Rob Borbidge became Premier of Queensland.

Just over a week later, Lewis phoned Bjelke-Petersen again and they spoke about: '... new Government members; particularly Borbidge, Cooper, Turner and Beanland; Fitzgerald, Crooke and their mongrel group; Gunn, Ahern, Dickie and other left-leaning journalists; need for loyalty.'

Introspection

Terry Lewis's decision to record his dreams in his prison diary was somewhat foreign to him. He had always been a man whose worth was measured by his actions and achievements. His work ethic was his expression to his family that he loved them. Having started out in the workforce aged 12, his view was always outward, and at times his almost manic busyness buffered him from any need for introspection.

The dream entries, and his time in prison, marginally changed that. In early 1996, Lewis offered the diary perhaps his most brutal self-assessment: 'I have carried a lot of things in my head over my lifetime – as have most other people – and until now never considered committing them to paper. They are thoughts that not everyone would agree with and might be considered by some to be a self-serving way of gaining sympathy. I can assure everybody that I past [sic] that stage a long time ago.'

Lewis wrote that he had always been 'conscious' of his humble upbringing in Ipswich. He said he was acutely aware of his lack of formal education, and had tried to make up for that handicap by undertaking university studies later in life. He conceded that he had always been shy and lacking in self-confidence but had tried to cover these afflictions 'by dint of hard work and trying to do my job to the best of my ability'.

He also noted that he was always 'very lonely' whenever he was away from home, be it for days or weeks, but did not reveal this to anyone because it could have been interpreted as a sign of weakness.

Lewis wrote that by recording his inner feelings he might be able to 'help future adults' avoid wasting time in search of success, and to enjoy their youth when they had the chance. He said he had had severe disappointments in life since 1987, the year of the inquiry. He admitted he was disappointed in 'the weakness of character' displayed by those he thought he could trust. He didn't think that human beings could stoop as low as a few of those 'despicable creatures'.

Having committed this to his diary, Lewis then took lunch – 'fish cake, macaroni and a banana'.

Halfway House

Any assistance Lewis might have imagined from a returned Coalition government didn't materialise in February and March of 1996, though he did speak again by telephone with Sir Joh Bjelke-Petersen, who told Lewis he had been 'speaking to messrs Borbidge, Beanland ...'

On Tuesday 9 April 1996, Lewis was on the move again – this time to the St Vincent de Paul Community Corrections Centre in South Brisbane. Community Corrections Director Greg Chambers reminded the media that Lewis had to serve half of his sentence – or seven years – before he was eligible for parole. 'This transferral is not special treatment,' he said, 'it is a step in the continuum to eventual release. Mr Lewis will remain at South Brisbane for 12 months, then he can apply for release to work, which will enable him to earn money in the community for 12 months while paying board to stay at the halfway house, then he will be considered for home detention before he is eligible for parole in 1998.'

Lewis says he met some decent people in the halfway house. 'There's the home and it's for homeless people if you like, they could come in there, they'd get breakfast, lunch and dinner on the ground floor,' he remembers. 'On the next couple of floors they've got beds for men to sleep overnight and then on the top floor there's this area that's contracted by the prison's department and run by St Vincent de Paul ...

'[They were] nearly all young people and 90 per cent of them, if not all, would leave in the morning to supposedly go to some work, some didn't. Some used to go and do some armed hold-ups ... who got caught. But most of them were there to go out to work, come back and stay the night and ... most of them could have the weekend off.'

During the week Lewis was transferred daily by mini-bus from the South Brisbane hostel to St Vinnies offices in Warry Street, Fortitude Valley, where he worked in an administrative position.

'I was very lucky, I had my own shower and toilet that I could clean, which I did ... they didn't have cleaners and that,' Lewis says. '[There was] a washing machine in a little room up there that I could do my laundry ... Hazel could come in and sit down in the common area for want of a better word, outside, and there I met some really very good fellows ...'

Seething

On Sunday 14 April, the *Sunday Mail* newspaper carried an extraordinary interview, brimming with venom, with former detective and assistant commissioner Tony Murphy.

Murphy had been provoked into speaking for the first time in several years courtesy of an unusual event. A criminal who had given evidence against Murphy at the Fitzgerald Inquiry had recently been involved in another trial, and been granted witness protection. At the latest trial, the criminal had been described variously as 'an extraordinary liar', a 'nut', a 'lunatic', 'psychotic' and 'grossly unreliable'. Even the judge had described him as a person of no credibility.

Murphy had a brilliant, and a long, memory. Just as Lewis's transfer to St Vinnies had recently been in the news, Murphy chimed in with his attack. He accused the Fitzgerald Inquiry of remaining 'mute' when it had evidence that could've cleared him and other police. 'I had to stand by while witnesses of the calibre of the indemnified witness now under protection gave evidence about me that was false and demonstrably false,' Murphy railed.

'In April 1988, this man gave a lengthy statement to the Fitzgerald Inquiry making very serious allegations against senior then and past serving police. In November 1988, he was interviewed by police in the presence of his solicitor and a Fitzgerald Inquiry legal officer. He made a statutory declaration withdrawing all the allegations and, in the plainest of language, admitted that all of them had been fabricated.

'I know that sworn document was passed on to the Fitzgerald Inquiry. Only four months later, in March 1989, the same witness again was given prominent media coverage with graphic and lurid accounts of how he had helped another criminal dispose of the bodies of the missing Brisbane woman Barbara McCulkin and her two daughters.'

It was typical Murphy. He paid enormous attention to detail and built logic through meticulously researched timelines. 'The part of this amazing saga I find particularly galling is the fact that in October 1988, when he made a sworn document admitting all these allegations against police, including me, were a complete fabrication, he also signed a document authorising the Fitzgerald Inquiry to allow the publication of his statutory declaration,' said Murphy.

'In December 1989, this witness was convicted in the Southport Magistrates Court of making false complaints ... I am still seething at the partisan conduct of that inquiry. While that witness, as far as I am aware, was not called at the inquiry, other persons with equally doubtful credentials were called to give evidence against me.'

He complained that a female with 'pages of criminal history' had sworn that she saw Murphy regularly at one of Gerry Bellino's illegal casinos, yet Murphy could prove he was living and working in Toowoomba, west of Brisbane, at the time.

'Another witness swore he saw me drinking in a Toowoomba hotel two or three times a week with an SP bookmaker from mid-1976,' Murphy added. 'I took up duty at Longreach in early February.'

The reporter Peter Hansen asked Murphy if there should be an inquiry into the inquiry.

'And give another $100 million to the legal fraternity?' he answered rhetorically. 'I'll give the subject a degree of prominence in a book in the not too distant future.'

It had been almost ten years since the inquiry had been called, and yet Murphy continued to fight to restore his name.

On Tuesday 16 April, Lewis wrote in his diary: 'Tony Murphy phoned; considers [journalist] Peter Hansen 100 per cent reliable ... had long talk with Lady Florence.'

Glorified

Piece by piece, there were increased attempts by the main players in the corruption saga to re-write history. Lewis did what he had always done best. He relentlessly lobbied support on the telephone. On Thursday 2 May 1996, if his diaries are accurate, he claimed to have phoned former director of prosecutions Desmond Sturgess, QC, and written down the famous legal eagle's comments. By Lewis's account, Sturgess told him: 'I have said some harsh things about you and others in the past but now should look to the future. I admired the way the Drugs laws were administered when you were there [as commissioner]. The Police Force has paid a terrible penalty from the Fitzgerald Inquiry. The media make the Police a whipping post. The morale of the Force is shot.' (Sturgess says that Lewis's entry sounded like something he would say at the time.)

Later that month, Tony Murphy paid Lewis another visit and they discussed Lewis doing an interview with local journalist Rod Henshaw. Lewis wrote: '… offer very appealing'.

Lewis had sought and been granted permission to take early morning walks in the vicinity of the hostel in South Brisbane. It was an area he knew well from his days walking the beat as a young police officer in the 1950s. Just off Riverside Drive used to be the old Killarney brothel in Lanfear Street, where the likes of prostitutes Shirley Brifman and Ada Bahnemann first started out.

It was a different South Brisbane, though, to the days of Commissioner Frank Bischof and his eager disciples. A gentrification was on the march, despite the lingering presence of industry on West End's northern reaches.

On Monday 1 July, Lewis met the journalist Rod Henshaw, and noted in his diary that he found him 'completely trustworthy'. Three days later he recorded an interview, which took about two hours.

Lewis was back in the hurley-burley, and his diaries revealed that he was enjoying the attention. The interview went to air on Monday 8 July, and elicited a storm of protest.

Police Minister Russell Cooper – though he had given Lewis permission to speak with Henshaw – blasted the former police commissioner, saying he had 'betrayed his position, the Queensland Police Service and the people'.

Cooper said he never had any doubts about Lewis's guilt, and said Lewis had nothing but a fair trial. He described the interview as 'laughable protestations of innocence'. In the interview, Lewis described Jack Herbert as 'the great destroyer'.

It provoked the ire of Peggy Herbert. 'We were both wondering why Terry didn't get up and give any evidence at his trial now that he is so vocal,' she said in a newspaper article.

Bill Gunn piped up, saying he was annoyed that Lewis was being 'glorified'.

Lewis was also annoyed: 'Rick Whitton phoned; *Courier-Mail* has shown the ultimate arrogance; never been such a witch hunt; John Jerrard said I would get out if admitted guilt, Rick disgusted with him and said why should I if not guilty?'

In a more detailed interview, Gunn described Lewis's assertion that he was set up by Herbert and others as a fiction. 'Being accused of having a vendetta by a convicted crook doesn't worry me at all,' Gunn said. 'He's just a sad and sorry old man who wanted to get some public sympathy.' Gunn said there was plenty of evidence, apart from Herbert, that showed Lewis was corrupt, including the testimony of former assistant commissioner Graeme Parker. 'I would also receive hundreds of calls every week from police who said Lewis was corrupt, but were too scared to be named or provide a statement for fear of losing their jobs.'

Five days after the controversial Lewis interview, colourful Sydney businessman Jack Rooklyn, 89, died at his home. Rooklyn was convicted in the Brisbane District Court in May 1992 of having bribed Lewis and Jack 'The Bagman' Herbert. He was fined $350,000 and saved from gaol by virtue of his age.

As the issue died down, Lewis kept lobbying. He continued to speak to Sir Joh on the phone, as he did with Tony Murphy. In early August, the corrupt Graeme Parker paid Lewis a visit, and another former officer phoned to report that he had seen '[Allen] Bulger driving a Yellow Cab, two weeks ago at Coorparoo'. Bulger had been charged with perjury following the Fitzgerald Inquiry, and been sentenced to 12 years in gaol, although he was paroled after less than four years. Lewis's source claimed to have seen Jack Herbert get into the cab and talk to Bulger for about 20 minutes. Lewis's informant said Herbert told Bulger he'd been to see his bank manager to borrow money for the purchase of another unit. Herbert allegedly said: 'Wish Terry would stop digging up the past as most people had forgotten.'

A couple of weeks later, journalist Rod Henshaw also dropped by and the pair discussed politics, police and the media. Lewis noted in his diary that Henshaw allegedly told him that several people believed Lewis was falsely convicted instead of the Mr Big, 'A.M [Anthony Murphy] … given another six months they would have stitched him up.'

A week after that, the man himself, Tony Murphy, visited Lewis and dropped off a short statement signed by Sir Joh Bjelke-Petersen on 20 August 1996, in relation to Bill Gunn and the details of Lewis being stood down as police commissioner.

Incredibly, Lewis was still trying to correct old records, building the point of his grievances with paperwork from players far removed from the moment. He was relentless. He phoned Des Sturgess who told him – according to Lewis's diary – that he needed strong legal argument about inadmissible evidence allowed at his trial.

Meanwhile, Jack Reginald Herbert, The Bagman, was still living in New Farm and taking his early morning walks in New Farm Park on the Brisbane River. A group of senior citizens who also enjoyed the park of a morning made formal complaints that it was potentially unsafe to exercise at the same time as Herbert, given he might still have some powerful, and potentially deadly, enemies. It was believed his witness protection had ceased around 1990.

Occasionally, Herbert and his wife Peggy were spotted about town in various Brisbane bars. Sometimes, Jack would nip into the Queens Arms Hotel in James Street, New Farm, for a beer.

Just as Lewis's life was beset with restrictions on one side of the river, the Herberts were granted permission to take a six-week holiday in the United Kingdom to catch up with friends and relatives.

Questions from the Outside In

What Terry Lewis could never control or be prepared for – no amount of diarising could stave them off – were the questions that came from the outside. In late 1997 *Courier-Mail* journalist Michael Ware began an intense inquiry into whether former Commissioner of Police, Terry Lewis, and other police had ever obstructed serious investigations into paedophilia.

Ware, a gun reporter under editor Chris Mitchell, ended up tracking down former Paedophile Task Force members Kym Goldup and Garnett Dickson. Goldup was living with her husband on the Gold Coast. 'I'd been contacted by a lot of journalists over the years and said I didn't know anything.' Goldup recalls her initial reaction to the revived media interest: 'I didn't want to relive it. Michael Ware said, "I know you do know something. I know this and this." I thought, who have you been talking to? So I got in touch with Garney. He said, "I think we can trust him."'

According to Goldup, she, Dickson and Ware met at Goldup's house in Parkwood on the Gold Coast. Soon after, Ware and the *Courier-Mail* started publishing a series of articles that sent shudders through government ranks. On Saturday 16 August they ran with a front-page story alleging that files taken from former commissioner Terry Lewis's safes by Fitzgerald Inquiry officials back in the late 1980s were potentially a political time bomb. 'The files contain material on alleged sexual behaviour involving top state and Federal Government advisors and senior public servants,' the newspaper said.

'Much of the material ... fails to provide hard evidence of criminal activity but reveals behaviour which warrants investigation.' Later articles also resurrected the perceived inaction by Commissioner Lewis in relation to the activities of former Senior Constable Dave Moore and radio celebrity Bill Hurrey in the early to mid 1980s.

Goldup says she's always wondered whether cooperating with the newspaper investigation was the right thing to do. 'Part of me does regret it,' she says. 'All it did was … [it] made the hierarchy very aware that there was still stuff out there we knew and had.'

As for Lewis, sitting over in South Brisbane, he was incensed. He described the paedophile articles as 'full of false accusations re sexual blackmail'.

The stories also rallied friends to Lewis's defence. His diary noted that former police officer Neal Freier phoned 're disgraceful article. A lot of people still love you.' Murphy also phoned to tell Lewis he'd been in touch with Alan Barnes and Pat Glancy. As the articles continued to be published, so the phone at the halfway house ran hot for Lewis.

Lewis said in no uncertain terms that the articles alleging he covered up paedophilia were nothing but a pack of lies, that he'd never interfered with any investigations, and that he was happy to assist in any inquiry if required.

In another call, Des Sturgess supposedly told Lewis that he 'was D. of Prosecutions when Moore and Hurrey charged and know that I never protected paedophiles …'.

Still, the *Courier-Mail* investigation had caused enough public disquiet to warrant official investigation.

It was yet another inquiry Lewis would have to face.

Project Triton

Just as the *Courier-Mail* was peering into some dark corners, revisiting a narrative thread that, on the surface, reached back to the 1950s, the

Children's Commission tabled in parliament its report – 'Paedophilia in Queensland'. The report looked into the perceived ineffectiveness by law enforcement agencies in the investigation and prosecution of offenders in relation to paedophilia, just as the *Courier-Mail* articles were asserting.

As a result of public debate, the Criminal Justice Commission (CJC) informed the Commissioner of the Queensland Police Service, Jim O'Sullivan, on 21 August 1997, that the CJC intended to investigate allegations of misconduct by police. The following day the CJC announced the establishment of a special task force investigation. It became known as Project Triton.

From 1 September the Triton team began their enquiries. Eventually, former District Court Judge Jack Kimmins was commissioned to preside over the investigation's public hearings.

The terms of reference included looking at whether former commissioner Terry Lewis allegedly kept secret files on possible criminal sexual behaviour by senior public officials for blackmail purposes, and if those files were seized by the Fitzgerald commission of inquiry from safes that were controlled by Lewis.

Another related to whether police had shown inactivity or had orchestrated a cover-up into allegations that children had been sexually abused and murdered during the filming of so-called 'snuff' movies in Queensland.

The Kimmins hearings were a sensation, coming a decade after the establishment of the Fitzgerald Inquiry. Queensland had moved on. Terry Lewis was in gaol. Rob Borbidge was Premier. Yet this ugly past was back at the centre of debate.

The inquiry heard that Lewis, when he was commissioner of police, had kept a 'treasure trove' of dirt files on the 'misbehaviour' of police up to the rank of inspector, as well as confidential files on the sexual activity of 'prominent figures', which were kept in a safe in the Juvenile Aid Bureau (JAB).

Former JAB officers were so concerned about the files, and the prospect of Lewis interfering with any investigations as they claimed he had done over the David Moore scandal, that they broke into the safe and copied the files.

Lewis's former personal assistant, Greg Early, was called. He said Lewis took files from his office in 1987 when he was stood aside as commissioner by Police Minister Bill Gunn. He said Lewis told him they were 'personal affairs'.

The next day, Fitzgerald Inquiry officers had raided Lewis's office. Early said he had 'never seen' a number of files Lewis kept, and didn't know if Lewis had kept a personal file on investigations into male brothels in the early to mid 1980s.

The inquiry further heard that a file relating to investigations into former senior constable Dave Moore had disappeared after it went to then Police Commissioner Terry Lewis's office.

Senior Sergeant Garnett Dickson was called to give evidence. Dickson said he had at one time briefed the CJC on paedophilia, and made them aware of certain files, and they hadn't seemed interested in what his investigations had uncovered.

'I did [so] because the main thrust of the inquiry was people in high places ... people in government,' he said. 'I mentioned that we had just done a large probe for the BCIQ (Bureau of Criminal Intelligence Queensland) called Probe Egret.

'Egret related to criminal paedophilia in Queensland. It was as thick as a phone book, that's the sort of information it contained. But they were not interested in that. They were going to do their own thing.'

Police Commissioner Jim O'Sullivan gave evidence before Kimmins. He said he was unaware whether any 'dirt files' had been part of the material seized by his taskforce when it raided Lewis's office. 'I was sent to police headquarters on various occasions by senior counsel attached to the Fitzgerald Inquiry with specific tasks,' he said. 'I seized material but did not inspect it.'

Lewis himself appeared before the inquiry, having been granted special leave from the St Vincent de Paul halfway house to do so, and denied he had ever kept any 'dirt files' on people, nor had he ever obstructed investigations into Moore in the early 1980s.

An earlier witness, former Juvenile Aid Bureau officer Mark McCoy, disagreed. McCoy believed Lewis had done everything he could to make sure no prosecution against Moore went ahead. 'I felt an eye was kept on us all the time,' McCoy told the inquiry.

The *Courier-Mail* reported that Lewis appeared much the same as he did before his fall from grace – 'the sagging features of a glum but not unfriendly bloodhound who used to be the jowl in the Crown of Queensland law enforcement'.

There was further evidence from former police officer Jim Slade in relation to a 'snuff' movie he claims to have seen – a film of a child being abused and murdered. Slade was interviewed by inquiry investigators but was not questioned before Kimmins during the hearings. He claimed he had seen the movie and that he believed it was made on the banks of the Brisbane River at Pinkenba.

The inquiry rolled into the New Year. In late January, the CJC reported that it had found no evidence that police had covered up paedophilia, and it had failed to prove that former commissioner Lewis or other officers had in any way interfered with investigations into paedophilia.

In February, the inquiry heard that detectives investigating paedophilia were warned that any search warrants issued on judicial officers had to be vetted first by senior police to ensure they were based on evidence.

In his ultimate final report, tabled in state parliament in September 1998, Kimmins, extraordinarily, found that in the course of his nine-month investigation, 'not one allegation had substance in fact'.

Kimmins said: '... those who prey upon and defile our young and innocent – and those who harbour such deviates – deserve nothing less than the full wrath of the community's condemnation and the fullest retribution prescribed by law ... [but the] public heralding of untested accusations can therefore be considered as heinous as paedophilia itself, particularly where the peddler of an accusation knows or ought to know that the accusation is untested, or worse, is unlikely to have any substance.'

CJC Chairman Frank Clair also echoed Kimmins when he said: 'It is regrettable that such rumours or scuttlebutt, to use the term that was used by Judge Kimmins, was widely and repeatedly circulated, eventually convincing some of its proponents of its authenticity.'

The *Courier-Mail*, which had a large role in triggering the inquiry, was outraged. It said in an editorial: 'The "scuttlebutt" which was swept under the carpet by churches, the police and others in positions of authority in the past right around the world, most certainly did not go away in this instance.

'The rash of cases of paedophilia before the courts in Queensland, relating to crimes committed in the 1960s and 70s, indicates dismissing the "scuttlebutt" as just that – rumour and innuendo unworthy of being taken seriously – merely leaves a generation of children without protection.'

Former deputy premier Bill Gunn fired back at the Kimmins inquiry, saying he had no doubt police had ignored paedophilia in the past.

The whole Kimmins experience left former Paedophile Taskforce officer Kym Goldup shattered. 'I think they broke Garney [Dickson] as well. They pretty much kept me and Garney apart.

'The other thing [was] if I said something, they'd say, "Where's the evidence for that?" There's a lot of things you know but you can't get a complainant. Paedophilia is one of those things ... you have to find a paedophile first, and then you have to find a complainant. It's very rare that a complainant comes to you.

'Garney always used to say to me they pick their mark, they'll take a kid off the street who is wearing rags, and they'll buy them the latest clothes and a ghetto blaster and a new skateboard and give them somewhere nice to sleep and so, of course, the kid's not going to make a complaint.'

Jim Slade was also angry his evidence about the 'snuff' movie was not believed. 'I was interviewed by these two guys from the Kimmins inquiry, and they were young solicitors, and I mean, you don't send young solicitors to interview a bloody guy who's done 20 years of undercover, and straightaway I knew that they were just out to trap me, you know?' says Slade. 'They weren't there to find out how, or where I saw it, or anything like that ...'

Slade says he later discovered that a civilian and a police officer who provided signed statements to the inquiry supporting Slade's version of events later recanted their statements. 'I mean, why would someone make up something about a snuff movie?' Slade asks. 'I got a real burn out of that.'

Once again, a commission of inquiry into Queensland paedophilia ended up shooting the messengers – in this case, Goldup, Dickson, journalist Michael Ware and the *Courier-Mail* newspaper. The hornet's nest kicked up by the charging of former constable Dave Moore and radio personality Bill Hurrey in the early 1980s was still echoing to the present, yet nothing stuck, despite the shadows and whispers.

Goldup says Ware's articles were spot on, yet his work was torn apart by Kimmins. She adds that the whole truth never had a chance of being exposed in the Kimmins inquiry. She claims the saga ruined her life.

'I bleed blue,' she says. 'I was a career police person. When I joined the police force I was most frightened of the baddies in the street. When I left the police service I was most frightened of the people I worked with.'

Home Sweet Home

In the New Year, Lewis continued to lobby lawyer Des Sturgess. He wanted a pardon, and still he was haunted by the past.

He had a visit from Sturgess on 22 January and they discussed Lewis's ambitions for a formal pardon or a new trial. He also talked about people he perceived as his enemies: Ross Dickson, Basil Hicks, Lorelle Saunders, John Huey, Jim Slade and Alec Jeppesen. The media personalities he loathed included Chris Masters, Phil Dickie and Quentin Dempster.

Lewis was formally granted home detention from 11 May 1998. The Queensland Community Corrections Board informed him that given his high profile, it was best he didn't engage in community service. The news sparked a brawl between the ALP and the Borbidge government. Opposition Leader Peter Beattie said that Lewis's release only six years and nine months into a 14-year sentence was hypocritical and made a mockery of the government's pretence to be tough on crime. Beattie said Police Minister Russell Cooper had broken the government's own declaration that serious criminals serve 80 per cent of their sentence. '[But here] we have a friend of the National Party, a serious criminal responsible for the corruption of a generation of police,' Beattie said. He also pointed out that Lewis had never shown remorse or admitted guilt for his corrupt behaviour.

Sir Joh Bjelke-Petersen, on the other hand, welcomed Lewis's release. Hazel Lewis said she was 'delighted' her husband was coming home.

Lewis says that upon his release the media was everywhere. 'I had to go from South Brisbane and the manager there agreed to drive me out to Toowong where the parole office was,' he recalls. 'Well, of course, outside St Vinnies at South Brisbane there must have been 40 media waiting for me to get in the car and I wouldn't talk to them. There were more of them out at Toowong and then when I got out to where

Hazel was living, there was a team of them there. But you know you're not going to gain anything by talking.'

On arriving home, Lewis had a short sleep. He says prison aged him considerably. 'You're not doing anything, it's mind boggling, [you're not] stretching the mind,' he says. 'It's very routine, mindless, endless.'

On that first night of freedom, Lewis was visited by one of his daughters, and recorded that he had 'mince, vegetables and pasta' for dinner. He then settled back to watch some television. He took in the news, and then caught most of that night's episode of *Heartbeat*, the British police drama set in the fictional village of Ashfordly in Yorkshire.

What may have escaped the scrupulous and attentive notice of civilian Terry Lewis, was that he was set free precisely nine years, almost to the minute, after the airing of Chris Masters' 'The Moonlight State', the investigative report that led to the Fitzgerald Inquiry.

On the night of his release from the halfway house, *Four Corners* broadcast a report called 'The Country Doctors', an investigation by reporter Liz Jackson into the secret culture of the International Monetary Fund.

Lewis missed it. He was in bed by 9.30 p.m.

2000s

Two Crusaders Lost, and a Rogue Too

In mid-2002, the former state member for South Brisbane, the lawyer Colin Bennett, was largely confined to his unit in Beaumont Towers on Dornoch Terrace at West End, in inner-Brisbane. For the previous 18 months Bennett, the firebrand anti-corruption crusader, whose agitation against men like Commissioner Frank Bischof in the 1960s ultimately resulted in the National Hotel inquiry and pre-empted the Fitzgerald Inquiry by almost a quarter of a century, had been cared for full-time by his daughter, Mary.

He sat in his chair facing the window and the view across the Brisbane River to the playing fields and sandstone buildings of the University of Queensland campus at St Lucia. He said decades of the rosary when the urge came upon him. On occasion, Mary would take her father for a walk through the streets that he had represented so passionately in parliament, or they might go out for a meal in a restaurant. At 83 his mind was still sharp.

Bennett often had occasion to pause and remember his extraordinary lifetime: a lawyer; a city councillor; a politician; a father who had lost a son in a tragic drowning accident at a local pool in 1959; a parliamentary bruiser and a brilliant debater; staunch Catholic with a social conscience that would see him representing those rejected by mainstream society. One of his most famous clients was, of course, brothel madam and prostitute Shirley Margaret Brifman, who had blown the whistle on corrupt police in 1971 and paid for the privilege with her life. At the time, Brifman had kept Bennett so busy he had his own dedicated 'Brifman briefcase'.

He had friends in the force as well as enemies. When police contacts learned of plans to get Bennett, they informed him. '[At one point] they were plotting to get him and make it look like an accident,' his daughter Mary recalls. 'They'd say, "Col, look, don't walk down George Street at this time on this night."

'He had an absolute commitment to justice and equity. He mixed with the elite of Queensland society but was always in support of the poor.'

In his last weeks, Mary says Bennett became reflective. He remembered the time, during the hearings of the Fitzgerald Inquiry, when he was regularly visited in the flat by Liberal MP and fellow lawyer Angus Innes. As the inquiry progressed, and background information was needed on various police and their activities during the 1950s and 60s, Innes would tap Bennett's extensive knowledge and his files. Invariably, Innes would leave Dornoch Terrace with a small Globite school case full of files from Bennett's voluminous records, and they would then be handed over to inquiry investigators for perusal.

Then Colin Bennett was gone.

Down at Parliament House in George Street, he was remembered as a man of courage. 'Col Bennett waged a long and fearless campaign against corrupt police commissioner Frank Bischof and two of his hand-picked detectives, Glen Hallahan and Tony Murphy, whom Col named in parliament,' said then Premier Peter Beattie in his motion of condolence in the House. 'Queensland was a corrupt place in those days. It was a place that really was a shame on the history of this state. It did require some people of courage to take on that corruption.

'It was a corruption that pervaded all sections of government and particularly the police service. It was very difficult for an honest man to break through. Col Bennett did.'

One year later, another famous corruption fighter passed away in his home town of Adelaide. Ray Whitrod, 88, the former ASIO agent, Commonwealth police commissioner, and Queensland commissioner of police from 1970 until his controversial resignation in late 1976, was an honest man who, unlike Col Bennett, did not break through.

When Whitrod resigned as commissioner, he fled south to Canberra and took up a post in academia, before ultimately returning to Adelaide. He only ever came back to Queensland twice – to give evidence before the Fitzgerald Inquiry and to deliver an academic paper.

Premier Peter Beattie said of Whitrod: 'Ray Whitrod should always be remembered as a brave, honest man who for six years fought to reform a corrupt police force.'

The *Courier-Mail* wrote in its editorial: 'Mr Whitrod's story should have been an uplifting one for the state. Instead, Queensland had to wait another 12 years for Tony Fitzgerald, QC, to expose the rot that had invaded many of its institutions.

'Mr Whitrod's memory would be best served if the government, judiciary, bureaucracy and, yes, the media of the day continued to recognise that a return to corruption is not only possible, but inevitable without proper vigilance.'

In a Gold Coast hospital, less than a year after Whitrod's passing, grafter and former Licensing Branch officer Jack Reginald Herbert died of a brain tumour. He was 79.

Herbert and his wife Peggy had left Brisbane for a quiet retirement on the Gold Coast, and were occasionally spotted at Jupiters Casino at Broadbeach. They lived in a small unit and Jack got around with the help of a motorised scooter. He read works of non-fiction and drank tea.

'I just enjoy life,' he said before his death. 'Peggy is good company and, yeah, I should go fishing.' He regretted that he got his wife so heavily involved in his corrupt activities. 'It weighed heavily on my shoulders that I involved her,' he said. 'But I've got to admit ... Tony Murphy once said, we had a bit of a party amongst Tony and myself and a few of the boys that were involved ... I think I've got [a picture of] him there giving Peggy a cuddle. And he said, "Peggy Herbert is as good as any policeman we know."

'They used to ring her for information and she knew who, how, why, what and all and she handled the money. I'm a bit of a persuasive sort of fellow and I persuaded her to take the bloody phone calls. And she knew all the fellows ... you know, she knew Terry, she knew [Frank] Bischof was involved, Don Lane used to come over and see us. I mean it was very hard to pick how safe you felt.'

When Herbert developed cancer, the meticulous Bagman organised his own funeral. 'I've written everything down for Peggy, what to do,' he said. 'I've contacted the funeral directors, believe it or not. I'm not being morbid but I'm just ... I'm getting some satisfaction out of arranging everything.

'And I've looked with Peggy at what's in the bank and she ... because she's never done anything like this. I've always done everything and I've got a few pages here, exactly setting it all out – one, two, three, four – on what to do.'

Few mourned The Bagman, although his death also earned an editorial in the *Courier-Mail*. 'No Queenslander who values the role of honesty in the governance of Queensland should feel overly sad about the passing of Jack Reginald Herbert,' it said. 'He was a thief and an extortionist whose prodigious skills at extracting graft and turning his fellow officers into crooks did enormous harm to the community standing of Queensland police.

'But it is also true that Queensland would be an altogether different place had Herbert not cut a deal with the Fitzgerald commission of inquiry ... while he made a major contribution to the history of the state, no one should fall for Herbert's attempts at portraying himself as some sort of mischievous rogue.'

Former Police Union president Ron Edington said that prior to Herbert's death former commissioner Terry Lewis had asked him to act as an intermediary and organise with Herbert to get a signed statement from The Bagman accepting all blame for police corruption.

'About two months before Jack died, Lewis rang me and asked if I would see Jack and ask him to get [Herbert's wife] Peggy to write a statement attributing all the blame for the corruption to Jack and Peg, and clearing Lewis and his wife, Hazel,' Edington told the *Courier-Mail*.

'I didn't mind doing what he asked. I checked it out first with a senior barrister. I put it to Jack and he was angry at the request. He said, "I've had to pay a penalty [loss of friends, property, money and reputation] and Lewis should pay his too."

'He was outraged that Lewis should suggest that Peggy cop the blame to clear his name.'

Lewis denied the Edington allegations. 'Ron makes up stories,' Lewis said. 'I haven't spoken to Herbert or any member of his family for 17 years. What would be the use?'

Despite this, it was clear Lewis reserved a special enmity for Herbert. He says: 'I was the sacrificial lamb, that's the part I found ... I could understand, if you like, for want of a better way of putting it, Herbert's objective. You know, get himself, his wife, his two kids off, and it doesn't matter who else I sacrifice ... the onus was just self-gain.'

Sue

Four months after Jack Herbert's death, more than ten years after he was imprisoned by a jury of his peers, Lewis attempted to sue the former legal team who had handled his appeal in 1991. He blamed the failed appeal on his barrister Shane Herbert.

Lewis's statement of claim, filed with Brisbane's Supreme Court, alleged that Shane Herbert had failed to adopt a key defence in the appeal that would have resulted in Lewis's convictions being quashed.

He suggested that Herbert had abandoned a defence pertaining to certain evidence alleged to have been incorrectly admitted in his trial before Judge Tony Healy. He had done this without the knowledge or permission of Lewis.

Lewis was suing for $470,000 – $450,000 as the value for the loss of a right to a fair trial, and $20,000 that was paid to Herbert.

The flamboyant Shane Herbert died from complications following a car crash. It was suspected Herbert was addicted to cocaine and heroin at the time he conducted Lewis's appeal. A blood test taken after the car crash contained traces of anti-depressants, tranquillisers, morphine and other drugs.

The *Courier-Mail* reported: 'Four months before his death, police had raided his inner Brisbane home and found 140g of marihuana, 0.02g of heroin, 30ml of methadone and 45 syringes, some of which had been used.' Herbert's wife pleaded guilty to possessing the drugs, although his family denied he was involved in drugs.

The *Courier-Mail* further noted that Lewis's court action named lawyers Ian Bruce Hillhouse and David Alan Burrough, as well as the estate of Lewis's former solicitor and at times confidant, Rick Glynn Whitton, who died in early 2004.

Both Hillhouse and Burrough rejected the claims. 'The firm denies the allegations as alleged by Mr Terence Lewis and is disappointed that such allegations are made 13 years after Mr Lewis's conviction and after the death of his appellate counsel, Mr Shane Herbert, QC, and solicitor Mr Rick Whitton,' they said in a statement. 'The firm intends to strenuously defend the claim and is confident the claim will be dismissed.'

The *Courier-Mail* reported: 'In their defence filed in the court, they allege Lewis's time to launch such a legal claim has expired, that the $450,000 Lewis paid them was inclusive of counsel's fees for the committal and that the defence omitted by Herbert would not have been successful, based on a recent legal precedent.'

In October 2004, the barrister Russell Hanson, QC, acting for Lewis's former legal team, told the Supreme Court that Lewis's attempt to sue his lawyers was a bid to 'rewrite history' and cast doubt over the numerous guilty verdicts Lewis suffered following his trial in 1991. He applied for the case to be struck off on the grounds of 'abuse of process'.

The world had moved on since Lewis's heyday and it was as if he had barely noticed.

Death of a Colossus

On the morning of Monday 18 April 2005, the ailing former Queensland premier, Sir Joh Bjelke-Petersen, was taken from the family home, Bethany, on the outskirts of Kingaroy, 210 kilometres north-west of Brisbane, to a private hospital in town, to die.

Two months earlier, the old man, 94, had survived a bout of pneumonia but was now deteriorating rapidly. He was rushed to the South Burnett Private Community Hospital in Markwell Street by ambulance. His wife, Lady Flo, told the press: 'I'm there beside him, supporting him and telling him Jesus loves him and God loves him. And, you know, when his time comes he's ready to go. He's never had any doubts at all. It's comforting for him – and I hope I go there myself later on.'

For some years, the former premier had lived with progressive supranuclear palsy, a neurological condition that affects speech, balance, swallowing and walking. Bjelke-Petersen's doctor said the palsy was paralysing Sir Joh's lungs. By the time he arrived at the hospital he was unable to eat or drink.

Dr Isabella Jonsson reportedly said Sir Joh was not putting up a huge fight this time round. 'I think he's probably ready to go, honestly – I mean there is a time in all our lives when things come to an end,' she said. 'It's not quality life for him anymore …'

Lady Flo added that when the time came, her husband's funeral would definitely be held in the Kingaroy Town Hall, just around the corner from the hospital. 'If people want to come to the funeral,' she said, 'they'll have to come to Kingaroy.'

As for his burial, Sir Joh himself had expressed the wish that he be interred at Bethany, near bushland where he enjoyed feeding wild birds. (The local council granted approval for the request.)

He died on Saturday 23 April. The next day, the *Sunday Mail* offered an editorial on the former premier's passing. 'It seems inconceivable that Queensland is today without Sir Joh Bjelke-Petersen,' it said. 'Joh, as most would remember him, played such a long and important role in our history that he was Queensland to many people.'

It paid tribute to Sir Joh's 'can-do philosophy' and how he encouraged 'the exploitation of the state's untapped potential'.

'Politically and socially, Joh's legacy is not so rich,' it continued. 'His self-belief and his impatience with contrary views made him an uncomfortable democrat. He inherited a disgraceful gerrymander and refined it to the unfair benefit of the National Party. His impatience with accepted processes and his need to wield absolute control made him peculiarly susceptible to cronyism and to the sort of corruption that ultimately destroyed his government and battered his reputation.'

It concluded, however, that Joh was 'a man for his times and a true colossus of Queensland politics'.

Then Premier Peter Beattie afforded Bjelke-Petersen a state funeral. 'There will be people who love him, and people who hate him but the fact is if you look at the total equation and you take the negative and the positive, he did a lot of good for this state,' Beattie said.

The funeral was slated for Tuesday 3 May, in the Kingaroy Town Hall. The vast bulk of Beattie's ALP Cabinet refused to attend the event. Former police commissioner Terry Lewis's wife, Hazel, refused to confirm their attendance. 'We do have some commitments this week,' she told the *Courier-Mail*. 'It's a long way and I think there'd be many important people up there. We really don't have to discuss our business with anyone.' (In fact, according to Lewis's diary, he telephoned Lady Flo on Friday 29 April, and 'extended our sympathy and reasons for not going to attend funeral; mainly media; countless phone calls and flowers; only one nasty one was female from ABC'.)

The funeral itself was broadcast live on local commercial television. Prime Minister at the time, John Howard, and a myriad of other national and state politicians, celebrities and friends filled the hall for the service. That morning Lewis took his dog Prince for a walk and did a load of washing.

He later watched the funeral on television. 'Large crowd; impressive ceremony,' he wrote in his diary.

In Kingaroy, Lewis's long-time mentor, friend, and the man who facilitated his rise to the top of the Queensland Police Force – and all the attendant benefits and honours that that entailed – was laid to rest.

Over in Winton Street, Stafford Heights, Lewis had a rookworst sandwich for lunch then spent the afternoon ironing '7 articles of clothing plus tablecloths'.

Dear Little Girl

In late September 2009, Hazel Lewis's long battle with health complications ended. She died in Brisbane's Prince Charles Hospital in the city's north after battling stress-induced diabetes for many years. She was 77.

For some years Terry and Hazel had been living in a house in Winton Street, Stafford Heights, north of the Brisbane CBD. Lewis says one of his sons won a Mater Prize home and two cars, and sold the prize home to give his parents some finances for a house. Eventually Hazel Lewis found the bargain in Stafford Heights, run down as it was.

Over the years, the Lewis's enjoyed their grandchildren, and Terry often kept busy with little jobs around the homes of his children. He was devoted to Hazel who, as she had done for their entire married lives, held the family together. Their little black and white pet terrier, Prince, was a great comfort to Hazel, and used to kiss her goodnight. In her final months, Hazel would say to her husband that she'd be alright 'if I could breathe'.

Her funeral service was held at the church the Lewis family once regularly attended – St Brigid's Catholic Church at Red Hill, not far from 12 Garfield Drive – and was attended by more than 100 people. Lewis delivered an emotional eulogy and said his 'dear little girl' would have been overwhelmed at the number of people in attendance. He said that his wife had been renowned for her 'goodwill, kindly feelings and warm affections'.

'She had been ill for several years, but her heart and health were broken by the events of 22 years ago,' Lewis added, referring to the start of the Fitzgerald Inquiry. 'She was my first girlfriend and my only wife. I never imagined her dying before me – it was the only thing she did wrong. I'll miss her every minute.'

On such a sombre occasion, in the great red-brick edifice of St Brigid's, Lewis continued to defend the Queensland Police. 'I've said it publicly before and I'll say it to the day I die – 95 per cent were the finest, 4 per cent were average and 1 per cent were a pain in the posterior.'

Later, the family and mourners headed over to Gambaro's Restaurant in Caxton Street, a short walk from the old police depot on Petrie Terrace, to reminisce.

Hindsight

As the decades rolled on, and the big and powerful of the Queensland Police Force of the 1960s and 1970s became old men, many of those mates continued to stay in touch. Brisbane-based Ron Edington, the former outspoken head of the Queensland Police Union in the early 1970s, spoke regularly with Tony Murphy who had settled at Robina on the Gold Coast.

'Well, Murphy ... rings me up quite regularly, you know, cause he's on a walker now, he can't walk ... and he reckons his memory's gone. Well, I've trapped him that many times, you know, caught him off-guard,' Edington jokes. He then offers an example of how he has tried to catch his old friend out. 'Remember the time you went down there, Tony, to try and get that old sheila for abortion and you parked the car outside and the old fellow came along? You had the fellow sitting in the back of the van, taking the photographs of the women going in to be aborted?'

'"Oh, yeah, yeah," he comes back, perfect. [But] he reckons he couldn't remember anything. Old Joh [Bjelke-Petersen] did the same. Old Joh said, "I can't remember that." He said that all the bloody way through his evidence.

'I tell you, he [Murphy] was that smart, he waited long enough ... to build [his house] ... built it on the lakes ... Robina, he reckons it's a bloody palace. He held onto it all the time before he was game to show his hand, you know ... he was just hanging off, hanging off and he waited all that time and what did it bring him? He can't go out, he's got bad back problems. Keeps on telling me that his memory's gone.

'I think he still has some fear that something might come up one bloody day, something's going to happen to him, he's had these many years of bad memory, he can't remember ... but I bet if he had a tin of fucking money hidden somewhere he'd fucking remember where that was.

'I've got a great mind to look into, to assess all these bastards. I always keep friendly with them ... that was always through the job I used to do, even if I thought they were my greatest fucking enemy, I'd still, you know, piss in their pocket.'

Lewis, too, has reassessed Murphy. 'I can't believe them not getting Murphy. I really, I just can't,' he says. 'You can hypothesise anything I suppose. Murphy went to work in the Licensing Branch. Why he did that – well I would never have done that over my dead body – I would sooner have gone back to uniform and done traffic duty or any bloody thing.'

Lewis points out that Jack Herbert had given evidence at the inquiry acknowledging that nobody who ever went into the Licensing Branch refused his invitation to be a part of The Joke. 'Murphy would have been the sub-inspector in charge in those days [Murphy was in the branch from 1966 to 1971] ... Herbert I think, by then, would either have been senior detective constable or detective sergeant and Murphy would have been senior to him ... so you could hardly leave him [Murphy] out of the picture, I would have thought,' says Lewis.

'I mean, this is probably ridiculous, but he'd [Murphy had] been there [for] four years, so obviously he and Herbert would have been very close, one way or another.'

Lewis says he never took a cent of corrupt money. 'I was offered six pound by a fellow living with a prostitute at Hamilton [in the 1950s] ... and I put a report in on that and that went to the Crown Law office and [I] never ever got it back,' he says. 'I'm not saying people didn't give me things. I had bloody grog sent to me and I had bloody food and casket tickets from time to time from people I had done things for and dinner from somebody who I'd done something for, nothing unlawful, they'd ring up and ask you could you expedite something or give them some advice or whatever.

'I had more grog and more food than you could, for 11 years ... I needn't have gone home ... I could have eaten out every bloody lunch and every dinner.'

Did he ever hear of the corrupt system known as The Joke?

'I never heard The Joke come up,' he says. 'I never, ever thought anything other than the Licensing Branch [was] a mob of bastards who had been getting a quid, but what are we going to do about it now?'

Did he ever consider that Tony Murphy's almost constant contact with him while he was in prison was anything other than the deeds of a concerned friend?

'I don't know what he said to me when he'd come. But one could hypothesise, I suppose, that he was coming to make sure I wasn't going to change my mind, if you like, and say, "Oh yes, I knew Murphy was a crook", or some bloody thing,' Lewis says.

Was it a fraudulent friendship?

'Oh, for a long time apparently,' Lewis reflects. 'Yet I still say ... I thought he was a bloody good detective. He was an effective one, if you like. But you could argue that ... was he effective? He put a lot of bad people out of business. And might have left a few people going in business ...'

Lewis still mentions the members of the public who approach him when he's doing his shopping or getting a haircut. 'I haven't had one person come and abuse me, not one,' Lewis says.

Still, the issue of Herbert's betrayal of their friendship still puzzles him. 'I don't think I was naive; I think I ... was a fairly worldly bloke, I just never suspected him of being a crook,' Lewis says. 'I mean, if I'd suspected him as a crook and I was getting a quid out of him, I would hope I wasn't so stupid as to be publicly seen with him [or] let him into my home and to go to places where I knew he'd be. I'm sure that any, well not any, but most intelligent corrupt top officials over the years have arranged to have the money delivered to them in the Bahamas, or something.'

For years after Hazel's death, Lewis continued to live at the Stafford Heights address. The two-level cream-brick house, with a twin garage and rock garden, radiated untouched Brisbane suburbia circa 1970s. It was the same inside, beyond the flyscreen – a spacious dining and lounge room, large, stuffed couches and armchairs, sideboards laden with framed photographs and memorabilia. On a shelf under the coffee table was a display of creamy coloured seashells. Vases were filled with plastic flowers and antimacassars were draped across the backs of the lounge chairs. In the lounge room, too, were large ledgers and albums that celebrated Lewis's police career.

Downstairs, Lewis used a corner room as his office. It too, was crowded with memorabilia from his days as a Knight of the Realm and as the Queensland police commissioner, shelves heavy with mementos and framed photographs of his family. There were police hats from all over the world, and a shelf of dusty spirit bottles.

In the corner was Lewis's desk. On it was a typewriter, pens, papers, a diary and a telephone. It was here he made notes, filed newspaper clippings, wrote letters, phoned friends and allies, and checked the voluminous documents kept in cardboard boxes in his garage and in a small storeroom behind his office. It was in the storeroom that he kept the full transcript of the Fitzgerald Inquiry, bound in red folders and prickled with hundreds of post-it notes. Here, Lewis submerged himself in the past to try and bring back, from the deep, proof of his innocence.

But outside, over in the city, the 21st century was in full swing.

If Lewis ever went to visit his old beats, when, as a member of the Consorting Squad in the 1950s he would check out the wooden cathouses of South Brisbane or the rough hotels along Stanley Street with their sawdust and menace, he would have found a boulevard of world-class art galleries and restaurants, the place still a hive of human movement – not sex and fights, but drama, culture and the spontaneous play of children at South Bank.

In the Treasury Building he would have discovered a casino in full bloom, and poker machines singing their peculiar song in pubs and clubs not only in Brisbane but throughout the entire state. Up at Petrie Terrace, where he trained in that stormy summer of 1948 and into 1949, before he was inducted into the police force, he would have seen not a training paddock and a cadet sleeping quarters, but supermarkets, cinemas, bottle shops and eateries, the old police radio shack a popular steak house.

As Lewis sifted through the past to clear his name, sex shops dotted throughout the suburbs, escort services and brothels were alive and well, and late at night you could take in stages of strippers in a club beneath Jo-Jo's restaurant in the heart of the city.

Brisbane was multifaceted and multicultural. It had moved beyond having, as its own little streak of exotic cuisine, the Lotus Room Chinese restaurant or the Playboy Club at Petrie Bight, where, in the 1960s, you could find men who liked to dress as women after dark. Gone was the infamous National Hotel. Gone was the illegal casino at 142 Wickham Street, now a massage house. Brisbane was now out and proud with a strong local gay and lesbian community. Books that criticised the government were no longer shredded. Street marches and protests were permitted.

The Gold Coast, which Lewis and his wife Hazel had so loved to visit each year over the Christmas holiday period, had lived up to its heathen potential, and was now a phantasmagoria of nightclubs and sex for sale. Drugs, fraud and youth violence flourished in the midst of the natural beauty of the coast.

Yet, each morning over in Winton Street, Lewis got up early, took his tea, and went to work at his downstairs desk, checking his diary, preparing for his day, mapping out who he had to see, what he needed to read, what files he had to check.

It was as if the old police commissioner had never left his office at Makerston Street.

Epilogue

It was a grey and wet Friday afternoon when they arrived to pay their respects. On Christmas Eve, 2010, clouds were scudding above the spire of the Sacred Heart Catholic Church at 50 Fairway Drive, Clear Island Waters, on the Gold Coast, the seat of the Surfers Paradise parish.

About an hour before the funeral, and the arrival of the coffin in a grey hearse, a lone police piper practised his bagpipe in preparation for the service. The mournful sound echoed across the bitumen and rifled through the exterior church pillars and up into the crowns of the nearby pale-skinned camphor laurels. 'It wasn't a bright, happy day,' says one journalist who was outside the church. 'It was rain, clouds, greyness. People were shuffling quickly to get inside.'

The occasion was the funeral service for the former assistant commissioner (crime) of the Queensland Police Force, Anthony 'Tony' Murphy, once the state's most famous detective. Murphy had gone from being a telegram boy at the Amberley Air Force Base south-west of Ipswich during the early years of World War II, joining the police and serving initially in the Photographic Section before rising to fame in the Consorting Squad in the 1950s. It was there he met and befriended two young policemen, Terence Murray Lewis and Glendon Patrick Hallahan. All three would become the favoured boys of Police Commissioner Frank 'Big Fella' Bischof in the late 1950s and early 1960s. The triumvirate would be whispered about down at the headquarters of the CIB at the corner of Elizabeth and George streets, up at the police depot on Petrie Terrace, in the lawyers' canteen at the Inns of Court at North Quay, and in the bordellos of South Brisbane, as the Rat Pack. They were three young kings, and they were going all the way to the top.

Throughout his career, there was talk of Murphy as an 'active' policeman, tenacious, unstoppable, with a brilliant memory and tactical mind. He inspired younger detectives, and he had a reputation for always securing evidence – the foundation stone of criminal convictions. It was always said – you never, ever wanted Tony Murphy on your tail.

Still, the talk was not always praise. It was rumoured he was one of Bischof's bagmen. That he had gone on the take and become a part of The Joke when he served in the Licensing Branch with Jack Reginald Herbert in the late 1960s. Then there were the perjury charges laid against him over his evidence before the National Hotel inquiry in 1963 and 1964. The murmurs that he was corrupt continued through to his retirement in late 1982, and were in part responsible for him leaving the force at just 55 years of age.

He settled with his family away from everything and virtually everyone, at Amity Point on North Stradbroke Island, to grow flowers. This was a place for the elderly, for recluses, for people who wanted to fall off the map. And yet still they talked about him, as if he were a myth, a legend.

Journalists would later analyse the systemic corruption discovered in the Queensland Police, and would allude to a central figure behind it. They talked about The Boss. They called him the Grey Ghost or the Grey Eminence.

More than 100 family, friends and former police colleagues attended Murphy's funeral service that miserable day. Former commissioner Terry Lewis was not among them.

During the service, then Assistant Commissioner of Police Paul Wilson said a few words. Outside, a handful of uniformed officers ensured that the ceremony was kept private. Afterwards, nobody commented to the media.

Murphy, 83, had passed away on Tuesday 21 December 2010, following a long illness. For several months he had been confined to his home after periodic visits to hospitals and nursing homes. Suffering from early signs of dementia he was attended to by part-time carers in the house he shared with his wife Maureen at Robina, the relatively new satellite suburb at the back of the Gold Coast.

Just weeks before he died, he was at home reminiscing about his years as one of Queensland's most recognisable policemen. Frail and thin, he would, on occasion, go through some of his old newspaper clippings and police photographs and documents that he'd salvaged from the past. To the end, he'd hosted a regular lunch with some of his retired colleagues who also lived on the Gold Coast.

Those who met Murphy at his peak from the 1950s through to the 1970s didn't fail to mention the man's sheer physical presence. He could instil fear without opening his mouth. Even much later, as an old man in a singlet and chequered pyjama pants, he still had steel in his voice that connected to the big, bullish, no-nonsense detective he had once been.

Murphy had always loathed the media, but on this day, he agreed to speak in what proved to be his final interview.

'How are you, Tony?'

'I'm just hanging in.'

'How old are you now?'

'Buggered if I know,' Murphy said. 'Born in 1927. I was sworn up in '48. I was a police cadet from 1944. A long while ago.'

'Former police commissioner Frank Bischof. What was he like?'

'A good fella, old Frank,' he replies. 'You could talk to him. I always thought highly of Frank Bischof. He treated us young kids alright. He was a snappy dresser. I can't remember much about him at all. Anyway, it was so long ago.'

'What about Glendon Patrick Hallahan?'

'We got on good together, as friends,' Murphy says.

'You were part of what was known as the Rat Pack?'

'That's right, yeah,' he recalls. 'He was good old Glen Patrick. A very interesting bloke. He never had any bloody flies on him at all.'

'Then along came former police commissioner Ray Whitrod, who sent you out to Longreach and Terry Lewis to Charleville.'

'I don't know whether it was Whitrod who did that, it could've been,' says Murphy. 'I didn't like him, but others did. I never got terribly wrapped up in Whitrod, but at the same time he never hurt me so I can't really complain about him. It's all ancient bloody history now.'

'Then Terry Lewis became Commissioner in 1976.'

'It's all in the past.'

'Do you remember the prostitute Shirley Margaret Brifman?'

'She was quite good, quite a reasonable sort of female, bit of a knockabout … she kicked around the bloody town.'

'Do you remember how she died?'

'Did she? I'd forgotten that. It's all water under the bridge.'

'She died of a suspected overdose of drugs in 1972.'

'I can't recall.'

'In a flat in Bonney Avenue, Clayfield.'

'I don't remember that. Anyway, it's all bloody history now, well and truly.'

'Did you like Terry Lewis?'

'Yes, my word,' he says. 'Found him a real good bloke. That was so many bloody years ago now, I can't remember the ins and outs …'

'What big cases did you work on, Tony?'

'It's so many years ago now, I don't remember those sorts of things.'

'Were you a powerful man in the force?'

'Buggered if I know.'

'Were you intimidating?'

'Maybe I was and maybe I wasn't,' he says. 'Hallahan and I and old Lewis too, we combined [to a] degree … we locked up quite a few of the nasties. It's all bloody water under the bridge.'

'Was the term "The Rat Pack" a friendly description of you, Hallahan and Lewis?'

'I don't think there was anything friendly about it,' he recalls. 'The bloody media put the boot in, that's my recollection. Friendly or not, I'm buggered if I know. I should contact him [Lewis] more often. I haven't contacted him for years and years. I haven't been in touch with old Terence Murray for bloody years.'

'Was he a good commissioner?'

'Oh yes,' says Murphy. 'None better. None better than Terence Murray Lewis. I got along well with old Jack Herbert.'

'Was he a rogue?'

'No, I think he's alright. He found his way around the town. I wouldn't say he was a rogue, old Jack, old Jack Reginald Herbert.'

'Do you have good memories of your police career?'

'No, I haven't,' he says. 'I haven't got good memories. I've got very poor memories. It's all in the past. It's long, long gone. It's ancient history that went out with the wind, I think.'

'You grew Geraldton Wax flowers over on North Stradbroke Island when you retired from the police force?'

'I never made any money out of them,' he says. 'It was something to occupy myself. It worked for a while. I don't know how many years ago that was. Yonks and yonks and yonks. That's many, many years ago, long forgotten …'

'Was Frank Bischof corrupt?'

'No, old Frank was alright. I never found him corrupt. Everybody was aware Frank Bischof wasn't to be messed around with. My mind's gone on the whole lot of them now …'

'Jack Herbert, what did you think of him rolling over at the Fitzgerald Inquiry?'

'I can't recall that. You been talking to Terry? He never mentioned that to me.'

'What did you think of the Fitzgerald Inquiry itself?'

'I wasn't very rapt,' he says. 'It's so long ago now ... I can't remember bloody much about the Fitzgerald Inquiry.'

'You were never called to give evidence before the inquiry?'

'I can't say if I was or wasn't. I might have been.'

'Terry went to gaol for 14 years.'

'I can't recall that.'

'He was found guilty of corruption.'

'Was he? My memory is gone,' Murphy says. 'My mind is absolutely bloody gone. My memory is long gone. I don't remember anything about myself let alone somebody else.'

'Do you remember perjury charges in relation to the National Hotel inquiry being laid against you after Shirley Brifman blew the whistle on corrupt police before she died? She was due to be a witness at your court case, but she died.'

'I don't remember that. No recollection whatever about her dying before or after, no recollection of that at all. I don't recall ever going to Shirley Brifman's house ... I don't recall.'

'What did you think of Police Minister Max Hodges, during the Whitrod era?'

'I never had time for Max Hodges. Ah yes, it's so long ago. It's remarkable how you come to find me. What are you doing a bloody book on? Who? Good luck to you. He [Terry Lewis] wouldn't be very happy about that would he, about his time in prison and all the rest of it? He never discussed anything with me about it. I've always thought the world of old Terry.'

'Who was corrupt in your time in the Queensland Police Force?'

'I can't bloody think of anyone.'

'Was the police life a good life?'

'It was certainly a busy life, it kept me occupied,' says Murphy. 'Oh, there'd be dozens of others I pinched … dozens of others … long, long gone out of my memory now.'

'Do you remember the Mr Asia drug syndicate in the late 1970s?'

'No, I do not. Do not. Mr Asia drug syndicate? No. I'm not saying it never happened, but I don't remember it.'

'You told journalist Brian Bolton that police had recordings relating to a big drug syndicate. Interviews with drug couriers Doug and Isabel Wilson. They were murdered after Bolton's story was published.'

'I don't remember that. I don't deny it happened. I knew Brian Bolton reasonably well.'

'Do you remember the National Hotel inquiry?'

'Not very well. It's all water under the bridge to me. It's all gone. I wouldn't know the time of day.'

'They say you were known as the Grey Ghost, the Grey Eminence.'

'The Grey Eminence?' he says. 'I never knew that. The Grey Eminence. That's news to me.'

★

It's all in the past.

It's all water under the bridge.

It's ancient bloody history.

Acknowledgements

The publication of the final volume of the Lewis trilogy marks the end of a five and a half year journey that has attracted the kindness and encouragement of many hundreds of people.

I would like to thank Terence Lewis for his contribution to the books. I have made every effort to present a balanced version of events in the trilogy, and as with the first two volumes – *Three Crooked Kings* and *Jacks and Jokers* – Lewis was offered a right of reply to all the major issues canvassed in *All Fall Down*.

I would like to pay tribute to writer and mate Doug Hall, who triggered the trilogy.

Many former State and Federal police officers generously gave of their time, and offered documentation and diaries for the books. Thanks to: Kym Goldup-Graham, Greg Deveney, Ross Dickson, Peter Gallagher, John 'Bluey' O'Gorman, Ron Edington, the family of the late Robert Walker, Barry Krosch, Les Lewis, Keith Smith, Peter Dautel, Ken Hoggett, the late John Huey, Geoff Pambroke, Ron Lewis, Arthur Volz, Bruce Wilby, the late Noel Creevey, Cliff Crawford, John Moller, Ian Hatcher, the late Abe Duncan, Fred Collins, Max Rogers, Brian Bennett, Bill Harrigan, Bob Sawford, Clive Small, David Marshall, John Cummins, Frank Rynne, Jim Shearer, John Morris, Ross Allan, Dennis Koch, the family of Merv Callaghan, the family of Don 'Buck' Buchanan, John Shobbrook and Ian Alcorn.

I owe a special thanks to Jim Slade and Peter Vassallo – two fine men.

I am especially grateful to Lewis' former personal assistant, Greg Early, for allowing me to make use of excerpts from his police diaries and his expansive unpublished memoir, and for his help with innumerable queries.

I am, once again, indebted to two great mates: former Licensing Branch officer Nigel Powell, for countless hours of support, advice and friendship – Nigel, you are the definition of integrity; and former Licensing Branch officer Kingsley Fancourt, a man who suffered much for his honesty, but whose actions contributed to changing the history of Queensland.

ACKNOWLEDGEMENTS

To those policemen and women, and their families, who offered information but chose to remain anonymous, I thank you.

I would like to pay tribute to the inspirational Mary Anne Brifman, who so generously welcomed me into her extraordinary life. The Brifman story haunts the trilogy and underpins much of the drama over more than 50 years, and its unfolding was only made possible due to Mary Anne's open heart and fierce intellect.

The political threads of the books were enriched by the cooperation of many former premiers, politicians and political operatives. Thank you to: former premier Mike Ahern, former premier Peter Beattie, Sir Llew Edwards, Paul Clauson, Terry White, Bill Hewitt, Brian Austin, Henry Palaszczuk, Paul Braddy, Russell Grenning, the family of the late Huan Fraser, Allen Callaghan, and the inestimable (Sir) Malcolm McMillan.

I would also like to thank former Chief Justice and now Governor of Queensland, Paul de Jersey, and his wife Kaye, the late Justice Bill Carter, Michael Forde, Terry O'Gorman and the late, great Colin Bennett. Thank you also to Gavin Rebetzke.

I would especially like to acknowledge the work and contribution to Queensland history of Tony Fitzgerald.

So many others from all walks of life made valuable contributions to the books. My thanks to: Anne Marie Tilley, Debbie Kilroy, Carol Scully, Leonie Bahnemann, Lee Kear, Richard Spencer, Peter Walsh, Lawrence and Andre Daws, Ken Lord, Ruth Whitrod Blackburn, Ian Whitrod, Mervyn Carey, Dr Paul Wilson, Dr Ross Fitzgerald, Paul Reynolds, Jean Hudson, John Hooper, John X. Berlin, Dr Harry Akers, Fred Komlosy and his family, Edgar Bourke, Keith Underwood, John Stopford, Tony Corrigan, Robert 'Dave' Berrick, Pat Gallagher, Vince Doyle, Mary, Judith and Christian Bennett and the Bennett family, and Bob Martin of Amity Point.

I am indebted to the hundreds of Queenslanders who have contacted me with their own tales from the eras covered by the books, some of which have enriched the text.

Again, I am enormously grateful to investigative journalists Chris Masters and Phil Dickie, whose work forms the bedrock of the trilogy.

Thank you, Chris and Phil, for your extreme generosity during the years of the project.

Thank you, also, to those inspirational scribes, Quentin Dempster and Evan Whitton, and to Bob Gordon, Greg Chamberlin, Peter James, Tony Koch, Alan Hall, Paul Weston, Ken 'Digger' Blanch, Matthew Fynes-Clinton, Jason Gagliardi, Michael McKenna, Alex Mitchell, Judith White, Phillip Knightley, Steve Bishop, Peter Morley, Michael Crutcher and David Fagan. I'd like to pay tribute to the memory of Tony Reeves. A special thanks to two great friends – Hedley Thomas and Des Houghton.

The books were largely made possible courtesy of the invaluable encouragement of my editors at News Queensland – Christopher Dore (*The Courier-Mail*), Peter Gleeson (*The Sunday Mail*) and Kylie Lang (*Qweekend* magazine). A big thank you to Alison Walsh, Phil Stafford, Anne-Maree Lyons, Frances Whiting, David Kelly, Russell Shakespeare, Leisa Scott and the wonderful Susan Johnson.

I owe more than I can express to Jean Bowra of Brisbane, who faithfully and professionally transcribed interviews over many years. Thank you, Jean.

Many books and documents have been important to the trilogy:

The Road to Fitzgerald and Beyond by Phil Dickie, UQP, 1989

In Place of Justice: An Analysis of a Royal Commission 1963–64 by Peter James, The Shield Press, 1974

The Sundown Murders by Peter James, Boolarong Publications, 1990

The Long Blue Line: A History of the Queensland Police by W. Ross Johnston, Boolarong Publications, 1992

The Bagman: Final Confessions of Jack Herbert by Jack Herbert with Tom Gilling, ABC Books, 2004

Before I Sleep: My Life Fighting Crime and Corruption by Ray Whitrod, UQP, 2001

The Prince and the Premier by David Hickie, Angus and Robertson, 1985

Trial and Error by Don Lane, Boolarong Publications, 1993

The Man They Called a Monster by Paul Wilson, Cassell Australia, 1981

A Life of Crime by Paul Wilson, Scribe, 1990

Reform in Policing: Lessons from the Whitrod Era by Jill M. Bolen, Hawkins Press, 1997

Don't You Worry About That! by Sir Joh Bjelke-Petersen, Angus and Robertson, 1990

Honest Cops: Revealing Accounts of Australians who Stood up to Corruption and Suffered the Consequences by Quentin Dempster, ABC Books, 1992

Crims in Grass Castles by Keith Moor, Penguin Books, 2009

Joh: The Life and Political Adventures of Johannes Bjelke-Petersen by Hugh Lunn, UQP, 1978

Inside Story by Chris Masters, Harper Collins, 1992

In the Arena: Memories of an A.L.P State Secretary in Queensland by Peter Beattie, edited by Brian Stevenson, Boolarong Publications, 1990

The Hillbilly Dictator: Australia's Police State by Evan Whitton, ABC Books, 1989

The Ayes Have It: The History of the Queensland Parliament by John Wanna and Tracey Arklay, ANU Press, 2010

Lock, Stock & Barrel: A Political Biography of Mike Ahern by Paul Reynolds, UQP, 2002

The Tangled Web by Des Sturgess, Bedside Books, 2001

A History of Queensland: From 1915 to the Early 1980s by Ross Fitzgerald, UQP, 1984

'An Investigation of the Dynamics of Cultural Policy Formation: The States' Patronage of Film Production in Australia, 1970–1988' by Thomas Vincent O'Donnell, RMIT University, 2005.

Thank you to former premier Peter Beattie for permission to quote from his Master of Arts thesis, 'The Window of Opportunity: The Fitzgerald Experiment and the Queensland Criminal Justice Commission 1987–1992' (QUT, November 1996).

Both the National Library's newspaper digitisation project, Trove, and Queensland Parliament's digitisation of Hansard, were of major importance to my research.

In addition, I wish to pay a special tribute to author Tom Gilling, author of Jack Herbert's memoir, *The Bagman*, for kindly providing me with the original interview cassettes he recorded with Herbert.

On a personal note, I would like to express my sincere love and thanks to Ron and Karen Condon, Marsha and Phil Pope and family, John Shakespeare and Anna-Lisa Backlund, Gillian Morris and Geof Hawke, Gary Morris and Jo Gaha, and Nick Morris and Clodagh Crowe and family. A special hug goes to Pat Rose, and to the memory of Victor Rose.

My publishers, University of Queensland Press, took on the Lewis trilogy before they (or any of us) understood the immensity of the job at hand, but over the years have carried out their role with the utmost professionalism and support. Thank you to CEO Greg Bain for having faith in the books. To Publisher Madonna Duffy, your guidance, duty of care and level of calm during the turbulent moments kept the project going – thank you, Madonna. I want to pay a special tribute to my editor, the brilliant Jacqueline Blanchard, who remained focused at all times and brought the books home. There is not a single page of the trilogy that does not bear her expertise. Thank you so much, Jacq. I owe gratitude also to Meredene Hill and the wonderful Bettina Richter.

Finally, all my love to my wife Katie Kate, who silently suffered my many absences during the years working on these books. Thank you, darling, for your affection and incredible forbearance. And to my beautiful children – Finnigan, Bridie Rose and Olly G. (Oliver George) – this, and everything, is for you.

Index

INDEX